RECURRENT NEURAL NETWORKS

Design and Applications

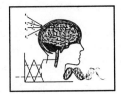

Edited by

L.R. Medsker

Departments of Physics and Computer
Science and Information Systems
American University
Washington, D.C.

L.C. Jain

Knowledge-Based Intelligent Engineering Systems Centre
Faculty of Information Technology
Director/Founder, KES
University of South Australia, Adelaide
The Mawson Lakes, SA
Australia

CRC Press
Boca Raton   London   New York   Washington, D.C.

Library of Congress Cataloging-in-Publication Data

Medsker, L.R.
   Recurrent neural networks: design and applications / by L.R. Medsker and L.C. Jain.
      p.   cm. — (The CRC Press international series on computational intelligence)
   Includes bibliographical references and index.
   ISBN 0-8493-7181-3 (alk. paper)
   1. Neural networks (Computer science) I. Jain, L.C. II. Title. III. Series.
QA76.87 M44   1999
006.3′2—dc21
                                                                                    99-049146
                                                                                        CIP

© 2000 by CRC Press LLC

No claim to original U.S. Government works
International Standard Book Number 0-8493-7181-3
Library of Congress Card Number 99-049146
Printed in the United States of America   2 3 4 5 6 7 8 9 0
Printed on acid-free paper

The CRC Press
International Series on Computational Intelligence

Series Editor
L.C. Jain, Ph.D., M.E., B.E., (Hons), Fellow I.E. (Australia)

H.-N. Teodorescu and A. Kandel
Dynamic Fuzzy Systems and Chaos Applications

L. Medsker and L.C. Jain
Recurrent Neural Networks: Design and Applications

L.C. Jain and A.M. Fanelli
Recent Advances in Artifical Neural Networks: Design and Applications

M. Russo and L.C. Jain
Fuzzy Learning and Applications

J. Liu
Multiagent Robotic Systems

M. Kennedy, R. Rovatti, and G. Setti
Chaotic Electronics in Telecommunications

H.-N. Teodorescu and L.C. Jain
Intelligent Systems and Techniques in Rehabilitation Engineering

I. Baturone, A. Barriga, C. Jimenez-Fernandez, D. Lopez, and S. Sanchez
Microelectronics Design of Fuzzy Logic-Based Systems

T. Nishida
Dynamic Knowledge Interaction

C.L. Karr
Practical Applications of Computational Intelligence for Adaptive Control

PREFACE

Recurrent neural networks have been an interesting and important part of neural network research during the 1990's. They have already been applied to a wide variety of problems involving time sequences of events and ordered data such as characters in words. Novel current uses range from motion detection and music synthesis to financial forecasting. This book is a summary of work on recurrent neural networks and is exemplary of current research ideas and challenges in this subfield of artificial neural network research and development. By sharing these perspectives, we hope to illuminate opportunities and encourage further work in this promising area.

Two broad areas of importance in recurrent neural network research, the architectures and learning techniques, are addressed in every chapter. Architectures range from fully interconnected to partially connected networks, including recurrent multilayer feedforward. Learning is a critical issue and one of the primary advantages of neural networks. The added complexity of learning in recurrent networks has given rise to a variety of techniques and associated research projects. A goal is to design better algorithms that are both computationally efficient and simple to implement.

Another broad division of work in recurrent neural networks, on which this book is structured, is the design perspective and application issues. The first section concentrates on ideas for alternate designs and advances in theoretical aspects of recurrent neural networks. Some authors discuss aspects of improving recurrent neural network performance and connections with Bayesian analysis and knowledge representation, including extended neuro-fuzzy systems. Others address real-time solutions of optimization problems and a unified method for designing optimization neural network models with global convergence.

The second section of this book looks at recent applications of recurrent neural networks. Problems dealing with trajectories, control systems, robotics, and language learning are included, along with an interesting use of recurrent neural networks in chaotic systems. The latter work presents evidence for a computational paradigm that has higher potential for pattern capacity and boundary flexibility than a multilayer static feedforward network. Other chapters examine natural language as a dynamic system appropriate for grammar induction and language learning using recurrent neural networks. Another chapter applies a recurrent neural network technique to problems in controls and signal processing, and other work addresses trajectory problems and robot behavior.

The next decade should produce significant improvements in theory and design of recurrent neural networks, as well as many more applications for the creative solution of important practical problems. The widespread application of recurrent neural networks should foster more interest in research and development and raise further theoretical and design questions.

THE EDITORS

Larry Medsker is a Professor of Physics and Computer Science at American University. His research involves soft computing and hybrid intelligent systems that combine neural network and AI techniques. Other areas of research are in nuclear physics and data analysis systems. He is the author of two books: *Hybrid Neural Network and Expert Systems* (1994) and *Hybrid Intelligent Systems* (1995). He co-authored with Jay Liebowitz another book on *Expert Systems and Neural Networks* (1994). One of his current projects applies intelligent web-based systems to problems of knowledge management and data mining at the U.S. Department of Labor. His Ph.D. in Physics is from Indiana University, and he has held positions at Bell Laboratories, University of Pennsylvania, and Florida State University. He is a member of the International Neural Network Society, American Physical Society, American Association for Artificial Intelligence, IEEE, and the D.C. Federation of Musicians, Local 161-710.

L.C. Jain is a Director/Founder of the Knowledge-Based Intelligent Engineering Systems (KES) Centre, located in the University of South Australia. He is a fellow of the Institution of Engineers Australia. He has initiated a postgraduate stream by research in the Knowledge-Based Intelligent Engineering Systems area. He has presented a number of keynote addresses at International Conferences on Knowledge-Based Systems, Neural Networks, Fuzzy Systems and Hybrid Systems. He is the Founding Editor-in-Chief of the *International Journal of Knowledge-Based Intelligent Engineering Systems* and served as an Associate Editor of the *IEEE Transactions on Industrial Electronics*. Professor Jain was the Technical chair of the ETD2000 International Conference in 1995, Publications Chair of the Australian and New Zealand Conference on Intelligent Information Systems in 1996 and the Conference Chair of the International Conference on Knowledge-Based Intelligent Electronic Systems in 1997, 1998 and 1999. He served as the Vice President of the Electronics Association of South Australia in 1997. He is the Editor-in-Chief of the International Book Series on Computational Intelligence, CRC Press USA. His interests focus on the applications of novel techniques such as knowledge-based systems, artificial neural networks, fuzzy systems and genetic algorithms and the application of these techniques.

ACKNOWLEDGMENTS

The editors thank Dr. R. K. Jain, University of South Australia, for his assistance as a reviewer. We are indebted to Samir Unadkat and Mãlina Ciocoiu for their excellent work formatting the chapters and to others who assisted: Srinivasan Guruswami and Aravindkumar Ramalingam. Finally, we thank the chapter authors who not only shared their expertise in recurrent neural networks, but also patiently worked with us via the Internet to create this book. One of us (L.M.) thanks Lee Giles, Ashraf Abelbar, and Marty Hagan for their assistance and helpful conversations and Karen Medsker for her patience, support, and technical advice.

Table of Contents

Chapter 5

Equivalence in Knowledge Representation: Automata, Recurrent Neural Networks, and Dynamical Fuzzy Systems... 99

C. Lee Giles, Christian W. Omlin, and K. K. Thornber

Chapter 6

Learning Long-Term Dependencies in NARX Recurrent Neural Networks..133

Tsungnan Lin, Bill G. Horne, Peter Tino, and C. Lee Giles

Chapter 9

Recurrent Autoassociative Networks: Developing Distributed Representations of Hierarchically Structured Sequences by Autoassociation 205

Ivelin Stoianov

Chapter 10

Comparison of Recurrent Neural Networks for Trajectory Generation 243

David G. Hagner, Mohamad H. Hassoun, and Paul B. Watta

Chapter 11

Training Algorithms for Recurrent Neural Nets that Eliminate the Need for Computation of Error Gradients with Application to Trajectory Production Problem

Malur K. Sundareshan, Yee Chin Wong, and Thomas Condarcure

Chapter 12

Training Recurrent Neural Networks for Filtering and Control.

Martin T. Hagan, Orlando De Jesús, and Roger Schultz

Chapter 1

INTRODUCTION

Samir B. Unadkat, Mãlina M. Ciocoiu and Larry R. Medsker

**Department of Computer Science and Information Systems
American University**

I. OVERVIEW

Recurrent neural networks have been an important focus of research and development during the 1990's. They are designed to learn sequential or time-varying patterns. A recurrent net is a neural network with feedback (closed loop) connections [Fausett, 1994]. Examples include BAM, Hopfield, Boltzmann machine, and recurrent backpropagation nets [Hecht-Nielsen, 1990].

Recurrent neural network techniques have been applied to a wide variety of problems. Simple partially recurrent neural networks were introduced in the late 1980's by several researchers including Rumelhart, Hinton, and Williams [Rummelhart, 1986] to learn strings of characters. Many other applications have addressed problems involving dynamical systems with time sequences of events.

Table 1 gives some other interesting examples to give the idea of the breadth of recent applications of recurrent neural networks. For example, the dynamics of tracking the human head for virtual reality systems is being investigated. The

Table 1. Examples of recurrent neural network applications.

Topic	Authors	Reference
Predictive head tracking for virtual reality systems	Saad, Caudell, and Wunsch, II	[Saad, 1999]
Wind turbine power estimation	Li, Wunsch, O'Hair, and Giesselmann	[Li, 1999]
Financial prediction using recurrent neural networks	Giles, Lawrence, Tsoi	[Giles, 1997]
Music synthesis method for Chinese plucked-string instruments	Liang, Su, and Lin	[Liang, 1999]
Electric load forecasting	Costa, Pasero, Piglione, and Radasanu	[Costa, 1999]
Natural water inflows forecasting	Coulibaly, Anctil, and Rousselle	[Coulibaly, 1999]

forecasting of financial data and of electric power demand are the objects of other studies. Recurrent neural networks are being used to track water quality and minimize the additives needed for filtering water. And, the time sequences of musical notes have been studied with recurrent neural networks.

Some chapters in this book focus on systems for language processing. Others look at real-time systems, trajectory problems, and robotic behavior. Optimization and neuro-fuzzy systems are presented, and recurrent neural network implementations of filtering and control are described. Finally, the application of recurrent neural networks to chaotic systems is explored.

A. RECURRENT NEURAL NET ARCHITECTURES

The architectures range from fully interconnected (Figure 1) to partially connected nets (Figure 2), including multilayer feedforward networks with distinct input and output layers. Fully connected networks do not have distinct input layers of nodes, and each node has input from all other nodes. Feedback to the node itself is possible.

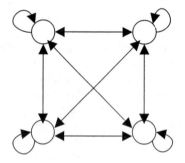

Figure 1. An example of a fully connected recurrent neural network.

Simple partially recurrent neural networks (Figure 2) have been used to learn strings of characters. Athough some nodes are part of a feedforward structure,

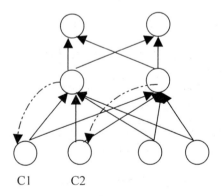

C1   C2

Figure 2. An example of a simple recurrent network.

other nodes provide the sequential context and receive feedback from other nodes. Weights from the context units (C1 and C2) are processed like those for the input units, for example, using backpropagation. The context units receive time-delayed feedback from, in the case of Figure 2, the second layer units. Training data consists of inputs and their desired successor outputs. The net can be trained to predict the next letter in a string of characters and to validate a string of characters.

Two fundamental ways can be used to add feedback into feedforward multilayer neural networks. Elman [Elman, 1990] introduced feedback from the hidden layer to the context portion of the input layer. This approach pays more attention to the sequence of input values. Jordan recurrent neural networks [Jordan, 1989] use feedback from the output layer to the context nodes of the input layer and give more emphasis to the sequence of output values. This book covers a range of variations on these fundamental concepts, presenting ideas for more efficient and effective recurrent neural networks designs and examples of interesting applications.

B. LEARNING IN RECURRENT NEURAL NETS

Learning is a fundamental aspect of neural networks and a major feature that makes the neural approach so attractive for applications that have from the beginning been an elusive goal for artificial intelligence. Learning algorithms have long been a focus of research (e.g., Nilsson [1965] and Mendel [1970]).

Hebbian learning and gradient descent learning are key concepts upon which neural network techniques have been based. A popular manifestation of gradient descent is back-error propagation introduced by Rumelhart [1986] and Werbos [1993]. While backpropagation is relatively simple to implement, several problems can occur in its use in practical applications, including the difficulty of avoiding entrapment in local minima. The added complexity of the dynamical processing in recurrent neural networks from the time-delayed updating of the input data requires more complex algorithms for representing the learning.

To realize the advantage of the dynamical processing of recurrent neural networks, one approach is to build on the effectiveness of feedforward networks that process stationary patterns. Researchers have developed a variety of schemes by which gradient methods, and in particular backpropagation learning, can be extended to recurrent neural networks. Werbos introduced the backpropagation through time approach [Werbos, 1990], approximating the time evolution of a recurrent neural network as a sequence of static networks using gradient methods. Another approach deploys a second, master, neural network to perform the required computations in programming the attractors of the original dynamical slave network [Lapedes and Farber, 1986]. Other techniques that have been investigated can be found in Pineda [1987], Almeida [1987], Williams and Zipser [1989], Sato [1990], and Pearlmutter [1989]. The various attempts to extend backpropagation learning to recurrent networks is summarized in Pearlmutter [1995].

II. DESIGN ISSUES AND THEORY

The first section of the book concentrates on ideas for alternate designs and advances in theoretical aspects of recurrent neural networks. The authors discuss aspects of improving recurrent neural network performance and connections with Bayesian analysis and knowledge representation.

A. OPTIMIZATION

Real-time solutions of optimization problems are often needed in scientific and engineering problems, including signal processing, system identification, filter design, function approximation, and regression analysis, and neural networks have been widely investigated for this purpose. The numbers of decision variables and constraints are usually very large, and large-scale optimization procedures are even more challenging when they have to be done in real time to optimize the performance of a dynamical system. For such applications, classical optimization techniques may not be adequate due to the problem dimensionality and stringent requirements on computational time. The neural network approach can solve optimization problems in running times orders of magnitude faster than the most popular optimization algorithms executed on general-purpose digital computers.

The chapter by Xia and Wang describes the use of neural networks for these problems and introduces a unified method for designing optimization neural network models with global convergence. They discuss continuous-time recurrent neural networks for solving linear and quadratic programming and for solving linear complementary problems and then focus on discrete-time neural networks. Assignment neural networks are discussed in detail, and some simulation examples are presented to demonstrate the operating characteristics of the neural networks.

The chapter first presents primal-dual neural networks for solving linear and quadratic programming problems (LP and QP) and develops the neural network for solving linear complementary problems (LCP). Following a unified method for designing neural network models, the first part of the chapter describes in detail primal-dual recurrent neural networks, with continuous time, for solving LP and QP. The second part of the chapter focuses on primal-dual discrete time neural networks for QP and LCP.

Although great progress has been made in using neural networks for optimization, many theoretical and practical problems remain unsolved. This chapter identifies areas for future research on the dynamics of recurrent neural networks for optimization problems, further application of recurrent neural networks to practical problems, and the hardware prototyping of recurrent neural networks for optimization.

B. DISCRETE-TIME SYSTEMS

Santos and Von Zuben discuss the practical requirement for efficient supervised learning algorithms, based on optimization procedures for adjusting the parameters. To improve performance, second order information is considered to minimize the error in the training. The first objective of their work is to describe systematic ways of obtaining exact second-order information for a range of recurrent neural network configurations, with a computational cost only two times higher than the cost to acquire first-order information. The second objective is to present an improved version of the conjugate gradient algorithm that can be used to effectively explore the available second-order information.

The dynamics of a recurrent neural network can be continuous or discrete in time. However, the simulation of a continuous-time recurrent neural network in digital computational devices requires the adoption of a discrete-time equivalent model. In their chapter, they discuss discrete-time recurrent neural network architectures, implemented by the use of one-step delay operators in the feedback paths. In doing so, digital filters of a desired order can be used to design the network by the appropriate definition of connections. The resulting nonlinear models for spatio-temporal representation can be directly simulated on a digital computer by means of a system of nonlinear difference equations. The nature of the equations depends on the kind of recurrent architecture adopted but may lead to very complex behaviors, even with a reduced number of parameters and associated equations.

Analysis and synthesis of recurrent neural networks of practical importance is a very demanding task, and second-order information should be considered in the training process. They present a low-cost procedure to obtain exact second-order information for a wide range of recurrent neural network architectures. They also present a very efficient and generic learning algorithm, an improved version of a scaled conjugate gradient algorithm, that can effectively be used to explore the available second-order information. They introduce a set of adaptive coefficients in replacement to fixed ones, and the new parameters of the algorithm are automatically adjusted. They show and interpret some simulation results.

The innovative aspects of this work are the proposition of a systematic procedure to obtain exact second-order information for a range of different recurrent neural network architectures, at a low computational cost, and an improved version of a scaled conjugate gradient algorithm to make use of this high-quality information. An important aspect is that, given the exact second-order information, the learning algorithm can be directly applied, without any kind of adaptation to the specific context.

C. BAYESIAN BELIEF REVISION

The Hopfield neural network has been used for a large number of optimization problems, ranging from object recognition to graph planarization to concentrator assignment. However, the fact that the Hopfield energy function is of quadratic order limits the problems to which it can be applied. Sometimes, objective functions that cannot be reduced to Hopfield's quadratic energy function can still be reasonably approximated by a quadratic energy function. For other problems, the objective function must be modeled by a higher-order energy function. Examples of such problems include the angular-metric TSP and belief revision, which is Abdelbar's subject in Chapter 4.

In his chapter, Abdelbar describes high-order recurrent neural networks and provides an efficient implementation data structure for sparse high-order networks. He also describes how such networks can be used for Bayesian belief revision and in important problems in diagnostic reasoning and commonsense reasoning under uncertainty.

D. KNOWLEDGE REPRESENTATION

Giles, Omlin, and Thornber discuss in their chapter neuro-fuzzy systems -- the combination of artificial neural networks with fuzzy logic -- which have become useful in many application domains. They explain, however, that conventional neuro-fuzzy models usually need enhanced representational power for applications that require context and state (e.g., speech, time series prediction, and control). Some of these applications can be readily modeled as finite state automata. Previously, it was proved that deterministic finite state automata (DFA) can be synthesized by or mapped into recurrent neural networks by directly programming the DFA structure into the weights of the neural network. Based on those results, they propose a synthesis method for mapping fuzzy finite state automata (FFA) into recurrent neural networks. This mapping is suitable for direct implementation in VLSI, i.e., the encoding of FFA as a generalization of the encoding of DFA in VLSI systems.

The synthesis method requires FFA to undergo a transformation prior to being mapped into recurrent networks. The neurons are provided with an enriched functionality in order to accommodate a fuzzy representation of FFA states. This enriched neuron functionality also permits fuzzy parameters of FFA to be directly represented as parameters of the neural network.

They also prove the stability of fuzzy finite state dynamics of the constructed neural networks for finite values of network weight and, through simulations, give empirical validation of the proofs. This proves the various knowledge equivalence representations between neural and fuzzy systems and models of automata.

E. LONG-TERM DEPENDENCIES

Gradient-descent learning algorithms for recurrent neural networks are known to perform poorly on tasks that involve long-term dependencies, i.e., those problems for which the desired output depends on inputs presented at times far in the past. Lin, Horne, Tino, and Giles discuss this in their chapter and show that the long-term dependencies problem is lessened for a class of architectures called NARX recurrent neural networks, which have powerful representational capabilities.

They have previously reported that gradient-descent learning can be more effective in NARX networks than in recurrent neural networks that have "hidden states" on problems including grammatical inference and nonlinear system identification. Typically the network converges much faster and generalizes better than other networks, and this chapter shows the same kinds of results.

They also present in this chapter some experimental results that show that NARX networks can often retain information for two to three times as long as conventional recurrent neural networks. They show that although NARX networks do not circumvent the problem of long-term dependenices, they can greatly improve performance on long-term dependency problems. They describe in detail some of the assumptions regarding what it means to latch information robustly and suggest possible ways to loosen these assumptions.

III. APPLICATIONS

This section looks at interesting modifications and applications of recurrent neural networks. Problems dealing with trajectories, control systems, robotics, and language learning are included, along with an interesting use of recurrent neural networks in chaotic systems.

A. CHAOTIC RECURRENT NETWORKS

Dayhoff, Palmadesso, and Richards present in their chapter work on the use of recurrent neural networks for chaotic systems. Dynamic neural networks are capable of a tremendous variety of oscillations, such as finite state oscillations, limit cycles, and chaotic behavior. The differing oscillations that are possible create an enormous repertoire of self-sustained activity patterns. This repertoire is very interesting because oscillations and changing activity patterns can potentially be exploited for computational purposes and for modeling physical phenomena.

In this chapter, they explore trends observed in a chaotic network when an external pattern is used as a stimulus. The pattern stimulus is a constant external input to all neurons in a single-layer recurrent network. The strength of the stimulus is varied to produce changes and trends in the complexity of the evoked oscillations. Stronger stimuli can evoke simpler and less varied oscillations. Resilience to noise occurs when noisy stimuli evoke the same or similar oscillations. Stronger stimuli can be more resilient to noise. They show examples of each of these observations. A pattern-to-oscillation map may eventually be exploited for pattern recognition and other computational purposes. In such a paradigm, the external pattern stimulus evokes an oscillation that is read off the network as the answer to a pattern association problem. They present evidence that this type of computational paradigm has higher potential for pattern capacity and boundary flexibility than a multilayer static feedforward network.

B. LANGUAGE LEARNING

The Kremer chapter examines the relationship between grammar induction or language learning and recurrent neural networks, asking how understanding formal language learning can help in designing and applying recurrent neural networks. The answer to this question comes in the form of four lessons: (1) training RNNs is difficult, (2) reducing the search space can accelerate or make learning possible, (3) ordering the search space can speed learning, and (4) ordering your training data helps. The chapter concerns dynamical recurrent neural networks, those that are presented with time-varying inputs and are designed to render outputs at various points in time. In this case, the operation of the network can be described by a function mapping an input sequence to an output value or sequence of values and is applied to the problem where inputs are selected from a discrete alphabet of valid values and output values fall into discrete categories. The problem of dealing with input sequences in which each item is selected from an input alphabet can also be cast as a formal language problem. This work uses recurrent neural networks to categorize subsets of an input language and reveals effective techniques for language learning.

C. SEQUENTIAL AUTOASSOCIATION

In spite of the growing research on connectionist Natural Language Processing (NLP), a number of problems need to be solved such as the development of proper linguistic representations. Natural language is a dynamic system with underlying hierarchical structure and sequential external appearance and needs an adequate hierarchical systematic way of linguistic representation. The development of global-memory recurrent neural networks, such as the Jordan Recurrent Networks [Jordan, 1986] and the Simple Recurrent Networks (SRN) by Elman [1990] stimulated the development of models that gradually build representations of their sequential input in this global memory

Stoianov in his chapter presents a novel connectionist architecture designed to build and process a hierarchical system of static distributed representations of complex sequential data. It follows upon the idea of building complex static representations of the input sequence but has been extended to reproduce these static representations in their original form by building unique representations for every input sequence. The model consists of sequential autoassociative modules called Recurrent Autoassociative Networks (RANs). Each of these modules learns to reproduce input sequences and as a side effect, develops static distributed representations of the sequences. If requested, these modules unpack static representations into their original sequential form. The complete architecture for processing sequentially represented hierarchical input data consists of a cascade of RANs. The input tokens of a RAN module from any but the lowest level in this cascade scheme are the static representations that the RAN module from the lower level has produced. The input data of the lowest level RAN module are percepts from the external world. The output of a module from the lowest level can be associated with an effector. Then, given a static representation set to the RAN hidden layer, this effector would receive commands sequentially during the unpacking process.

RAN is a recurrent neural network that conforms to the dynamics of natural languages, and RANs produce representations of sequences and interpret them by unpacking back to their sequential form. The more extended architecture, a cascade of RANs, resembles the hierarchy in natural languages. Furthermore, given a representative training environment, this architecture has the capacity to develop the distributed representations in a systematic way. He argues that RANs provide an account of systematicity, and therefore that the RAN and the RAN cascade can participate in a more global cognitive model, where the distributed representations they produce are extensively transformed and associated.

This chapter includes a discussion of hierarchy in dynamic data, and a small RAN example is presented for developing representations of syllables. Although the model solves the problem of developing representations of hierarchically structured sequences, some questions remain open, especially for developing an autonomous cognitive model. Nevertheless, the suggested model may be an important step in connectionist modeling.

D. TRAJECTORY PROBLEMS

An important application of recurrent neural networks is the modeling of dynamic systems involving trajectories, which are good examples of events with specific required time relationships. Typical test cases are the famous nonlinear and autonomous dynamic systems of the circle and the figure-eight.

The difficulty in training recurrent networks often results in the use of approximations that may result in inefficient training. Sundareshan, Wong, and Condarcure in their chapter describe two alternate learning procedures that do not require gradient evaluations. They demonstrate the performance of the two algorithms by use of a complex spatiotemporal learning task to produce continuous trajectories. They show significant advantages in implementation.

They describe two distinct approaches. One uses concepts from the theory of learning automata and the other is based on the classical simplex optimization approach. They demonstrate the training efficiency of these approaches with the task of spatiotemporal signal production by a trained neural network. The complexity of this task reveals the unique capability of recurrent neural networks for approximating temporal dynamics.

In their chapter, Hagner, Hassoun, and Watta compare different network architectures and learning rules, including single-layer fully recurrent networks and multilayer networks with external recurrence: incremental gradient descent, conjugate gradient descent, and three versions of the extended Kalman filter. The circle trajectory is shown to be relatively easily learned while the figure-eight trajectory is difficult. They give a qualitative and quantitative analysis of the neural net approximations of these internally and externally recurrent autonomous systems.

E. FILTERING AND CONTROL

Recurrent networks are more powerful than nonrecurrent networks, particularly for uses in control and signal processing applications. The chapter by Hagan, De Jesús, and Schultz introduces Layered Digital Recurrent Networks (LDRN), develops a general training algorithm for this network, and demonstrates the application of the LDRN to problems in controls and signal processing. They present a notation necessary to represent the LDRN and discuss the dynamic backpropagaion algorithms that are required to compute training gradients for recurrent networks. The concepts underlying the backpropagation-through-time and forward perturbation algorithms are presented in a unified framework, and are demonstrated for a simple, single-loop recurrent network. They also describe a general forward perturbation algorithm for computing training gradients for the LDRN.

Two application sections discuss dynamic backpropogation: implementation of the general dynamic backpropogation algorithm and the application of a neurocontrol architecture to the automatic equalization of an acoustic transmitter. A section on nonlinear filtering demonstrates the application of a recurrent filtering network to a noise-cancellation application.

F. ADAPTIVE ROBOT BEHAVIOR

The chapter by Ziemke discusses the use of recurrent neural networks for robot control and learning and investigates its relevance to different fields of research, including cognitive science, AI, and the engineering of robot control systems. Second-order RNNs, which so far only rarely have been used in robots, are discussed in particular detail, and their capacities for the realization of adaptive robot behavior are demonstrated and analyzed experimentally.

IV. FUTURE DIRECTIONS

This book represents the breadth and depth of interest in recurrent neural networks and points to several directions for ongoing research. The chapters address both new and improved algorithms and design techniques and also new applications. The topics are relevant to language processing, chaotic and real-time systems, optimization, trajectory problems, filtering and control, and robotic behavior.

Research in recurrent neural networks has occurred primarily in the 1990's, building on important fundamental work in the late 1980's. The next decade should produce significant improvements in theory and design as well as many more applications for the creative solution of important practical problems. The widespread application of recurrent neural networks should foster more interest in research and development and raise further theoretical and design questions. The ongoing interest in hybrid systems should also result in new and more powerful uses of recurrent neural networks.

REFERENCES

Almeida, L. B., A learning rule for asynchronous perceptrons with feedback in a combinatorial environment, *Proceedings of the IEEE 1st Annual International Conference on Neural Networks*, San Diego, 609, 1987.

Costa, M., Pasero, E., Piglione, F, and Radasanu, D., Short term load forecasting using a synchronously operated recurrent neural network, *Proceedings of the International Joint Conference on Neural Networks*, 1999.

Coulibay, P., Anctil, F., and Rousselle, J., Real-time short-term water inflows forecasting using recurrent neural networks, *Proceedings of the International Joint Conference on Neural Networks*, 1999.

Elman, J. L., Finding structure in time, *Cognitive Science*, 14, 179, 1990.

Fausett, L., *Fundamentals of Neural Networks*, Prentice Hall, Englewood Cliffs, NJ, 1994.

Giles, C. L., Lawrence, S., Tsoi, A.-C., Rule inference for financial prediction using recurrent neural networks, *IEEE Conference on Computational Intelligence for Financial Engineering*, IEEE Press, 253, 1997.

Hecht-Nielsen, R., *Neurocomputing*, Addison-Wesley, Reading, PA, 1990.

Jordan, M., Generic constraints on underspecified target trajectories, *Proceedings of the International Joint Conference on Neural Networks*, 1, 217, 1989.

Lapedes, A. and Farber, R., Programming a massively parallel computation universal system: static behavior, in *Neural Networks for Computing*, Denker, J. S., Ed., AIP Conference Proceedings, 151, 283, 1986.

Li, S., Wunsch II, D. C., O'Hair, E., and Giesselmann, M. G., Wind turbine power estimation by neural networks with Kalman filter training on a SIMD parallel machine, *Proceedings of the International Joint Conference on Neural Networks*, 1999.

Liang, S.-F., Su, A. W. Y., and Lin, C.-T., A new recurrent-network-based music synthesis method for Chinese plucked-string instruments - pipa and qiu, *Proceedings of the International Joint Conference on Neural Networks*, 1999.

Mendel, J. M. and Fu, K. S., Eds., *Adaptive, Learning and Pattern Recognition Systems*, Academic, New York, 1970.

Nilsson, N. J., *Learning Machines: Foundations of Trainable Pattern Classifying Systems*, McGraw-Hill, New York, 1965.

Pearlmutter, B., Learning state space trajectories in recurrent neural networks, *Neural Computation*, 1, 263, 1989.

Pearlmutter, B., Gradient calculations for dynamic recurrent neural networks: A survey, *IEEE Transactions on Neural Networks*, 6, 1212, 1995.

Pineda, F. J., Generalization of backpropagation in recurrent neural networks, *Physical Review Letters*, 59 (19), 2229, 1987.

Introduction

Rumelhart, D. E., Hinton, G. E., and Williams, R. J., Learning internal representations by error propagation, in *Parallel Distributed Processing: Explorations in the Microstructure of Cognition*, Rumelhart, D. E. and McClelland, J. L., Eds., MIT Press, Cambridge, 45, 1986.

Saad, E. W., Caudell, T. P., and Wunsch II, D. C., Predictive head tracking for virtual reality, *Proceedings of the International Joint Conference on Neural Networks*, 1999.

Sato, M., A real time running algorithm for recurrent neural networks, *Biological Cybernetics*, 62, 237, 1990.

Werbos, P., Backpropagation through time: what it does and how to do it, *Proceedings of the IEEE*, 78, 1550, 1990.

Werbos, P., *The Roots of Backpropagation: From Ordered Derivatives to Neural Networks and Political Forecasting*, Wiley, New York, 1993.

Williams, R. and Zipser, D., A learning algorithm for continually running fully recurrent neural networks, *Neural Computation*, 1, 270, 1989.

Chapter 2

RECURRENT NEURAL NETWORKS FOR OPTIMIZATION: THE STATE OF THE ART

Youshen Xia and Jun Wang

Department of Mechanical & Automation Engineering
The Chinese University of Hong Kong
Shatin, New Territories, Hong Kong

I. INTRODUCTION

Optimization problems arise in a wide variety of scientific and engineering applications including signal processing, system identification, filter design, function approximation, regression analysis, and so on. In many practical optimization problems such as the planning of power systems and routing of telecommunication systems, the numbers of decision variables and constraints are usually very large. It is even more challenging when a large-scale optimization procedure has to be performed in real time to optimize the performance of a dynamical system. For such applications, classical optimization techniques may not be competent due to the problem dimensionality and stringent requirement on computational time. One possible and very promising approach to real-time optimization is to apply artificial neural networks. Neural networks are composed of many massively connected neurons. Resembling more or less their biological counterparts in structures, artificial neural networks are representational and computational models composed of interconnected simple processing elements called artificial neurons. In processing information, the processing elements in an artificial neural network operate concurrently and collectively in a parallel and distributed fashion. Because of the inherent nature of parallel and distributed information processing in neural networks, the convergence rate of the solution process is not decreasing as the size of the problem increases. Furthermore, unlike other parallel algorithms, neural networks can be implemented physically in designated hardware such as application-specific integrated circuits where optimization is carried out in a truly parallel and distributed manner. This feature is particularly desirable for real-time optimization in decentralized decision-making situations. Neural networks are promising computational models for solving large-scale optimization problems in real time. Therefore, the neural network approach can solve optimization problems in running times at the orders of magnitude much faster than the most popular optimization algorithms executed on general-purpose digital computers.

Neural network research stemmed back from McCulloch and Pitts' pioneering work a half century ago. Since then, numerous neural network models have been developed. One of the well-known classic neural network models is the Perceptron developed by Rosenblatt. The Perceptron is a single-layer adaptive feedforward network of threshold logic units, which possess some learning capability.

Another important early neural network model is the Adaline which is a one-layer linear network using the delta learning rule for learning. The Perceptron and Adaline were designed primarily for the purpose of pattern classification. Given a set of input-output training patterns, the Perceptron and Adaline could learn from the exemplar patterns and adapt their parametric representations accordingly to match the patterns. The limitation of the Perceptron and Adaline is that they could only classify linearly separable patterns because, among others, they lacked an internal representation of stimuli.

The first attempt to develop analog circuits for solving linear programming problems was perhaps Pyne in 1956 [Pyne, 1956]. Soon after, some other circuits were proposed for solving various optimization problems. In 1986, Tank and Hopfield [Hopfield and Tank, 1985; Tank and Hopfield, 1986] introduced a linear programming neural network implemented by using an analog circuit which is well suited for applications that require on-line optimization. Their seminal work has inspired many researchers to investigate alternative neural networks for solving linear and nonlinear programming problems. Many optimization neural networks have been developed. For example, Kennedy and Chua [Kennedy and Chua, 1988] proposed a neural network for solving nonlinear programming problems. This network inculde the Tank and Hopfield network as a special case. The disadvantages of this network is that it contains penalty parameters and thus its equilibrium points correspond to approximate optimal solutions only. To overcome the shortcoming, Rodríguez-Vázquez et al. [1990] proposed a switched-capacitor neural network for solving a class of optimization problems. This network is suitable when the optimal solution lies in the feasible region only. Otherwise, the network may have no equilibrium point. Wang [Wang, 1994] proposed a deterministic annealing neural network for solving convex programming. This network guarantees an optimal solution can be obtained. Yet, the given sufficient condition is not easy to be verfied sometimes. From the optimization point of view, most of the methods employed by these existing neural networks belong to either the penalty function method or Lagrangian method. For more discussion on the advantages and disadvantages of these models and their modification, see Cichocki and Unbehauen [1993]. More recently, using the gradient and projection methods Bouzerdoum and Pattison [Bouzerdoum and Pattison, 1993] presented a neural network for solving quadratic optimization problems with bounded variables only. The network has the good performance in computation and implementation but can not solve general linear and quadratic programming problems. By the dual and projection methods Xia and Wang developed some neural networks for solving general linear and quadratic programming problems. These new neural networks have shown to be of good performance in computation and implementation.

Organized in two parts, this chapter is going to discuss the primal-dual neural networks for solving linear and quadratic programming problems (LP and QP) and develop the neural network for solving linear complementary problems (LCP). Following a unified method for designing neural network models, the first part of this chapter describes in detail primal-dual recurrent neural networks, with continuous time, for solving LP and QP. The second part of this chapter focuses on primal -dual discrete time neural networks for QP and LCP. The discrete assignment neural networks are described in detail.

II. CONTINUOUS-TIME NEURAL NETWORKS FOR QP AND LCP

A. PROBLEMS AND DESIGN OF NEURAL NETWORKS

1. Problem Statement

We consider convex quadratic programming with bound contraints:

$$
\begin{aligned}
\text{Minimize} \quad & \frac{1}{2}x^T Ax + c^T x \\
\text{subject to} \quad & Dx = b, \\
& 0 \leq x \leq d
\end{aligned}
\tag{1}
$$

where $x \in \Re^n$ is the vector of decision variables, $A \in \Re^{n \times n}$ is a positive semidefinite matrix, $b \in \Re^m, c \in \Re^n, d \in \Re^n$ are constant column vectors, $D \in \Re^{m \times n}$ is a coefficient matrix, $m \leq n$. When $d = \infty$, (1) become a standard quadratic programming:

$$
\begin{aligned}
\text{Minimize} \quad & \frac{1}{2}x^T Ax + c^T x \\
\text{subject to} \quad & Dx = b, x \geq 0
\end{aligned}
\tag{2}
$$

When $A = 0$, (1) becomes linear programming with bound contraints:

$$
\begin{aligned}
\text{Minimize} \quad & c^T x \\
\text{subject to} \quad & Dx = b, \\
& 0 \leq x \leq d
\end{aligned}
\tag{3}
$$

We consider also linear complementary problems below: Find a vector $z \in R^l$ such that

$$
z^T(Mz + q) = 0, (Mz + q) \geq 0, z \geq 0
\tag{4}
$$

where $q \in R^l$, and $M \in R^{l \times l}$ is a positive semidefinite matrix but not necessarily symmetric. LCP has been recognized as a unifying description of a wide class of problems including LP and QP, fixed point problems and bimatrix equilibrium points [Bazaraa, 1990]. In electrical engineering applications, it is used for the analysis and modeling of piecewise linear resistive circuits [Vandenberghe, 1989].

2. Design of Neural Networks

A neural network can operate in either continuous-time or discrete-time form. A continuous- time neural network described by a set of ordinary differential equations enables us to solve optimization problems in real time due to the massively parallel operations of the computing units and due to its real-time convergence rate. In comparison, discrete-time models can be considered as special cases of discretization of continuous-time models. Thus, in this part, we first discuss continuous-time neural networks.

The procedure of a continuous-time neural network design to optimization usually begins with the formulation of an energy function based on the objective function and constraints of the optimization problem under study. Ideally, the minimum of a formulated energy function corresponds to the optimal solution (minimum or maximum, whatever applicable) of the original optimization problem. Clearly, a convex energy function should be used to eliminate local minima. In nontrivial constrained optimization problems, the minimum of the energy function has to satisfy a set of prespecified constraints. The majority, if not all, of the existing neural network approaches to optimization formulates an energy function by incorporating objective function and constraints through functional transformation and numerical weighting. Functional transformation is usually used to convert constraints to a penalty function to penalize the violation of constraints. Numerical weighting is often used to balance constraint satisfaction and objective minimization (or maximization). The way the energy function is formulated plays an important role in the optimization problem-solving procedure based on neural networks.

The second step in designing a neural network for optimization usually involves the derivation of a dynamical equation (also known as state equation or motion equation) of the neural network based on a formulated energy function. The dynamical equation of a neural network prescribes the motion of the activation states of the neural network. The derivation of a dynamical equation is crucial for success of the neural network approach to optimization. A properly derived dynamical equation can ensure that the state of neural network reaches an equilibrium and the equilibrium state of the neural network satisfies the constraints and optimizes the objective function of the optimization problems under study. Presently, the dynamical equations of most neural networks for optimization are derived by letting the time derivative of a state vector to be directly proportional to the negative gradient of an energy function.

The next step is to determine the architecture of the neural network in terms of the neurons and connections based on the derived dynamical equation. An activation function models important characteristics of a neuron. The range of an activation function usually prescribes the domain of state variables (the state space of the neural network). In the use of neural networks for optimization, the activation function depends on the feasible region of decision variables delimited by the constraints of the optimization problem under study. Specifically, it is necessary for the state space to include the feasible region. Any explicit bound on decision variables can be realized by properly selecting the range of activation functions. The activation function is also related to the energy function. If the gradient-based method is adopted in deriving the dynamical equation, then the convex energy function requires an increasing activation function. Precisely, if the steepest descent method is used, the activation function should be equal to the derivative of the energy function. Figure 1 illustrates four examples of energy functions and corresponding activation functions, where the linear activation function can be used for unbounded variables.

The last step in developing neural networks for optimization is usually devoted

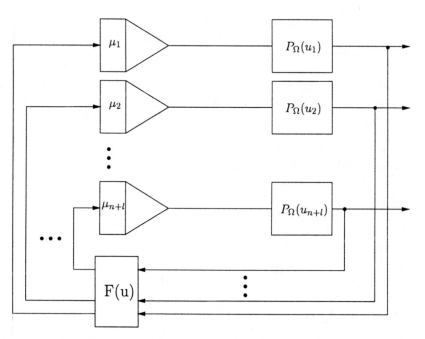

Figure 1. A block diagram of the neural network model in (5) (Xia, Y. and Wang, J., A general method for designing optimization neural networks with global converge nce, *IEEE Transactions on Neural Networks*, ©1998 IEEE)

to simulation to test the performance of the neural network. Simulations can be performed numerically using commercial software packages or self-programmed simulators. Simulation can also be implemented physically in hardware (e.g., using off-the-shelf electronic components).

In summary, to formulate a optimization problem in terms of a neural network, there are two types of methods. One approach commonly used in developing an optimization neural network is to first convert the constrained optimization problem into an associated unconstrained optimization problem, and then design a neural network that solves the unconstrained problem with gradient methods. Another approach is to construct a set of differential equations such that their equilibrium points correspond to the desired solutions and then find an appropriate Lyapunov function such that all trajectory of the systems converges to some equilibrium points. Combining the above two types of methods, we give a deterministic procedure to be used directly to construct neural network models [Xia and Wang, 1998].

Step 1. Find a continuous function $\Phi : \Omega \subset R^{n+l} \to R$ such that its minima correspond to the exact or approximate solutions to P, where $\Omega = \{u = (u_1, ..., u_{n+l})^T | u_i$ satisfies some interval constraints and P denotes one of (1)-(4).}

Step 2. Construct a continuous vector valued function $F : \Omega \subset R^{n+l} \to R^{n+l}$ such that the functions $F(u)$ and $\Phi(u)$ satisfy

(I) if u^* is a minimizer of Φ, then $F(u^*) = 0$,

(II) $(u - u^*)^T F(u) \leq -\alpha(\Phi(u) - \Phi(u^*)), \forall u \in \Omega$

where $F(u)$ satisfies local Lipschitz conditions, $\alpha > 0$ and fixed.

Step 3. Let the neural network model for solving P be represented by the following dynamic systems

$$\frac{du}{dt} = \Lambda F(u), \quad u \in \Omega \tag{5}$$

where $\Lambda = diag(\mu_1, ..., \mu_{n+l})$, and $\mu_i > 0$ which is to scale the convergence rate of (5).

Step 4. Based on the systems in (5), design the neural network architecture for solving P.

A block diagram of the neural network is shown in Fig. 1, where the projection operator $P_\Omega(u)$ enforces state vector u in Ω, which is defined by $P_\Omega(u) = [P_\Omega(u_1), ..., P_\Omega(u_{n+l})]^T$ and for $i \in L - I$, $P_\Omega(u_i) = u_i$; for $i \in I$,

$$P_\Omega(u_i) = \begin{cases} d_i & u_i < d_i \\ u_i & d_i \geq u_i \geq h_i \\ h_i & u_i > h_i \end{cases}$$

where $L = \{1, ..., n + l\}$ and $I \subset L$.

3. Theoretical Result of the Method

About the proposed method, we have the theoretical results below [Xia and Wang, 1998].

Theorem 1. Any neural network derived from the proposed method is stable in the sense of Lyapunov and globally convergent to an exact or approximate solution to P.

Proof. Without loss of generality we assume that the set of minimizers of P is unbounded, and thus the set of global minimizers of Φ is unbounded.

First, we know from the first step of the method that an exact or approximate solution to P corresponds to a minimizer of Φ, and from the second step that $F(u) = 0$ if and only if u is a minimizer of Φ. Thus it follows that $F(u) = 0$ if and only if u is an exact or an approximate solution to P. That is, the equilibrium points of the system in (5) correspond to exact or approximate solutions to P.

Next, by the existence theory of ordinary differential equations [Miller and Michel, 1982], we see that for any an initial point taken in Ω there exists a unique and continuous solution $u(t) \subset \Omega$ for the systems in (5) over $[t_0, T)$ since the function $F(u)$ satisfies local Lipschitz conditions.

Now, we consider the positive definite function

$$V(u) = \frac{1}{2}\|\Lambda_1(u - u^*)\|_2^2, \quad u \in \Omega$$

where $\Lambda_1 = diag(\mu_1^{-\frac{1}{2}}, ..., \mu_{n+l}^{-\frac{1}{2}})$ and u^* is a fixed minimizer of Φ. From condition (II) we have

$$\begin{aligned}
\frac{d}{dt}V(u) &= \frac{dV}{du}\frac{du}{dt} = (u - u^*)^T \Lambda_1^2 \Lambda F(u) \\
&= (u - u^*)^T F(u) \le -\alpha(\Phi(u) - \Phi(u^*)) \le 0. \quad (6)
\end{aligned}$$

Thus

$$\|u(t) - u^*\|_2 \le \beta\|u(t_0) - u^*\|_2 \quad \forall t \in [t_0, T)$$

where β is a positive constant. Then the solution $u(t)$ is bounded on $[t_0, T)$, and thus $T = \infty$. Moreover, the system in (5) is Lyapunov stable at each equilibrium point.

On the other hand, since $\lim_{k\to\infty} V(u^k) = +\infty$ whenever the sequence $u^k \subset \hat{\Omega}$ and $\lim_{k\to\infty}\|u^k\| = +\infty$, by Lemma 2 we see that all level sets of V are bounded though all level sets of Φ are unbounded, thus $\hat{\Omega} = \{u \in \Omega | V(u) \le V(u^0)\}$ is bounded. Because $V(u)$ is continuously differentiable on the compact set $\hat{\Omega}$ and $\{u(t)|t \ge t_0\} \subset \hat{\Omega}$, it follows from the LaSalle's invariance principle that trajectories $u(t)$ converge to Σ, the largest invariant subset of the following set

$$E = \{u \in \hat{\Omega} \mid \frac{dV}{dt} = 0\}.$$

Note that if $dV/dt = 0$, then $(u - u^*)^T F(u) = 0$. So $-\alpha(\Phi(u) - \Phi(u^*)) \ge 0$ by condition (II). Thus $\Phi(u) = \Phi(u^*)$ and u is an equilibrium point of the system in (7); i.e.,

$$\frac{du}{dt} = \Lambda F(u) = 0.$$

19

Conversely, if $du/dt = 0$, then $F(u) = 0$, and $dV/dt = (u - u^*)^T F(u) = 0$. So $du/dt = 0$ if and only if $dV/dt = 0$. Hence

$$E = \{u \in \hat{\Omega} | \frac{du}{dt} = 0\}$$

Finally, let $\lim_{k \to \infty} u(t_k) = \hat{u}$, then $\hat{u} \in \Omega^*$. Therefore, for $\forall \epsilon > 0$ there exists $q > 0$ such that

$$\|\Lambda_1(u(t_k) - \hat{u})\| < \epsilon \quad k \geq q$$

Note that (6) holds for each $u^* \in \Omega^*$, then $\|\Lambda_1(u(t) - \hat{u})\|$ is decreasing as $t \to \infty$. It follows that

$$\|\Lambda_1(u(t) - \hat{u})\|_2 \leq \|\Lambda_1(u(t_{k_q}) - \hat{u})\|_2 < \epsilon \quad t \geq k_q,$$

then

$$\lim_{t \to \infty} \|\Lambda_1(u(t) - \hat{u})\|_2 = 0.$$

So

$$\lim_{t \to \infty} u(t) = \hat{u}.$$

Remark: From Theorem 1 we see that any neural network designed by using the proposed method is globally stable and convergent. Following the proposed method we will derive two neural network models for QP and LCP, in which equilibrium points give exact solutions and there is no need for penalty or variable parameter in the models.

B. PRIMAL-DUAL NEURAL NETWORKS FOR LP AND QP

1. Neural Network Models

From the dual theory we see that the dual problem of (1) is as follows

$$\text{Maximize} \quad b^T y - \frac{1}{2}x^T Ax - d^T v$$
$$\text{subject to} \quad Ax - D^T y + c + v \geq 0, \tag{7}$$
$$v \geq 0$$

where $y \in \Re^m, v \in \Re^n$ are the vectors of dual decision variables. By the complementary slackness theorem [Bertsekas, 1982], x^* and (y^*, v^*) are optimal solutions respectively to the primal problem (1) and the dual problem (7) if and only if x^* and (y^*, v^*) satisfy $Dx^* = b, 0 \leq x^* \leq d, v^* \geq 0$, and the following complementary conditions

$$\begin{cases} (v^*)^T(d - x^*) = 0 \\ (x^*)^T(Ax^* - D^T y^* + c + v^*) = 0 \end{cases} \tag{8}$$

It is easy to see that (8) is equivalent to the equation of projection

$$x^* = P_\Omega(x^* - Ax^* + D^T y^* - c)$$

where $\Omega = \{x \in \Re^n | 0 \leq x \leq d\}, P_\Omega(x) = [P_\Omega(x_1), P_\Omega(x_2), \ldots, P_\Omega(x_n)]^T$, and for $i = 1, 2, \ldots, n$,

$$P_\Omega(x_i) = \begin{cases} 0, & \text{if } x_i < 0 \\ x_i, & \text{if } 0 \leq x_i \leq d_i \\ d_i, & \text{if } x_i > d_i \end{cases}.$$

In Xia [1995], through improving the structure of the modifying extragradient algorithm [Marcotte, 1991], we proposed the following primal-dual neural network model for solving (2)

$$\frac{d}{dt}\begin{pmatrix} x \\ y \end{pmatrix} = -\left\{ \begin{array}{c} D^T(Dx - b) + \beta_0[2Ax - D^T y + c \\ -A(x - Ax + D^T y - c)^+] \\ \beta_0[D(x - Ax + D^T y - c)^+ - b] \end{array} \right\} \qquad (9)$$

and the following model for solving (3)

$$\frac{d}{dt}\begin{pmatrix} x \\ y \end{pmatrix} = -\left\{ \begin{array}{c} D^T(Dx - b) - \beta_1(D^T y + c) \\ \beta_1[DP_\Omega(x + D^T y - c) - b] \end{array} \right\}, \qquad (10)$$

respectively, where $x \in \Omega, y \in R^m$, $\beta_1 = \|x - P_\Omega(x + D^T y - c)\|_2^2$, $\beta_0 = \|x - (x - Ax + D^T y - c)^+\|_2^2$, $(x)^+ = \{[x_1]^+, \ldots, [x_l]^+\}^T$, and $[x_i]^+ = \max\{0, x_i\}$. Here, directly extending the structure of the above two models we can obtain the following neural network model for solving (1)

$$\frac{d}{dt}\begin{pmatrix} x \\ y \end{pmatrix} = -\left\{ \begin{array}{c} D^T(Dx - b) + \beta[2Ax - D^T y + c \\ -AP_\Omega(x - Ax + D^T y - c)] \\ \beta[DP_\Omega(x - Ax + D^T y - c) - b] \end{array} \right\} \qquad (11)$$

where $x \in \Omega, y \in R^m$, and $\beta = \|x - P_\Omega(x - Ax + D^T y - c)\|_2^2$. For simplicity, eqn. (11) can be written as follows:

$$\frac{d}{dt}\begin{pmatrix} x \\ y \end{pmatrix} = -\left\{ \begin{array}{c} Bx - q + \beta v(x, y) \\ \beta[Dg(x, y) - b] \end{array} \right\} \qquad (12)$$

where $B = D^T D, q = D^T b, v(x, y) = 2Ax - D^T y + c - Ag(x, y)$, and $g(x, y) = P_\Omega(x - Ax + D^T y - c)$. The primal-dual neural network consists of a multivariable system with an excitation function $v(x, y)$ and a multivariable decaying system $g(x, y)$ with a time-varying parameter β. Figure 2 illustrates the architecture of the primal-dual network.

2. Global Convergence and Stability

First, we introduce two lemmas.

Lemma 1. Let $u^* \in \Omega, u \in \Re^n$, then

$$[P_\Omega(u) - u^*]^T[u - u^*] \geq \|u^* - P_\Omega(u)\|_2^2.$$

21

Proof. See [Gafni and Bertsekas, 1984].

Lemma 2. Let $\Phi_0(x,,y) = \|Dx-b\|_2^2 + \|P_\Omega(x-Ax+D^Ty-c)-x\|_2^4$. Then $\Phi_0(x,,y) \geq 0$ and $\Phi_0(x,,y) = 0$ if and only if (x,y) is an optimal solution to the original and dual problems, and if $\Phi_0(x,,y) = 0$, then (x,y) is an equilibrium point of the system (11).

Proof. From (4) and the structure of the system (11) it is easy to know the conclusion of Lemma 2.

Theorem 2. Assume that the original problem has an optimal solution. Then the primal-dual network (11) is stable in the sense of Lyapunov and globally convergent to a point corresponding to the optimal solution of both (1) and (7).

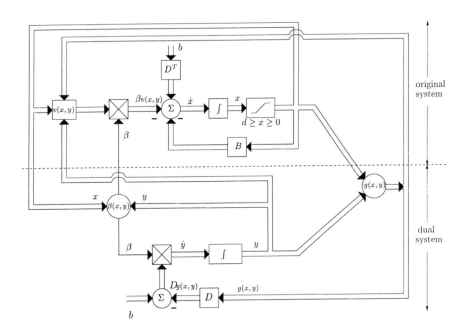

Figure 2. A block diagram of the neural network model in (12)

Proof. Let $(x_0, y_0) \in \Omega \times \Re^m$ be an any given initial point. Since the projection function $P_\Omega(x - Ax + D^Ty - c)$ is Lipschitz continuous in $\Re^{n+m}$,

$$F(x,y) = \left\{ \begin{array}{c} D^T(Dx-b) + \beta[A(x - P_\Omega(x-Ax+D^Ty-c)) \\ +Ax - D^Ty - c] \\ \beta[DP_\Omega(x-Ax+D^Ty-c) - b] \end{array} \right\}$$

is also Lipschitz continuous. From the existence theory of ordinary differential equation we see that there exists a unique and continuous solution $w(t) = (x(t), y(t))$ with $w(0) = (x_0, y_0)$ for (11) on some interval $[0,\infty)$. Let $w^* =$

(x^*, y^*), where x^* and y^* is an optimal solution to (1) and (7), respectively. Then

$$
\begin{aligned}
& - \quad (w(t) - w^*)^T F(x, y) \\
& = \quad \begin{pmatrix} x - x^* \\ y - y^* \end{pmatrix}^T \begin{pmatrix} D^T(Dx - b) + \beta[2Ax - D^Ty + c \\ -AP_\Omega(x - Ax + D^Ty - c)] \\ \beta[DP_\Omega(x - Ax + D^Ty - c) - b] \end{pmatrix} \\
& = \quad \|Dx - b\|_2^2 + \beta(x - x^*)^T\{A[x - P_\Omega(x - Ax + D^Ty - c)] \\
& + \quad (Ax - D^Ty + c)\} + \beta(y - y^*)^T D[P_\Omega(x - Ax + D^Ty - c) - x] \\
& + \quad \beta(y - y^*)^T(Dx - b) \\
& = \quad \|Dx - b\|_2^2 + \beta[x - P_\Omega(x - Ax + D^Ty - c)]^T[Ax - D^Ty + c] \\
& + \quad \beta(x - x^*)^T D^T(y - y^*) \\
& + \quad \beta[x - P_\Omega(x - Ax + D^Ty - c)]^T[D^Ty^* - Ax^* - c] \\
& + \quad \beta(x - x^*)^T(Ax - D^Ty + c)
\end{aligned}
$$

On one hand, using the same optimal value of both (1) and (7) we obtain that

$$
\begin{aligned}
& - \quad (w(t) - w^*)^T F(x, y) \\
& \geq \quad \|Dx - b\|_2^2 + \beta[x - P_\Omega(x - Ax + D^Ty - c)]^T[Ax - D^Ty + c] \\
& + \quad \beta(x - x^*)^T A^T(x - x^*)
\end{aligned}
$$

On the other hand, from Lemma 1 we let $u = x - Ax + D^Ty - c, u^* = x$, then

$$[P_\Omega(x - Ax + D^Ty - c) - x]^T[x - Ax + D^Ty - c - x] \geq \|x - P_\Omega(x - Ax + D^Ty - c)\|_2^2.$$

Therefore,

$$
\begin{aligned}
& - \quad (w(t) - w^*)^T F(x, y) \\
& \geq \quad \|Dx - b\|_2^2 + \beta\|x - P_\Omega(x - Ax + D^Ty - c)\|_2^2 + (x - x^*)^T A(x - x^*) \\
& \geq \quad \Phi_0(x, y)
\end{aligned}
$$

since $\beta = \|x - P_\Omega(x - Ax + D^Ty - c)\|_2^2$ and A is a positive semidefinite matrix. So

$$(w(t) - w^*)^T F(x, y) \leq -(\Phi_0(x, y) - \Phi_0(x^*, y^*)). \tag{13}$$

So $\Phi_0(x, y)$ and $F(x, y)$ satisfy the conditions (I) and (II). By Theorem 1 we can obtain the proof of Theorem 2.

C. NEURAL NETWORKS FOR LCP

1. Neural Network Model

According to Kinderlehrer [1980], z^* is a solution to (4) if and only if z^* satisfies the following equation

$$P_\Omega(z - Mz - q) = z \tag{14}$$

23

where $\Omega = \{z \in R^l | z \geq 0\}$ and $P_\Omega(\cdot)$ denotes the projection onto the set Ω. In Wang [1998] we proposed the following neural network model

$$\frac{dz}{dt} = F(z) = (I + M^T)((z - Mz - q)^+ - z) \tag{15}$$

The system described by (15) can be easily realized by a recurrent neural network with a two-layer structure shown in Fig. 3 where the vector z is the network output, $\beta q = (q_i)$ is the network input vector, and $(I + M^T) = (m_{ij})$ and $M = (w_{ij})$ are weighted connections. We see from Fig. 3 that the proposed neural network can be implemented only by using simple hardware without analog multipliers for variables or penalty parameter. The circuit realizing the recurrent neural network consists of $2l^2 + 3l$ simple summers, l integrators, and $2l^2$ weighted connections. The projection operator $(\cdot)^+$ may be implemented by using a piecewise activation function [Bouzerdoum and Pattison, 1993].

2. Global Convergence and Stability

Using Theorem 1 we can obtain the following result.

Theorem 3. Assume that $\Omega^* = \{z \in R^l | z$ satisfies (4)$\}$ is a nonempty set. Then the neural network of (15) is stable in the sense of Lyapunov and globally convergent to a solution to (4).

Proof. We see first that $z^* \in \Omega^*$ if and only if $\Phi(z^*) = 0$ where $\Phi(z) = z - (z - Mz - q)^+$. Therefore, $\Phi(u)$ and $F(u)$ satisfy the first step and condition (I) in the second step. By the fact that $(u - Mu - q)^+$ is the projection of $(x - Mx - q)$ onto Ω and x^* is in Ω, using Lemma 2 we have

$$[z^* - (u - Mu - q)^+]^T[Mz + q - z + (u - Mu - q)^+] \geq 0, \forall z \in R^l.$$

Since z^* is a solution to (4), then

$$\{(u - Mu - q)^+ - z^*\}^T\{Mz^* + q\} \geq 0, \quad \forall z \in R^l.$$

Adding the two resulting inequalities yields

$$\{z^* - (u - Mu - q)^+\}^T\{Mz - Mx^* + (u - Mu - q)^+ - z\} \geq 0,$$

then

$$(z^* - z)^T M(z^* - z) \leq (z - z^*)^T(I + M^T)(z - (u - Mu - q)^+)$$
$$- \|z - (u - Mu - q)^+\|_2^2.$$

Noting that $(z - z^*)^T M(z - z^*) \geq 0$, it follows that

$$(z - z^*)^T (I + M^T)(z - (u - Mu - q)^+)\} \leq -\|z - (u - Mu - q)^+\|_2^2,$$

thus

$$(z - z^*)^T F(z) \leq -(\Phi(z) - \Phi(z^*)).$$

So $\Phi(z)$ and $F(z)$ satisfy conditions (I) and (II). By Theorem 1 we can obtain the proof of Theorem 3.

III. DISCRETE-TIME NEURAL NETWORKS FOR QP AND LCP

In many operations, discrete-time neural networks are preferable to their continuous-time counterparts because of the availability of design tools and the compatibility with computers and other digital devices. In this section, we discuss discrete-time neural networks. Generally speaking, a discrete-time neural network model can be obtained from a continuous-time one by converting differential equations into appropriate difference equations though discretization. However, the resulting discrete-time model is usually not guaranteed to be globally convergent to optimal solutions. In addition, difficulties may arise in selecting design parameters since the parameters may not be bounded in a small range. Moreover, it is not straightforward to realize variable parameters in hardware implementation of neural networks.

In this section, we present discrete-time recurrent neural networks with fixed design parameters. These networks are readily realized in digital circuits, and the proposed recurrent neural networks are guaranteed to globally converge to an optimal solution.

A. NEURAL NETWORKS FOR QP AND LCP

We first consider the relation between LCP and the following QP

$$\begin{aligned}
&\text{minimize} \quad \frac{1}{2}x^T A x + c^T x \\
&\text{subject to} \quad Dx \geq b, \quad x \geq 0.
\end{aligned} \tag{16}$$

It is easy to see that its dual problem is

$$\begin{aligned}
&\text{maximize} \quad b^T y - \frac{1}{2}x^T A x \\
&\text{subject to} \quad D^T y - A x \leq c, \quad y \geq 0
\end{aligned} \tag{17}$$

where $y \in R^m$. From Lagrangian duality [Bertsekas, 1982], one can see that x^*, y^* is an optimal solution to (16),(17), respectively, if and only if (x^*, y^*) satisfies

$$\begin{aligned}
c + A^T x - D^T y \geq 0, \quad x \geq 0, \quad x^T(c + A^T x - D^T y) = 0, \\
Dx - b \geq 0, \quad y \geq 0, \quad y^T(Dx - b) = 0.
\end{aligned} \tag{18}$$

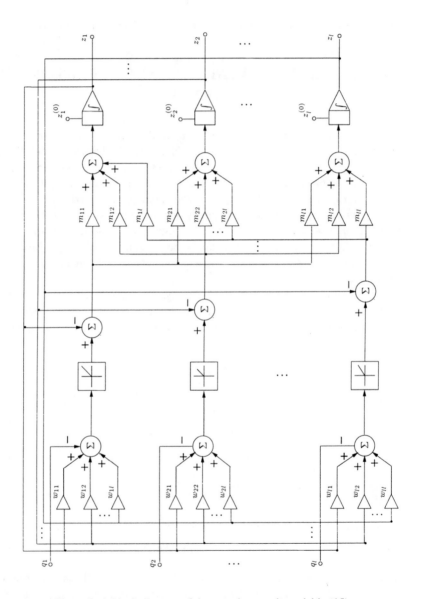

Figure 3. A block diagram of the neural network model in (15)

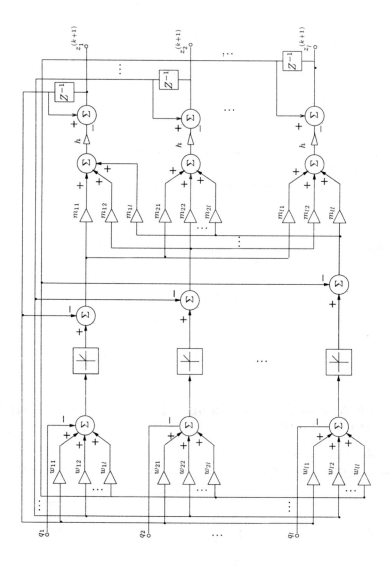

Figure 4. A block diagram of the neural network model in (19)

Let

$$M = \begin{bmatrix} A & -D^T \\ D & 0 \end{bmatrix}, \quad q = \begin{bmatrix} c \\ -b \end{bmatrix}.$$

Then the problem (16) and (17) may become an LCP problem. Therefore, we discuss only discrete-time neural network for LCP.

Applying the Euler formula to the proposed neural network model

$$\frac{dz}{dt} = (I + M^T)((z - Mz - q)^+ - z),$$

we can get the following discrete-time neural network

$$z(k+1) = z(k) - hF(z(k)) \quad k = 1, 2, \dots \tag{19}$$

where $F(z) = (I + M^T)((z - Mz - q)^+ - z)$ and $h > 0$ is a fixed design parameter. Figure 4 shows its digital implementation.

For (19) we have the following theoretical result.

Theorem 4. If $h < \frac{2}{\|I+M^T\|^2}$, then sequence $\{z(k)\}$ generated by the discrete-time network of (19) is globally convergent to an optimal solution of the problem (16) and (17).

Proof. From the proof of the paper [Solodov and Tseng, 1996] we see that when $h = 2\|F(z(k))\|^{-2}\|r(z(k))\|^2$, where $r(z) = ((z - Mz - q)^+ - z)$, the sequence $\{z(k)\}$ generated by the discrete-time network of (19) is globally convergent to an optimal solution of the problem (16) and (17). Since

$$\|(I + M^T)r\|^2 \leq \|I + M^T\|^2\|r\|^2,$$

$$\frac{2}{\|I + M^T\|^2} \leq 2\|F(z(k))\|^{-2}\|r(z(k))\|^2.$$

Thus the conclusion of Theorem 4 holds.

B. PRIMAL-DUAL NEURAL NETWORK FOR LINEAR ASSIGNMENT

1. Problem Formulation

The assignment problem can be formulated as the following zero-one integer linear program:

$$\text{minimize} \quad \sum_{i=1}^{n}\sum_{j=1}^{n} c_{ij}x_{ij}, \tag{20}$$

$$\text{subject to} \quad \sum_{i=1}^{n} x_{ij} = 1, \quad j = 1, 2, \dots, n; \tag{21}$$

$$\sum_{j=1}^{n} x_{ij} = 1, \quad i = 1, 2, \dots, n; \tag{22}$$

$$x_{ij} \in \{0, 1\}, \quad i, j = 1, 2, \dots, n. \tag{23}$$

where c_{ij} and x_{ij} are respectively the cost coefficient and decision variable associated with assigning entity i to position j. In general, a cost coefficient can be positive representing a loss or negative representing a gain. The decision variable is defined such that $x_{ij} = 1$ if and only if entity i is assigned to position j. The objective function (20) to be minimized is the total cost for the assignment. Constraint (21) ensures that exactly one entity is assigned to each position; i.e., each column of x_{ij} has only one decision variable being 1. Constraint (22) ensures that each entity is assigned to exactly one position; i.e., each row of x_{ij} has only one decision variable being 1. Constraint (23) is the zero-one integrality constraint on decision variables. The assignment problem has a unique solution for almost all the cost coefficient matrix $[c_{ij}]$, and thus the uniqueness of the solution of (20)-(23) is assumed throughout this paper. It is well known, from the optimal solution point of view, that if the optimal solution is unique, then the assignment problem is equivalent to a linear programming problem by replacing the zero-one integrality constraints (23) with nonnegativity constraints, due to the total unimodularity property [Bazaraa et al., 1990]:

$$x_{ij} \geq 0, \quad i, j = 1, 2, \ldots, n. \tag{24}$$

We can therefore obtain the solution of (20)-(23) by solving its equivalent linear program which has also a unique solution. Based on the primal assignment problem, the dual assignment problem can be formulated as follows:

$$\text{maximize} \quad \sum_{i=1}^{n} (u_i + v_i) \tag{25}$$

$$\text{subject to} \quad u_i + v_j \leq c_{ij}, \ i, j = 1, 2, \ldots, n; \tag{26}$$

where u_i and v_i denote the dual decision variables. The number of decision variables and inequality constraints in the dual assignment problem is $2n$ and n^2, respectively. According to the duality theorem in optimization theory [Bazaraa et al., 1990], the value of the objective function at its maximum is equal to the total cost of the primal assignment problem at its minimum; i.e., no duality gap.

2. Neural Network Models

In this section, we discuss the existing primal-dual assignment networks [Wang and Xia, 1998] for solving the primal and dual assignment problems.

Consider the following energy function:

$$
\begin{aligned}
E(x, u, v) = & \frac{1}{2} \left\{ \sum_{i=1}^{n} \left[\sum_{j=1}^{n} c_{ij} x_{ij} - (u_i + v_i) \right] \right\}^2 + \frac{1}{2} \sum_{i=1}^{n} \left[\sum_{j=1}^{n} x_{ij} - 1 \right]^2 \\
& + \frac{1}{2} \sum_{j=1}^{n} \left[\sum_{i=1}^{n} x_{ij} - 1 \right]^2 + \frac{1}{4} \sum_{i=1}^{n} \sum_{j=1}^{n} (x_{ij}^2 - |x_{ij}| x_{ij}) \\
& + \frac{1}{4} \sum_{i=1}^{n} \sum_{j=1}^{n} [c_{ij} - (u_i + v_j)] \left[c_{ij} - (u_i + v_j) - |c_{ij} - (u_i + v_j)| \right]
\end{aligned}
\tag{27}
$$

where $x = (x_{11}, \cdots, x_{ij}, \cdots, x_{nn})^T \in R^{n^2}$, $v = (v_1, \cdots, v_i, \cdots, v_n)^T \in R^n$, and $u = (u_1, \cdots, u_i, \cdots, u_n)^T \in R^n$. The first term in eqn. (27) is the squared duality gap, the second and third terms are respectively for the equality constraints (21) and (22) and the fourth term is for the nonnegativity constraint (24) in the primal assignment problem, the last term is for the inequality constraint (26) in the dual assignment problem. Clearly, the function $E(x, u, v)$ is continuously differentiable, convex, and nonnegative on R^{n^2+2n}. By the duality theorem, x^* and (u^*, v^*) are optimal solutions respectively to the primal problem and the dual problem if and only if $E(x^*, u^*, v^*) = 0$.

The continuous-time version of the primal-dual assignment network is tailored from the ones for general linear programming [Xia, 1996]. If we let the time derivative of a state variable equal the partial derivative of the energy function defined in eqn. (27) with respect to the state variable, the dynamic equation of the continuous-time primal-dual assignment network is defined in the following differential equations: for $i, j = 1, 2, \ldots, n$;

$$
\frac{dx_{ij}}{dt} = -\mu\{c_{ij}\sum_{p=1}^{n}(\sum_{q=1}^{n} c_{pq}x_{pq} - u_p - v_p) + \frac{1}{2}(x_{ij} - |x_{ij}|)
$$

$$
+ \sum_{l=1}^{n}(x_{il} + x_{lj}) - 2\} \tag{28}
$$

$$
\frac{du_i}{dt} = -\mu\{-\sum_{p=1}^{n}(\sum_{q=1}^{n} c_{pq}x_{pq} - u_p - v_p) - \frac{1}{2}\sum_{l=1}^{n}(c_{il} - u_i - v_l
$$

$$
- |c_{il} - u_i - v_l|)\} \tag{29}
$$

$$
\frac{dv_i}{dt} = -\mu\{-\sum_{p=1}^{n}(\sum_{q=1}^{n} c_{pq}x_{pq} - u_p - v_p) - \frac{1}{2}\sum_{l=1}^{n}(c_{li} - u_l - v_i
$$

$$
- |c_{li} - u_l - v_i|)\} \tag{30}
$$

where $\mu > 0$ is a design parameter which scales the convergence rate of the continuous-time assignment network.

Since $s - |s| = 2\min\{0, s\}$ and $\max\{0, s\} = -\min\{0, -s\}$, the above equations can be rewritten as follows:

$$
\frac{dx_{ij}}{dt} = -\mu\{c_{ij}\sum_{p=1}^{n}(\sum_{q=1}^{n} c_{pq}x_{pq} - u_p - v_p) + (x_{ij})^-
$$

$$
+ \sum_{l=1}^{n}(x_{il} + x_{lj}) - 2\} \tag{31}
$$

$$
\frac{du_i}{dt} = -\mu\{-\sum_{p=1}^{n}(\sum_{q=1}^{n} c_{pq}x_{pq} - u_p - v_p) + \sum_{l=1}^{n}(u_i + v_l - c_{il})^+\} \tag{32}
$$

$$
\frac{dv_i}{dt} = -\mu\{-\sum_{p=1}^{n}(\sum_{q=1}^{n} c_{pq}x_{pq} - u_p - v_p) + \sum_{l=1}^{n}(u_l + v_i - c_{li})^+\}, \tag{33}
$$

where $(s)^+ = \max\{0, s\}$ and $(s)^- = \min\{0, s\}$.

Based also on the energy function (27), the discrete-time version of the primal-dual assignment network is defined in the following difference equations: for $i, j = 1, 2, \cdots, n$;

$$
\begin{aligned}
x_{ij}^{(k+1)} &= x_{ij}^{(k)} - h\{c_{ij} \sum_{p=1}^{n}(\sum_{q=1}^{n} c_{pq} x_{pq}^{(k)} - u_p^{(k)} - v_p^{(k)}) + (x_{ij}^{(k)})^- \\
&+ \sum_{l=1}^{n}(x_{il}^{(k)} + x_{lj}^{(k)}) - 2\}
\end{aligned}
\tag{34}
$$

$$
\begin{aligned}
u_i^{(k+1)} &= u_i^{(k)} + h\{\sum_{p=1}^{n}(\sum_{q=1}^{n} c_{pq} x_{pq}^{(k)} - u_p^{(k)} - v_p^{(k)}) \\
&- h \sum_{l=1}^{n}(u_i^{(k)} + v_l^{(k)} - c_{il})^+\}
\end{aligned}
\tag{35}
$$

$$
\begin{aligned}
v_i^{(k+1)} &= v_i^{(k)} + h\{\sum_{p=1}^{n}(\sum_{q=1}^{n} c_{pq} x_{pq}^{(k)} - u_p^{(k)} - v_p^{(k)}) \\
&- h \sum_{l=1}^{n}(u_l^{(k)} + v_i^{(k)} - c_{li})^+\},
\end{aligned}
\tag{36}
$$

where $h > 0$ is a design parameter to be given. For convenience, let

$$
\xi^{(k)} = \sum_{p=1}^{n}(\sum_{q=1}^{n} c_{pq} x_{pq}^{(k)} - u_p^{(k)} - v_p^{(k)}),
\tag{37}
$$

$$
y_{ij}^{(k)} = \sum_{l=1}^{n}(x_{il}^{(k)} + x_{lj}^{(k)}),
\tag{38}
$$

$$
\gamma_i^{(k)} = \sum_{l=1}^{n}(u_i^{(k)} + v_l^{(k)} - c_{il})^+,
\tag{39}
$$

$$
\delta_i^{(k)} = \sum_{l=1}^{n}(u_l^{(k)} + v_i^{(k)} - c_{li})^+.
\tag{40}
$$

Then eqns. (34)-(36) can be rewritten as: for $i, j = 1, 2, \cdots, n$;

$$
x_{ij}^{(k+1)} = x_{ij}^{(k)} - h\left[\xi^{(k)} c_{ij} + (x_{ij}^{(k)})^- + y_{ij}^{(k)} - 2\right]
\tag{41}
$$

$$
u_i^{(k+1)} = u_i^{(k)} + h\left[\xi^{(k)} - \gamma_i^{(k)}\right]
\tag{42}
$$

$$
v_i^{(k+1)} = v_i^{(k)} + h\left[\xi^{(k)} - \delta_i^{(k)}\right]
\tag{43}
$$

Figure 5 illustrates the architectures of the primal-dual assignment networks defined in auxiliary equations (37)-(40) (Figure 5(a)), differential equations (31-33) (Figure 5(b)), and difference equations (22)-(24) (Figure 5(c)). It shows that

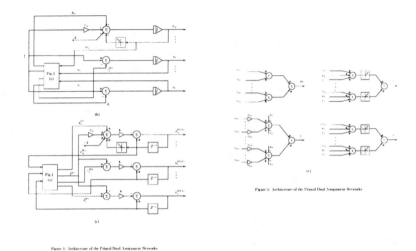

Figure 1: Architecture of the Primal-Dual Assignment Networks

Figure 5. Architectures of the primal-dual assignment networks (Wang, J. and Xia, Y., Analysis and Design of Primal-Dual Assignment Networks, *IEEE Transactions on Neural Networks*, ©1998 IEEE)

the primal-dual assignment networks are composed of a number of adders, limiters, and time delays or integrators only.

3. Global Convergence

The global convergence property of the continuous-time counterpart is proven in Xia [1996]. In this section, we shall show that the discrete-time assignment network with a constant design parameter is globally convergent to an exact solution to the primal-dual assignment problem. First, some lemmas are needed to be introduced.

Lemma 3. Let $\varphi(x) = \frac{1}{2}(x^2 - |x|x), x \in R$. Then $\varphi'(x) = x - |x|$. For any $x, y \in R$,

$$\varphi(x) \leq \varphi(y) + \varphi'(y)(x - y) + (x - y)^2. \tag{44}$$

Proof. Consider two cases as follows.
(i) For any $y \geq 0, \varphi(y) = 0$ and $\varphi'(y) = 0$. Thus,
  a) if $x \geq 0, \varphi(x) \leq (x - y)^2$, so (44) holds;
  b) if $x < 0, \varphi(x) = x^2 \leq (x - y)^2$, so (44) also holds.
(ii) For $y < 0, y^2 + 2y(x - y) + (x - y)^2 = x^2$, so (44) holds.

Lemma 4. Let $\varphi(x) = \frac{1}{2}[(a_0x + b_0)^2 - |a_0x + b_0|(a_0x + b_0)], x \in R$. For any $x, y \in R$,

$$\varphi(x) \leq \varphi(y) + \varphi'(y)(x - y) + a_0^2(x - y)^2. \tag{45}$$

Proof. Let $z_1 = a_0 x + b_0, z_2 = a_0 y + b_0$, then $\varphi(x) = \varphi_1(z_1) = \frac{1}{2}(z_1^2 - |z_1|z_1)$ and $\varphi(y) = \varphi_1(z_2) = \frac{1}{2}(z_2^2 - |z_2|z_2)$. Thus, by Lemma 3 we have

$$\varphi(x) = \varphi_1(z_1) \leq \varphi_1(z_2) + \varphi_1'(z_2)(z_1 - z_2) + (z_1 - z_2)^2.$$

Hence

$$\varphi(x) \leq \varphi(y) + \varphi'(y)(x - y) + a_0^2(x - y)^2.$$

Lemma 5. Let $\Phi(x) = \frac{1}{2}x^T(x - |x|), x \in R^n$. For any $x, y \in R^n$,

$$\Phi(x) \leq \Phi(y) + \nabla\Phi(y)^T(x - y) + \|x - y\|_2^2. \tag{46}$$

where $\nabla\Phi(y)$ is the gradient of $\Phi(y)$.

Proof. Note that

$$\Phi(x) = \frac{1}{2}\sum_{i=1}^{n} x_i(x_i - |x_i|).$$

Then $\forall x, y \in R^n$, by Lemma 1 we have

$$\Phi(x) \leq \sum_{i=1}^{n} \left[\frac{1}{2}y_i(y_i - |y_i|) + (y_i - |y_i|)(x_i - y_i) + (x_i - y_i)^2 \right].$$

Thus we have (46).

Lemma 6. Let $\Phi(y) = \frac{1}{2}(c - A^T y)^T\{(c - A^T y) - |c - A^T y|)\}$, where $A \in R^{n \times m}$ and $y \in R^m$. For any $y, z \in R^m$,

$$\Phi(z) \leq \Phi(y) + \nabla\Phi(y)^T(z - y) + (z - y)^T A A^T(z - y). \tag{47}$$

Proof. By Lemma 4 and Lemma 5, we have (47).

Lemma 7. Let $w = (x, u, v)^T, w' = (x', u', v')^T \in R^{n^2+2n}$, and $E(x, u, v)$ be defined in Section III. For any w, w'

$$E(w) \leq E(w') + \nabla E(w')^T(w - w') + (w - w')^T H(w - w'), \tag{48}$$

where

$$H = \left[\begin{array}{cc} A^T A + cc^T + I & -cb^T \\ -bc^T & AA^T + bb^T \end{array} \right],$$

$c = [c_{11}, c_{12}, \ldots, c_{1n}, c_{21}, c_{22}, \ldots, c_{2n}, \ldots, c_{n1}, c_{n2}, \ldots, c_{nn}]^T, b = (1, \cdots, 1)^T \in R^{2n}$, and A is the $2n \times n^2$ constraint matrix in the assignment problem whose (i, j) column is $e_i + e_{n+j}$, e_p is a vector in R^{2n} with the p-th element being 1 and others being 0, for $i, j, p = 1, \cdots, n$.

Proof. Let

$$E_1(w) = \frac{1}{2}\left\{\sum_{i=1}^{n}\left[\sum_{j=1}^{n}c_{ij}x_{ij} - (u_i + v_i)\right]\right\}^2 +$$

$$\frac{1}{2}\left\{\sum_{i=1}^{n}\left[\sum_{j=1}^{n}x_{ij} - 1\right]^2 + \sum_{j=1}^{n}\left[\sum_{i=1}^{n}x_{ij} - 1\right]^2\right\}$$

and

$$E_2(w) = \frac{1}{2}\sum_{i=1}^{n}\sum_{j=1}^{n}(x_{ij}^2 - |x_{ij}|x_{ij}) +$$

$$\frac{1}{2}\sum_{i=1}^{n}\sum_{j=1}^{n}[c_{ij} - (u_i + v_j)][c_{ij} - (u_i + v_j) - |c_{ij} - (u_i + v_j)|].$$

By using the second-order Taylor formula, we have

$$E_1(w) = E_1(w') + \nabla E_1(w')^T(w - w') + (w - w')^T\nabla^2 E_1(w')(w - w'),$$

where

$$\nabla^2 E_1(w') = \begin{bmatrix} cc^T + A^T A & -cb^T \\ -bc^T & bb^T \end{bmatrix}.$$

In addition, we see from Lemma 3 and Lemma 4 that

$$E_2(w) \leq E_2(w') + \nabla E_2(w')^T(w - w') + (w - w')^T H_1(w - w').$$

where

$$H_1 = \begin{bmatrix} I & 0 \\ 0 & AA^T \end{bmatrix},$$

Since $E(w) = E_1(w) + E_2(w)$, we obtain (48).

Lemma 8. $E(w)$ defined in Lemma 4 is continuously differentiable and convex on R^{n^2+2n}, and for $\forall w, w' \in R^{n^2+2n}$

$$(w - w')^T\nabla E(w') \leq E(w) - E(w').$$

Proof. See Ortega [1970].

Lemma 9. Let A be defined in Lemma 7. The maximum eigenvalue of AA^T is $2n$.

Proof. Since A is a $2n \times n^2$ matrix whose (i, j) column is $e_i + e_{j+n}$ for $i, j = 1, 2, \ldots, n$, then

$$AA^T = \sum_{i=1}^{n}\sum_{j=1}^{n}(e_i + e_{j+n})(e_i + e_{j+n})^T$$

$$= \sum_{i=1}^{n}\sum_{j=1}^{n}(e_i e_i^T + e_{j+n}e_{j+n}^T + e_i e_{j+n}^T + e_{j+n}e_i^T)$$

$$= \sum_{i=1}^{n}\sum_{j=1}^{n}(e_i e_i^T + e_{j+n}e_{j+n}^T) + \sum_{i=1}^{n}\sum_{j=1}^{n}(e_i e_{j+n}^T + e_{j+n}e_i^T)$$

$$= \sum_{i=1}^{n}\sum_{j=1}^{n}(e_i e_i^T + e_{j+n}e_{j+n}^T) + \sum_{i=1}^{n}\sum_{j=1}^{n}(e_i e_{j+n}^T + e_{j+n}e_i^T).$$

It is easy to see that

$$\sum_{i=1}^{n}\sum_{j=1}^{n}(e_i e_i^T + e_{j+n}e_{j+n}^T) = n\sum_{i=1}^{n} e_i e_i^T + n\sum_{i=n+1}^{2n} e_{i+n}e_{i+n}^T$$

$$= 2n\sum_{i=1}^{2n} e_i e_i^T = 2nI_{2n\times 2n},$$

where $I_{2n\times 2n}$ is a $2n \times 2n$ identity matrix. In addition, we have

$$\sum_{i=1}^{n}\sum_{j=1}^{n}(e_i e_{j+n}^T + e_{j+n}e_i^T) = \sum_{i=1}^{n} e_i \sum_{j=1}^{n} e_{j+n}^T + \sum_{j=1}^{n} e_{j+n} \sum_{i=1}^{n} e_i^T.$$

Let $\eta_1 = \sum_{i=1}^{n} e_i$ and $\eta_2 = \sum_{j=1}^{n} e_{j+n}$, then $\eta_1^T \eta_2 = \eta_2^T \eta_1 = 0$ and $\eta_1^T \eta_1 = \eta_2^T \eta_2 = n$. Thus $(\eta_1 \eta_2^T + \eta_2 \eta_1^T)(\eta_1 + \eta_2) = n(\eta_1 + \eta_2)$. Hence n is an eigenvalue of $\eta_1 \eta_2^T + \eta_2 \eta_1^T$.

Assuming that n is not the maximum eigenvalue of $\eta_1 \eta_2^T + \eta_2 \eta_1^T$, then there exists $\epsilon > 0$ such that

$$\begin{pmatrix} 0 & U \\ U & 0 \end{pmatrix}\begin{pmatrix} v_1 \\ v_2 \end{pmatrix} = (n+\epsilon)\begin{pmatrix} v_1 \\ v_2 \end{pmatrix}$$

where $v_1, v_2 \in R^n$ and

$$U = \begin{pmatrix} 1 & 1 & \ldots, 1 \\ 1 & 1 & \ldots, 1 \\ \vdots & \vdots & \ddots, \vdots \\ 1 & 1 & \ldots, 1 \end{pmatrix}_{n\times n}.$$

Thus

$$Uv_1 = (n+\epsilon)v_2$$
$$Uv_2 = (n+\epsilon)v_1,$$

and $U^2 v_2 = (n+\epsilon)Uv_1 = (n+\epsilon)^2 v_2$. Since the maximum eigenvalue of U^2 is n^2,

$$n^2 < (n+\epsilon)^2 \le n^2,$$

which is contradictory. Therefore, the maximum eigenvalue of $\eta_1\eta_2^T + \eta_2\eta_1^T$ is n and thus the maximum eigenvalue of AA^T is $2n$. The proof is complete.

Using the above lemmas, we shall establish the result of global convergence for the discrete-time assignment network.

Theorem 5. If $h < \frac{1}{2\lambda_H}$ where λ_H is a maximum eigenvalue of the matrix H defined in Lemma 7, then sequence $\{x^{(k)}, u^{(k)}, v^{(k)}\}$ generated by the discrete-time assignment network is globally convergent to an optimal solution of the primal-dual assignment problem.

Proof. Let $\{w^{(k)}\} = \{x^{(k)}, u^{(k)}, v^{(k)}\}$. First, by Lemma 7 we have $E(w^{(k+1)}) \leq E(w^{(k)}) + \nabla E(w^{(k)})^T(w^{(k+1)} - w^{(k)}) + (w^{(k+1)} - w^{(k)})^T H(w^{(k+1)} - w^{(k)})$. Since $w^{(k+1)} - w^{(k)} = -h\nabla E(w^{(k)})$,

$$0 \leq E(w^{(k)}) + \nabla E(w^{(k)})^T(-h\nabla E(w^{(k)})) + h^2\nabla E(w^{(k)})^T H\nabla E(w^{(k)}),$$

hence

$$-E(w^{(k)}) \leq -h\|\nabla E(w^{(k)})\|_2^2 + h^2\lambda_H\|\nabla E(w^{(k)})\|_2^2.$$

Therefore, from Lemma 8 we obtain

$$
\begin{aligned}
\|w^{(k+1)} - w^*\|_2^2 &= \|w^{(k)} - w^*\|_2^2 - 2h(w^{(k)} - w^*)^T\nabla E(w^{(k)}) \\
&\quad + h^2\|\nabla E(w^{(k)})\|_2^2 \\
&\leq \|w^{(k)} - w^*\|_2^2 - 2h^2 E(w^{(k)}) + h^2\|\nabla E(w^{(k)})\|_2^2 \\
&\leq \|w^{(k)} - w^*\|_2^2 - 2h^2\|\nabla E(w^{(k)})\|_2^2 \\
&\quad + 2h^3\lambda_H\|\nabla E(w^{(k)})\|_2^2 + h^2\|E(w^{(k)})\|_2^2 \\
&\leq \|w^{(k)} - w^*\|_2^2 - h^2\|\nabla E(w^{(k)})\|_2^2(1 - 2h\lambda_H)
\end{aligned}
$$

where $w^* = (x^*, u^*, v^*)^T$ is an optimal solution to the primal and dual assignment problem. Since

$$H = \begin{bmatrix} A^T A + I & 0 \\ 0 & AA^T \end{bmatrix} + \begin{bmatrix} c \\ -b \end{bmatrix}[c^T, -b^T],$$

and H is a symmetric positive semi-definite matrix, thus $\lambda_H > 0$. So, when $\nabla E(w^{(k)}) \neq 0$ (i.e., $w^{(k)}$ is not an optimal solution), it follows that

$$\|w^{(k+1)} - w^*\|_2 < \|w^{(k)} - w^*\|_2. \tag{49}$$

Thus, $\{w^{(k)}\}$ is bounded. On the other hand, using the above second inequality we have

$$h^2\|\nabla E(w^{(k)})\|_2^2(1 - 2h\lambda_H) \leq \|w^{(k)} - w^*\|_2^2 - \|w^{(k+1)} - w^*\|_2^2,$$

so

$$\sum_{k=1}^{\infty} \|\nabla E(w^{(k)})\|_2^2 < +\infty.$$

Thus $\lim_{k \to \infty} \|\nabla E(w^{(k)})\|_2 = 0$. Since $\{w^{(k)}\}$ is bounded, there is a sequence $\{k_i\}$ such that

$$\lim_{i \to \infty} w^{(k_i)} = \hat{w}.$$

Then

$$\lim_{i \to \infty} \|\nabla E(w^{(k_i)})\|_2 = \|\nabla E(\hat{w})\|_2 = 0,$$

and thus $E(\hat{w}) = 0$. So $\hat{w} = (\hat{x}, \hat{u}, \hat{v})^T$ is an optimal solution to the primal and dual assignment problem. In view of (30), the sequence $\{w^{(k)}\}$ has only one limit point, so

$$\lim_{k \to \infty} w^{(k)} = \hat{w}.$$

The above analytical result shows that the constant design parameter of the discrete-time assignment network is bounded in a small range. The following theorem will illustrate that for any fixed initial step h_0 there is a number $l > 0$ such that $\frac{1}{2^l} h_0 < \frac{1}{\lambda_H}$, and hence the assignment network is definitely convergent to optimal solution to the primal-dual assignment problem in finite steps.

Theorem 6. If $h < 1/[2(4n + \|c\|_2^2 + 1)]$, then sequence $\{w^{(k)}\}$ generated by the discrete-time assignment network is globally convergent to an optimal solution of the primal-dual assignment problem.

Proof. Since

$$H = \begin{bmatrix} A^T A + I & 0 \\ 0 & A A^T \end{bmatrix} + \begin{bmatrix} c \\ -b \end{bmatrix} [c^T, -b^T],$$

and H is the sum of two symmetric matrices, according to Courant Fischer Min-max Theorem [Wang, 1995],

$$\lambda_H \leq \lambda + \|c\|_2^2 + 2n$$

where λ is the maximum eigenvalue of

$$\begin{bmatrix} A^T A + I & 0 \\ 0 & A A^T \end{bmatrix}.$$

In view that $A^T A$ and $A A^T$ have the same nonzero eigenvalues, according to Lemma 9, we have $\lambda = 2n + 1$. Hence

$$\lambda_H \leq 4n + \|c\|_2^2 + 1.$$

Then from Theorem 5, we can complete the proof.

IV. SIMULATION RESULTS

In order to demonstrate the effectiveness and efficiency of the proposed neural networks, in this section, we discuss the simulation results through four examples.

Recurrent Neural Networks for Optimization

The simulation is conducted on matlab, the ordinary differential equation solver engaged is ode45s.

Example 1. Consider the following quadratic program (the equivalent to the one in Kennedy and Chua [1988]) with the only optimal solution $x^* = (5.0, 5.0)$:

$$\text{Minimize} \quad x_1^2 + x_2^2 + x_1 x_2 - 30x_1 - 30x_2$$

$$\text{subject to} \quad \frac{5}{12}x_1 - x_2 \le \frac{35}{12},$$

$$\frac{5}{2}x_1 + x_2 \le \frac{35}{2},$$

$$-x_1 \le 5,$$

$$x_2 \le 5.$$

This problem is equivalent to

$$\text{Minimize} \quad x_1^2 + x_2^2 + x_1 x_2 - 30x_1 - 30x_2$$

$$\text{subject to} \quad \frac{5}{12}x_1 - x_2 + x_3 = \frac{35}{12},$$

$$\frac{5}{2}x_1 + x_2 + x_4 = \frac{35}{2},$$

$$-5 \le x_1 \le 7, -5 \le x_2 \le 5, 0 \le x_3 \le 10, 0 \le x_4 \le 35.$$

We use the system (11) to solve the above problem. Figure 6 shows the transient behavior of the primal-dual network which globally converges to the optimal solution.

Example 2. Consider the convex quadratic program (16) where

$$D = \begin{bmatrix} -5/12 & 1 \\ -5/2 & -1 \\ 1 & 0 \\ 0 & -1 \end{bmatrix}, A = \begin{bmatrix} 2 & 1 \\ 1 & 2 \end{bmatrix}, b = \begin{bmatrix} -35/12 \\ -35/2 \\ -5 \\ -5 \end{bmatrix}, c = \begin{bmatrix} -30 \\ -30 \end{bmatrix}$$

Its exact solution is $(5, 5)^T$. We use the systems (15) and (19) to solve the above problem. All simulation results show that the solution trajectory always converges to unique point $z^* = (5.000, 5.000, 0, 6.000, 0, 9.000)^T$ which corresponds to the optimal solution $(5, 5)^T$. For example, let $B = 5I$, and starting point is $(-10, 10, 0, 0, 0, 0)^T$. Figure 7 shows the transient behavior of the continuous-time neural network for this starting point. In the discrete-time case, taking step size $h = 0.08$, respective trajectories of the initial point $(-10, 10, 0, 0, 0, 0)^T$ are shown in Figure 8.

Example 3. Consider the classical linear complementary problem which was taken from Hertog [1994]. M is an 10×10 upper triangular matrix

$$M = \begin{bmatrix} 1 & 2 & 2 & \cdots & 2 \\ 0 & 1 & 2 & \cdots & 2 \\ 0 & 0 & 1 & \cdots & 2 \\ \vdots & \vdots & \vdots & \ddots & \vdots \\ 0 & 0 & 0 & \cdots & 1 \end{bmatrix}$$

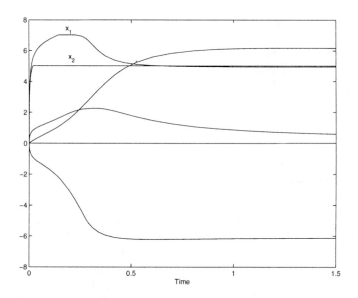

Figure 6. Transient behaviors of the primal-dual network of (14) in Example 1

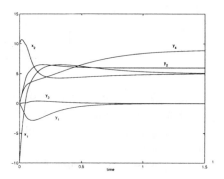

Figure 7. Transient behaviors of the primal-dual network of (15) in Example 2

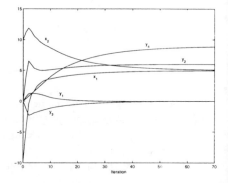

Figure 8. Transient behaviors of the primal-dual network of (19) in Example 2

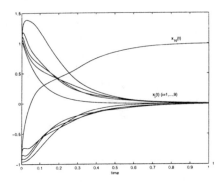

Figure 9. Transient behaviors of the recurrent neural network of (15) in Example 3

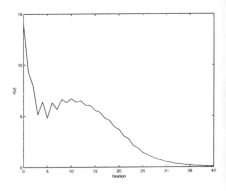

Figure 10. Transient behaviors of the recurrent neural network of (19) in Example 3

and $q = (-1, ..., -1)^T \in R^10$. The solution of the problem is $u^* = (0, ..., 0, 1)^T \in R^10$. We use the systems (15) and (19) to solve the above problem. The simulation results show that the trajectory of the system always globally converges to the solution $(0, ..., 1)^T$. For example, let $B = 5I$, and the initial point is $(1, -1, ..., 1, 1, -1)^T \in R^{10}$, respectively. Figure 9 shows the transient behaviors of the continuous-time neural network for this initial point. In the discrete-time case, taking $n = 80$ and step size $h = 0.016$, then the error $r(u) = \|P_\Omega(u - \beta(Mu + q)) - u\|$ along the trajectory of the zero initial point is shown in Figure 10.

Example 4: Consider the sorting problem used in Wang [1995, 1997] (Example 1): rank 10 items $\{-1.3, 1.7, 0.5, 2.2, -2.6, 1.5, -0.6, 0.9, -1.2, 1.1\}$ in ascending order. Let $s_j = 11 - j$ for $j = 1, 2, ..., 10$. Accordingly, the cost coefficient matrix can be defined as follows.

$$[c_{ij}] = \begin{pmatrix} -13.0 & -11.7 & -10.4 & -9.1 & -7.8 & -6.5 & -5.2 & -3.9 & -2.6 & -1.3 \\ 17.0 & 15.3 & 13.6 & 11.9 & 10.2 & 8.5 & 6.8 & 5.1 & 3.4 & 1.7 \\ 5.0 & 4.5 & 4.0 & 3.5 & 3.0 & 2.5 & 2.0 & 1.5 & 1.0 & 0.5 \\ 22.0 & 19.8 & 17.6 & 15.4 & 13.2 & 11.0 & 8.8 & 6.6 & 4.4 & 2.2 \\ -26.0 & -23.4 & -20.8 & -18.2 & -15.6 & -13.0 & -10.4 & -7.8 & -5.2 & -2.6 \\ 15.0 & 13.5 & 12.0 & 10.5 & 9.0 & 7.5 & 6.0 & 4.5 & 3.0 & 1.5 \\ -6.0 & -5.4 & -4.8 & -4.2 & -3.6 & -3.0 & -2.4 & -1.8 & -1.2 & -0.6 \\ 9.0 & 8.1 & 7.2 & 6.3 & 5.4 & 4.5 & 3.6 & 2.7 & 1.8 & 0.9 \\ -12.0 & -10.8 & -9.6 & -8.4 & -7.2 & -6.0 & -4.8 & -3.6 & -2.4 & -1.2 \\ 11.0 & 9.9 & 8.8 & 7.7 & 6.6 & 5.5 & 4.4 & 3.3 & 2.2 & 1.1 \end{pmatrix}$$

The sorting problem can be formulated as the assignment problem [Wang, 1995]. The decision variable is defined as that $x_{ij} = 1$ if item i with numerical key r_i is in the j-th position of the sorted list. The cost coefficients of the assignment problem for sorting are defined as $c_{ij} = r_i s_j$ where r_i and s_j denote respectively the numerical key of the i-th item to be sorted and the nonzero weighting parameter for the j-th position in the desired list.

Simulations have been conducted with the initial values of all variables to be zero for both continuous-time and discrete-time assignment networks. Figure 11 illustrates the transient behavior of the energy function of the continuous-time assignment network with $\mu = 10^8$ and variable time-steps. Figure 12 depicts the transient behaviors of the discrete-time assignment network with three different

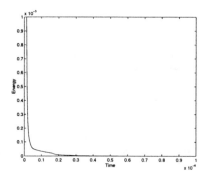

Figure 11. Transient behaviors of the continuous-time network of (14) in Example 4 (Wang, J. and Xia, Y., Analysis and design of primal-dual assignment networks, *IEEE Transactions on Neural Networks*, ©1998 IEEE)

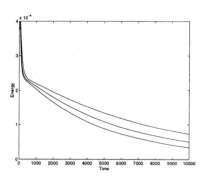

Figure 12. Transient behaviors of the discrete-time network of (14) in Example 4 (Wang, J. and Xia, Y., Analysis and design of primal-dual assignment networks, *IEEE Transactions on Neural Networks*, ©1998 IEEE)

step lengths h. Specifically, the line decreasing at the fastest rate corresponds to $h = 0.25$, the slowest line $h = 0.15$, in-between $h = 0.20$. Note that every step size $h > 1/(2\lambda_H)$. All the values of the energy function converge to zero.

V. CONCLUDING REMARKS

Neural networks have been proposed for optimization in a variety of application areas such as design and layout of very large scale integrated (VLSI) circuits. The nature of parallel and distributed information processing makes recurrent neural networks viable for solving complex optimization problems in real time. One of the salient features of neural networks is their suitability for hardware implementation, in which the convergence rate is not increasing statistically as the size of the problem increases.

Although great progress has been made in using neural networks for optimization, many theoretical and practical problems remain unsolved. Many avenues are open for future work. For example, the existing neural networks have not yet been shown to be capable of solving nonconvex optimization problems. Neither could the existing neural networks be guaranteed to obtain the optimial solutions to NP-hard combinatorial optimization problems. Further investigations should aim at the indepth analysis of the dynamics of recurrent neural networks for solving nonconvex and discrete optimization problems, the wide applications of recurrent neural networks to practical problems for real-time design and planning, and the hardware prototyping of recurrent neural networks for optimization.

REFERENCES

Baiocchi, C. and Capelo, A., *Variational and Quasi-variational Inequalities: Applications to Free Boundary Problems*, John Wiley and Sons, New York, 1988.

Bazaraa, M. S., Jarvis, J. J., and Sherali, H. D., *Linear Programming and Network Flows* (2nd Ed.), John Wiley & Sons, New York, NY, 1990.

Bertsekas, D. P., *Constrained Optimization and Largrange Multiplier Methods*, Academic Press, New York, 1982.

Bouzerdoum, A. and Pattison, T. R., Neural network for quadratic optimization with bound constraints, *IEEE Transactions on Neural Networks*, 4, 293, 1993.

Chua, L. O. and Lin, G. N., Nonlinear Programming without Computation, *IEEE Transactions on Circuits and Systems*, 31, 182, 1984.

Cichocki, A. and Unbehauen, R., Switched-Capacitor Neural Networks for Differential Optimization, *International Journal of Circuit Theory and Applications*, 19, 161, 1991.

Cichocki, A. and Unbehauen, R., *Neural Networks for Optimization and Signal Processing*, John Wiley, New York, 1993.

Cottle, R. W., Pang, J.-S., and Stone, R. E., *The Linear Complementarity Problem*. Academic Press, Boston, 1992.

Dennis, J. B., *Mathematics Programming and Electrical Networks*. Chapman and Hall, London, 1959.

Gafni, E. M. and Bertsekas, D. P., Two-metric projection methods for constrained optimization, *SIAM J. Control and Optimization*, 22, 936, 1984.

Glazos, M. P., Hui, S., and Zak, S. H., Sliding models in solving convex programming problems, *SIAM J. Control and Optimization*, 36(2), 680, 1998.

Hertog, D., *Interior Point Approach to Linear, Quadratic and Convex Programming: Algorithms and Complexity*, Kluwer Academic Publishers, Boston, MA, 1994.

Hopfield, J. J. and Tank, D. W., Neural Computation of Decisions in Optimization Problems, *Biological Cybernetics*, 52(3), 141, 1985.

Kinderlehrer, D. and Stampcchia, G., *An Introduction to Variational Inequalities and Their Applications*, Italy, Academic Press, 1980.

Kennedy, M. P. and Chua, L. N., Unifying the Tank and Hopfield Linear Programming Circuit and the Canonical Nonlinear Programming Circuit of Chua and Lin, *IEEE Transactions on Circuits and Systems*, 34(2), 210, 1987.

Kennedy, M. D. and Chua, L. N., Neural networks for nonlinear programming, *IEEE Transactions on Circuits and Systems*, 35(5), 554, 1988.

Lillo, W. E., Loh, M. H., Hui, S., and Zăk, S. H., On solving constrained optimization problems with neural networks: A penalty method approach, *IEEE Transactions on Neural Networks*, 4(6), 931, 1993.

Maa, C. Y. and Shanblatt, M. A., A Two-Phase Optimization Neural Network, *IEEE Transactions on Neural Networks*, 3(6), 1003, 1992.

Maa, C. Y. and Shanblatt, M. A., Linear and quadratic programming neural network analysis, *IEEE Transactions on Neural Networks*, 3, 580, 1992.

Marcotte, P., Application of Khobotov's algorithm to variational inequalities and network equilibrium problems, *Information Systems in Operations Research*, 29, 258, 1991.

Miller R. K. and Michel, A. N., *Ordinary Differential Equations*, Academic Press, New York, 1982.

More, J. J. and Toroaldo, G., On the solution of large quadratic programming problems with bound constraints, *SIAM J. Optimization*, 1(1), 93, 1991.

Ortega, J. M. and Rheinboldt, W. G., *Iterative Solution of Nonlinear Equations in Several Variables*, Academic Press, New York, 1970.

Pang, J. S., A posteriori error bounds for the linearly-constrained variational inequality problem, *Mathematics of Operations Research*, 12, 474, 1987.

Pyne, I. B., Linear programming on an electronic analogue computer. *Transactions of the American Institute of Electrical Engineering*, 75, 139, 1956.

Rodríguez-Vázquez, A., Domínguez-Castro, R., Rueda, A., Huertas, J. L., Sánchez-Sinencio, E., Nonlinear switched-capacitor 'neural networks' for optimization problems, *IEEE Transactions on Circuits and Systems*, 37(3), 384, 1990.

Rybashov, M. V., The gradient method of solving convex programming problems on electronic analogue computers. *Automation Remote Control*, 26(11), 1886, 1965.

Solodov, M. V. and Tseng, P., Modified projection-type methods for monotone variational inequalities, *SIAM J. Control and Optimization*, 2, 1814, 1996.

Sudharsanan, S. and Sundareshan, M., Exponential stability and a systematic synthesis of a neural network for quadratic minimization, *Neural Networks*, 4(5), 599, 1991.

Tank, W. D. and Hopfield, J. J., Simple neural optimization networks: an A/D converter, signal decision circuit, and a linear programming circuit, *IEEE Transactions on Circuits and Systems*, 33(5), 533, 1986.

Vandenberghe, L., Moor, B. L., and Vandewalle, J., The generalized linear complementarity problem applied to the complete analysis of resistive piecewise-linear circuits, *IEEE Transactions on Circuits and Systems*, 36(11), 1391, 1989.

Wang, J., A deterministic annealing neural network for convex programming, *Neural Networks*, 7(4), 629, 1994.

Wang, J., Analysis and design of an analog sorting network, *IEEE Transactions on Neural Networks*, 6(4), 962, 1995.

Wang, J., Primal and dual assignment networks, *IEEE Transactions on Neural Networks*, 8, 784, 1997.

Wang, J. and Xia, Y., Analysis and Design of Primal-Dual Assignment Networks, *IEEE Transactions on Neural Networks*, 9, 183, 1998.

Wu, X., Xia, Y., Li,J., and Chen, W. K., A high performance neural network for solving linear and quadratic programming problems, *IEEE Transactions on Neural Networks*, 7, 643, 1996.

Xia, Y., A new neural network for solving linear programming problems and its applications," *IEEE Transactions on Neural Networks*, 7, 525, 1996.

Xia, Y., A new neural network for solving linear and quadratic programming problems, *IEEE Transactions on Neural Networks*, 7, 1544, 1996.

Xia, Y., Neural network for solving extended linear programming problems, *IEEE Transactions on Neural Networks*, 8, 525, 1997.

Xia Y. and Wang J., Neural network for solving linear programming problems with bounded variables, *IEEE Transactions on Neural Networks*, 6, 515, 1995.

Xia, Y. and Wang, J., A General method for designing optimization neural networks with global convergence, *IEEE Transactions on Neural Networks*, 9, 1998.

Zhang, S. and Constantinides, A. G., Lagrange Programming Neural Networks, *IEEE Transactions on Circuits and Systems II: Analog and Digital Signal Processing*, 39(7), 441, 1992.

Zhang, S., Zhu, X., and Zou, L. H., Second-Order Neural Networks for Constrained Optimization, *IEEE Transactions on Neural Networks*, 3(6), 1021, 1992.

Chapter 3

EFFICIENT SECOND-ORDER LEARNING ALGORITHMS FOR DISCRETE-TIME RECURRENT NEURAL NETWORKS

Eurípedes P. dos Santos and Fernando J. Von Zuben

School of Electrical and Computer Engineering (FEEC)
State University of Campinas (Unicamp)
Brazil

I. INTRODUCTION

Artificial neural networks can be described as computational structures built up from weighted connections among simple and functionally similar nonlinear processing units or nodes, denoted artificial neurons. A class of neural network architectures that has been receiving a great deal of attention in the last few years is that of recurrent neural networks. They can be classified as being globally or partially recurrent.

Globally recurrent neural networks have arbitrary feedback connections, including neurons with self-feedback. On the other hand, partially recurrent neural networks have their main structure non-recurrent, or recurrent but with restrictive properties associated with the feedback connections, like fixed weights or local nature. The presence of feedback allows the generation of internal representations and memory devices, both essential to process spatio-temporal information.

The dynamics presented by a recurrent neural network can be continuous or discrete in time. The analysis of dynamic behavior using already stated theoretical results for continuous dynamic systems and the generation of new results regarding stability of continuos-time recurrent neural networks seem to be the most important appeals to the use of continuous dynamics [Jin, 1995]. However, the simulation of a continuous-time recurrent neural network in digital computational devices requires the adoption of a discrete-time equivalent model.

In this chapter, we will study discrete-time recurrent neural network architectures, implemented by the use of one-step delay operators in the feedback paths. In doing so, digital filters of a desired order can be used to design the network, by a proper definition of connections [Back, 1991]. The resulting nonlinear models for spatio-temporal representation can be directly simulated on a digital computer, by means of a system of nonlinear difference equations. The nature of the equations depends on the kind of recurrent architecture adopted. As a well-known result from signal processing theory, recurrent connections may lead to very complex behaviors, even with a reduced number of parameters and associated equations [Oppenheim, 1999].

Globally and partially recurrent neural networks were shown to perform well in a wide range of applications that involve dynamic and sequential processing [Haykin, 1999]. However, analysis [Kolen, 1994] and synthesis [Cohen, 1992] of recurrent neural networks of practical importance is a very demanding task. As a consequence, the process of weight adjustment in supervised learning is much more demanding in the recurrent case [Williams, 1989], and the availability of recurrent neural networks of practical importance has to be associated with the existence of efficient training algorithms, based on optimization procedures for adjusting the parameters. To improve performance, second-order information should be considered in the training process [Campolucci, 1998, Chang, 1999, Von Zuben, 1995].

So, in what follows, after a brief motivation for using recurrent neural networks and second-order learning algorithms, a low-cost procedure to obtain exact second-order information for a wide range of recurrent neural network architectures will be presented. After that, a very efficient and generic learning algorithm will be described. We will propose an improved version of a scaled conjugate gradient algorithm [Narenda, 1990], that can effectively be used to explore the available second-order information. The original algorithm will be improved based on the detection of important limitations. Basically, we introduce a set of adaptive coefficients to replace fixed ones. These new parameters of the algorithm are automatically adjusted and do not represent additional items to be arbitrarily determined by the user. Finally, some simulation results will be obtained and interpreted.

II. SPATIAL × SPATIO-TEMPORAL PROCESSING

Supervised learning in the context of artificial neural networks can be associated with the use of optimization-based techniques to adjust the network parameters [Poggio, 1990]. The objective is to minimize a cost function, i.e., a function of the input-output data available for learning, that somehow defines the desired behavior to be achieved.

At first glance, neural networks can be divided into two classes: static (non-recurrent) and dynamic (recurrent) networks. Static neural networks are those whose outputs are linear or nonlinear functions of its inputs, and for a given input vector, the network always generates the same output vector. These nets are suitable for processing of spatial patterns. In this case, the relevant information is distributed throughout the spatial coordinates associated with the variables that compose the set of input learning patterns. Typical problems with remarkable spatial dependencies can be found in the areas of pattern recognition and function approximation [Bishop, 1995].

In contrast, dynamic neural networks are capable of implementing memories which gives them the possibility of retaining information to be used later. Now, the network can generate diverse output vectors in response to the same input vector, because the response may also depend on the actual state of the existing memories. By their inherent characteristic of memorizing past information, for long or short-term periods, dynamic networks are good candidates to process patterns with spatio-temporal dependencies, for example, signal processing with

48

emphasis on identification and control of nonlinear dynamic systems [Jin, 1995, Kim, 1997], and nonlinear prediction of time series [Connor, 1994, Von Zuben, 1997].

III. COMPUTATIONAL CAPABILITY

Multilayer perceptron [Haykin, 1999] is a widespread example of a static (non-recurrent) neural network architecture. The main reason it is so effective in worldwide spatial processing applications is the existence of two complementary existential results, with immediate practical effects: a proof of its universal approximation capability [Hornik, 1989] and an effective way to use first- and second-order information, once available, for adjusting the parameters (generally based on the backpropagation algorithm) [Battiti, 1992, van der Smagt, 1994].

However, in the case of recurrent neural network architectures, there are no equivalent *practical* results concerning universal approximation capability with respect to spatio-temporal patterns. A great number of the recurrent neural network architectures, particularly the ones convertible to NARX architectures, share the *existential* property of being capable of simulating Turing machines [Siegelmann, 1997, Siegelmann, 1991], where a Turing machine is an abstraction defined to be functionally as powerful as any computer. However, this very important existential result does not provide any insight about how to achieve the desired behavior, which is why we are faced with so many different architectures to deal with spatio-temporal problems, each one devoted to the specific nature of the problem at hand [Frasconi, 1992, Haykin, 1999].

In spite of some attempts to discover unifying aspects in various architectures [Nerrand, 1993, Tsoi, 1997], the diversity of available architectures that can potentially be applied to solve a given spatio-temporal problem is still commonplace.

In this chapter, we will not try to overcome this troublesome aspect of design. Instead, we will concentrate efforts on developing a generic procedure to obtain first- and second-order information for adjusting the parameters, directly applicable to a wide range of recurrent neural network architectures. Once the first- and second-order information is available, it is important to point out that the same optimization algorithm can be applied, without any kind of modification, to any kind of recurrent (or non-recurrent) neural network architecture.

IV. RECURRENT NEURAL NETWORKS AS NONLINEAR DYNAMIC SYSTEMS

A dynamic system is composed of two parts: the state and the dynamic. The state is formally defined as a multivariate vector of variables, parameterized with respect to time, such that the current value of the state vector summarizes all the information about the past behavior of the system considered necessary to uniquely describe its future behavior, except for the possibly existing external effects produced by inputs applied to the system. The set of possible states is denoted the state space of the system. The dynamic, assumed here to be deterministic, describes how the state evolves through time, and the sequence of states is known as the trajectory in the state space. It is possible to define four classes of dynamic systems [Kolen, 1994], according to the scheme presented in Figure 1.

In essence, the class of recurrent neural networks to be discussed in this chapter is the one characterized by the discrete dynamic and continuous state. The resulting system of difference equations corresponds to a complex nonlinear parametric dynamic system that can exhibit a wide range of behaviors, not produced by static systems.

| | | State space | |
		continuous	discrete
d y n a m i c	continuous	system of differential equations	spin glasses
	discrete	system of difference equations	automata

Figure 1. Classes of dynamic systems

For recurrent neural network with these properties, there are two functional uses [Haykin, 1999]:

- associative memory and
- input-output mapping network.

For example, when globally recurrent neural networks are constrained to have symmetric connections (or some equivalent restrictive property), their asymptotic behaviors are dominated by fixed-point attractors, with guaranteed convergence to stable states from any initial condition. This property can be explored to produce associative memories, as is the case in Hopfield-type neural networks [Li, 1988].

Without such a constraint, the connective structure may assume a wide range of configurations, so that the corresponding recurrent neural network is able to present more complex behaviors than fixed points. The trajectory in the state space will be influenced by a set of attractors and repellers, with arbitrary multiplicity and properly distributed across the state space, each one belonging to one of the following types: fixed point, limit cycle, quasi-periodic, or chaotic [Ott, 1993].

The analysis of computational simulations often considers only the attractors, because the repellers can not be observed. Once the state has reached one attractor, it will stay there indefinitely, unless an external force pushes the state away. When the trajectory of an autonomous system reaches an attractor, we say that the system is in a stationary state. Both continuous and discrete dynamics are able to present the four types of stationary behavior mentioned above.

So, the dynamical complexity of a recurrent neural network can be measured in terms of the number, type, and relative position of attractors and repellers in the state space. Some preliminary results are already available to synthesize, in a closed form, recurrent neural networks in terms of specific position and extension of a reduced number of attractors and repellers in the state space [Cohen, 1992]. However, in the case of complex configurations of attractors and repellers, and when the description of the dynamic system to be synthesized can not be done in terms of attractors and repellers, the only available way of performing the task is by means of supervised learning.

The formalism of attractors and repellers plays an important role in the study of recurrent neural network stability [Haykin, 1999]. In the analysis of dynamic system theory, in addition to stability, controllability and observability are fundamental aspects. If we can control the dynamic behavior of the recurrent neural network, using external inputs if necessary, then we say that the dynamic is controllable. If we can observe the result of the control applied to the network, then we say that the dynamic is observable. Levin and Narendra [Levin, 1993] have presented important results associated with local controllability and local observability of recurrent neural networks.

V. RECURRENT NEURAL NETWORKS AND SECOND-ORDER LEARNING ALGORITHMS

As stated in the previous section, this chapter will treat recurrent neural networks as input-output mapping networks, giving rise to the necessity of establishing an association between the desired input-output behavior and a specific configuration for the neural network parameters (connective configuration). Unfortunately, this association can not be determined a priori or in a closed form. Then, a desired dynamic behavior should be produced by means of an effective learning process (this procedure is also known as dynamic reconstruction [Haykin, 1999]) responsible for discovering this association, which may not be unique.

As supervised learning should be applied to achieve the desired behavior, the success of the task will depend on two conditions:
- the desired behavior must belong to the range of dynamic behaviors that can be produced by the recurrent neural network and
- the supervised learning process must be capable of finding a desired set of parameter values that will give the final connective configuration to the neural network.

Certainly, the most widespread supervised learning mechanisms for neural networks are those using first-order (gradient) information. In this case, the first-order partial derivatives, or sensitivities, associated with some error measure (based on the difference between the network outputs and some target sequences), are computed with respect to the parameters of the network. Later, this available local information related to the error surface is then used to minimize the error.

As widely reported in the literature, despite their widespread use, the gradient-descent method and its variants are characterized by their slow rate of convergence and in some cases, require the arbitrary setting of learning parameters, such as learning rates, before the beginning of the optimization task [Battiti, 1992]. An inadequate choice may raise difficulties or even prevent the success of the adjustment.

Moreover, specifically in the case of recurrent neural networks, there can be at least one hard additional problem that may trap the gradient-based optimization process: the existence of feedback along the processing makes the error surface present highly nonlinear spots [Pearlmutter, 1995]. This characteristic of the error surface is motivated by the possibility of migrating between two qualitatively distinct nonlinear behaviors merely by means of tuning the feedback gain. For example, even small changes in the network parameters, dictated by the learning algorithm itself, may guide the dynamics of the network to change from stable fixed points to unstable ones, which causes a sudden jump in the error measure. Of course, here we are considering an implicit hypothesis that first-order optimization methods do not work properly out of smooth areas in continuous error surfaces.

In general, these undesirable aspects are the main reasons for the poor average performance of first-order learning algorithms. These problems become even more evident in the case of very demanding tasks, where the network behavior must consider simultaneously a great number of correlated specifications (for example, many attractors and repellers). Examples of these kinds of problems are becoming more frequent in system identification and time series prediction tasks.

To improve performance, second-order information should be considered in the training process. One of the most elaborated second-order algorithms for search in multidimensional nonlinear surfaces is the conjugate gradient method, which was proved to be remarkably effective in dealing with general objective functions and is considered among the best general purpose optimization methods presently available.

Given a procedure to obtain second-order information for any kind of recurrent neural network architecture, the learning procedure can be directly applied without any adaptation to the specific context. That is why the first objective of this work is to describe systematic ways of obtaining exact second-order information for a range of recurrent neural network architectures.

In addition to that, the algorithms to be proposed in a coming section present a computational cost (memory usage and processing time) only two times higher than the cost to acquire first-order information.

VI. RECURRENT NEURAL NETWORK ARCHITECTURES

As already stated, the natural way of investigating the dynamic behavior of recurrent neural networks is to consider them as nonlinear dynamic systems. Let a nonlinear discrete-time stationary dynamic system be represented by the state space equations:

$$\begin{cases} \mathbf{x}_p(k+1) = \mathbf{f}_p\big(\mathbf{x}_p(k), \mathbf{u}(k)\big) \\ \mathbf{y}_p(k) = \mathbf{h}_p\big(\mathbf{x}_p(k), \mathbf{u}(k)\big) \end{cases} \tag{1}$$

where k is the discrete instant of time, $\mathbf{x}_p \in \mathfrak{R}^n$, $\mathbf{u} \in \mathfrak{R}^m$, and $\mathbf{y}_p \in \mathfrak{R}^r$ are the state, input, and output vectors, respectively; $\mathbf{f}_p : \mathfrak{R}^n \times \mathfrak{R}^m \rightarrow \mathfrak{R}^n$ and $\mathbf{h}_p : \mathfrak{R}^n \times \mathfrak{R}^m \rightarrow \mathfrak{R}^r$ are continuous vector-valued functions representing the state transition mapping and output mapping, respectively. This state space representation is very general and can describe a large range of important nonlinear dynamic systems. Notice that the output equation is a static mapping.

System identification is a fundamental and challenging research area involving nonlinear dynamic systems, and a common approach to identify systems represented by equation (1) is to adopt parameterized models for the unknown maps $\mathbf{f}_p$ and $\mathbf{h}_p$. In this case, there is a growing amount of research about the use of neural networks to model some important subclasses of nonlinear dynamic systems, subsumed within the class of models represented by equation (1). In the literature, attention has been paid to the analysis and synthesis of neural networks models structured in the form of nonlinear auto-regressive moving average (NARMA) models. In this context, there are two main approaches to synthesize NARMA models. The first one assumes that the dynamic behavior of the system output is governed by a finite set of available input-output measurements. Then, an obvious route to modeling is to choose the NARMA model as a feedforward neural network of the form:

$$\mathbf{y}_m(k) = \hat{\mathbf{g}}_m\big(\mathbf{y}_p(k-1), \cdots, \mathbf{y}_p(k-n), \mathbf{u}(k), \cdots, \mathbf{u}(k-m)\big) \tag{2}$$

where $\hat{\mathbf{g}}_m$ represents the input-output map performed by the static neural network and $\mathbf{y}_m$ is the output of the model. This is a kind of series-parallel model and presumes a fairly good knowledge of the actual system structure. This scheme of adaptation has been denoted as equation-error approach by the system identification community and is designated as teacher forcing in the neural network parlance. More recently, in view of its peculiar characteristics, Williams [Williams, 1990] coined it as the conservative approach, when related to neural control.

The second approach to construct neural network NARMA models is argued to be used in situations where the use of past input-output information together with a feedforward nonlinear mapping is not able to satisfactorily represent the actual dynamic system. A typical situation is the use of these static neural network NARMA models when the map $\mathbf{h}_p$ in equation (1) has no inverse. In this case, the representation capability of the model can be improved by the use of a recurrent neural network. If the recurrent paths include the outputs, we have a parallel model. As an example, consider the parallel NARMA model given by the following equation:

$$\mathbf{y}_m(k) = \hat{\mathbf{g}}_m\big(\mathbf{y}_m(k-1), \cdots, \mathbf{y}_m(k-n), \mathbf{u}(k), \cdots, \mathbf{u}(k-m)\big) \tag{3}$$

Again, $\hat{\mathbf{g}}_m$ represents the feedforward input-output mapping performed by the neural network, but now the outputs always depend on past values of themselves. In this case, the adaptation of the neural network parameters should be realized by a dynamic learning algorithm. When adjusting the model parameters in this way, we are using the output error approach, raised in the system identification area. Some results in the literature have pointed out that parallel models may give improved performance when compared to their series-parallel counterparts, particularly in the case of noisy systems [Shink, 1989]. This improvement occurs because the parallel model prevents the presence of noisy outputs in the composition of the input vector.

In spite of the more powerful representation capabilities associated with parallel models, few results are available in terms of stability analysis, and more effective learning algorithms are required. Because of the aforementioned characteristics, the use of parallel models in tasks related to neural network identification and control is called liberal approach [Williams, 1990].

Figures 2 to 4 show the three most popular recurrent neural network architectures for spatio-temporal processing, where the neural network parameters are left implicit. In Figure 2 we have the globally recurrent neural network architecture (GRNN). In this architecture, the output of each hidden neuron is used to generate the feedback information. If the feedback paths, indicated by the bold arrows, are removed, then a simpler architecture is produced, called local recurrent neural network (LRNN). When the network outputs are the signals used in the feedback loops, as in Figure 3, we have the output-feedback recurrent neural network (OFRNN) or Jordan network. If all the outputs of the existing neurons are used for feedback, the resulting architecture is the most general and is called a fully recurrent neural network (FRNN), as shown in Figure 4.

With different degrees of extension, all these recurrent neural network architectures have attracted the interest of researches [Tsoi, 1994]. A brief look at Figures 3 and 4 can indicate that OFRNN and FRNN are networks that have to be trained following the liberal approach. There are few results concerning the FRNN architecture, because the high flexibility of its dynamic behavior is not so easy to be accessed [Williams, 1990].

On the other hand, the generality of the GRNN architecture and its universal approximation property have been proved [Jin, 1995]. Another important result obtained is that GRNN and OFRNN are equivalent architectures, if their output neurons are linear [Tsoi, 1997].

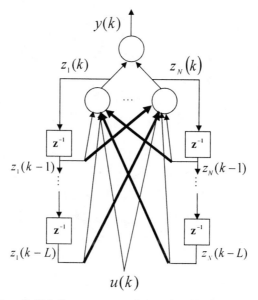

Figure 2. Globally recurrent neural network architecture (GRNN)

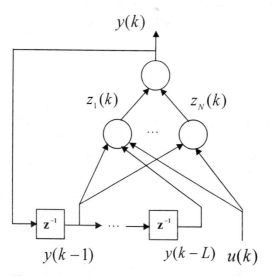

Figure 3. Output-feedback recurrent neural network (OFRNN)

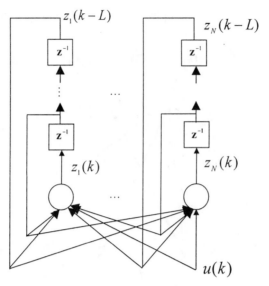

Figure 4. Fully recurrent neural network (FRNN)

VII. STATE SPACE REPRESENTATION FOR RECURRENT NEURAL NETWORKS

The formulations adopted in this work for the learning algorithms are strongly based on matrix manipulations. Hence, in this section a state space representation, valid for each of the three architectures described above, is briefly presented. In the sequel, we take Figures 2 to 4 as guidelines, and we consider that in each architecture there is one hidden layer containing N neurons, M external inputs, and O linear output units. Also, the nonlinear activation function is supposed to be the same for all hidden neurons.

The state variables for any architecture in Figures 2 to 4 can be immediately selected as the set of variables responsible for the memory storage in the recurrent neural network. They are just the past signals available from the tapped delay lines of length L. To make the exposure clear, we can first write the following scalar equations at a particular discrete time instant k:

$$s_i(k) = \sum_{j=1}^{D}\sum_{l=1}^{L} a_{il}^{j} x_j(k-l) + \sum_{m=0}^{M} b_{im} u_m(k), \quad i = 1,2,\cdots,N \qquad (4)$$

$$z_i(k) = f(s_i(k)), \quad i = 1,2,\cdots,N \qquad (5)$$

$$y_r(k) = \sum_{p=0}^{N} c_{rp} z_p(k), \quad r = 1, 2, \cdots, O \tag{6}$$

where the signals $s_i(k)$, $z_i(k)$, and $y_r(k)$ are hidden neurons weighted sums, hidden neurons outputs, and network outputs, respectively. The a_{il}^j's are the weights in the feedback loops, the b_{im}'s are the external inputs gains, and the c_{rp}'s are the weights between the hidden and the output layer. In these equations, $z_0(k)$ and $u_0(k)$ are the bias inputs. The actual values for the state variables x_j's, and the total number of signals to be used to feed the tapped delay lines, D, depends on the recurrent network architecture. We have $x_j(t) = z_j(t)$, with $D = N$ for the GRNN and LRNN architectures. Following the same idea, we have $x_j(t) = y_j(t)$, with $D = O$ for the OFRNN. For the FRNN, we also have $x_j(t) = z_j(t)$, with $D = N$. The FRNN network has all its units in a unique layer, and the output neurons (visible neurons) correspond to a subset of these units. Then, the parameters c_{rp} in equation (6) are constants (not adjustable parameters), taking the value 1 if $p=r$ and the value 0 otherwise. In this architecture, the bias inputs for all neurons are removed from the set of output weights and accounted for in the set of input weights.

A matrix formulation for equations (4) to (6) can be obtained as done in what follows:

$$s(k) = \mathbf{A}x(k) + \mathbf{B}u(k) \tag{7}$$

$$z(k) = \mathbf{F}(s(k)) = [f(s_1(k)), \cdots, f(s_N(k))]^T \tag{8}$$

$$y(k) = \mathbf{C}\begin{bmatrix} z(k) \\ 1 \end{bmatrix} \tag{9}$$

where

$$x(k) = [x_1(k-1), \cdots, x_1(k-L), \cdots, x_D(k-1), \cdots, x_D(k-L)]^T \tag{10}$$

$$u(k) = [u_1(k), \cdots, u_M(k), 1]^T \tag{11}$$

$$y(k) = [y_1(k), \cdots, y_O(k)]^T \tag{12}$$

The entries with value 1 in the vectors appearing in equations (9) and (11) correspond to the bias input. If the network of interest is a FRNN, the bias input must be removed from equation (9). Matrices **A**, **B**, and **C** are formed from the weights a_{il}^{j}'s, b_{im}'s, and c_{rp}'s, respectively, that appear in equations (4) and (6). These matrices have dimensions $(N, D.L)$, $(N, M+1)$, and $(O, N+1)$, respectively.

VIII. SECOND-ORDER INFORMATION IN OPTIMIZATION-BASED LEARNING ALGORITHMS

Supervised learning in an artificial neural network can be formulated as an unconstrained nonlinear optimization problem, where the network parameters are the free independent variables to be adjusted, and an error measure is the dependent variable. The error measure or cost function depends on the network parameters and on the error between the neural network outputs and the desired behaviors dictated by the training examples.

In general, the training examples are in the form of input-output pairs that can be the samples obtained from trajectories generated from some dynamic system, possibly with a nonlinear behavior.

The goal of the supervised learning is to adjust the network parameter so that the trajectories generated by the neural network match the given desired trajectories. Additionally, the trained neural network is required to perform properly when subjected to patterns not seen in the training phase.

Let $\mathbf{w} \in R^{NP}$ be the column vector containing all the neural network weights or adjustable parameters. Also, consider the vectors $\mathbf{y}(k)$ and $\mathbf{y}_d(k)$, as the neural network output and desired output, respectively. Formally the optimization based learning process is defined by the following equations:

$$\min_{\mathbf{w}} E_T(\mathbf{w}) \tag{13}$$

$$E_T(\mathbf{w}) = \sum_{k=1}^{P} E^k(\mathbf{w}) \tag{14}$$

$$E^k(\mathbf{w}) = \frac{1}{2}(\mathbf{y}(k) - \mathbf{y}_d(k))^T (\mathbf{y}(k) - \mathbf{y}_d(k)) \tag{15}$$

where P is the horizon of time to be considered.

In classical optimization methods, the search for the vector **w** that solves the minimization problem (13) is conducted in an iterative set of steps. In each step, given the actual vector **w,** the optimization procedure can use only information extracted from the cost function to generate a new vector that is a better estimation of the optimal solution.

To see which information is of practical concern, consider the following Taylor series expansion for the error measure around a point **w** in the error surface:

$$\mathbf{E_T}(\mathbf{w}+\Delta\mathbf{w}) = \mathbf{E_T}(\mathbf{w}) + \nabla\mathbf{E_T}(\mathbf{w})^T \cdot \Delta\mathbf{w} + \frac{1}{2!}\Delta\mathbf{w}^T \cdot \mathbf{H}(\mathbf{w}) \cdot \Delta\mathbf{w} + \mathbf{O}\left(\|\Delta\mathbf{w}\|^2\right) \quad (16)$$

where $\nabla\mathbf{E_T}(\mathbf{w})$ is the gradient vector with components $\partial\mathbf{E_T}/\partial w_i$, $\mathbf{H}(\mathbf{w})$ is the Hessian matrix with components $\partial^2\mathbf{E_T}/\partial w_i\partial w_j$, and $\mathbf{O}\left(\|\Delta\mathbf{w}\|^2\right)$ represent the terms with order higher than two in $\Delta\mathbf{w}$.

Optimization methods that use only objective function evaluation to solve problem (13) form the family of direct search methods. In these methods, some mechanism is used to generate new candidate points and the objective function is used to select the best one. If, at each step, the method uses function evaluations and the first-order information contained in the gradient vector to generate a new point in the search space, it is in the family of steepest descent methods. These methods are characterized by their relative simplicity but slow rate of convergence to a local minimum.

Methods that depend on the information present in the Hessian matrix are second-order methods. These methods work on the hypotheses that a quadratic model is a good local approximation to the objective function. The most representative method in this family is the Newton's method, where, at each step, the inverse of the Hessian matrix is used to generate a new point.

Certainly, the use of higher order information about the error surface can be an effective way of generating improved solutions at each step of the optimization process. It is well known that a second-order method has rate of convergence superior to the one produced by a first-order method [Luenberger, 1989]. But, when dealing with highly nonlinear large-scale optimization problems, practical aspects related with excessive computational burden, numerical errors in matrix operations, and the need for large matrix storage can make such a kind of second-order methods unfeasible to be implemented. In such a situation, even a first-order method is a better choice.

In general, these aspects are frequently present in the supervised neural network learning, where the search space is highly nonlinear and of large dimension. Maybe these are the main reasons for the widespread use of the backpropagation algorithm, in spite of its slowness and oscillatory behavior associated with the use of a fixed learning rate [Jacobs, 1988].

IX. THE CONJUGATE GRADIENT ALGORITHM

Fortunately, all the disadvantages of second-order methods, discussed in the previous section, can be adequately eliminated. To do that, we will employ one of the most effective second-order methods for search in multidimensional nonlinear surface: the conjugate gradient method (CGM). The CGM can be regarded as being somewhat intermediate between the method of steepest descent and Newton's method. It is motivated by the desire to accelerate the typically slow convergence associated with steepest descent, while maintaining simplicity by avoiding the requirements associated with the evaluation, storage, and inversion of the Hessian matrix (or at least the solution of the corresponding system of equations), as required by Newton's method. The storage requirements for the original CGM are for the actual weights, the actual and the immediately previous gradient vector, and two successive search direction vectors.

Originally, the CGM was designed to minimize a quadratic objective function. As an example, consider the quadratic function obtained if the term $O\left(\|\Delta w\|^2\right)$ in equation (16) is neglected. Adopting the hypothesis of a quadratic model, the CGM works as follows:

- given two distinct directions d_1 and d_2, they are said to be **H**-orthogonal, or conjugate with respect to a symmetric matrix **H**, if $d_1^T H d_2 = d_2^T H d_1 = 0$.
- the CGM is obtained by selecting the successive directions as conjugate with respect to the Hessian matrix. The first direction is set to the current negative gradient vector, and subsequent directions are not specified beforehand but determined sequentially at each step of the iteration.
- the new gradient vector is computed, and linearly combined with previous direction vectors, to obtain a new conjugate direction along which to move.

A. THE ALGORITHM

Initialization: Set random initial values to w^o and an arbitrarily small value to ε.

Step 1: Starting at w^o, compute $g^o = \nabla E_T(w^o)$ and set $d^o = -g^o$.

Step 2: For $k = 0, \Lambda \cdots, NP-1$:

a) Compute $H(w^j)$;

b) Set $w^{j+1} = w^j + \alpha^j d^j$, with $\alpha^j = \dfrac{-(g^j)^T d^j}{(d^j)^T H(w^j) d^j}$; $\qquad$ (17)

c) Compute $g^{j+1} = \nabla E_T(w^{j+1})$;

d) Unless $k = NP-1$, set $d^{j+1} = -g^{j+1} + \beta^j d^j$, $\qquad$ (18)

$\qquad$ where $\beta^j = \dfrac{(g^{j+1})^T H(w^j) d^j}{(d^j)^T H(w^j) d^j}$. $\qquad$ (19)

Step 3: If $E_T(w^{NP}) > \varepsilon$, replace w^o by w^{NP} and go back to step 1.

For problems where the cost function is exactly quadratic, the Hessian **H** is a constant matrix. It can be proved that in this situation, if **H** is positive definite, the CGM described above converges to the solution in at most NP iterations. In the everyday practice, this analytical result may, in some sense, be different due to inevitable numerical errors that are carried over in successive iterations of the method.

B. THE CASE OF NON-QUADRATIC FUNCTIONS

Adopting the already mentioned hypothesis of local quadratic model, the CGM can be extended to general nonlinear objective functions. A nice justification for this assumption is that, near any local optimum, a great variety of nonlinear functions can be well approximated by quadratic functions. This property can be inferred from the Taylor series expansion in equation (16). However, in dealing with general nonlinear functions, the computation of the scalars α^j and β^j, in equations (17) and (19), requires the calculation of the Hessian matrix at each new point generated by the algorithm. Further, a problem of major concern is that the definiteness property of the Hessian matrix may change from one point to another. It is important to stress the occurrence of the Hessian matrix in the denominator of the expression for the step-length α^j. If, at a given point of the search process, the matrix $\mathbf{H}(\mathbf{w}^j)$ is negative definite, then it is likely that α^j will be negative, resulting in a step along a direction that increases the cost function, instead of decreasing it as expected.

In general, the need for the evaluation of the full Hessian matrix at each new point generated by the CGM is a computational demanding process. This dependence can be suppressed by adopting the following alternatives for the calculation of α^j and β^j.

The step-length α^j can be obtained by solving the following one-dimensional minimization problem

$$\alpha^j = \arg\min_{\alpha} E_T\left(\mathbf{w}^j + \alpha \mathbf{d}^j\right) \tag{20}$$

Thus, the value of α used at step j is just the one obtained by minimizing the cost function along the line defined by $\mathbf{w}^j + \alpha \mathbf{d}^j$.

Two particular alternative expressions for β^j, that do not use the Hessian matrix, are of special concern in this work. First, using the definition for α^j and β^j given in equations (17) and (19) and the orthogonality property between the gradient at step j and all the previous conjugate directions, the following expression can be obtained:

$$\beta^j_{PR} = \frac{\left(\mathbf{g}^{j+1}\right)^T \left(\mathbf{g}^{j+1} - \mathbf{g}^j\right)}{\left(\mathbf{g}^j\right)^T \mathbf{g}^j} \tag{21}$$

This is known as the Polak-Ribiere expression, and can be further simplified using the orthogonality property between the gradient at step j and all the previous gradients, resulting in the Fletcher-Reeves expression:

$$\beta_{FR}^{j} = \frac{\left(g^{j+1}\right)^{T} g^{j+1}}{\left(g^{j}\right)^{T} g^{j}} \tag{22}$$

If the cost function is exactly quadratic, the two expressions for β^{j}, in equations (21) and (22), are equivalent. In the case of more general nonlinear objective functions, the Polak-Ribiere expression is argued to give better results, when compared with the Fletcher-Reeves expression [Johansson, 1992]. This is explained by the fact that, in situations where the algorithm is producing successive points with very little reduction in the objective function, the successive gradient vectors g^{j+1} and g^{j} are approximately equal in module. Thus, the orthogonality property between gradients is lost, and the Polak-Ribiere expression gives a nearly zero value to β^{j}. A small β^{j} has the effect of ruling out the previous search direction and forces a major contribution of the new gradient in the generation of the next search direction, as indicated by the expression in equation (18).

The two alternative expressions described above lead to a CGM that uses only function evaluations and gradient calculations, eliminating the need of the Hessian matrix. But there are some drawbacks associated with the line-search phase necessary to solve problem (20): it is known that the performance of the CGM is sensitive to the accuracy used in the solution of this line-search problem. If the line-search is carried out with great accuracy, the overall performance of the main algorithm will depend on the computations spent on function evaluations used in the line-search phase. On the other hand, a coarse line-search process will produce wrong values for the step-length α^{j}, affecting the orthogonality property between gradients and conjugate directions. Some criteria have been proposed to stop the line-search process when a sufficiently accurate solution for the step-length has been obtained. But these criteria, together with a line-search procedure, introduce problem-dependent parameters that must be specified by the user.

Regardless of the full calculation of the Hessian matrix or the use of line-search procedures, as the algorithm takes its course, the search directions are no longer H-conjugate. To alleviate this problem, it is a common practice to reinitialize the direction of search to the negative of the current gradient, after the completion of NP iterations. This restart strategy is the simplest one, but more sophisticated strategies can be found in the literature [Bazaraa, 1992].

C. SCALED CONJUGATE GRADIENT ALGORITHM

Moller [Moller, 1993] proposed an effective CGM, called scaled conjugate gradient method (SCGM). In the SCGM, no line search is required and it is considered a procedure to handle the occurrence of negative definite Hessian matrices, at any point in the search space.

The SCGM uses the fact that the Hessian matrix appears in the expression for α^{j} multiplied by a vector d^{j} (see equation (17)). The product of the Hessian

$\mathbf{H}(w^k)$ by an arbitrary vector $\mathbf{v}$ can be calculated efficiently with the aid of the following finite difference approximation

$$\mathbf{H}(\mathbf{w}^k)\mathbf{v} \approx \frac{\nabla\mathbf{E}_T(\mathbf{w}^k + \sigma^k\mathbf{v}) - \nabla\mathbf{E}_T(\mathbf{w}^k)}{\sigma^k}, \quad 0 < \sigma^k \ll 1. \tag{23}$$

In the limit, this approximation tends to the true value of the product $\mathbf{H}(\mathbf{w}^k)\mathbf{v}$. Here, the trick is to avoid the line-search phase, firstly calculating the approximation to the product $\mathbf{H}(\mathbf{w}^k)\mathbf{v}$ by equation (23), and then using equation (17) to obtain α^j.

If in some point $\mathbf{w}^k$, the Hessian matrix is negative definite, the use of a possibly negative step-length α^j is avoided by adding a positive scale parameter λ to the diagonal of $\mathbf{H}(\mathbf{w}^k)$. If λ is sufficiently large, the Hessian matrix is guaranteed to be positive definite, yielding a positive α^j. Taking a large value for λ implies a small step size in the direction of search $\mathbf{d}^j$, that is, the first-order information will predominate over the second-order information. In a similar way, if the scale parameter λ has a small value, the second-order information will have a major influence than the first-order one in the final value of α^j. To allow the adaptation of λ during the optimization process, the SCGM includes steps inherited from trust region methods that decrease λ in regions where the quadratic model is a good local approximation and increase λ in regions where the quadratic approximation is poor. Detailed description of all the steps in the SCGM can be founded in Moller [Moller, 1993].

X. AN IMPROVED SCGM METHOD

As reported in Moller [Moller, 1993], the SCGM has superior performance when compared with the conventional CGM. In using the original SCGM on highly complex nonlinear surfaces, as those associated with recurrent neural networks, we have observed some problems in the method, regarding the production of negative values for the parameters α^j and β^j. The use of a negative value of α^j, as already stated, indicates that the algorithm is taking a step in a direction that leads to an increase in the objective function. This is a contradictory situation, since we want to minimize the cost function. Also it is known that the convergence of any CGM using the Polak-Ribiere expression for β^j (see equation (21)) is not guaranteed. To alleviate these problems we propose the adoption of a hybridization in the choice of the value to be used for β^j. Another important improvement that can be introduced into the SCGM is the exact evaluation of the product $\mathbf{H}(\mathbf{w}^j)\mathbf{v}$. At least theoretically, the use of equation (23) is subject to numerical and roundoff problems. In this equation, there are conflicting requirements, as for example the need of small values for σ^j in order to obtain a good approximation to the product $\mathbf{H}(\mathbf{w}^j)\mathbf{v}$, confronted with precision lost when $\mathbf{v}$ is multiplied by a small value of σ^j and used in the sum $\mathbf{w}^j + \sigma^j\mathbf{v}$. Fortunately, the problem related to the exact computation of the product involving the Hessian matrix and an arbitrary vector was entirely solved by Pearlmutter [Pearlmutter, 1994]. Using a differential operator it is possible to compute the product of $\mathbf{H}(\cdot)$ with any desired vector without approximations, and also to avoid the calculation and storage of the Hessian itself.

In the context of recurrent neural networks of practical importance, the application of the SCGM [Moller, 1993], together with the result of Pearlmutter [Pearlmutter, 1994], was firstly considered in Von Zuben and Netto [Von Zuben, 1995] and posteriorly in Campolucci *et al.* [Campolucci, 1998].

A. HYBRIDIZATION IN THE CHOICE OF β^j

It is known that any conjugate gradient method using the Fletcher-Reeves expression (see equation (22)) is globally convergent. The same property can not be guaranteed when using the Polak-Ribiere expression (see equation (21)) [Shewchuk, 1994]. But, as largely reported in the literature, the use of the Polak-Ribiere expression generally leads to superior results [Touati-Ahmed, 1990]. In this chapter, we adopt an idea in some sense similar to one proposed in Touati-Ahmed and Storey [Touati-Ahmed, 1990]. Consider the expressions for β_{PR}^j and β_{FR}^j given in equations (21) and (22), respectively. Our choice for β^j is computed as follows:

If j = *NP*-1,

$$\beta^j = 0; \ \mathbf{d}^{j+1} = -\mathbf{g}^{j+1}; \ j = 0;$$

else

>**If ($\beta_{PR}^j > 0$) and ($\beta_{PR}^j < \beta_{FR}^j$),**
>
>>$$\beta^j = \beta_{PR}^j;$$
>>
>>$$\mathbf{d}^{j+1} = -\mathbf{g}^{j+1} + \beta^j\mathbf{d}^j;$$
>>
>>**If $-\mathbf{g}^{j+1}(\mathbf{d}^{j+1})^T < 0$,**
>>
>>>$$\beta^j = 0; \ \mathbf{d}^{j+1} = -\mathbf{g}^{j+1}; \ j = 0;$$
>>
>>**else**
>>
>>>$$j = j+1;$$
>>
>>**end**
>
>**else if $\beta_{PR}^j > \beta_{FR}^j$,**

$$\beta^{j} = \beta^{j}_{FR} ;$$

$$\mathbf{d}^{j+1} = -\mathbf{g}^{j+1} + \beta^{j}\mathbf{d}^{j} ;$$

If $-\mathbf{g}^{j+1}\left(\mathbf{d}^{j+1}\right)^{T} < 0$,

$$\beta^{j} = 0; \ \mathbf{d}^{j+1} = -\mathbf{g}^{j+1}; \ j = 0;$$

else

$$j = j+1;$$

end

else

$$\beta^{j} = 0; \ \mathbf{d}^{j+1} = -\mathbf{g}^{j+1} ; \ j = 0;$$

end

end

B. EXACT MULTIPLICATION BY THE HESSIAN [PEARLMUTTER, 1994]

Expanding $\nabla E_{T}(\cdot)$ around a point $\mathbf{w} \in R^{NP}$ yields:

$$\nabla E_{T}(\mathbf{w} + \Delta\mathbf{w}) = \nabla E_{T}(\mathbf{w}) + \mathbf{H}(\mathbf{w}) \cdot \Delta\mathbf{w} + \mathbf{O}\left(\|\Delta\mathbf{w}\|^{2}\right) \qquad (24)$$

where $\Delta\mathbf{w}$ is a small perturbation. Choosing $\Delta\mathbf{w} = \alpha\mathbf{v}$, where α is a small real number and $\mathbf{v} \in R^{NP}$ is an arbitrary vector, we can compute $\mathbf{H}(\mathbf{w})\mathbf{v}$ as follows;

$$\mathbf{H}(\mathbf{w})\mathbf{v} = \frac{1}{\alpha}\left[\nabla E_{T}(\mathbf{w} + \alpha\mathbf{v}) - \nabla E_{T}(\mathbf{w}) + \mathbf{O}\left(\alpha^{2}\right)\right] =$$
$$\frac{\nabla E_{T}(\mathbf{w} + \alpha\mathbf{v}) - \nabla E_{T}(\mathbf{w})}{\alpha} + \mathbf{O}\left(\alpha^{2}\right) \qquad (25)$$

Taking the limit as $\alpha \to 0$,

$$\mathbf{H}(\mathbf{w})\mathbf{v} = \lim_{\alpha \to 0} \frac{\nabla E_{T}(\mathbf{w} + \alpha\mathbf{v}) - \nabla E_{T}(\mathbf{w})}{\alpha} = \frac{\partial}{\partial\alpha}\nabla E_{T}(\mathbf{w} + \alpha\mathbf{v})\Big|_{\alpha=0} \qquad (26)$$

Now, it is necessary to introduce a transformation to convert an algorithm that computes the gradient of the system into one that computes the expression in equation (26). Defining the operator

$$\Psi_{\mathbf{v}}\{f(\mathbf{w})\} \equiv \frac{\partial}{\partial\alpha}f(\mathbf{w} + \alpha\mathbf{v})\Big|_{\alpha=0} \qquad (27)$$

we have $\Psi_v\{\nabla E_T(w)\} = H(w)v$ and $\Psi_v\{w\} = v$. Because $\Psi_v\{\cdot\}$ is a differential operator, it obeys the usual rules of differentiation.

XI. THE LEARNING ALGORITHM FOR RECURRENT NEURAL NETWORKS

To apply the improved SCGM to recurrent neural network learning, we need to compute $\nabla E_T(w)$ and the product $H(w)v$ for each step j. Consider again the recurrent neural network architectures presented in section 6. Let a, b, and c be the column vectors obtained from piling the lines of the matrices A, B, and C, respectively. The ordering in which the lines are taken to form the piles may be arbitrary, as long as the favored order is always adopted from then on. Thus, following the dimensions adopted for the architectures, we can write $a \in R^{(N.D.L)}$, $b \in R^{(N.(M+1))}$, and $c \in R^{(O.(N+1))}$. Remember that, if the architecture is a FRNN, matrix C and its corresponding vector c do not have adjustable parameters.

Now, the vector $w \in R^{NP}$, that contains all the weights of a particular architecture, can be expressed as $w = \begin{bmatrix} a^T & b^T & c^T \end{bmatrix}^T$ and has a total number of parameters given by $NP=(N.D.L) + (N.(M+1)) + O.(N+1)$.

Given the gradient vector $\nabla E_T(w)$ of the error measure defined in equation (14), its decomposition to produce the partial gradient vectors with respect to a, b, and c, are columns vectors denoted by $\nabla E_T^a(w)$, $\nabla E_T^b(w)$, and $\nabla E_T^c(w)$, respectively. Following the same notation adopted in the formation of w, the vector $\nabla E_T(w)$ can now be expressed as

$$\nabla E_T(w) = \left[\left(\nabla E_T^a\right)^T \ \left(\nabla E_T^b\right)^T \ \left(\nabla E_T^c\right)^T \right]^T .$$

The vector v, considered in the calculus of the product $H(w)v$, has the same dimension of w. Actually, v will always be taken as the search direction d^j, to be defined at each iteration of the improved SCGM. Thus, v can be used to generate three matrices, V_a, V_b, and V_c, with the same dimensions as the matrices A, B, and C, respectively. The process used to distribute the elements of v into the matrices V_a, V_b, and V_c must be the inverse of the one adopted to form w.

To help in further developments, in what follows we will define generic vectors and matrices. Considering the column vectors $\Phi = [\phi_1, \cdots, \phi_H]^T$ and $g = [g_1(\Phi), \cdots, g_P(\Phi)]^T$, we define the following matrices:

$$\Lambda(\mathbf{g}) = \text{block diagonal}\{g_i, i = 1, \cdots, P\} = \begin{bmatrix} g_1 & 0 & 0 & \cdots & 0 \\ 0 & g_2 & 0 & \cdots & 0 \\ \cdot & \cdot & \cdot & \cdot & \cdot \\ 0 & 0 & 0 & \cdots & g_P \end{bmatrix}$$

$$\Pi(\Phi) = \text{block diagonal}\{[\phi_1, \cdots, \phi_H]\} = \begin{bmatrix} \phi_1 & \cdots & \phi_H & 0 & \cdots & & & & 0 \\ 0 & \cdots & 0 & \phi_1 & \cdots & \phi_H & 0 & \cdots & 0 \\ \cdot & \cdot & \cdot & \cdot & \cdot & \cdot & \cdot & \cdot & \cdot \\ 0 & \cdots & & & & & 0 & \phi_1 & \cdots & \phi_H \end{bmatrix}$$

$\mathbf{J}_\Phi(\mathbf{g})$ = Jacobian matrix of $\mathbf{g}$ with respect to Φ :

$$\mathbf{J}_\Phi(\mathbf{g}) = \begin{bmatrix} \dfrac{\partial g_1}{\partial \phi_1} & \dfrac{\partial g_1}{\partial \phi_2} & \cdots & \dfrac{\partial g_1}{\partial \phi_H} \\ \dfrac{\partial g_2}{\partial \phi_1} & \dfrac{\partial g_2}{\partial \phi_2} & \cdots & \dfrac{\partial g_2}{\partial \phi_H} \\ \cdot & \cdot & & \cdot \\ \dfrac{\partial g_P}{\partial \phi_1} & \dfrac{\partial g_P}{\partial \phi_2} & \cdots & \dfrac{\partial g_P}{\partial \phi_H} \end{bmatrix}$$

$\overline{\mathbf{C}}, \overline{\mathbf{V}}_\mathbf{c}$: matrices obtained from $\mathbf{C}$, and $\mathbf{V}_c$, respectively, by removing the last column. In $\mathbf{C}$, this column contains the bias of the output units.

In the following development the equations for the derivative of the error, measured with respect to the network parameters, will be presented through matrix manipulations.

A. COMPUTATION OF $\nabla E_T(\mathbf{w})$

The operator ∇ is a linear differential operator, and its application to equation (14) results in the following equation:

$$\nabla E_T(\mathbf{w}) = \sum_{k=1}^{P} \nabla E^k(\mathbf{w}) \tag{28}$$

Since we are adopting batch learning, the network parameters are updated only after the presentation of all the training patterns. In this case, the total gradient is the sum of the partial gradients calculated at each time step k. In the sequel, we will present the equations for the calculation of partial gradients. Each partial gradient can also be broken into its components, corresponding to vectors $\mathbf{a}$, $\mathbf{b}$, and $\mathbf{c}$. Thus, we can write:

67

Efficient Second-Order Learning Algorithms

$$\nabla E^k(\mathbf{w}) = \left[\left(\nabla E_a^k\right)^T \ \left(\nabla E_b^k\right)^T \ \left(\nabla E_c^k\right)^T \right]^T \tag{29}$$

Using the definition for $\mathbf{E}^k(\mathbf{w})$, given in equation (15), and the state space representation, given in equations (7) to (12), the following equations can be written:

$$\mathbf{J}_c(\mathbf{z}(k)) = \Lambda\left(\dot{\mathbf{F}}(\mathbf{s}(k))\right)\mathbf{A}\mathbf{J}_c(\mathbf{x}(k)) \tag{30}$$

$$\mathbf{J}_c(\mathbf{y}(k)) = \overline{\mathbf{C}}\mathbf{J}_c(\mathbf{z}(k)) + \Pi\left(\begin{bmatrix} \mathbf{z}(k) \\ 1 \end{bmatrix}\right) \tag{31}$$

$$\left[\nabla E_c^k\right]^T = \left[\mathbf{y}(k) - \mathbf{y}_d(k)\right]^T \mathbf{J}_c(\mathbf{y}(k)) \tag{32}$$

$$\mathbf{J}_a(\mathbf{z}(k)) = \Lambda\left(\dot{\mathbf{F}}(\mathbf{s}(k))\right)\{\mathbf{A}\mathbf{J}_a(\mathbf{x}(k)) + \Pi(\mathbf{x}(k))\} \tag{33}$$

$$\mathbf{J}_a(\mathbf{y}(k)) = \overline{\mathbf{C}}\mathbf{J}_a(\mathbf{z}(k)) \tag{34}$$

$$\left[\nabla E_a^k\right]^T = \left[\mathbf{y}(k) - \mathbf{y}_d(k)\right]^T \mathbf{J}_a(\mathbf{y}(k)) \tag{35}$$

$$\mathbf{J}_b(\mathbf{z}(k)) = \Lambda\left(\dot{\mathbf{F}}(\mathbf{s}(k))\right)\left\{ \mathbf{A}\mathbf{J}_b(\mathbf{x}(k)) + \Pi\left(\begin{bmatrix} \mathbf{u}(k) \\ 1 \end{bmatrix}\right) \right\} \tag{36}$$

$$\mathbf{J}_b(\mathbf{y}(k)) = \overline{\mathbf{C}}\mathbf{J}_b(\mathbf{z}(k)) \tag{37}$$

$$\left[\nabla E_b^k\right]^T = \left[\mathbf{y}(k) - \mathbf{y}_d(k)\right]^T \mathbf{J}_b(\mathbf{y}(k)) \tag{38}$$

B. COMPUTATION OF H(w)v

Given a vector $\mathbf{v}$, with the properties already mentioned, the computation of $\mathbf{H}(\mathbf{w})\mathbf{v} = \Psi_v\{\nabla E_T(\mathbf{w})\}$ requires the application of the derivative operator $\Psi_v\{\cdot\}$ to every calculation done to obtain $\nabla E_T(\mathbf{w})$. Applying $\Psi_v\{\cdot\}$ to equations (7) to (9), we get

$$\Psi_v\{\mathbf{s}(k)\} = \mathbf{A}\Psi_v\{\mathbf{x}(k)\} + \mathbf{V}_a\mathbf{x}(k) + \mathbf{B}\Psi_v\{\mathbf{u}(k)\} + \mathbf{V}_b\mathbf{u}(k) \tag{39}$$

$$\Psi_v\{\mathbf{z}(k)\} = \Lambda\left(\dot{\mathbf{F}}(\mathbf{s}(k))\right)\Psi_v\{\mathbf{s}(k)\} \tag{40}$$

$$\Psi_v\{y(k)\} = \mathbf{C}\begin{bmatrix} \Psi_v\{z(k)\} \\ 0 \end{bmatrix} + \mathbf{V_c}\begin{bmatrix} z(k) \\ 1 \end{bmatrix} \tag{41}$$

Now, applying the operator $\Psi_v\{\cdot\}$ to equation (28) results in the following equation:

$$\Psi_v\{\nabla E_T(\mathbf{w})\} = \sum_{k=1}^{P} \Psi_v\{\nabla E^k(\mathbf{w})\} \tag{42}$$

This equation leads to the conclusion that the total product $H(w)v$ can be computed by adding the results of applying the operator $\Psi_v\{\cdot\}$ to each partial gradient computed at time step k. Following these guidelines, we obtain:

$$\begin{aligned}\Psi_v\{J_c(z(k))\} = \Lambda\{\Lambda[\ddot{F}(s(k))]\Psi_v(s(k))\}AJ_c(x(k)) \\ + \Lambda(\dot{F}(s(k)))[A\Psi_v\{J_c(x(k))\} + V_a J_c(x(k))]\end{aligned} \tag{43}$$

$$\Psi_v\{J_c(y(k))\} = \overline{C}\Psi_v\{J_c(z(k))\} + \overline{V}_c J_c(z(k)) + \Pi\left(\begin{bmatrix} \Psi_v\{z(k)\} \\ 0 \end{bmatrix}\right) \tag{44}$$

$$\Psi_v\left\{\left[\nabla E_c^k\right]^{\Gamma}\right\} = [y(k) - y_d(k)]^{\Gamma}\Psi_v\{J_c(y(k))\} + \Psi_v\{y(k)\}J_c(y(k)) \tag{45}$$

$$\begin{aligned}\Psi_v\{J_a(z(k))\} = \Lambda\{\Lambda[\ddot{F}(s(k))]\Psi_v(s(k))\}\{AJ_a(x(k)) + \Pi(x(k))\} \\ + \Lambda(\dot{F}(s(k)))[A\Psi_v\{J_a(x(k))\} + V_a J_a(x(k)) + \Pi(\Psi_v\{x(k)\})]\end{aligned} \tag{46}$$

$$\Psi_v\{J_a(y(k))\} = \overline{C}\Psi_v\{J_a(z(k))\} + \overline{V}_c J_a(z(k)) \tag{47}$$

$$\Psi_v\left\{\left[\nabla E_a^k\right]^{\Gamma}\right\} = [y(k) - y_d(k)]^{\Gamma}\Psi_v\{J_a(y(k))\} + \Psi_v\{y(k)\}J_a(y(k)) \tag{48}$$

$$\begin{aligned}\Psi_v\{J_b(z(k))\} = \Lambda\{\Lambda[\ddot{F}(s(k))]\Psi_v(s(k))\}\left\{AJ_b(x(k)) + \Pi\left(\begin{bmatrix} u(k) \\ 1 \end{bmatrix}\right)\right\} \\ + \Lambda(\dot{F}(s(k)))\begin{bmatrix} A\Psi_v\{J_b(x(k))\} + V_a J_b(x(k)) \\ + \Pi\left(\begin{bmatrix} \Psi_v\{u(k)\} \\ 0 \end{bmatrix}\right) \end{bmatrix}\end{aligned} \tag{49}$$

$$\Psi_v\{J_b(y(k))\} = \overline{C}\Psi_v\{J_b(z(k))\} + \overline{V}_c J_b(z(k)) \tag{50}$$

69

$$\Psi_v\left\{\left[\nabla E_b^k\right]^T\right\} = \left[y(k) - y_d(k)\right]^T \Psi_v\{J_b(y(k))\} + \Psi_v\{y(k)\}J_b(y(k)) \qquad (51)$$

XII. SIMULATION RESULTS

To show the gain in performance obtained with the proposed hybrid SCGM, we establish a comparison with the original SCGM with exact second-order information, considered to be the best second-order algorithm already proposed in the literature. We take two examples: one concerning nonlinear system identification, and the other a time series prediction. In simulations involving recurrent neural networks with the same architectures, the competing algorithms were initialized with the same set of weights. In all situations, the weights were generated from a symmetric uniform distribution in the range [-0.2,0.2].

The error criterion used in all the simulations is that indicated in equation (14). The network parameters were adapted by presenting the patterns in a batch (epoch-wise) mode. As the main objective is to access the convergence aspects of both versions of the SCGM, major attention is given to the error curves in the learning process.

Nonlinear System Identification: The nonlinear plant used in the generation of the training patterns is the same used in Example 3 of Narendra and Parthasarathy [Narenda, 1990]. The training set consists of 1000 samples of input-output pairs, generated according to the guidelines adopted there. The neural network identifiers receive $u(k)$ as input and have $y_p(k+1)$ as desired output. We carried out simulations with the three recurrent architectures. To exemplify, Figure 5 shows the errors curves obtained in the training of a neural net with the OFRNN architecture. We adopted 5 (five) hidden neurons and tapped delay lines of length L = 5. The curve with solid line corresponds to the hybrid SCGM, and the curve with dotted line corresponds to the conventional one. This figure shows that the hybrid SCGM reached the local minimum of the error surface in a reduced number of epochs when compared with the original SCGM.

Time Series Prediction: In this task, we take as training patterns 1000 points of a time series generated from the Lorentz equations, with the same conditions described in Ergezinger and Thomsen [Ergezinger, 1995]. In Figure 6, we show the curves of the error measure for the same recurrent network with the FRNN architecture. The net has 10 (ten) hidden neurons and tapped delay lines of length L = 1. Again the hybrid SCGM (solid line) takes advantage over the original SCGM (doted line).

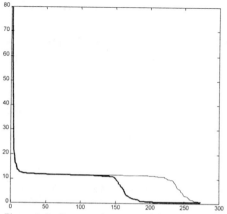

Figure 5. Performance in a system identification task

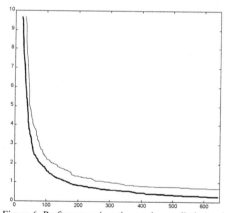

Figure 6. Performance in a time series prediction task

XIII. CONCLUDING REMARKS

Based on the results presented above, we state that globally and partially recurrent neural networks can be applied to represent complex dynamic behaviors. This chapter investigated input-output mapping networks, so that the desired dynamic behavior has to be produced by means of an effective supervised learning process.

The innovative aspects of this work are the proposition of a systematic procedure to obtain exact second-order information for a range of different recurrent neural network architectures, at a low computational cost, and an improved version of a scaled conjugate gradient algorithm to make use of this high-quality information. An important aspect is that, given the exact second-order information, the learning algorithm can be directly applied, without any kind of adaptation to the specific context.

ACKNOWLEDGMENTS

Eurípedes P. dos Santos acknowledges CAPES (DS-44/97-0), and Fernando J. Von Zuben CNPq (300910/96-7) and FAPESP (98/09939-6), for their support.

REFERENCES

Back, A. D. and Tsoi. A. C., FIR and IIR synapses, a new neural network architecture for time series modeling, *Neural Computation*, 3: 375, 1991.

Battiti, R., First- and second-order methods for learning: between steepest descent and Newton's method, *Neural Computation*, 4(2), 141, 1992.

Bazaraa, M. S., Sherali, H. D., and Shetty, C. M., *Nonlinear Programming: Theory and Algorithms*, John Wiley & Sons, New York, 1992.

Bishop, C. M., *Neural Networks for Pattern Recognition*. Oxford Univ. Press, New York, 1995.

Campolucci, P., Simonetti, M., Uncini, A., and Piazza, F., New second-order algorithms for recurrent neural networks based on conjugate gradient, *IEEE International Joint Conference on Neural Networks*, 384, 1998.

Chang, W.-F. and Mak, M.-W., A conjugate gradient learning algorithm for recurrent neural networks, *Neurocomputing*, 24, 173, 1999.

Cohen, M. A., The construction of arbitrary stable dynamics in nonlinear neural networks, *Neural Networks*, 5(1), 83, 1992.

Connor, J. T., Martin, R. D., and Atlas, L. E., Recurrent neural networks and robust time series prediction, *IEEE Transactions on Neural Networks*, 5(2), 240, 1994.

Ergezinger, S. and Thomsen, E., An accelerated learning algorithm for multilayer perceptrons: optimization layer by layer, *IEEE Transactions on Neural Networks*, 6(1), 31, 1995.

Frasconi, P., Gori, M., and Soda, G., Local feedback multilayered networks, *Neural Computation*, 4, 121, 1992.

Haykin, S., *Neural Networks – A Comprehensive Foundation*. Prentice Hall, Englewood Cliffs, NJ, 1999.

Hornik, K., Stinchcombe, M., and White, H., Multi-layer feedforward networks are universal approximators, *Neural Networks*, 2(5), 359, 1989.

Jacobs, R. A., Increased rates of convergence through learning rate adaptation, *Neural Networks*, 1, 295, 1988.

Jin, L., Nikiforuk, P. N., and Gupta, M. M., Approximation capability of feedforward and recurrent neural networks, in Gupta, M. M., and Sinha, N. K., Eds., *Intelligent Control Systems: Concepts and Applications*, IEEE Press, 235, 1995.

Johansson, E. M., Dowla, F. U., and Goodman, D. M., Backpropagation learning for multilayred feed-foward neural networks using the conjugate gradient method. *International Journal of Neural Systems*, 2(4): 291, 1992.

Kim, Y. H., Lewis, F. L., and Abdallah, C. T., A dynamic recurrent neural-network-based adaptive observer for a class of nonlinear systems, *Automatica*, 33(8), 1539, 1997.

Kolen, J. F., *Exploring the Computational Capabilities of Recurrent Neural Networks*, Ph.D. Thesis, The Ohio State University, Columbus, 1994.

Levin, A. V. and Narendra, K. S., Control of nonlinear dynamical systems using neural networks – controllability and stabilization, *IEEE Transactions on Neural Networks*, 4(2), 192, 1993.

Levin, A. V. and Narendra, K. S., Control of nonlinear dynamical systems using neural networks – Part II: observability, identification, and control, *IEEE Transactions on Neural Networks*, 7(1), 30, 1996.

Li, J. H., Michel, A. N., and Porod, W., Qualitative analysis and synthesis of a class of neural networks, *IEEE Transactions on Circuits and Systems*, 35(8), 976, 1988.

Luenberger, D. G., *Linear and Nonlinear Programming*. Addison-Wesley Publishing Company, Reading, MA, 1989.

Moller, M. F., A scaled conjugate gradient algorithm for fast supervised learning, *Neural Networks*, 6(4), 525, 1993.

Narendra, K. S. and Parthasarathy, K., Identification and control of dynamical systems using neural networks, *IEEE Transactions on Neural Networks*, 1(1), 4, 1990.

Nerrand, O., Roussel-Ragot, P., Personnaz, L., and Dreyfus, G., Neural networks and nonlinear adaptive filtering: unifying concepts and new algorithms. *Neural Computation*, 5(2), 165, 1993.

Oppenheim, A. V. and Schafer, R. W., *Discrete-Time Signal Processing*, Prentice-Hall, Englewood Cliffs, NJ, 1999.

Ott, E., *Chaos in Dynamical Systems*. Cambridge University Press, London, 1993.

Pearlmutter, B. A., Fast exact multiplication by the Hessian. *Neural Computation*, 6(1), 147, 1994.

Pearlmutter, B. A., Gradient calculations for dynamic recurrent neural networks: a survey, *IEEE Transactions on Neural Networks*, 6(5), 1212, 1995.

Poggio, T. and Girosi, F., Networks for approximation and learning, *Proceedings of the IEEE*, 78(9), 1481, 1990.

Shewchuk, J. R., An introduction to the conjugate gradient method without the agonizing pain, School of Computer Science, Carnegie Mellon University, Pittsburgh, August 4, 1994.

Shink, J. J., Adaptive IIR filtering, *IEEE ASSP Magazine*, 4, 21, 1989.

Siegelmann, H. T. and Sontag, E. D., Turing computability with neural nets, *Applied Mathematics Letters*, 4, 77, 1991.

Siegelmann, H. T., Horne, B. G., and Giles, C. L., Computational capabilities of recurrent NARX neural networks, *IEEE Transactions on Systems, Man, and Cybernetics, Part B: Cybernetics*, 27, 208, 1997.

Touati-Ahmed, D. and Storey, C., Efficient hybrid conjugate gradient techniques, *Journal of Optimization Theory and Applications* 64(2), 379, 1990.

Tsoi, A. C. and Back, A. D., Discrete time recurrent neural network architectures: a unifying review, *Neurocomputing*, 15, 183, 1997.

Tsoi, A. C. and Back, A. D., Locally recurrent globally feedforward networks: a critical review of architectures, *IEEE Transactions on Neural Networks*, 5(2): 229, 1994.

van der Smagt, P. P., Minimisation methods for training feedforward neural networks, *Neural Networks*, 7(1), 1, 1994.

Von Zuben, F. J. and Netto, M. L. A, Second-order training for recurrent neural networks without teacher-forcing, *Proceedings of the IEEE International Conference on Neural Networks*, 2, 801, 1995.

Von Zuben, F. J. and Netto, M. L. A., Recurrent neural networks for chaotic time series prediction, in Balthazar, J.M., Mook, D.T., and Rosário, J.M., Eds., *Nonlinear Dynamics, Chaos, Control, and Their Applications to Engineering Sciences*, 1, 347, 1997.

Williams, R. J., Adaptive state representation and estimation using recurrent connectionist networks, in Miller, W.T., Sutton, R.S., and Werbos, P., Eds., *Neural Networks for Control*, MIT Press, Cambridge, 1990.

Williams, R. J. and Zipser, D., A learning algorithm for continually running fully recurrent neural networks, *Neural Computation*, 1, 270, 1989.

Chapter 4

DESIGNING HIGH ORDER RECURRENT NETWORKS FOR BAYESIAN BELIEF REVISION

Ashraf M. Abdelbar

Department of Computer Science
American University in Cairo

I. INTRODUCTION

The Hopfield neural network has been used for a large number of optimization problems, ranging from object recognition [Lin *et al.*, 1991] to graph planarization [Takefuji and Lee, 1989] to concentrator assignment [Tagliarini and Page, 1987]. However, the fact that the Hopfield energy function is of quadratic order limits the problems to which it can be applied. Sometimes, objective functions which cannot be reduced to Hopfield's quadratic energy function can still be reasonably approximated by a quadratic energy function. For other problems, the objective function must be modeled by a higher-order energy function. Examples of such problems include the angular-metric TSP [Aggarwal *et al.*, 1997] and belief revision, which is our subject here.

In this chapter, we describe high-order recurrent neural networks and provide an efficient implementation data structure for sparse high-order networks. We then describe how such networks can be used for Bayesian belief revision, an important problem in diagnostic reasoning and in commonsense reasoning. We begin by introducing belief revision and reasoning under uncertainty.

II. BELIEF REVISION AND REASONING UNDER UNCERTAINTY

A. REASONING UNDER UNCERTAINTY

Humans exhibit the ability to assimilate and reason with information that is incomplete, contradictory, or subject to change. For example, most men have no trouble comprehending that, when their wives ask their opinion on a new hairstyle, they are expected to both "be honest" and "say that they love it." Similarly, if a man is driving his car, believing the car to be in fourth gear, and finds the car unable to accelerate, he is able to consider the possibility that the car is in fact in second gear. Reasoning with uncertainty is the branch of artificial intelligence that is concerned with modeling this facet of human cognition.

Conventional first-order logic is inadequate for this task. Statements are either known to be true, known to be false, or not known to be one way or the other. Further, once a statement is known to be true (or false), it stays true (or false) forever. One approach to reasoning with uncertainty is to use higher-order nonmonotonic logic [Ginsberg, 1987; Marek and Truszczynski, 1993; Reiter, 1987; Shoham, 1987]. For example, modal logic [Konyndyk, 1986; Popkorn, 1994] augments predicate logic with modal operators which take whole sentences as arguments. With modal logic, it is possible, for example, to distinguish between a statement which is false but has the potential of being true (such as Johnny is a straight-A student) and a statement which is by necessity false (such as Johnny has three eyes and six legs).

Another approach is to use numerical representations of uncertainty which may or may not be based on the probability calculus. Methods in this school can frequently be formalized in terms of belief functions. A belief function, $BEL(A)$, measures the degree to which all the evidence we have supports the hypothesis A. For this reason, numerical approaches to uncertainty are sometimes also referred to as the theory of evidence [Yager et al., 1994]. Belief functions are usually defined to have a value within the interval $[0, 1]$. In addition, a plausibility function is defined as

$$PLAUS(A) = 1 - BEL(\neg A) , \qquad (1)$$

and measures the degree to which our belief in $\neg A$ leaves room for belief in A. Note that unlike probability functions,

$$BEL(A) + PLAUS(A) \neq 1 . \qquad (2)$$

The only requirement is that

$$BEL(A) + PLAUS(A) \leq 1 . \qquad (3)$$

If for a particular hypothesis A, $BEL(A) = 0$ and $PLAUS(A) = 1$, this indicates complete ignorance. While if $BEL(A) = 1$ and $PLAUS(A) = 1$, or $BEL(A) = 0$ and $PLAUS(A) = 0$, this indicates with absolute certainty that A is true, or that A is false, respectively. The most popular non-probabilistic approach to belief functions is the Dempster-Shafer theory [Dempster, 1967; Kofler and Leondes, 1994; Shafer, 1976; Shafer, 1986; Shafer and Logan, 1987]. It is also possible to define belief functions in terms of fuzzy sets [Zadeh, 1979; Zadeh, 1994, Zadeh and Kacprzyk, 1992; Zimmerman, 1991] or in terms of rough sets [Pawlak, 1991; Pawlak, 1992; Pawlak et al., 1995].

Belief functions which are defined probabilistically are called *Bayesian belief functions*. A Bayesian belief function $BEL(A)$ is defined as

$$BEL(A) = P(A|\mathcal{E}) , \qquad (4)$$

where $\mathcal{E}$ denotes the available evidence. Pearl [1988] gives examples of how Dempster-Shafer belief functions can lead to counterintuitive reasoning. He argues convincingly that probability can be considered a "faithful guardian of common sense." Lindley [1987] contends that the probability calculus is "the only satisfactory description of uncertainty." However, there have been two primary criticisms of probabilistic approaches to representing uncertainty. The first is that there is no way to distinguish between complete ignorance and complete uncertainty. With Dempster-Shafer belief functions,

$$\begin{aligned} BEL(A) &= 0 \\ PLAUS(A) &= 1 \end{aligned} \tag{5}$$

indicate total ignorance; the evidence we have gives us no reason to believe A nor to disbelieve A. However,

$$BEL(A) = PLAUS(A) = 0.5 \tag{6}$$

indicate total uncertainty; the evidence we have provides equal support to A and $\neg A$. However, in the Bayesian formalism,

$$P(A|\mathcal{E}) = P(\neg A|\mathcal{E}) = 0.5, \tag{7}$$

indicates that A and $\neg A$ are equally likely given $\mathcal{E}$; this could be because $\mathcal{E}$ supports both hypotheses equally or because it provides support to neither. The other criticism of the Bayesian formalism has historically been that the need to consider probabilistic dependencies makes probability calculations unfeasible. However, this has largely changed with the advent of Bayesian belief networks, which provide a natural and concise graphical representation of probabilistic dependencies.

B. BAYESIAN BELIEF NETWORKS

Incarnations of Bayesian belief networks seem to have been around for some time. They have been called influence diagrams, knowledge maps, and causal diagrams. However, Judea Pearl has been largely credited with standardizing and popularizing Bayesian belief networks with his 1988 book [Pearl, 1988]. Given a set of random variables representing events or hypotheses in a given problem domain, a Bayesian belief network is a triple (V, E, P), where V is a set of nodes such that each node is identified with a domain variable, (V, E) specify a directed acyclic graph (DAG), and P is a set of probability distributions which specify for each node $v \in V$ the probability of each possible instantiation of v given each possible instantiation of $v's$ parents $\pi(v)$, and such that (V, E) is a *minimal independency map* of the domain variables. This requirement that a Bayesian belief network's underlying DAG be a minimal independency map of the problem domain is what allows computations on belief networks to be greatly simplified.

The definition of an independency map, or *I-map*, is based on the notion of conditional independence. If X, Y, and Z are disjoint sets of random variables,

X and Y are conditionally independent given Z, written $I(X, Z, Y)$ if for any possible instantiations of x, y, and z, of X, Y, and Z, respectively,

$$P(x|y \wedge z) = P(x|z), \tag{8}$$

whenever

$$P(y \wedge z) > 0. \tag{9}$$

Furthermore, if D is a DAG and X, Y, and Z are three disjoint sets of nodes of D, Z is said to *d-separate* X and Y, denoted $<X, Z, Y>$, if every path from a member of X to a member of Y is blocked by a member of Z. If D is a DAG where each node of D represents a random variable, then D is an independency map if $I(X, Z, Y)$ is implied by $<X|Z|Y>$. Finally, a DAG is a minimal I-map if the removal of any edge from the DAG renders the DAG no longer an I-map.

x	y	z	v	P(v | x,y,z)
T	T	T	T	0.34
T	T	T	F	0.66
T	T	F	T	0.80
T	T	F	F	0.20
T	F	T	T	0.23
T	F	T	F	0.77
T	F	F	T	0.65
T	F	F	F	0.35
F	T	T	T	0.95
F	T	T	F	0.05
F	T	F	T	0.55
F	T	F	F	0.45
F	F	T	T	0.10
F	F	T	F	0.90
F	F	F	T	0.25
F	F	F	F	0.75

Figure 1. Example of a local probability distribution with redundancies.

Based on the requirement that a Bayesian belief network be an I-map, the joint probability of any instantiation $\mathcal{A}$ of the nodes of a belief network (V, E, P) can be computed according to

$$P(\mathcal{A}) = \prod_{v \in V} P(\mathcal{A}(v)|\mathcal{A}(\pi(v))). \tag{10}$$

The correctness of this equation relies on the network being an I-map; while the minimality requirement enforces conciseness.

For a belief network (V, E, P), the set of probability distributions P specifies for each node v the probability of every possible instantiation of v given every possible instantiation of $\pi(v)$. Thus, if v is a binary-valued node and has two parents, x and y, which are also binary-valued, then v's probability distribution would be similar to Figure 1. However, Figure 1 contains some redundant information since for any given fixed instantiation $\mathcal{I}$ of $\pi(v)$,

$$P(v = \mathbf{T}|\mathcal{I}(\pi(v))) = 1 - P(v = \mathbf{F}|\mathcal{I}(\pi(v))). \tag{11}$$

Therefore, it is sufficient for binary-valued nodes to specify the probability of one truth assignment for each possible instantiation of the parents, as shown in Figure 2. In general, for a discrete node with k possible instantiations, it is necessary and sufficient to specify $k - 1$ probabilities for each possible instantiation of the parents.

x	y	z	v	P(v | x,y,z)
T	T	T	T	0.34
T	T	F	T	0.80
T	F	T	T	0.23
T	F	F	T	0.65
F	T	T	T	0.95
F	T	F	T	0.55
F	F	T	T	0.10
F	F	F	T	0.25

Figure 2. Example of a local probability distribution without redundancies.

C. BELIEF REVISION

Suppose a grocery store clerk sees a man come into his store carrying a gun. Based on the observed evidence ("man in store with gun"), the clerk may develop the belief that he is about to be the victim of a robbery. If the evidence set is augmented with the observation that the "gunman" is carrying a policeman's badge, the clerk may then revise his belief.

Formally, belief revision is the problem of finding the most plausible explanation for the current evidence at hand. This has applications in many areas of AI. For example, in natural language understanding, the evidence would be the natural language text and the possible explanations would be the possible meanings of the text [Charniak and Shimony, 1994; Hobbs et al., 1993]; in medical diagnosis, the evidence would be the symptoms and lab results and the explanations would be the possible diagnoses [Shachter, 1986]. For Bayesian belief networks, belief revision is the problem of finding the most probable explanation for a given set of evidence. In other words, given a set of observances, represented as a partial assignment $\mathcal{E}$ to a subset of the network variables, the objective is to find the network assignment $\mathcal{A}$ which maximizes the conditional probability $P(\mathcal{A}|\mathcal{E})$. Because it maximizes the posterior probability, $\mathcal{A}$ is called the *maximum a posteriori* assignment and the belief revision problem on Bayesian belief networks is often called the MAP assignment problem, or simply the MAP problem.

From Bayes' theorem we know that

$$P(\mathcal{A}|\mathcal{E}) = \frac{P(\mathcal{A})P(\mathcal{E}|\mathcal{A})}{P(\mathcal{E})}, \tag{12}$$

and since $P(\mathcal{E})$ is constant, maximizing $P(\mathcal{A}|\mathcal{E})$ is equivalent to maximizing $P(\mathcal{A})$ subject to the constraint that $\mathcal{E} \subseteq \mathcal{A}$. If $\mathcal{E}$ is empty, then we are simply interested in finding the network assignment with highest unconditional probability $P(\mathcal{A})$.

D. APPROACHES TO FINDING MAP ASSIGNMENTS

An important indicator of complexity for a belief network is whether it is *singly-connected* or *multiply-connected*. A singly-connected network is a network in which, for any pair of nodes, there is only one directed path connecting them. An alternative definition is that it is a network in which the underlying undirected graph is also acyclic. A multiply-connected network is a network in which there is more than one directed path connecting at least one pair of nodes.

For singly-connected networks, Pearl [Pearl, 1986; Pearl, 1988] has developed an algorithm, based on message passing, for finding the optimal MAP in linear time. The problem of finding MAPs on multiply-connected networks is **NP**-hard [Shimony, 1994] and even approximating the optimal MAP within a constant factor is **NP**-hard [Abdelbar and Hedetniemi, 1998]. Existing methods for finding exact MAPs on multiply-connected networks all have exponential complexity in the worst case. Simulated annealing [Abdelbar and Hedetniemi, 1997; Abdelbar and Attia, 1999; Geman and Geman, 1984], genetic algorithm [Abdelbar and Hedetniemi, 1997; Abdelbar and Attia, 1999; Rojas-Guzman and Kramer, 1993; Rojas-Guzman and Kramer, 1994], and integer programming approaches [Abdelbar, 1998; Abdelbar, 1999; Santos, 1994; Santos and Santos, 1996] for the problem are currently being investigated.

III. HOPFIELD NETWORKS AND MEAN FIELD ANNEALING

A. OPTIMIZATION AND THE HOPFIELD NETWORK

A recurrent neural network is one whose underlying topology of inter-neuronal connections contains at least one cycle. The Hopfield network [Hopfield, 1982; Hopfield, 1984] is perhaps the best known network of this class. The underlying topology of a Hopfield network is a graph: each weighted connection is either a binary connection T_{ij} between two neurons i and j or a unary connection I_i involving a single neuron i. A neuron in the Hopfield network is governed by

$$\frac{du_i}{dt} = \sum_{j \neq i} T_{ij} V_j + I_i \,, \tag{13}$$

and

$$V_i = g(u_i) \,, \tag{14}$$

where g is a (typically sigmoidal) activation function. The Hopfield network is a member of the Cohen-Grossberg [Cohen and Grossberg, 1983] family of dynamical systems. Under the requirements that the T_{ij} matrix be symmetric and with a zero-diagonal, and that the activation function g be monotonically non-decreasing and with a sufficiently high slope, the neurons of a Hopfield network will tend towards a collective state which minimizes the energy function

$$E = -\sum_{i=1}^{n} I_i V_i - \sum_{i=1}^{n} \sum_{j<i} T_{ij} V_i V_j \ . \tag{15}$$

The Hopfield network is used for optimization by constructing the T_{ij} and I_i connections such that the minimum points of the energy function correspond to the optimal solutions of the problem at hand. Many optimization problems can be described by an objective function that is to be minimized or maximized and a set of constraints that must be satisfied. These two components of the energy function can be constructed separately and then superimposed to form the overall energy function:

$$E = E^{obj} + \beta E^{cons} \ , \tag{16}$$

where E^{cons} and E^{obj} represent the energy functions corresponding to the constraints and objectives, respectively, and β is a manually-tuned scaling constant.

Certain types of constraints are encountered so frequently in the context of different problems that special design rules have been developed for their handling. Tagliarini et al.'s [Tagliarini et al., 1991] k-out-of-n rule deals with the case where it is desired to select exactly k out of an ensemble of n neurons.

In the energy function

$$E = \left(k - \sum_i V_i \right)^2 + \left(\sum_i V_i (1 - V_i) \right) \ , \tag{17}$$

the first term is minimized when the sum of the V_i's is k and the second term when all the V_i's have digital values. With some algebraic manipulation, it is easy to see that equation (17) has the same minimum points as

$$E = -\frac{1}{2} \sum_i \sum_{j \neq i} (-2) V_i V_j - \sum_i V_i (2k - 1) \ . \tag{18}$$

Correspondingly, the k-out-of-n rule prescribes that we assign T_{ij} to (-2) for every pair of neurons and assign I_i to $(2k - 1)$ for every neuron in the ensemble. This design rule can be applied to simultaneous constraints and the energy functions produced by each application of the rule can be superimposed to produce the overall E^{cons} [Page and Tagliarini, 1988].

B. BOLTZMANN MACHINE

Like the Hopfield network, the Boltzmann machine [Hinton and Sejnowski, 1986] can be used for optimization. The energy function of the Boltzmann machine is the same as that of the Hopfield network but, unlike the deterministic Hopfield network, the Boltzmann machine employs stochastic neurons. The activation level u_i of a neuron i in the Boltzmann machine is computed according to equation (13) as in the Hopfield network, but the output V_i of a neuron i is a binary-valued random variable with distribution:

$$P(V_i = 1) = \frac{1}{1 + e^{-\frac{u_i}{T}}} , \tag{19}$$

where T is a parameter known as the *temperature*. Initially, the temperature is set to a relatively high value and then, over time, it is gradually decreased according to some *annealing schedule*.

Note that when T is close to infinity, the probability is close to 0.5 regardless of the value of u_i; this corresponds to a random walk through weight space. On the other hand, when T is very low, network behavior becomes very similar to the discrete version of the Hopfield network.

The choice of annealing schedule for a Boltzmann machine is central to network performance. A well-known theoretical result by Geman and Geman [1984] holds that if the rate of decay of the temperature is no faster than logarithmic, the network is guaranteed to eventually converge to a global optimum. However, this schedule is very slow in practice and is rarely used. A commonly used schedule, first proposed by Kirkpatrick *et al.*[1983], is to reduce the temperature by a fixed fraction f after every iteration,

$$T^{new} = T^{old} * f . \tag{20}$$

C. MEAN FIELD ANNEALING

Mean field theory [Peterson and Hartman, 1989] can be used to obtain a deterministic approximation to the Boltzmann machine. In this variation, the output V_i of a neuron i is deterministically approximated to be

$$V_i = \tanh\left(\frac{u_i}{T}\right) , \tag{21}$$

where T is the annealing temperature. This mean field approximation, often called the deterministic Boltzmann machine, has been observed to produce faster convergence than the stochastic Boltzmann machine [Peterson and Anderson, 1987].

IV. HIGH ORDER RECURRENT NETWORKS

A High Order Recurrent Network (HORN) is a recurrent network whose underlying topology is a hypergraph, i.e., it allows weighted hyperedges which connect more than two neurons. The degree of a hyperedge is the number of neurons it connects; the order of a HORN is the largest hyperedge degree in the topology. We will use the notation $T^{(d)}_{i_1 \ldots i_d}$ to denote the weight of the dth-degree edge connecting neurons $i_1 \ldots i_d$. A HORN is symmetric if

$$T^{(d)}_{i_1 \ldots i_d} = T^{(d)}_{i_{h(1)} \ldots i_{h(d)}} , \tag{22}$$

for any permutation h of the integers $1 \ldots d$. By default, a HORN is assumed to be symmetric unless otherwise specified.

A kth-order HORN minimizes a kth-order energy function [Pinkas, 1995]:

$$
\begin{aligned}
E \;=\; &-\sum_{1 \leq i_1 < i_2 < \ldots < i_k \leq n} T^{(k)}_{i_1 \ldots i_k} V_{i_1} \ldots V_{i_k} \\
&-\sum_{1 \leq i_1 < i_2 < \ldots < i_{k-1} \leq n} T^{(k-1)}_{i_1 \ldots i_{k-1}} V_{i_1} \ldots V_{i_{k-1}} \\
&-\ldots-\sum_{1 \leq i \leq n} T^{(1)} V_i ,
\end{aligned}
\tag{23}
$$

where n is the number of neurons. For example, the energy function of a fourth-order HORN has the form:

$$
\begin{aligned}
E \;=\; &-\sum_{i=1}^{n}\sum_{j=i+1}^{n}\sum_{k=j+1}^{n}\sum_{l=k+1}^{n} T^{(4)}_{ijkl} V_i V_j V_k V_l - \sum_{i=1}^{n}\sum_{j=i+1}^{n}\sum_{k=j+1}^{n} T^{(3)}_{ijk} V_i V_j V_k \\
&-\sum_{i=1}^{n}\sum_{j=i+1}^{n} T^{(2)}_{ij} V_i V_j - \sum_{i=1}^{n} T^{(1)}_{i} V_i .
\end{aligned}
\tag{24}
$$

If S_d denotes the set of all sequences $j_1, \ldots, j_d$, such that $1 \leq j_a \leq n$, for $a = 1, \ldots, d$, and $j_a \neq j_b$ if $a \neq b$, then, each neuron is governed by

$$\frac{du_i}{dt} = \sum_{d=1}^{k} \sum_{s \in S_d, i \in s} T^{(d)}_s \prod_{j \in s, j \neq i} V_j . \tag{25}$$

In the new notation of this section, equation (13) would be expressed as:

$$\frac{du_i}{dt} = \sum_{j \neq i} T^{(2)}_{ij} V_j + T^{(1)}_i . \tag{26}$$

The relationship between the output V_i and the activation level u_i of a neuron i can follow the form either of the Hopfield network, of the stochastic Boltzmann machine, or of the mean field theory Boltzmann machine.

In a 1995 paper, Gadi Pinkas [Pinkas, 1995] shows that it is possible to transform a kth-order network to a strongly equivalent quadratic-order network with an increase in the number of neurons. Although it is often more efficient in practice to simulate the high-order networks directly, Pinkas' transformation provides an important theoretical foundation for HORNs because of the Hopfield network's relationship to the Cohen-Grossberg family.

We will now briefly review the Pinkas transformation. Given a kth-order network, each kth-order connection $T_{i_1...i_k}^{(k)}$ is replaced by a number of lower-order connections in a manner that depends on the sign of the weight of $T_{i_1...i_k}^{(k)}$.

If the weight of $T_{i_1...i_k}^{(k)}$ is positive, then it is replaced by $(k+1)$ second- and first-order connections and a new hidden neuron is added. If we let h denote the new hidden neuron, then the $(k+1)$ connections are created as follows:

1. For every $j = 1, ..., k$, a connection $T_{i_j h}^{(2)}$ is added and its weight is set according to

$$T_{i_j h}^{(2)} = 2T_{i_1...i_k}^{(k)}. \tag{27}$$

2. A connection $T_h^{(1)}$ is added and its weight is set according to

$$T_h^{(1)} = -(2k-1)T_{i_1...i_k}^{(k)}. \tag{28}$$

If, on the other hand, the weight of $T_{i_1...i_k}^{(k)}$ is negative, then $(k-2)$ new hidden neurons are needed. If we let $h_3...h_k$ denote the $(k-2)$ new hidden neurons, then the low-order connections are created as follows:

1. For every $j = k, ..., 3$, perform the following steps:

    (a) For $\ell = 1, ..., j-1$, a new connection $T_{i_\ell h_j}^{(2)}$ is added and its weight is set according to

$$T_{i_\ell h_j}^{(2)} = -2T_{i_1...i_k}^{(k)}. \tag{29}$$

    (b) A new connection $T_{i_j h_j}^{(2)}$ is created and its weight is set according to

$$T_{i_j h_j}^{(2)} = 2T_{i_1...i_k}^{(k)}. \tag{30}$$

    (c) A connection $T_{h_j}^{(1)}$ is created and its weight is set according to

$$T_{h_j}^{(1)} = (2j-3)T_{i_1...i_k}^{(k)}. \tag{31}$$

2. A connection $T_{i_1 i_2}^{(2)}$ is created and its weight is set according to

$$T_{i_1 i_2}^{(2)} = T_{i_1...i_k}^{(k)}. \tag{32}$$

In this manner, an arbitrary k^{th}-order network can always be converted to a strongly equivalent second-order network.

V. EFFICIENT DATA STRUCTURES FOR IMPLEMENTING HORNS

The most common implementation of a Hopfield network stores the T_{ij} and I_i connections in two-dimensional and one-dimensional arrays, respectively. To fire a neuron, say neuron i, we can use

```
1.              delta_u = I [i] ;
2.              for j = 1 to n do
3.                      if j ≠ i then
4.                              delta_u += T [i,j] * V [j] ;
5.              od ;
```

For a HORN with dense connections, a similar approach can be adopted, using a d-dimensional array for each $T^{(d)}$. To fire a neuron, we would then have $k - 1$ nested loops, which means a computational complexity of $O(n^k)$ to fire all n neurons once.

However, for some applications such as belief revision, the HORNs of interest are sparsely-connected, that is, the majority or even the vast majority of possible connections have a connection weight of 0. For such HORNs, we propose the following data structure, which is meant to be very fast at the expense of redundance in storage.

We use an array of records, where each record holds three fields:

```
degree :  integer ;
neurons:  array [1..k] of integer ;
weight :  real ;
```

The size of the array of records is set to the maximum number of non-zero connections in the entire network, which we will denote as m. We then duplicate this array n times. This gives us the following declaration, which is illustrated in Figure 3:

```
Conn :   array [1..n,1..m] ;
```

For each neuron i, the one-dimensional array Conn [i] holds the connections in which i participates. Each record Conn [i,j] stores the specifications of one connection in which i participates. The array Conn [i,j].neurons holds the neurons which participate in the connection **not including neuron i itself**. Since the entire Conn [i] deals with connections which involve i, there is no need to include i in the neurons array of each record; in addition the exclusion of i makes it possible to avoid including an if-statement between lines 4 and 5 in the pseudo-code below.

To fire neuron i, we can use

```
1.  delta_u = 0 ;
```

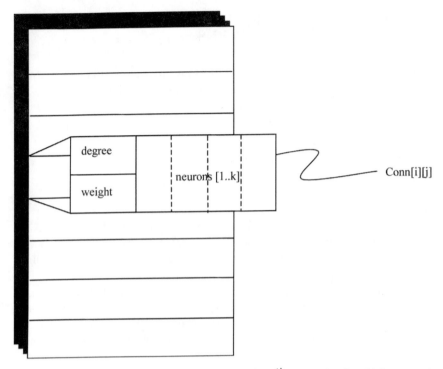

Figure 3. Each record Conn [i][j] describes the jth connection in which neuron i participates.

```
2.    for j = 1 to m [i] do
3.            factor = Conn [i,j].weight ;
4.            for a = 1 to Conn [i,j].degree - 1 do
5.                    factor *= V [Conn [i,j].neurons[a]] ;
6.            od ;
7.            delta_u += factor ;
8.    od ;
```

We can now fire a neuron in $O(mr)$, where r is the average connection degree of the HORN, and all neurons can be fired in $O(nmr)$.

VI. DESIGNING HORNS FOR BELIEF REVISION

Bayesian belief networks are themselves essentially connectionist structures (and interestingly they meet most generic definitions of a neural network). Let us go back for a moment to the example probability distribution table shown in Figure 1. Consider for example the sixth line of this table. This line associates a probability of 0.77 with the combination of four hypotheses: that x is true, that y is false, that z is true, and that v is false. Each line in the probability table of a belief network node with in-degree d connects $d + 1$ hypotheses. For this reason, a Bayesian belief network with a maximum in-degree of k will require a HORN of order $(k + 1)$.

Here, we present an algorithm for constructing a HORN for a given Bayesian belief network with discrete-valued (not necessarily binary) variables and a given evidence set.

Let $B = (U, E, P)$ and $\mathcal{E}$ be a Bayesian belief network and associated evidence set, respectively. For $U = v_1, \ldots, v_n$, let $\mathcal{D}(v_i)$ be the finite domain from which variable v can be instantiated. We will assume that, for each $v \in U$, each distribution P_v is in the form of a table, where each line ℓ in the table is in the form of a set of assignments $\{(x \rightarrow r)|x \in \{v\} \cup \pi(v), r \in \mathcal{D}(x)\}$, and we will let $P(\ell)$ denote the probability associated with line ℓ.

We construct a neural network with $\left(\sum_{v \in U} |\mathcal{D}(v)|\right)$ neurons: a neuron v_r is associated with every $r \in \mathcal{D}(v)$ for every $v \in U$. For each $v \in U$ and for each $\ell \in P_v$, we create a connection

$$T^{(d)}_{i_1 i_2 \ldots i_d} = \log P(\ell) , \tag{33}$$

where $d = |\ell|$, and $i_a = x_r$ where $(x \rightarrow r) \in \ell$, for $a = 1, \ldots, d$.

Let the evidence be represented as a set of assignments. For each assignment $(x \rightarrow r) \in \mathcal{E}$ where $r \in \mathcal{D}(x)$:

1. Let x_r be the neuron corresponding to the instantiation r of x. Since the evidence requires x to take the value r, we can consider V_{x_r} to be clamped to 1. Therefore, we can replace every connection $T^{(d)}_{i_1 i_2 \ldots i_d}$ such that $i_a = x_r$ for some $a \in 1, \ldots, d$, with the connection $T^{(d-1)}_{i_1 \ldots i_{a-1} i_{a+1} \ldots i_d}$, letting the new connection retain the weight of the removed connection.

2. We can now remove neuron x_r (which now corresponds to a fact rather than a hypothesis) from the network and permanently assign V_{x_r} to 1.

3. For each $s \in (\mathcal{D}(x) - \{r\})$, let x_s be the neuron corresponding to the instantiation s of x. Since the evidence requires x to take on a value different from s, we can consider V_{x_s} to be clamped to 0. Therefore, we can prune every connection $T^{(d)}_{i_1 i_2 \ldots i_d}$ such that $i_b = x_s$ for some $b \in 1, \ldots, d$.

4. We can now remove neuron x_s and permanently assign V_{x_s} to 0.

In this manner, we construct a connection corresponding to every line in every probability table in the belief network. Let these connections constitute E^{obj}. We illustrate the E^{obj} connections with a small numerical example. Consider the binary-valued belief network shown in Figure 4. Figure 5 shows the Conn [i] arrays that would be constructed for the evidence $\{(x \rightarrow \mathbf{T})\}$ assuming the neuron associations $(V_1 : w_{\mathbf{T}}, V_2 : w_{\mathbf{F}}, V_3 : x_{\mathbf{T}}, V_4 : x_{\mathbf{F}}, V_5 : y_{\mathbf{T}}, V_6 : y_{\mathbf{F}}, V_7 : z_{\mathbf{T}}, V_8 : z_{\mathbf{F}})$.

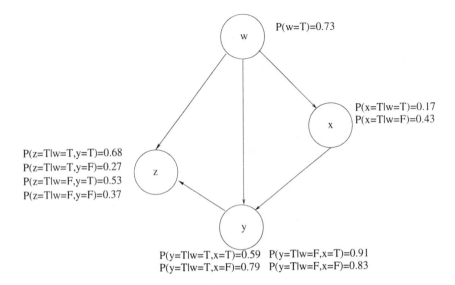

Figure 4. A small belief network

An assignment $\mathcal{V}$ to the HORNs V vector will induce a belief network assignment $\mathcal{A}$,

$$\mathcal{A} = \{(v \to r) | v \in U, V_{v_r} = 1\}, \tag{34}$$

under the two constraints that all V_i's have digital values and that exactly one of $\{V_{v_r} | r \in \mathcal{D}(v)\}$ is equal to 1 for every $v \in U$. An assignment $\mathcal{V}$ is said to be feasible if it induces a belief network assignment $\mathcal{A}$.

Theorem: *Let $\mathcal{V}_1$ and $\mathcal{V}_2$ be two feasible neural network assignments such that $\mathcal{V}_1$ yields a lower value for E^{obj} than $\mathcal{V}_2$. Then, if $\mathcal{A}_1$ and $\mathcal{A}_2$ are the two belief network assignments induced by $\mathcal{V}_1$ and $\mathcal{V}_2$, respectively, then $P(\mathcal{A}_1|\mathcal{E}) > P(\mathcal{A}_2|\mathcal{E})$.*

Proof: Maximizing $P(\mathcal{A}|\mathcal{E})$ is equivalent to maximizing $P(\mathcal{A})$ under the constraint $\mathcal{E} \subseteq \mathcal{A}$; the containment of $\mathcal{E}$ in $\mathcal{A}$ is guaranteed by the clamping of V_{x_r} to 1 for every $(x \to r) \in \mathcal{E}$. Every connection in the HORN corresponds to a line in the probability table of some node. Let P_v be the probability distribution for an arbitrary $v \in U$. For any assignment $\mathcal{A}$, there is exactly one $\ell \in P_v$ such that $\ell \in \mathcal{A}$. Therefore, E^{obj} consists of exactly U non-zero terms. Each non-zero connection has a weight

$$T^{(d)}_{i_1 i_2 \ldots i_d} = \log P(\ell), \tag{35}$$

for some $\ell \in P_v$ for some $v \in U$ and such that $\ell \in \mathcal{A}$. This means

$$E^{obj} = -\sum_{v \in U} \log P(\mathcal{A}(v)|\mathcal{A}(\pi(v))),$$

degree	neurons		w
1			log 0.73
2	5		log 0.59
2	6		log 0.41
3	5	7	log 0.68
3	5	8	log 0.32
3	6	7	log 0.27
3	6	8	log 0.73

Conn [1]

degree	neurons		w
1			log 0.27
2	5		log 0.91
2	6		log 0.09
3	5	7	log 0.53
3	5	8	log 0.47
3	6	7	log 0.37
3	6	8	log 0.63

Conn [2]

degree	neurons		w
2	1		log 0.59
2	2		log 0.91
3	1	7	log 0.68
3	1	8	log 0.32
3	2	7	log 0.53
3	2	8	log 0.47

Conn [5]

degree	neurons		w
2	1		log 0.41
2	2		log 0.09
3	1	7	log 0.27
3	1	8	log 0.73
3	2	7	log 0.37
3	2	8	log 0.63

Conn [6]

degree	neurons		w
3	1	5	log 0.68
3	1	6	log 0.27
3	2	5	log 0.53
3	2	6	log 0.37

Conn [7]

degree	neurons		w
3	1	5	log 0.32
3	1	6	log 0.73
3	2	5	log 0.47
3	2	6	log 0.63

Conn [8]

Figure 5. The Conn arrays that result from applying the algorithm to the belief network shown in Figure 4 with $\mathcal{E} = \{(x \to \mathbf{T})\}$

	min	max	avg
Nodes	10	20	13.33
Maximum in-degree	2	4	3.095
Maximum out-degree	3	7	4.905
Average degree	2.2	3.87	3.11
Total number of entries in all probability tables	50	216	121.33
Ratio of number of evidence nodes to total nodes	0	0.9	0.5738
Number of neural network iterations	10	101	51.381

Figure 6. Summary of experimentation

$$= -\log \prod_{v \in U} P\left(\mathcal{A}\left(v\right) | \mathcal{A}\left(\pi\left(v\right)\right)\right) = -\log P\left(\mathcal{A}\right). \tag{36}$$

Therefore, minimizing E^{obj} is equivalent to maximizing $P\left(\mathcal{A}\right)$.

What remains is to construct connections, which we will call E^{cons}, to enforce the feasibility constraints. This can be achieved using the standard k-out-of-n design rule. The two components, E^{cons} and E^{obj}, are then combined according to equation (16) with an appropriate choice of weighting constant β.

Using mean field annealing, with the schedule of (20), this technique has found the optimal assignments for a collection of twenty belief networks and evidence sets with the characteristics shown in Figure 6. For each belief network and evidence set, extensive experimentation, however, is required to obtain good values for the three parameters: β, initial temperature T_0, and temperature cooling factor f. Performance is especially sensitive to β and f. It is hoped that heuristics can be developed for automatically setting β according to the probability values of the network. Alternatively, techniques such as genetic optimization could be used to automate the parameter selection problem.

VII. CONCLUSION

Belief revision is the problem of finding the most plausible explanation for a given set of observances. In the context of Bayesian belief networks, belief revision becomes the problem of finding the network assignment $\mathcal{A}$ with maximum posterior probability $P(\mathcal{A}|\mathcal{E})$, where $\mathcal{E}$ is a partial network assignment corresponding to the observed evidence. Exact techniques for multiply-connected belief networks run in time exponential in the size of the network graph's minimum loop-cutset: the smallest set of vertices whose removal renders the network graph acyclic. For multiply-connected networks in which the loop-cutset is small, traditional methods can be used. However, for large heavily-connected networks, other methods are needed.

In this chapter, we began by describing High Order Recurrent Networks (HORNs) and reviewing a transformation which allows HORNs to be transformed to quadratic-order networks with equivalent energy functions. This was followed by the description of an efficient data structure for the software implementation of HORNs. We then showed how HORNs could be used for belief revision on belief networks.

Using the Pinkas transformation described in Section 4, the high order networks produced by our method can be converted to equivalent Hopfield networks and Boltzmann machines; this is of significance because of the potential for the hardware implementation of these networks [Schneider and Card, 1993; Schneider and Card, 1998].

ACKNOWLEDGMENT

I would like to thank my graduate student, Mr. Murad Assaggaf, for invaluable assistance and contributions.

REFERENCES

Abdelbar, A.M. A linear constraint satisfaction approach to Bayesian networks, *Proceedings IEEE International Joint Conference on Neural Networks,* 504, 1999.

Abdelbar, A.M. An algorithm for finding MAPs for belief networks through cost-based abduction, *Artificial Intelligence*, 104, 331, 1998.

Abdelbar, A.M. and Attia, S. Finding most probable explanations using simulated annealing as a genetic operator, *Proceedings World Multiconference on Systemics, Cybernetics and Informatics*, 8, 131, 1999.

Abdelbar, A.M. and Hedetniemi, S.M. Approximating MAPs for belief networks is NP-hard and other theorems, *Artificial Intelligence*, 102, 21, 1998.

Abdelbar, A.M. and Hedetniemi, S.M. A parallel hybrid genetic algorithm simulated annealing approach to finding probable explanations on Bayesian belief networks, *Proceedings IEEE International Conference on Neural Networks,* **I**, 450, 1997.

Aggarwal, A. Coppersmith, D. Khanna, S. Motwani, R. and Schieber, B. The angular-metric traveling salesman problem, *Proceedings Eighth Annual ACM-SIAM Symposium on Discrete Algorithms*, 221, 1997.

Charniak, E. and Shimony, S. Cost-based abduction and MAP explanation, *Artificial Intelligence*, 66, 345, 1994.

Cohen, M.A. and Grossberg, S. Absolute stability of global pattern formation and parallel memory storage by competitive neural networks, *IEEE Transactions on Systems, Man, and Cybernetics,* 13, 815, 1983.

Dempster, A.P. Upper and lower probabilities induced by a multivalued mapping, *Annals of Mathematical Statistics,* 38, 157, 1967.

Geman, S. and Geman, D. Stochastic relaxation, Gibbs distributions, and the Bayesian restoration of images, *IEEE Transactions on Pattern Recognition and Machine Intelligence,* 6, 721, 1984.

Ginsberg, M.L. *Readings in Nonmonotonic Reasoning,* Morgan Kauffman, San Mateo, 1987.

Hinton, G.E. and Sejnowski, T.J. Learning and re-learning in Boltzmann machines, in: J.L. McClelland, D.E. Rumelhart, and the PDP Research Group, eds., *Parallel Distributed Processing: Explorations in the Microstructure of Cognition* **I**, MIT Press, Cambridge, 282, 1986.

Hobbs, J.R. Stickel, M.E. Appelt, D.E. and Martin, P. Interpretation as abduction, *Artificial Intelligence*, 63, 69, 1993.

Hopfield, J.J. Neurons with graded response have collective computational properties like those of two-state neurons, *Proceedings National Academy of Science*, 81, 3088, 1984.

Hopfield, J.J. Neural networks and physical systems with emergent collective computational abilities, *Proceedings National Academy of Science*, 79, 2554, 1982.

Kirkpatrick, S. Gelatt, D. and Vecchi, M. Optimization by simulated annealing, *Science*, 220, 621, 1983.

Kofler, E.T. and Leondes, C.T. Algorithmic modifications to the theory of evidential reasoning, *Journal of Algorithms*, 17, 269, 1994.

Konyndyk, K. *Introductory Modal Logic*, Notre Dame Press, Notre Dame, 1986.

Lin, W-C. Liao, F-Y. Tsao, C-K. and Lingutla, T. A hierarchical multiple-view approach to three-dimensional object recognition, *IEEE Transactions on Neural Networks*, 2, 84, 1991.

Lindley, D.V. The probability approach to the treatment of uncertainty, *Statistical Science*, 2, 17, 1987.

Marek, V.W. and Truszczynski, M. *Nonmonotonic Logic*, Springer-Verlag, Berlin, 1993.

Page, E.W. and Tagliarini, G.A. Algorithm development for neural networks, *Proceedings SPIE Symposium Innovative Science and Technology*, 880, 11, 1988.

Pawlak, Z. Grzymala-Busse, J. Slowinski, R. and Ziark, W. Rough sets, *Communications of the ACM*, 38, 88, 1995.

Pawlak, Z. Rough sets: A new approach to vagueness, in: L. Zadeh, and J. Kacprzyk, eds., *Fuzzy Logic for the Management of Uncertainty*, John Wiley & Sons, New York, 1992.

Pawlak, Z. *Rough Sets*, Kluwer Academic, Dordrecht, 1991.

Pearl, J. *Probabilistic Reasoning in Intelligent Systems: Networks of Plausible Inference*, Morgan-Kaufmann, San Mateo, 1988.

Pearl, J. Fusion, propagation, and structuring in belief networks, *Artificial Intelligence*, 29, 241, 1986.

Peterson, C. and Hartman, E. Explorations of the mean field theory learning algorithm, *Neural Networks*, 2, 475, 1989.

Peterson, C. and Anderson, J.R. A mean field theory learning algorithm for neural networks, *Complex Systems*, 1, 995, 1987.

Pinkas, G. Reasoning, nonmonotonicity and learning in connectionist networks that capture propositional knowledge, *Artificial Intelligence*, 77, 203, 1995.

Popkorn, S. *First Steps in Modal Logic*, Cambridge University Press, Cambridge, 1994.

Reiter, R. Nonmonotonic reasoning, *Annual Review of Computer Science*, 147, 1987.

Rojas-Guzman, C. and Kramer, M.A. "GALGO: A Genetic ALGOrithm decision support tool for complex uncertain systems modeled with Bayesian belief networks," *Proceedings Ninth Annual Conference on Uncertainty in AI*, 368, 1993.

Rojas-Guzman, C. and Kramer, M.A. Remote diagnosis and monitoring of complex industrial systems using a genetic algorithms approach, *Proceedings IEEE International Symposium on Industrial Electronics*, 363, 1994.

Santos Jr., E. A linear constraint satisfaction approach to cost-based abduction, *Artificial Intelligence*, 65, 1, 1994.

Santos Jr., E. and Santos, E.S. Polynomial solvability of cost-based abduction, *Artificial Intelligence*, 86, 157, 1996.

Schneider, C.R. and Card, H.C., Analog hardware implementation issues in deterministic Boltzmann machines, *IEEE Transactions on Circuits and Systems II*, 45, 352, 1998.

Schneider, C.R. and Card, H.C. Analog CMOS deterministic Boltzmann circuits, *IEEE Journal Solid-State Circuits*, 28, 907, 1993.

Shachter, R.D. Evaluating inference diagrams, *Operations Research*, 34, 871, 1986.

Shafer, G. The combination of evidence, *International Journal of Intelligent Systems*, 1, 155, 1986.

Shafer, G. *A Mathematical Theory of Evidence*, Princeton University Press, Princeton, 1976.

Shafer, G. and Logan, R. Implementing Dempster's rule for heirarchial evidence, *Artificial Intelligence*, 33, 271, 1987.

Shimony, E. Finding MAPs for belief networks is NP-hard, *Artificial Intelligence*, 68, 399, 1994.

Shoham, Y. Nonmonotonic logics: Meaning and utility, *Proceedings International Joint Conference on Artificial Intelligence*, 388, 1987.

Tagliarini, G. and Page, E.W. A neural-network solution to the concentrator assignment problem, *Proceedings IEEE Conference on Neural Information Processing Systems—Natural and Synthetic*, 775, 1987.

Tagliarini, G. Fury-Christ, J. and Page, E.W. Optimization using neural networks, *IEEE Transactions on Computers*, 40, 1347, 1991.

Takefuji, Y. and Lee, K-C. A near optimum parallel planarization algorithm, *Science*, 245, 1221, 1989.

Yager, R. Fedrizzi, M. and Kacprzyk, J. *Advances in the Dempster-Shafer Theory of Evidence,* John Wiley & Sons, New York, 1994.

Zadeh, L. Fuzzy logic, neural networks and soft computing, *Communications of the ACM*, 37, 77, 1994.

Zadeh, L. and Kacprzyk, J. *Fuzzy Logic for the Management of Uncertainty*, John Wiley & Sons, New York, 1992.

Zadeh, L. A theory of approximate reasoning, in: J. Hayes, D. Michie, and L.I. Mikulich, eds., *Machine Intelligence* **9**, Halstead Press, New York, 149, 1979.

Zimmerman, H-J. *Fuzzy Set Theory and Its Applications*, Kluwer Academic, Boston, 1991.

Chapter 5

EQUIVALENCE IN KNOWLEDGE REPRESENTATION: AUTOMATA, RECURRENT NEURAL NETWORKS, AND DYNAMICAL FUZZY SYSTEMS

C. Lee Giles

NEC Research Institure and
UMIACS, University of Maryland

Christian W. Omlin

Department of Computer Science,
University of Stellenbosch, South Africa

K. K. Thornber

UMIACS, University of Maryland

I. INTRODUCTION

A. MOTIVATION

As our applications for intelligent systems become more ambitious, our processing models become more powerful. One approach to increasing this power is through hybrid systems - systems that include several different models' intelligent processing [Giles, 1998a]. There has also been an increased interest in hybrid systems as more applications with hybrid models emerge [Bookman, 1993]. However, there are many definitions of hybrid systems [Hendler, 1991, Honavar, 1994, Sun, 1997].

One example of hybrid systems is in combining artificial neural networks and fuzzy systems (see Bezdek [1992], Herrmann [1995], Palaniswami [1995], Kasabov [1996]). Fuzzy logic [Zadeh, 1965] provides a mathematical foundation for approximate reasoning; fuzzy logic has proven very successful in a variety of applications [Berenji, 1992, Bonissone, 1995, Chiu 1991, Corbin, 1994, Franquelo, 1996, Hardy, 1994, Kickert, 1976, Lee, 1990, Pappis, 1977, Yang, 1995]. The parameters of adaptive fuzzy systems have clear physical meanings that facilitate the choice of their initial values. Furthermore, rule-based information can be incorporated into fuzzy systems in a systematic way.

Artificial neural networks propose to simulate on a small scale the information processing mechanisms found in biological systems that are based on the cooperation and computation of artificial neurons that perform simple operations, and on their ability to learn from examples. Artificial neural networks have become valuable computational tools in their own right for tasks such as pattern recognition, control, and forecasting (for more information on neural networks, please see various textbooks [Bishop, 1995, Cichocki, 1993, Haykin, 1998]). Recurrent neural networks (RNNs) are dynamical systems with temporal state representations; they are computationally quite powerful [Siegelmann, 1995, Siegelmann, 1999] and can be used in many different temporal processing models and applications [Giles, 1998].

Fuzzy finite state automata (FFA), fuzzy generalizations of deterministic finite state automata, [1] have a long history [Santos, 1968, Zadeh, 1971]. The fundamentals of FFA have been discussed in Gaines [1976] without presenting a systematic machine synthesis method. Their potential as design tools for modeling a variety of systems is beginning to be exploited in various applications [Kosmatopoulso, 1996, Mensch, 1990]. Such systems have two major characteristics: (1) the current state of the system depends on past states and current inputs, and (2) the knowledge about the system's current state is vague or uncertain.

Finally, the proofs of representational properties of artificial intelligence, machine learning, and computational intelligence models are important for a number of reasons. Many users of a model want guarantees about what it can do theoretically, i.e., its performance and capabilities; others need this for justification of use and acceptance of the approach. The capability of *representing* a model, say a fuzzy finite automata (FFA), in an intelligent system can be viewed as a foundation for the problem of *learning* that model from examples (if a system cannot represent a FFA, then it certainly will have difficulty learning a FFA).

Since recurrent neural networks are nonlinear dynamical systems, the proof of their capability to represent FFA amounts to proving that a neural network representation of fuzzy states and transitions remains stable for input sequences of arbitrary length and is robust to noise. Neural networks that have been *trained* to behave like FFA do not necessarily share this property, i.e., their internal representation of states and transitions may become unstable for sufficiently long input sequences Omlin [1996a]. Finally, with the extraction of knowledge from trained neural networks, the methods discussed here could potentially be applied to incorporating and refining [Maclin, 1993] fuzzy knowledge previously encoded into recurrent neural networks.

B. BACKGROUND

A variety of implementations of FFA have been proposed, some in digital systems [Grantner, 1994, Khan, 1995]. However, here we give a proof that such implementations in sigmoid activation RNNs are stable, i.e. guaranteed to converge to the correct prespecified membership. This proof is based on previous work of stably mapping deterministic finite state automata (DFA) in recurrent neural networks reported in Omlin [1996]. In contrast to DFA, a *set* of FFA states can be occupied to *varying degrees* at any point in time; this fuzzification of states gener-

---

[1] Finite state automata also have a long history as theoretical [Hopcroft, 1979] and practical [Ashar, 1992] models of computation and were some of the earliest implementations of neural networks [Klenne, 1956, Minsky, 1967]. Besides automata, other symbolic computational structures can be used with neural networks [Fu, 1994, Giles 1998].

ally reduces the size of the model, and the dynamics of the system being modeled is often more accessible to a direct interpretation.

From a control perspective, fuzzy finite state automata have been shown to be useful for modeling fuzzy dynamical systems, often in conjunction with recurrent neural networks [Cellier, 1995, Kosmatopoulso, 1995, Kosmatopoulso, 1995a, Kosmatopoulso, 1996, Kosmatopoulso, 1996a]. There has been much work on the learning, synthesis, and extraction of finite state automata in recurrent neural networks, see for example Casey [1996], Cleeremans [1989], Elman [1990], Frasconi [1996], Giles [1992], Pollack [1991], Watrous [1992], and Zeng [1993]. A variety of neural network implementations of FFA have been proposed [Grantner, 1994, Grantner, 1993, Khan, 1995, Unal, 1994]. We have previously shown how fuzzy finite state automata can be mapped into recurrent neural networks with second-order weights using a *crisp* representation[2] of FFA states [Omlin, 1998]. That encoding required a transformation of a FFA into a deterministic finite state automaton that computes the membership functions for strings; it is only applicable to a restricted class of FFA that have *final states*. The transformation of a fuzzy automaton into an equivalent deterministic acceptor generally increases the size of the automaton and thus the network size. Furthermore, the fuzzy transition memberships of the original FFA undergo modifications in the transformation of the original FFA into an equivalent DFA that is suitable for implementation in a second-order recurrent neural network. Thus, the direct correspondence between system and network parameters is lost which may obscure the natural fuzzy description of systems being modeled.

The existence of a crisp recurrent network encoding for all FFA raises the question of whether recurrent networks can also be *trained* to compute the fuzzy membership function, and how they represent FFA states internally. Based on our theoretical analysis, we know that they have the ability to represent FFA in the form of equivalent deterministic acceptors. Recent work reported in [Blanco, 1997] addresses these issues. Instead of augmenting a second-order network with a linear output layer for computing the fuzzy string membership as suggested in Omlin [1998], they chose to assign a distinct output neuron to each fuzzy string memberships μ_i occurring in the training set. Thus, the number of output neurons became equal to the number of distinct membership values μ_i. The fuzzy membership of an input string was then determined by identifying the output neuron whose activation was highest after the entire string had been processed by a network. Thus, they transformed the fuzzy inference problem into a classification problem with multiple classes or classifications. This approach lessens the burden on the training and improves the accuracy and robustness of string membership computation.

Apart from the use of multiple classes, training networks to compute the fuzzy string membership is identical to training networks to behave like DFA. This was verified empirically through information extraction methods [Casey, 1996, Omlin, 1996a] where recurrent networks trained on fuzzy strings develop a crisp internal

---

[2] A *crisp* mapping is one from a fuzzy to a nonfuzzy variable.

representation of FFA, i.e., they represent FFA in the form of equivalent deterministic acceptors.[3] Thus, our theoretical analysis *correctly predicted* the knowledge representation for such trained networks.

C. OVERVIEW

In this chapter, we present a method for encoding FFA using a *fuzzy* representation of states.[4] The objectives of the FFA encoding algorithm are (1) ease of encoding FFA into recurrent networks, (2) the direct representation of "fuzziness," i.e., the fuzzy memberships of individual transitions in FFA are also parameters in the recurrent networks, and (3) achieving a fuzzy representation by making only minimal changes to the underlying architecture used for encoding DFA (and crisp FFA representations).

Representation of FFA in recurrent networks requires that the internal representation of FFA states and state transitions be stable for indefinite periods of time. We will demonstrate how the stability analysis for neural DFA encodings carries over to and generalizes the analysis of stable neural FFA representations.

In high-level VLSI design a DFA (actually finite state machines) is often used as the first implementation of a design and is mapped into sequential machines and logic [Ashar, 1992]. Previous work has shown how a DFA can be readily implemented in recurrent neural networks and how neural networks have been directly implemented in VLSI chips [Akers, 1990, Sheu, 1995, Mead, 1989]. Thus, with this approach FFA could be readily mapped into electronics and could be useful for applications, such as real-time control (see, e.g., Chiu [1991])[5] and could potentially be applied to incorporate a priori knowledge into recurrent neural networks for knowledge refinement [Giles, 1993].

The remainder of this chapter is organized as follows: Fuzzy finite state automata are introduced in Section 2. The fuzzy representation of FFA states and transitions in recurrent networks are discussed in Section 3. The mapping "fuzzy automata $\rightarrow$ recurrent network" proposed in this paper requires that FFA be transformed into a special form before they can be encoded in a recurrent network. The transformation algorithm can be applied to arbitrary FFA; it is described in Section 4. The recurrent network architecture for representing FFA is described in Section 5. The stability of the encoding is derived in Section 6. A discussion of simulation results in Section 7 and a summary of the results and possible directions for future research in Section 8 conclude this chapter.

---

[3]The equivalence of FFA and deterministic acceptors was first discussed in Thomason [1974] and first used for encoding FFA in Omlin [1998].

[4]For reasons of completeness, we have included the main results from Omlin [1996] which laid the foundations for this and other papers [Omlin, 1996c, Omlin, 1998] Thus, by necessity, there is some overlap.

[5]Alternative implementations of FFA have been proposed (see, e.g., Grantner [1993]). The method proposed uses recurrent neurons with sigmoidal discriminant functions and a fuzzy internal representation of FFA states.

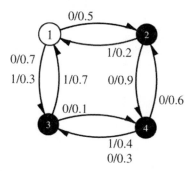

Figure 1. **Example of a Fuzzy Finite State Automaton:** A fuzzy finite state automaton is shown with weighted state transitions. State 1 is the automaton's start state. A transition from state q_j to q_i on input symbol a_k with weight θ is represented as a directed arc from q_j to q_i labeled a_k/θ. Note that transitions from states 1 and 4 on input symbols '0' are fuzzy ($\delta(1, 0, .) = \{2, 3\}$ and $\delta(4, 0, .) = \{2, 3\}$).

II. FUZZY FINITE STATE AUTOMATA

In this section, we give a formal definition of FFA [Dubois, 1980] and illustrate the definition with an example.

Definition 2.1 *A fuzzy finite state automaton (FFA) M is a 6-tuple $M = < \Sigma, Q,$ $R, Z, \delta, \omega >$ where $\Sigma = \{a_1, \ldots, a_m\}$ is the alphabet, $Q = \{q_1, \ldots, q_n\}$ is a set of states, $R \in Q$ is the automaton's fuzzy start state,*[6] *Z is a finite output alphabet, $\delta : \Sigma \times Q \times [0, 1] \rightarrow Q$ is the fuzzy transition map, and $\omega : Q \rightarrow Z$ is the output map.*[7]

Weights $\theta_{ijk} \in [0, 1]$ define the 'fuzziness' of state transitions, i.e., a FFA can simultaneously be in different states with a different degree of certainty. The particular output mapping depends on the nature of the application. Since our goal is to construct a fuzzy representation of FFA states and their stability over time, we will ignore the output mapping ω for the remainder of this discussion, and not concern ourselves with the language $L(M)$ defined by M. For a possible definition, see Dubois [1980]. An example of a FFA over the input alphabet $\{0, 1\}$ is shown in Figure 1.

---

[6] In general, the start state of a FFA is fuzzy, i.e., it consists of a set of states that are occupied with varying memberships. It has been shown that a restricted class of FFA whose initial state is a single crisp state is equivalent with the class of FFA described in Definition 2.1 [Dubois, 1980]. The distinction between the two classes of FFA is irrelevant in the context of this paper.

[7] This is in contrast to stochastic finite state automata where there exists no ambiguity about which is an automaton's current state. The automaton can only be in exactly one state at any given time and the choice of a successor state is determined by some probability distribution. For a discussion of the relationship between probability and fuzziness, see for instance Thomas [1995].

III. REPRESENTATION OF FUZZY STATES

A. PRELIMINARIES

The current fuzzy state of a FFA M is a collection of states $\{q_i\}$ of M that are occupied with different degrees of fuzzy membership. A fuzzy representation of the states in a FFA thus requires knowledge about the membership of each state q_i. This requirement then dictates the representation of the current fuzzy state in a recurrent neural network. Because the method for encoding FFA in recurrent neural networks is a generalization of the method for encoding DFA, we will briefly discuss the DFA encoding algorithm.

B. DFA ENCODING ALGORITHM

We make use of an algorithm used for encoding deterministic finite state automata (DFA) [Omlin, 1996, Omlin, 1996c]. For encoding DFA, we use discrete-time, second-order recurrent neural networks with sigmoidal discriminant functions that update their current state according to the following equations:

$$S_i^{(t+1)} = g(\alpha_i(t)) = \frac{1}{1 + e^{-\alpha_i(t)}}, \qquad \alpha_i(t) = b_i + \sum_{j,k} W_{ijk} S_j^{(t)} I_k^{(t)}, \quad (1)$$

where b_i is the bias associated with hidden recurrent state neurons S_i, W_{ijk} is a second-order weight, and I_k denotes the input neuron for symbol a_k. The indices i, j, and k run over all state and input neurons, respectively. The product $S_j^{(t)} I_k^{(t)}$ corresponds directly to the state transition $\delta(q_j, a_k) = q_i$. The architecture is illustrated in Figure 2.

DFA can be encoded in discrete-time, second-order recurrent neural networks with sigmoidal discriminant functions such that the DFA and constructed network accept the same regular language [Omlin, 1996]. The desired finite state dynamics are encoded into a network by programming a small subset of all available weights to values $+H$ and $-H$; this leads to a nearly orthonormal internal DFA state representation for sufficiently large values of H, i.e., a one-to-one correspondence between current DFA states and recurrent neurons with a high output. Since the magnitude of all weights in a constructed network is equal to H, the equation governing the dynamics of a constructed network is of the special form

$$S_i^{(t+1)} = g(x, H) = \frac{1}{1 + e^{H(1-2x)/2}} \qquad (2)$$

where x is the input to neuron S_i.

The objective of mapping DFA into recurrent networks is to assign DFA states to neurons and to program the weights such that the assignment remains stable for input sequence of arbitrary length, i.e., exactly one neuron corresponding to the current DFA state has a high output at any given time. Such stability is trivial for recurrent networks whose neurons have hard-limiting (or "step function") discriminant functions. However, this is not obvious for networks with continuous, sigmoidal discriminant functions. The nonlinear dynamical nature of recurrent networks makes it possible for intended internal DFA state representations to become unstable, i.e., the requirement of a one-to-one correspondence between DFA

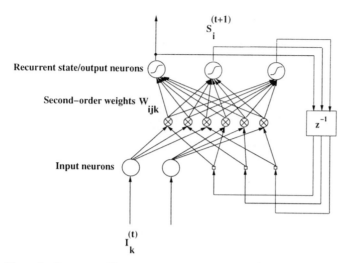

Figure 2. **Recurrent Network Architecture for Deterministic Finite State Automata:**
The recurrent state neurons are connected and implement the stable finite state dynamics.
One of the recurrent neurons also is the dedicated network output neuron (i.e., the neuron
which by its output value classifies whether or not a given string is a member of a regular
language).

states and recurrent neurons may be violated for sufficiently long input sequences.
We have previously demonstrated that it is possible to achieve a stable internal
DFA state representation that is *independent* of the string length: In constructed
networks, the recurrent state neurons always operate near their saturation regions
for sufficiently large values of H; as a consequence, the internal DFA state representation remains stable indefinitely. The internal representation of fuzzy states
proposed in this paper is a generalization of the method used to encode DFA states
since FFA may be in several states at the same time. We will apply the same tools
and techniques to prove stability of the internal representation of fuzzy states in
recurrent neural networks.

C. RECURRENT STATE NEURONS WITH VARIABLE OUT-PUT RANGE

We extend the functionality of recurrent state neurons in order to represent
fuzzy states as illustrated in Figure 3. The main difference between the neuron
discriminant function for DFA and FFA is that the neuron now receives as inputs
the weight strength H, the signal x that represents the collective input from all
other neurons, and the transition weight θ_{ijk}, where $\delta(q_j, a_k, \theta_{ijk}) = q_i$; we will
denote this triple with (x, H, θ_{ijk}). The value of θ_{ijk} is different for each of the
states that collectively make up the current fuzzy network state. This is consistent
with the definition of FFA.

The following generalized form of the sigmoidal discriminant function $g(.)$
will be useful for representing FFA states:

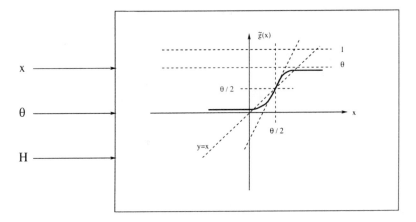

Figure 3. **Neuron Discriminant Function for Fuzzy States**: A neuron is represented figuratively by the box and receives as input the collective signal x from all other neurons, the weight strength H, and the fuzzy transition membership θ to compute the function $\tilde{g}(x, H, \theta) = \frac{\theta}{1 + e^{H(\theta - 2x)/2\theta}}$. Thus, the sigmoidal discriminant function used to represent FFA states has a variable output range.

$$S_i^{(t+1)} = \tilde{g}(x, H, \theta_{ijk}) = \frac{\theta_{ijk}}{1 + e^{H(\theta_{ijk} - 2x)/2\theta_{ijk}}} \tag{3}$$

Compared to the discriminant function $g(.)$ for the encoding of DFA, the weight H that programs the network state transitions is strengthened by a factor $1/\theta_{ijk}$ $(0 < \theta_{ijk} \leq 1)$; the range of the function $\tilde{g}(.)$ is squashed to the interval $[0, \theta_{ijk}]$, and it has been shifted towards the origin. Setting $\theta_{ijk} = 1$ reduces the function (3) to the sigmoidal discriminant function (2) used for DFA encoding.

More formally, the function $\tilde{g}(x, H, \theta)$ has the following important invariant property that will later simplify the analysis:

Lemma 3.1 $\tilde{g}(\theta x, H, \theta) = \theta\ \tilde{g}(x, H, 1) = \theta\ g(x, H)$.

Proof. $\tilde{g}(\theta x, H, \theta) = \dfrac{\theta}{1 + e^{H(\theta - 2\theta x)/2\theta}} = \dfrac{\theta}{1 + e^{H(1 - 2x)/2}} = \theta\ \tilde{g}(x, H, 1) = \theta\ g(x, H)$.

Thus, $g(x, H)$ can be obtained by scaling $\tilde{g}(x, H, 1)$ uniformly in the $x-$ and $y-$directions by a factor θ.

The above property of $\tilde{g}$ allows a stability analysis of the internal FFA state representation similar to the analysis of the stability of the internal DFA state representation.

106

D. PROGRAMMING FUZZY STATE TRANSITIONS

Consider state q_j of FFA M and the fuzzy state transition $\delta(q_j, a_k, \{\theta_{ijk}\}) = \{q_{i_1} \ldots q_{i_r}\})$. We assign recurrent state neuron S_j to FFA state q_j and neurons $S_{i_1} \ldots S_{i_r}$ to FFA states $q_{i_1} \ldots q_{i_r}$. The basic idea is as follows: The activation of recurrent state neuron S_i represents the certainty θ_{ijk} with which some state transition $\delta(q_j, a_k, \theta_{ijk}) = q_i$ is carried out, i.e., $S_i^{t+1} \simeq \theta_{ijk}$. If q_i is not reached at time $t + 1$, then we have $S_i^{t+1} \simeq 0$.

We program the second-order weights W_{ijk} as follows:

$$W_{ijk} = \begin{cases} +H & \text{if } q_i \in \delta(q_j, a_k, \theta_{ijk}) \\ 0 & \text{otherwise} \end{cases} \tag{4}$$

$$W_{jjk} = \begin{cases} +H & \text{if } q_j \in \delta(q_j, a_k, \theta_{jjk}) \\ -H & \text{otherwise} \end{cases} \tag{5}$$

$$b_i = -H/2 \ if \ q_i \in M. \tag{6}$$

Setting W_{ijk} to a large positive value will ensure that S_i^{t+1} will be arbitrarily close to θ_{ijk} and setting W_{jjk} to a large negative value will guarantee that the output S_j^{t+1} will be arbitrarily close to 0. This is the same technique used for programming DFA state transitions in recurrent networks [Omlin, 1996] and for encoding partial prior knowledge of a DFA for rule refinement [Omlin, 1996b].

IV. AUTOMATA TRANSFORMATION

A. PRELIMINARIES

The above encoding algorithm leaves open the possibility for ambiguities when a FFA is encoded in a recurrent network as follows: Consider two FFA states q_j and q_l with transitions $\delta(q_j, a_k, \theta_{ijk}) = \delta(q_l, a_k, \theta_{ilk}) = q_i$ where q_i is one of all successor states reached from q_j and q_l, respectively, on input symbol a_k. Further assume that q_j and q_l are members of the set of current FFA states (i.e., these states are occupied with some fuzzy membership). Then, the state transition $\delta(q_j, a_k, \theta_{ijk}) = q_i$ requires that recurrent state neuron S_i have dynamic range $[0, \theta_{ijk}]$ while state transition $\delta(q_l, a_k, \theta_{ilk}) = q_i$ requires that state neuron S_i asymptotically approach θ_{ilk}. For $\theta_{ijk} \neq \theta_{ilk}$, we have ambiguity for the output range of neuron S_i.

Definition 4.1 *We say an ambiguity occurs at state q_i if there exist two states q_j and q_l with $\delta(q_j, a_k, \theta_{ijk}) = \delta(q_l, a_k, \theta_{ilk}) = q_i$ and $\theta_{ijk} \neq \theta_{ilk}$. A FFA M is called __ambiguous__ if an ambiguity occurs for any state $q_i \in M$.*

B. TRANSFORMATION ALGORITHM

That ambiguity could be resolved by testing all possible paths through the FFA and identifying those states for which the above described ambiguity can occur. However, such an endeavor is computationally expensive. Instead, we propose to resolve that ambiguity by transforming any FFA M.

Input: FFA $M = <\Sigma, Q, R, Z, \delta, \omega>$ with $\Sigma = \{a_1, \ldots, a_M\}$ and $Q = \{q_1, \ldots, q_N\}$.
Output: FFA $M' = <\Sigma, Q', R', Z, \delta', \omega>$ with $\Sigma = \{a_1, \ldots, a_M\}$ and $Q' = \{q_1, \ldots, q_N, q_{N+1}, \ldots, q_X\}$ with the properties

        (1) $M \equiv M'$ and

        (2) there exist no two states q_j and q_l in M' with $\delta(q_j, a_k, \theta_{ijk}) = \delta(q_l, a_k, \theta_{ilk}) = q_i$ with $\theta_{ijk} \neq \theta_{ilk}$.

Algorithm:

1. $X \leftarrow N$; $list \leftarrow Q$;

        while $list \neq \emptyset$ **do**

2. $list \leftarrow list \setminus \{q_i\}$;

           for $k = 1 \ldots M$ **do**

3. $visit \leftarrow \emptyset$;

               for $j = 1 \ldots N$ **do**

4.   **if** $\delta(q_j, a_k, \cdot) = q_i$ **then** $visit \leftarrow visit \cup \{q_j\}$;

               end

5. $class \leftarrow \{q_l \in visit \mid \delta(q_l, a_k, \theta_{ilk}) = q_i$ with $\theta_{ilk} = \theta_{ik}\}$;

6. $visit \leftarrow visit \setminus \{class\}$;

               while $class \neq \emptyset$ **do**

7. $class \leftarrow \{q_l \in visit \mid \delta(q_l, a_k, \theta_{ilk}) = q_i$ with $\theta_{ilk} = \theta_{ik}\}$;

8. $visit \leftarrow visit \setminus \{class\}$;

9. $X \leftarrow X + 1$;

10. $Q \leftarrow Q \cup \{q_X\}$;   /* create new FFA state q_X */

                 for each q_j in class **do**

11. $\delta(q_j, a_k, \theta_{ijk}) \leftarrow q_X$;   /* change transition */

                     for $l = 1 \ldots N$ **do**

                       for $k = 1 \ldots M$ **do**

12. $\delta(q_X, a_k, \theta_{lXk}) \leftarrow \delta(q_i, a_k, \theta_{lik})$;

                       /* implies $\theta_{lXk} \leftarrow \theta_{lik}$ */

                       end

                     end

                 end

               end

           end

        end

    end

Figure 4. **Algorithm for FFA Transformation.**

Before we state the transformation theorem, and give the algorithm, it will be useful to define the concept of equivalent FFA.

Definition 4.2 *Consider a FFA M that is processing some string $s = \sigma_1 \sigma_2 \ldots \sigma_L$ with $\sigma_i \in \Sigma$. As M reads each symbol σ_i, it makes simultaneous weighted state transitions $\Sigma \times Q \times [0,1]$ according to the fuzzy transition map $\delta(q_j, a_k, \theta_{ijk}) = q_i$. The set of distinct weights $\{\theta_{ijk}\}$ of the fuzzy transition map at time t is called the* <u>*active weight set*</u>.

Note that the active weight set can change with each symbol σ_i processed by M. We will define what it means for two FFA to be equivalent:

Definition 4.3 *Two FFA M and M' with alphabet Σ are called* <u>*equivalent if their active weight sets are at all times identical for any string $s \in \Sigma^*$.*</u>

We will prove the following theorem:

Theorem 4.1 *Any FFA M can be transformed into an equivalent, unambiguous FFA M'.*

The trade-off for making the resolution of ambiguities computationally feasible is an increase in the number of FFA states. The algorithm that transforms a FFA M into a FFA M' such that $L(M) = L(M')$ is shown in Figure 4. Before we prove the above theorem, we will discuss an example of FFA transformation.

C. EXAMPLE

Consider the FFA shown in Figure 5a with four states and input alphabet $\Sigma = \{0,1\}$; state q_1 is the start state.[8] The algorithm initializes the variable 'list' with all FFA states, i.e., list=$\{q_1, q_2, q_3, q_4\}$. First, we notice that no ambiguity exists for input symbol '0' at state q_1 since there are no state transitions $\delta(., 0, .) = q_1$. There exist two state transitions that have state q_1 as their target, i.e. $\delta(q_2, 1, 0.2) = \delta(q_3, 1, 0.7) = q_1$. Thus, we set the variable $visit = \{q_2, q_3\}$. According to Definition 4.1, an ambiguity exists since $\theta_{121} \neq \theta_{131}$. We resolve that ambiguity by introducing a new state q_5 and setting $\delta(q_3, 1, 0.7) = q_5$. Since $\delta(q_3, 1, 0.7)$ no longer leads to state q_1, we need to introduce new state transitions leading from state q_5 to the target states $\{q\}$ of all possible state transitions: $\delta(q_1, ., .) = \{q_2, q_3\}$. Thus, we set $\delta(q_5, 0, \theta_{250}) = q_2$ and $\delta(q_5, 1, \theta_{351}) = q_3$ with $\theta_{250} = \theta_{210}$ and $\theta_{351} = \theta_{311}$. One iteration through the outer loop thus results in the FFA shown in Figure 5b. Consider Figure 5d which shows the FFA after 3 iterations. State q_4 is the only state left that has incoming transitions $\delta(., a_k, \theta_{4.k}) = q_4$ where not all values $\theta_{4.k}$ are identical. We have $\delta(q_2, 0, 0.9) = \delta(q_6, 0, 0.9) = q_4$; since these two state transition do not cause an ambiguity

---

[8]The FFA shown in Figure 5a is a special case in that it does not contain any fuzzy transitions. Since the objective of the transformation algorithm is to resolve ambiguities for states q_i with $\delta(\{q_{j_1}, \ldots, q_{j_r}\}, a_k, \{, \theta_{ij_1 k}, \ldots, \theta_{ij_r k}\}) = q_i$, fuzziness is of no relevance; therefore, we omitted it for reasons of simplicity.

for input symbol '0', we leave these state transitions as they are. However, we also have $\delta(q_2, 0, \theta_{420}) = \delta(q_3, 0, \theta_{430}) = \delta(q_7, 0, \theta_{470}) = q_4$ with $\theta_{430} = \theta_{470} \neq \theta_{420} = 0.9$. Instead of creating new states for both state transitions $\delta(q_3, 0, \theta_{430})$ and $\delta(q_7, 0, \theta_{470})$, it suffices to create one new state q_8 and to set $\delta(q_3, 0, 0.1) = \delta(q_7, 0, 0.1) = q_8$. States q_6 and q_7 are the only possible successor states on input symbols '0' and '1', respectively. Thus, we set $\delta(q_8, 0, 0.6) = q_6$ and $\delta(q_8, 1, 0.4) = q_7$. There exist no more ambiguities and the algorithm terminates (Figure 5e).

D. PROPERTIES OF THE TRANSFORMATION ALGORITHM

We have shown with an example how the algorithm transforms any FFA M into a FFA M' without ambiguities. We now need to show that the algorithm correctly transforms M into M', i.e., we need to show that M and M' are equivalent. In addition, we also need to demonstrate that the algorithm terminates for any input M.

First, we prove the following property of the transformation algorithm:

Lemma 4.1 *Resolution of an ambiguity does not result in a new ambiguity.*

Proof. Consider the situation illustrated in Figure 6a. Let q_i, q_j, q_l, q_m be four FFA states and let there be an ambiguity at state q_i on input symbol a_k, i.e. $\delta(q_j, a_k, \theta_{ijk}) = \delta(q_l, a_k, \theta_{ilk}) = q_i$ with $\theta_{ijk} \neq \theta_{ilk}$. Furthermore, let $\delta(q_i, a_{k'}, \theta_{mik'}) = q_m$. The ambiguity is resolved by creating a new state q_X. We arbitrarily choose the state transition $\delta(q_l, a_k, \theta_{ilk}) = q_i$ and set $\delta(q_l, a_k, \theta_{Xlk}) = q_X$ with $\theta_{Xlk} = \theta_{ilk}$. This removes the ambiguity at state q_i. We now need to introduce a new state transition $\delta(q_X, a'_k, \theta_{mXk'}) = q_m$. By observing that $\theta_{mXk'} = \theta_{mik}$ we conclude that no new ambiguity has been created at state q_m following the resolution of the ambiguity at state q_i.

We observe that M' is not unique, i.e. the order in which states are visited and the order in which state transition ambiguities are resolved determine the final FFA M'. Consider the FFA in Figure 5a. In our example, if we had chosen to change transition $\delta(q_2, 1, 0.2) = q_1$ instead of state transition $\delta(q_3, 1, 0.7) = q_1$, then the resulting FFA M' would have been different. However, all possible transformations M' share a common invariant property.

Lemma 4.2 *The number of states in M' is constant regardless of the order in which states are visited and state transition ambiguities are resolved.*

Proof. To see that the lemma's claim holds true, we observe that resolving an ambiguity consists of creating a new state for each set of states $\{q_j\}$ with $\delta(q_j, a_k, \theta_{ijk}) = q_i$ with $\forall j \neq j' : \theta_{ijk} \neq \theta_{ij'k}$. Since resolving the ambiguity for any state q_i does not introduce new ambiguities (see Lemma 4.1), the number of newly created states depends only on the number FFA states with ambiguities.

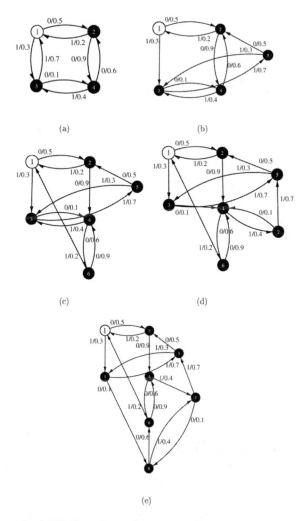

Figure 5. **Example of FFA Transformation:** Transition weight ambiguities are resolved in a sequence of steps: (a) the original FFA; there exist ambiguities for all four states; (b) the ambiguity of transition from state 3 to state 1 on input symbol 1 is removed by adding a new state 5; (c) the ambiguity of transition from state 4 to state 2 on input symbol 0 is removed by adding a new state 6; (d) the ambiguity of transition from state 4 to state 3 on input symbol 1 is removed by adding a new state 7; (e) the ambiguity of transition from states 3 and 7 - both transition have the same fuzzy membership - to state 4 is removed by adding a new state 8.

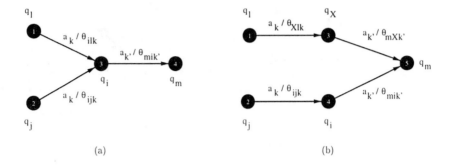

(a)   (b)

Figure 6. **Resolution of Ambiguities:** The transition ambiguity from states q_l and q_j to state q_i on input symbol a_k is resolved by adding a new state q_X and adjusting the transition as shown.

The following definitions will be convenient:

Definition 4.4 *The outdegree* $d_{out}(q_i)$ *of a state* q_i *in FFA* M *is the maximum number of states* q_j *for which we have* $\delta(q_i, a_k, \theta_{ijk}) = \{q_j\}$ *for fixed* a_k *with* $\theta_{jik} > 0$ *where the maximum is taken over all symbols* a_k. *The maximum outdegree* $D_{out}(M)$ *of some FFA* M *is the maximum over all* $d_{out}(q_i)$ *with* $q_i \in M$.

Definition 4.5 *The indegree* $d_{in}(q_i)$ *of a state* q_i *in FFA* M *is the maximum number of states* q_j *for which we have* $\delta(\{q_j\}, a_k, \theta_{ijk}) = q_i$ *for fixed* a_k *with* $\theta_{ijk} > 0$ *where the maximum is taken over all symbols* a_k. *The maximum indegree* $D_{in}(M)$ *of some FFA* M *is the maximum over all* $d_{in}(q_i)$ *with* $q_i \in M$.

We can give a very loose upper bound for the number of states in M' as follows:

Lemma 4.3 *For a FFA* M *with* N *states and* K *input symbols, the transformed FFA has at most* $D_{in}KN(N-1)$ *states.*

Proof. Consider some arbitrary state q_i of M. It can have at most $D_{in}N$ incoming transitions for input symbol a_k. The resolution of ambiguity for state q_i requires that all but one transition $\delta(., a_k, \theta_{i.k})$ lead to a new state. In the case where the fuzzy transition memberships $\theta_{i.k}$ are all different, $N-1$ new states are created per ambiguous state. Thus, for K input symbols, at the most, $D_{in}KN(N-1)$ new states are created.

The results in Table 1 show the size of randomly generated FFA M with input alphabet $\{0, 1\}$, the maximum outdegree $D_{out}(M)$, the upper bound on the size of transformed FFA M', and average and standard deviation of actual sizes for transformed FFA M' taken over 100 experiments. The random FFA M were generated by connecting each state of M to at most D_{out} other states for given input symbol. We observe that the average actual size of transformed FFA depends on the maximum outdegree $D_{out}(M)$ and appears to be linear in N and D_{out}. Lemma 4.3 has the following corollary:

Corollary 4.1 *The FFA transformation algorithm terminates for all possible FFA.*

Proof. The size of the set *list* in the algorithm decreases monotonically with each iteration. Thus, the outer while loop terminates when list $= \emptyset$. Likewise, the inner while loop terminates since there is only a finite number of states q_l in the set 'class' and the size of that set monotonically decreases with each iteration. Thus, the algorithm terminates.

We now return to the proof of Theorem 4.1. We have already proven that applying the FFA transformation algorithm results in a FFA where no ambiguities exist. It is easy to see that the transformed FFA M' is equivalent with the original FFA M, since no new fuzzy transition memberships have been added, and the algorithm leaves unchanged the order in which FFA transitions are executed. This completes the proof of Theorem 4.1.

The above transformation algorithm removes all ambiguities for incoming transitions. However, a minor adjustment for the neural FFA encoding is needed. Given a FFA state q_i with $\delta(q_j, a_k, \theta_{ijk}) = q_i$ and $\delta(q_j, a_k, .) \neq q_i$, the corresponding weight W_{iik} is set to $-H$. We also need to specify an implicit value $\theta_{iik} > 0$ for the neural FFA encoding even though we have $\theta_{iik} = 0$ in the FFA. In order to be consistent with regard to neurons with variable output range, we set $\theta_{iik} = \theta_{ijk}$.

V. NETWORK ARCHITECTURE

The architecture for representing FFA is shown in Figure 7. A layer of sparsely connected recurrent neurons implements the finite state dynamics. Each neuron S_i of the state transition module has a dynamical output range $[0, \theta_{ijk}]$ where θ_{ijk} is the rule weight in the FFA state transition $\delta(q_j, a_k, \theta_{ijk}) = q_i$. Notice that each neuron S_i is only connected to pairs (S_i, I_k) for which $\theta_{ijk} = \theta_{ij'k}$ since we assume that M is transformed into an equivalent, unambiguous FFA M' prior to the network construction. The weights W_{ijk} are programmed as described in Section 3.D. Each recurrent state neuron receives as inputs the value S_j^t and an output range value θ_{ijk}; it computes its output according to Equation (3).

size of M	$D_{out}(M)$	upper limit on size of M'	average size of M'	standard deviation
10	1	180	12	2
	2	360	16	5
	3	540	19	15
	4	720	25	29
	5	900	28	84
20	1	760	25	6
	2	1520	32	19
	3	2280	40	40
	4	3040	50	191
	5	3800	68	278
30	1	1740	38	7
	2	3480	49	27
	3	5220	61	64
	4	6960	84	266
	5	8700	111	578
40	1	2400	51	6
	2	4800	65	29
	3	7200	85	104
	4	9600	117	342
	5	12000	154	1057
50	1	4900	65	14
	2	9800	84	41
	3	14700	107	217
	4	19600	154	704
	5	24500	198	1478
100	1	19800	129	26
	2	39600	161	64
	3	59400	215	285
	4	78800	309	1845
	5	98600	401	3916

Table 1. **Scaling of Transformed FFA:** The results show the increase of the size of FFA M due to its transformation into a FFA M' without ambiguities as a function of the size of M and the maximum outdegree $D_{out}(M)$. The FFA were randomly generated and the average was computed over 100 transformations. The average size of transformed FFA appears to be linear in N and D_{out}.

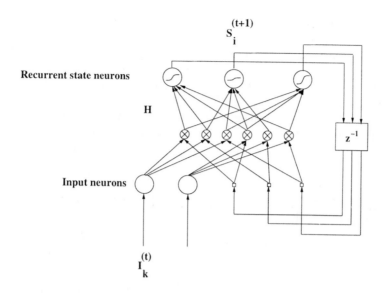

Figure 7. **Network Architecture for FFA Representation**: The architecture for representing FFA differs from that for DFA in that (1) the recurrent state neurons have variable output range, (2) the resolution of ambiguities causes a sparser interconnection topology, and (3) there is no dedicated output neuron.

VI.   NETWORK STABILITY ANALYSIS

A.   PRELIMINARIES

In order to demonstrate how the FFA encoding algorithm achieves stability of the internal FFA state representation for indefinite periods of time, we need to understand the dynamics of signals in a constructed recurrent neural network.

We define stability of an internal FFA state representation as follows:

Definition 6.1 *A fuzzy encoding of FFA states with transition weights* $\{\theta_{ijk}\}$ *in a second-order recurrent neural network is called* <u>*stable*</u> *if only state neurons corresponding to the set of current FFA states have an output greater than* $\theta_{ijk}/2$ *where* θ_{ijk} *is the dynamic range of recurrent state neurons, and all remaining recurrent neurons have low output signals less than* $\theta_{ijk}/2$ *for all possible input sequences.*

It follows from this definition that there exists an upper bound $0 < \phi^- < \theta_{ijk}/2$ for low signals and a lower bound $\theta_{ijk}/2 < \phi^+ < \theta_{ijk}$ for high signals in networks that represent stable FFA encodings. The ideal values for low and high signals are 0 and θ_{ijk}, respectively.

A detailed analysis of all possible network state changes in Omlin [1996] revealed that, for the purpose of demonstrating stability of internal finite state representations, it is sufficient to consider the following two worst cases: (1) A neuron that does not correspond to a current fuzzy automaton state receives the same residual low input from all other neurons that it is connected to, and that value is identical for all neurons. (2) A neuron that changes its output from low to high at the next time step receives input only from one other neuron (i.e., the neuron which corresponds to the current fuzzy automaton state), and it may inhibit itself. In the case of FFA, a neuron S_i undergoing a state change from $S_i^t \approx 0$ to $S_I^{t+1} \approx \theta_{ijk}$ may receive principal inputs from more than one other neuron. However, any additional input only serves to strengthen high signals. Thus, the case of a neuron receiving principal input from exactly one other neuron represents a worst case.

B. FIXED POINT ANALYSIS FOR SIGMOIDAL DISCRIMINANT FUNCTION

Here, we summarize without proofs some of the results that we used to demonstrate stability of neural DFA encodings; details of the proofs can be found in [Omlin, 1996].

In order to guarantee low signals to remain low, we have to give a tight upper bound for low signals that remains valid for an arbitrary number of time steps:

Lemma 6.1 *The low signals are bounded from above by the fixed point $[\phi_f^-]_\theta$ of the function f*

$$\begin{cases} f^0 = 0 \\ f^{t+1} = \tilde{g}(r \cdot f^t) \end{cases} \tag{7}$$

where $[\phi_f^-]_\theta$ represents the fixed point of the discriminant function $\tilde{g}()$ with variable output range θ, and r denotes the maximum number of neurons that contribute to a neuron's input. For reasons of simplicity, we will write ϕ_f^- for $[\phi_f^-]_\theta$ with the implicit understanding that the location of fixed points depends on the particular choice of θ. This lemma can easily be proven by induction on t.

It is easy to see that the function to be iterated in Equation (7) is $f(x, H, \theta, r) = \dfrac{\theta}{1 + e^{H(\theta - 2rx)/2\theta}}$. The graphs of the function for $\theta = 1.0$ are shown in Figure 9 for different values of the parameter r. It is obvious that the location of fixed points depends on the particular values of θ. We will show later in this section that the conditions that guarantee the existence of one or three fixed points are *independent* of the parameter θ.

The function $f(x, H, \theta, r)$ has some desirable properties:

Lemma 6.2 *For any $H > 0$, the function $f(x, H, \theta, r)$ has at least one fixed point ϕ_f^0.*

Lemma 6.3 *There exists a value $H_0^-(r)$ such that for any $H > H_0^-(r)$, $f(x, H, \theta, r)$ has three fixed points $0 < \phi_f^- < \phi_f^0 < \phi_f^+ < \theta$.*

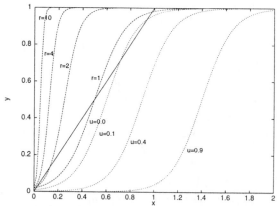

Figure 8. **Fixed Points of the Sigmoidal Discriminant Function:** Shown are the graphs of the function $f(x, H, 1, r) = \frac{1}{1+e^{H(1-2rx)/2}}$ (dashed graphs) for $H = 8$ and $r = \{1, 2, 4, 10\}$ and the function $p(x, u) = \frac{1}{1+e^{H(1-2(x-u))/2}}$ (dotted graphs) for $H = 8$ and $u = \{0.0, 0.1, 0.4, 0.9\}$. Their intersection with the function $y = x$ shows the existence and location of fixed points. In this example, $f(x, r)$ has three fixed points for $r = \{1, 2\}$, but only one fixed point for $r = \{4, 10\}$ and $p(x, u)$ has three fixed points for $u = \{0.0, 0.1\}$, but only one fixed point for $u = \{0.4, 0.9\}$.

Lemma 6.4 *If $f(x, H, \theta, r)$ has three fixed points ϕ_f^-, ϕ_f^0, and ϕ_f^+, then*

$$\lim_{t \to \infty} f^t = \begin{cases} \phi_f^- & x_0 < \phi_f^0 \\ \phi_f^0 & x_0 = \phi_f^0 \\ \phi_f^+ & x_0 > \phi_f^0 \end{cases} \qquad (8)$$

where x_0 is an initial value for the iteration of $f(.)$.

The above lemma can be proven by defining an appropriate Lyapunov function P and showing that P has minima at ϕ_f^- and ϕ_f^+.[9]

The basic idea behind the network stability analysis is to show that neuron outputs never exceed or fall below some fixed points ϕ^- and ϕ^+, respectively. The fixed points ϕ_f^- and ϕ_f^+ are only valid upper and lower bounds on low and high signals, respectively, if convergence toward these fixed points is monotone. The following corollary establishes monotone convergence of f^t towards fixed points:

---

[9]Lyapunov functions can be used to prove the stability of dynamical systems [Khalil, 1992]. For a given dynamical system S, if there exists a function P - we can think of P as an energy function - such that P has at least one minimum, then S has a stable state. Here, we can choose $P(x_i) = (x_i - \phi)_f)^2$ where x_i is the value of $f(.)$ after i iterations and ϕ is one of the fixed points. It can be shown algebraically that, for $x_0 \neq \phi_f^0$, $P(x_i)$ decreases with every step of the iteration of $f(.)$ until a stable fixed point is reached.

Corollary 6.1 *Let $f^0, f^1, f^2, \ldots$ denote the finite sequence computed by successive iteration of the function f. Then we have $f^0 < f^1 < \ldots < \phi_f$ where ϕ_f is one of the stable fixed points of $f(x, H, \theta, r)$.*

With these properties, we can quantify the value $H_0^-(r)$ such that for any $H > H_0^-(r)$, $f(x, H, \theta, r)$ has three fixed points. The low and high fixed points ϕ_f^- and ϕ_f^+ are the bounds for low and high signals, respectively. The larger r, the larger H must be chosen in order to guarantee the existence of three fixed points. If H is not chosen sufficiently large, then f^t converges to a unique fixed point $\theta/2 < \phi_f < \theta$. The following lemma expresses a quantitative condition that guarantees the existence of three fixed points:

Lemma 6.5 *The function $f(x, H, \theta, r) = \frac{\theta}{1+e^{H(\theta-2rx)/2\theta}}$ has three fixed points $0 < \phi_f^- < \phi_f^0 < \phi_f^+ < \theta$ if H is chosen such that*

$$H > H_0^-(r) = \frac{2(\theta + (\theta - x) \, log(\frac{\theta-x}{x}))}{\theta - x}$$

where x satisfies the equation

$$r = \frac{\theta^2}{2x(\theta + (\theta - x) \, log(\frac{\theta-x}{x}))}.$$

Proof. We only present a sketch of the proof; for a complete proof, see Omlin [1996]. Fixed points of the function $f(x, H, \theta, r)$ satisfy the equation $\frac{\theta}{1+e^{H(\theta-2rx)/2\theta}} = x$. Given the parameter r, we must find a minimum value $H_0^-(r)$ such that $f(x, H, \theta, r)$ has three fixed points. We can think of x, r, and H as coordinates in a three-dimensional Euclidean space. Then the locus of points (x, r, H) satisfying relation the above equation is a curved surface. What we are interested in is the number of points where a line parallel to the x-axis intersects this surface.

Unfortunately, the fixed point equation cannot be solved explicitly for x as a function of r and H. However, it can be solved for either of the other parameters, giving the intersections with lines parallel to the r-axis or the H-axis:

$$r = r(x, \theta, H) = \frac{\theta}{2x} - \frac{\theta \, log(\frac{\theta-x}{x})}{Hx} \tag{9}$$

$$H = H(r, \theta, x) = \frac{2\theta \, log(\frac{\theta-x}{x})}{\theta - 2rx} \tag{10}$$

The contours of these functions show the relationship between H and x when r is fixed (Figure 9). We need to find the point on each contour where the tangent is parallel to the x-axis, which will indicate where the transition occurs between one and three solutions for $f(x, H, \theta, r) = x$. Solving $\frac{\partial r(x,\theta,H)}{\partial x} = 0$, we obtain the conditions of the lemma.

Even though the location of fixed points of the function f depends on H, r, and θ, we will use $[\phi_f]_\theta$ as a generic name for any fixed point of a function f.

Similarly, we can quantify high signals in a constructed network:

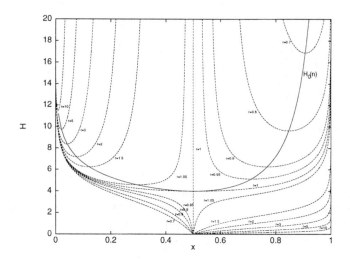

Figure 9. **Contour Plot of** $f(x, H, \theta, r) = x$: The contour plots (dotted graphs) show therelationship between H and x for various values of r and fixed value $\theta = 1$. If H is chosen such that $H > max(H_0^-(r), H_0^+(r))$ (solid graphs), then a line parallel to the x-axis intersects the surface satisfying $f(x, H, \theta, r) = x$ in three points which are the fixed points of $f(x, \theta, r)$.

Lemma 6.6 *The high signals are bounded from below by the fixed point $[\phi_h^+]_\theta$ of the function*

$$\begin{cases} h^0 = 1 \\ h^{t+1} = \tilde{g}(h^t - f^t) \end{cases} \tag{11}$$

Notice that the above recurrence relation couples f^t and h^t which makes it difficult, if not impossible, to find a function $h(x, \theta, r)$ which when iterated gives the same values as h^t. However, we can bound the sequence $h^0, h^1, h^2, \ldots$ from below by a recursively defined function p^t - i.e. $\forall t : p^t \le h^t$ - which decouples h^t from f^t.

Lemma 6.7 *Let $[\phi_f]_\theta$ denote the fixed point of the recursive function f, i.e., $\lim_{t \to \infty} f^t = [\phi_f]_\theta$. Then the recursively defined function p*

$$\begin{cases} p^0 = 1 \\ p^{t+1} = \tilde{g}(g^t - [\phi_f]_\theta) \end{cases} \tag{12}$$

has the property that $\forall t : p^t \le h^t$.

Then, we have the following sufficient condition for the existence of two stable fixed points of the function defined in Equation (11):

Lemma 6.8 *Let the iterative function p^t have two stable fixed points and $\forall t : p^t \leq h^t$. Then the function h^t also has two stable fixed points.*

The above lemma has the following corollary:

Corollary 6.2 *A constructed network's high signals remain stable if the sequence $p^0, p^1, p^2, \ldots$ converges towards the fixed point $\theta/2 < [\phi_p^+]_\theta < \theta$.*

Since we have decoupled the iterated function h^t from the iterated function f^t by introducing the iterated function p^t, we can apply the same technique to p^t for finding conditions for the existence of fixed points as in the case of f^t. In fact, the function that when iterated generates the sequence $p^0, p^1, p^2, \ldots$ is defined by

$$p(r, \theta, x) = \frac{\theta}{1 + e^{H(\theta - 2(x - [\phi_f^-]_\theta))/2\theta}} = \frac{\theta}{1 + e^{H'(\theta - 2r'x))/2\theta}} \tag{13}$$

with

$$H' = H(1 + 2[\phi_f^-]_\theta), \quad r' = \frac{1}{1 + 2[\phi_f^-]_\theta}. \tag{14}$$

We can iteratively compute the value of $[\phi_p]_\theta$ for given parameters H and r. Thus, we can repeat the original argument with H' and r' in place of H and r to find the conditions under which $p(r, x)$ and thus $g(r, x)$ have three fixed points.

Lemma 6.9 *The function $p(x, [\phi_f^-]_\theta) = \dfrac{1}{1 + e^{H(\theta - 2(x - [\phi_f^-]_\theta))/2\theta}}$ has three fixed points $0 < [\phi_p^-]_\theta < [\phi_p^0]_\theta < [\phi_p^+]_\theta < 1$ if H is chosen such that*

$$H > H_0^+(r) = \frac{2(\theta + (\theta - x) \, log(\frac{\theta - x}{x}))}{(1 + 2[\phi_f^-]_\theta)(\theta - x)}$$

where x satisfies the equation

$$\frac{1}{1 + 2[\phi_f^-]_\theta} = \frac{\theta^2}{2x(\theta + (\theta - x) \, log(\frac{\theta - x}{x}))}.$$

Since there is a collection of fuzzy transition memberships θ_{ijk} involved in the algorithm for constructing fuzzy representations of FFA, we need to determine whether the conditions of Lemmas 6.5 and 6.9 hold true for all rule weights θ_{ijk}. The following corollary establishes a useful invariant property of the function $H_0(x, r, \theta)$:

Corollary 6.3 *The value of the minima $H(x, r, \theta)$ depends only on the value of r and is independent of the particular values of θ:*

$$\inf H(x, r, \theta) = \inf \frac{2\theta \, log(\frac{\theta - x}{x})}{\theta - 2rx} = H_0(r) \tag{15}$$

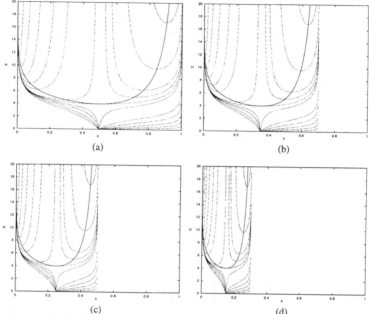

(a)　　　　　　　　　(b)

(c)　　　　　　　　　(d)

Figure 10. **Invariant Fixed Points:** The contour plots illustrating the existence and location of fixed points of the function $\tilde{g}(x, H, \theta, r) = \frac{\theta}{1 + e^{H(\theta - 2rx)/2\theta}}$ are shown for (a) $\theta = 1.0$, (b) $\theta = 0.7$, (c) $\theta = 0.5$, and (d) $\theta = 0.3$. The location of fixed points depends on the value of θ, but the condition on H and r for the existence of one vs. two stable fixed points is independent of θ. The scaling of the graphs illustrates that invariant property.

Proof. The term $log(\frac{\theta - x}{x})$ scales the function $H(x, r, \theta)$ along the x-axis. We introduce a scaling factor ϵ and set $\theta' = \epsilon\theta$ and $x' = \epsilon x$. Then, Equation (10) becomes

$$H_\epsilon(x', r, \theta') = \frac{2\epsilon\theta\, log(\frac{\epsilon\theta - \epsilon x}{\epsilon x})}{\epsilon\theta - 2r\epsilon x} = \frac{2\epsilon\theta\, log(\frac{\theta - x}{x})}{\epsilon(\theta - 2rx)} = \frac{2\theta\, log(\frac{\theta - x}{x})}{\theta - 2rx} = H(x, r, \theta)$$

(16)

for fixed r. Thus the values of $H(x, r, \theta)$ are identical for fixed values of r, and their local minima have the same values independent of θ.

The relevance of the above corollary is that there is no need to test conditions for all possible values of θ in order to guarantee the existence of fixed points. The graphs in Figure 10 illustrate that invariant property of the sigmoidal discriminant function.

We can now proceed to prove stability of low and high signals, and thus stability of the fuzzy representation of FFA states, in a constructed recurrent neural network.

121

C. NETWORK STABILITY

The existence of two stable fixed points of the discriminant function is only a necessary condition for network stability. We also need to establish conditions under which these fixed points are upper and lower bounds of stable low and high signals, respectively.

Before we define and derive the conditions for network stability, it is convenient to apply the result of Lemma 3.1 to the fixed points of the sigmoidal discriminant function (Section 3.C):

Corollary 6.4 *For any value θ with $0 < \theta \le 1$, the fixed points $[\phi]_\theta$ of the discriminant function*

$$\frac{\theta}{1 + e^{H(\theta - 2rx)/2\theta}}$$

have the following invariant relationship:

$$[\phi]_\theta = \theta \, [\phi]_1$$

Proof. By definition, fixed points ϕ of $\tilde{g}(.)$ have the property that $[\phi]_\theta = \tilde{g}[(\phi)]_\theta$. According to Lemma 3.1, we also have

$$[\phi]_\theta = \tilde{g}([\phi]_\theta) = \tilde{g}([\phi]_\theta, H, \theta) = \theta \, \tilde{g}(\theta[\phi]_1, H, 1) = \theta \, \tilde{g}([\phi]_1) = \theta \, [\phi]_1$$

because the invariant scaling property applies to all points of the function $\tilde{g}$, including its fixed points. Thus, we do not have to consider the conditions separately for all values of θ that occur in a given FFA.

We now redefine stability of recurrent networks constructed from DFA in terms of fixed points:

Definition 6.2 *An encoding of DFA states in a second-order recurrent neural network is called* <u>stable</u> *if all the low signals are less than $[\phi_f^0]_{\theta_i}$, and all the high signals are greater than $[\phi_h^0]_{\theta_i}$ for all θ_i of all state neurons S_i.*

We have simplified $\theta_{i..}$ to θ_i because the output of each neuron S_i has a fixed upper limit θ for a given input symbol, regardless which neurons S_j contribute residual inputs. We note that this new definition is stricter than what we gave in Definition 6.1. In order for the low signal to remain stable, the following condition has to be satisfied:

$$-\frac{H}{2} + Hr[\phi_f^-]_{\theta_j} < [\phi_f^0]_{\theta_j} \tag{17}$$

Similarly, the following inequality must be satisfied for stable high signals:

$$-\frac{H}{2} + H[\phi_h^+]_{\theta_j} - H[\phi_f^-]_{\theta_i} > [\phi_h^0]_{\theta_i} \tag{18}$$

The above two inequalities must be satisfied for all neurons at all times. Instead of testing for all values θ_{ijk} separately, we can simplify the set of inequalities as follows:

Lemma 6.10 *Let θ_{min} and θ_{max} denote the minimum and maximum, respectively, of all fuzzy transition memberships θ_{ijk} of a given FFA M. Then, inequalities (17) and (18) are satisfied for all transition weights θ_{ijk} if the inequalities*

$$-\frac{H}{2} + Hr[\phi_f^-]_{\theta_{max}} < [\phi_f^0]_{\theta_{min}} \tag{19}$$

$$-\frac{H}{2} + H[\phi_h^+]_{\theta_{min}} - H[\phi_f^-]_{\theta_{max}} > [\phi_h^0]_{\theta_{max}} \tag{20}$$

are satisfied.

Proof. Consider the two fixed points $[\phi_f^-]_{\theta_{min}}$ and $[\phi_h^-]_{\theta_{max}}$. According to Corollary 6.4, we have

$$[\phi_f^-]_{\theta_{min}} = \theta_{min}[\phi_f^-]_1 < \theta_{ijk}[\phi_f^-]_1 < \theta_{max}[\phi_f^-]_1 = [\phi_f^-]_{\theta_{max}}$$

Thus, if inequalities (19) and (20) are not violated for $[\phi_f^-]_{\theta_{min}}$ and $[\phi_f^-]_{\theta_{max}}$, then they will not be violated for $\theta_{min} \leq \theta_{ijk} \leq \theta_{max}$ either. We can rewrite inequalities (19) and (20) as

$$-\frac{H}{2} + Hr\,\theta_{max}[\phi_f^-]_1 < \theta_{min}[\phi_f^0]_1 \tag{21}$$

and

$$-\frac{H}{2} + H\theta_{min}[\phi_h^+]_1 - H\theta_{max}[\phi_f^-]_1 > \theta_{max}[\phi_h^0]_1 \tag{22}$$

Solving inequalities (21) and (22) for $[\phi_f^-]_1$ and $[\phi_h^+]_1$, respectively, we obtain conditions under which a constructed recurrent network implements a given FFA. These conditions are expressed in the following theorem:

Theorem 6.1 *For some given unambiguous FFA M with n states and m input symbols, let r denote the maximum number of transitions to any state over all input symbols of M. Furthermore, let θ_{min} and θ_{max} denote the minimum and maximum, respectively, of all transitions weights θ_{ijk} in M. Then, a sparse recurrent neural network with n state and m input neurons can be constructed from M such that the internal state representation remains stable if*

(1) $[\phi_f^-]_1 < \dfrac{1}{r\,\theta_{max}}\left(\dfrac{1}{2} + \theta_{min}\dfrac{[\phi_f^0]_1}{H}\right),$

(2) $[\phi_h^+]_1 > \dfrac{1}{\theta_{min}}\left(\dfrac{1}{2} + \theta_{max}[\phi_f^-]_1 + \dfrac{[\phi_h^0]_1}{H}\right),$

(3) $H > max(H_0^-(r), H_0^+(r)).$

Furthermore, the constructed network has at most $3mn$ second-order weights with alphabet $\Sigma_w = \{-H, 0, +H\}$, $n + 1$ biases with alphabet $\Sigma_b = \{-H/2\}$, and maximum fan-out $3m$.

For $\theta_{min} = \theta_{max} = 1$, conditions (1)-(3) of the above theorem reduce to those found for stable DFA encodings [Omlin, 1996]. This is consistent with a crisp representation of DFA states.

VII. SIMULATIONS

In order to test our theory, we constructed a fuzzy encoding of a randomly generated FFA with 100 states (after the execution of the FFA transformation algorithm) over the input alphabet $\{0, 1\}$. We randomly assigned weights in the range $[0, 1]$ to all transitions in increments of 0.1. The maximum indegree was $D_{in}(M) = r = 5$. We then tested the stability of the fuzzy internal state representation on 100 randomly generated strings of length 100 by comparing, at each time step, the output signal of each recurrent state neuron with its ideal output signal (since each recurrent state neuron S_i corresponds to a FFA state q_i, we know the degree to which q_i is occupied after input symbol a_k has been read: either 0 or θ_{ijk}). A histogram of the differences between the ideal and the observed signal of state neurons for selected values of the weight strength H over all state neurons and all tested strings is shown in Figure 11. As expected, the error decreases for increasing values of H. We observe that the number of discrepancies between the desired and the actual neuron output decreases 'smoothly' for the shown values of H (almost no change can be observed for values up to $H = 6$). The most significant change can be observed by comparing the histograms for $H = 9.7$ and $H = 9.75$: The existence of significant neuron output errors for $H = 9.7$ suggests that the internal FFA representation is highly unstable. For $H \geq 9.75$, the internal FFA state representation becomes stable. This discontinuous change can be explained by observing that there exists a critical value $H_0(r)$ such that the number of stable fixed points also changes discontinuously from one to two for $H < H_0(r))$ and $H > H_0(r))$, respectively (see Figure 11). The 'smooth' transition from large output errors to very small errors for most recurrent state neurons (Figure 11a-e) can be explained by observing that not all recurrent state neurons receive the same number of residual inputs; some neurons may not receive any residual input for some given input symbol a_k at time step t; in that case, the low signals of those neurons are strengthened to $\tilde{g}(0, H, \theta_{i.k}) \simeq 0$ (note that strong low signals imply strong high signals by Lemma 6.7).

VIII. CONCLUSIONS

Theoretical work that proves representational relationships between different computational paradigms is important because it establishes the equivalences of those models. Previously it has been shown that it is possible to deterministically encode fuzzy finite state automata (FFA) in recurrent neural networks by transforming any given FFA into a deterministic acceptor which assign string membership [Omlin, 1998]. In such a deterministic encoding, only the network's classification of strings is fuzzy, whereas the representation of states is *crisp*. The correspondence between FFA and network parameters - i.e., fuzzy transition memberships and network weights, respectively - is lost in the transformation.

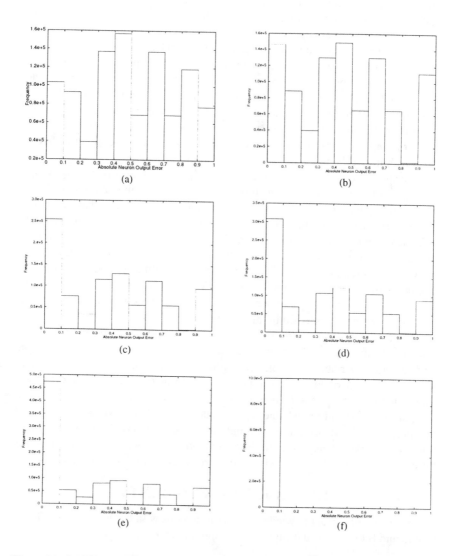

Figure 11. **Stability of FFA State Encoding:** The histograms shows the absolute neuron output error of a network with 100 neurons that implements a randomly generated FFA and reads 100 randomly generated strings of length 100 for different values of the weight strength H. The error was computed by comparing, at each time step, the actual with the desired output of each state neuron. The distribution of neuron output signal errors are for weight strengths (a) $H = 6.0$, (b) $H = 9.0$, (c) $H = 9.60$, (d) $H = 9.65$, and (e) $H = 9.70$, and (f) $H = 9.75$.

Here, we have demonstrated analytically and empirically that it is possible to encode FFA in recurrent networks *without* transforming them into deterministic acceptors. The constructed network directly represents FFA states with the desired fuzziness. That representation requires (1) a slightly increased functionality of sigmoidal discriminant functions (it only requires the discriminants to accommodate variable output range), and (2) a transformation of a given FFA into an equivalent FFA with a larger number of states. (We have found empirically that the increase in automaton size is roughly proportional to $N * K$ where N and K are the automaton and alphabet size, respectively.) In the proposed mapping FFA $\rightarrow$ recurrent network, the correspondence between FFA and network parameters remains intact; this can be significant if the physical properties of some unknown dynamic, nonlinear system are to be derived from a trained network modeling that system. Furthermore, the analysis tools and methods used to demonstrate the stability of the crisp internal representation of DFA carried over and generalized to show stability of the internal FFA representation.

We speculate that other encoding methods are possible and that it is an open question as to which encoding methods are better. One could argue that, from a engineering point of view, it may seem more natural to use radial basis functions to represent fuzzy state membership (they are often used along with triangular and trapezoidal membership functions in the design of fuzzy systems) instead of sigmoidal discriminant functions (DFA can be mapped into recurrent neural networks with radialbasis functions [Frasconi, 1996]). It is an open question how mappings of FFA into recurrent neural networks with radial basis discriminant functions would be implemented and how such mappings would compare to the encoding algorithm described in this work.

The usefulness of training recurrent neural networks with fuzzy state representation from examples to behave like a FFA - the variable output range θ can be treated as a variable parameter and an update rule similar to that for network weights can be derived - and whether useful information can be extracted from trained networks has yet to be determined. In particular, it would be interesting to compare training and knowledge representation of networks whose discriminant functions have fixed and variable output ranges, respectively. Discriminant functions with variable neuron output range may open the door to novel methods for the extraction of symbolic knowledge from recurrent neural networks.

IX.   ACKNOWLEDGMENTS

We would like to acknowledge useful discussions with K. Bollacker, D. Handscomb and B.G. Horne and suggestions from the referees.

REFERENCES

Akers, L., Ferry, D., Grondin, R., Synthetic neural systems in VLSI. In *An Introduction to Neural and Electronic Systems*. Academic Press, 317, 1990.

Ashar, P., Devadas, S., Newton, A., *Sequential Logic Synthesis.* Kluwer Academic Publishers, Norwell, 1992.

Berenji, H., Khedkar, P., Learning and fine tuning fuzzy logic controllers through reinforcement. *IEEE Transactions on Neural Networks*, (3)5, 724, 1992.

Bezdek, J., Fuzzy logic and neural networks. *IEEE Transactions on Neural Networks*, 3, 1992. Special Issue.

Bishop, C., *Neural Networks for Pattern Recognition.* Oxford University Press, 1995.

Blanco, A., Delgado, M., Pegalajar, M., Fuzzy grammar inference using neural networks. Tech. Rep., Department of Computer Science and Artificial Intelligence, University of Granada, Spain, 1997.

Bonissone, P., Badami, V., Chiang, K., Khedkar, P., Marcelle, K., Schutten, M., Industrial applications of fuzzy logic at General Electric. *Proceedings of the IEEE*, (83)3, 450, 1995.

Bookman, L., Sun, R., Architectures for integrating symbolic and neural processes. *Connection Science*, 5(3,4), 1993. Special Issue.

Casey, M., The dynamics of discrete-time computation, with application to recurrent neural networks and finite state machine extraction. *Neural Computation*, 8(6), 1135, 1996.

Cellier, F., Pan, Y., Fuzzy adaptive recurrent counterpropagation neural networks: A tool for efficient implementation of qualitative models of dynamic processes. *J. Systems Engineering*, 5(4), 207, 1995.

Chiu, S., Chand, S., Moore, D., Chaudhary, A., Fuzzy logic for control of roll and moment for a flexible wing aircraft. *IEEE Control Systems Magazine*, 11(4), 42, 1991.

Cichocki, A., Unbehauen, R., Eds. *Neural Networks for Optimization and Signal Processing.* John Wiley, New York, 1993.

Cleeremans, A., Servan-Schreiber, D., McClelland, J., Finite state automata and simple recurrent neural networks. *Neural Computation*, 1(3), 372, 1989.

Corbin, J., A fuzzy logic-based financial transaction system. *Embedded Systems Programming*, 7(12), 24, 1994.

Dubois, D., Prade, H., *Fuzzy Sets and Systems: Theory and Applications*, Vol. 144 of *Mathematics in Science and Engineering*. Academic Press, 220, 1980.

Elman, J., Finding structure in time. *Cognitive Science*, 14, 179, 1990.

Franquelo, L., Chavez, J., Fasy: A fuzzy-logic based tool for analog synthesis. *IEEE Transactions on Computer-Aided Design of Integrated Circuits*, 15(7), 705, 1996.

Frasconi, P., Gori, M., Maggini, M., Soda, G., Representation of finite state automata in recurrent radial basis function networks. *Machine Learning*, 23, 5, 1996.

Fu, L.-M., *Neural Networks in Computer Intelligence*. McGraw-Hill, Inc., New York, 1994.

Gaines, B., Kohout, L., The logic of automata. *International Journal of General Systems*, 2, 191, 1976.

Giles, C., Gori, M., Eds. *Adaptive Processing of Sequences and Data Structures*. Lecture Notes in Artificial Intelligence. Springer-Verlag, 1998.

Giles, C., Miller, C., Chen, D., Chen, H., Sun, G., Lee, Y., Learning and extracting finite state automata with second-order recurrent neural networks. *Neural Computation*, 4(3), 393, 1992.

Giles, C., Omlin, C., Extraction, insertion and refinement of symbolic rules in dynamically driven recurrent neural networks. *Connection Science*, 5(3,4), 307, 1993.

Giles, C., Sun, R., Zurada, J., Neural networks and hybrid intelligent models: Foundations, theory, and applications. *IEEE Transactions on Neural Networks*, 9(5), 721, 1998. Special Issue.

Grantner, J., Patyra, M., VLSI implementations of fuzzy logic finite state machines. In *Proceedings of the Fifth IFSA Congress*, 781, 1993.

Grantner, J., Patyra, M., Synthesis and analysis of fuzzy logic finite state machine models. In *Proc. of the Third IEEE Conf. on Fuzzy Systems*, I, 205, 1994.

Hardy, T. L., Multi-objective decision-making under uncertainty fuzzy logic methods. Tech. Rep. TM 106796, NASA, Washington, D.C., 1994.

Haykin, S., *Neural Networks, A Comprehensive Foundation*. Prentice Hall, Englewood Cliffs, NJ, 1998.

Hendler, J., Developing hybrid symbolic/connectionist models. In *Advances in Connectionist and Neural Computation Theory*, Barnden, J., Pollack, J., Eds. Ablex Publishing, 1991.

Herrmann, C., A hybrid fuzzy-neural expert system for diagnosis. In *Proc. of the Fourteenth International Joint Conf. on Artificial Intelligence*, I, 494, 1995.

Honavar, V., Uhr, L., Eds., *Artificial Intelligence and Neural Networks: Steps toward Principled Integration*. Academic Press, 1994.

Hopcroft, J., Ullman, J., *Introduction to Automata Theory, Languages, and Computation*. Addison-Wesley Publishing Company, Inc., Reading, PA, 1979.

Kasabov, N., *Foundations of Neural Networks, Fuzzy Systems, and Knowledge Engineering*. MIT Press, Cambridge, 1996.

Khalil, H., *Nonlinear Systems*. Macmillan Publishing Company, New York, 1992.

Khan, E., Unal, F., Recurrent fuzzy logic using neural networks. In *Advances in fuzzy logic, neural networks, and genetic algorithms*, Furuhashi, T., Ed., Lecture Notes in AI. Springer-Verlag, 1995.

Kickert, W. J. M., van Nauta Lemke, H., Application of a fuzzy controller in a warm water plant. *Automatica*, 12(4), 301, 1976.

Kleene, S., Representation of events in nerve nets and finite automata. In *Automata Studies*, Shannon, C., McCarthy, J., Eds. Princeton University Press, Princeton, NJ, 3, 1956.

Kosmatopoulos, E., Christodoulou, M., Structural properties of gradient recurrent high-order neural networks. *IEEE Transactions on Circuits and Systems*, 42(9), 592, 1995.

Kosmatopoulos, E., Christodoulou, M., Neural networks for identification of fuzzy dynamical systems: An application to identification of vehicle highway systems. In *Proceedings of the 4th IEEE Mediterranean Symposium on New Directions in Control and Automation*, 23, 1996.

Kosmatopoulos, E., Christodoulou, M., Recurrent neural networks for approximation of fuzzy dynamical systems. *International Journal of Intelligent Control and Systems*, 1(2), 223, 1996a.

Kosmatopoulos, E., Polycarpou, M., Christodoulou, M., Ioannou, P., High-order neural networks for identification of dynamical systems. *IEEE Transactions on Neural Networks*, 6(2), 422, 1995a.

Lee, C., Fuzzy logic in control systems: fuzzy logic controller. *IEEE Transactions on Man, Systems, and Cybernetics*, 20(2), 404, 1990.

Maclin, R., Shavlik, J., Using knowledge-based neural networks to improve algorithms: Refining the Chou-Fasman algorithm for protein folding. *Machine Learning*, 11, 195, 1993.

Mead, C., *Analog VLSI and Neural Systems*. Addison-Wesley, Reading, PA, 1989.

Mensch, S., Lipp, H., Fuzzy specification of finite state machines. In *Proceedings of the European Design Automation Conference*, 622, 1990.

Minsky, M., *Computation: Finite and Infinite Machines*. Prentice-Hall, Inc., Englewood Cliffs, NJ, 1967.

Omlin, C., Giles, C., Constructing deterministic finite-state automata in recurrent neural networks. *Journal of the ACM*, 43(6), 937, 1996.

Omlin, C., Giles, C., Extraction of rules from discrete-time recurrent neural networks. *Neural Networks*, 9(1), 41, 1996a.

Omlin, C., Giles, C., Rule revision with recurrent neural networks. *IEEE Transactions on Knowledge and Data Engineering*, 8(1), 183, 1996b.

Omlin, C., Giles, C., Stable encoding of large finite-state automata in recurrent neural networks with sigmoid discriminants. *Neural Computation*, 8(7), 675, 1996c.

Omlin, C., Thornber, K., Giles, C., Fuzzy finite-state automata can be deterministically encoded into recurrent neural networks. *IEEE Transactions on Fuzzy Systems*, 6(1), 76, 1998.

Palaniswami, M., Attikiouzel, Y., Marks, R., Fogel, D., Eds. *Computational Intelligence: A Dynamic System Perspective*. IEEE Press, Piscataway, NJ, 1995.

Pappis, C., Mamdani, E., A fuzzy logic controller for a traffic junction. *IEEE Transactions on Systems, Man, and Cybernetics*, 7(10), 707, 1977.

Pollack, J., The induction of dynamical recognizers. *Machine Learning*, 7(2/3), 227, 1991.

Santos, E., Maximin automata. *Information and Control*, 13, 363, 1968.

Sheu, B. J., *Neural Information Processing and VLSI*. Kluwer Academic Publishers, Boston, 1995.

Siegelmann, H., Sontag, E., On the computational power of neural nets. *Journal of Computer and System Sciences*, 50(1), 132, 1995.

Siegelmann, H. T., *Neural Networks and Analog Computation: Beyond the Turing Limit*. Birkhauser, Boston, 1999.

Sun, R., Learning, action, and consciousness: A hybrid approach towards modeling consciousness. *Neural Networks*, 10(7), 1317, 1997.

Thomas, S. F., *Fuzziness and Probability*. ACG Press, Wichita, KS, 1995.

Thomason, M., Marinos, P., Deterministic acceptors of regular fuzzy languages. *IEEE Transactions on Systems, Man, and Cybernetics*, 3, 228, 1974.

Unal, F., Khan, E., A fuzzy finite state machine implementation based on a neural fuzzy system. In *Proceedings of the Third International Conference on Fuzzy Systems*, 3, 1749, 1994.

Watrous, R., Kuhn, G., Induction of finite-state languages using second-order recurrent networks. *Neural Computation*, 4(3), 406, 1992.

Yang, X., Kalambur, G., Design for machining using expert system and fuzzy logic approach. *Journal of Materials Engineering and Performance*, 4(5), 599, 1995.

Zadeh, L., Fuzzy sets. *Information and Control*, 8, 338, 1965.

Zadeh, L., Fuzzy languages and their relation to human and machine intelligence. Tech. Rep. ERL-M302, Electronics Research Laboratory, University of California, Berkeley, 1971.

Zeng, Z., Goodman, R., Smyth, P., Learning finite state machines with self-clustering recurrent networks. *Neural Computation*, 5(6), 976, 1993.

Chapter 6

LEARNING LONG-TERM DEPENDENCIES IN NARX RECURRENT NEURAL NETWORKS

Tsungnan Lin

NEC Research Institute and
Department of Electrical Engineering, Princeton University

Bill G. Horne

NEC Research Institute

Peter Tino

NEC Research Institute and
Dept. of Computer Science and Engineering
Slovak Technical University

C. Lee Giles

NEC Research Institute and
UMIACS, University of Maryland

I. INTRODUCTION

Recurrent Neural Networks (RNNs) are capable of representing arbitrary non-linear dynamical systems [Seidl, 1991, Siegelmann, 1995, Sontag, 1992]. However, learning simple behavior can be quite difficult using gradient descent. For example, even though these systems are Turing equivalent, it has been difficult to get them to successfully learn small finite state machines from example strings encoded as temporal sequences. Recently, it has been demonstrated that at least part of this difficulty can be attributed to long–term dependencies, i.e., when the desired output of a system at time T depends on inputs presented at times $t \ll T$. This was noted by Mozer who reported that RNNs were able to learn short term musical structure using gradient based methods [Mozer, 1992], but had difficulty capturing global behavior. These ideas were recently formalized by Bengio *et al.* [Bengio, 1994], who showed that if a system is to latch information robustly, then the fraction of the gradient due to information n time steps in the past approaches zero as n becomes large.

Several approaches have been suggested to circumvent the problem of vanishing gradients. For example, gradient–based methods can be abandoned completely in favor of alternative optimization methods [Bengio, 1994, Puskorius, 1994]. However, the algorithms investigated so far either perform just as poorly on problems involving long–term dependencies, or, when they are better, require far more computational resources [Bengio, 1994]. Another possibility is to modify conventional gradient-descent by more heavily weighing the fraction of the gradient due to information far in the past, but there is no guarantee that such a modified algorithm would converge to a minimum of the error surface being searched [Bengio, 1994]. As an alternative to using different learning algorithms, one suggestion has been to alter the input data so that it represents a reduced description that makes global features more explicit and more readily detectable [Mozer, 1992, Schmidhuber, 1992a, Schmidhuber, 1992]. However, this approach may fail if short term dependencies are equally as important. Hochreiter also proposes a specific architectural approach which utilizes high order units [Hochreiter, 1995]. Finally, it has been suggested that a network architecture that operates on multiple time scales might be useful for tackling this problem [Gori, 1994, Hihi, 1996].

In this paper, we also propose an architectural approach to deal with long–term dependencies. We focus on a class of architectures based upon Nonlinear AutoRegressive models with eXogenous inputs (NARX models), which are therefore called *NARX recurrent neural networks* [Chen, 1990, Narendra, 1990]. (However, there is no reason that this method cannot be extended to other recurrent architectures.) This is a powerful class of models which has recently been shown to be computationally equivalent to Turing machines [Siegelmann, 1996]. It has been demonstrated that they are well suited for modeling nonlinear systems such as heat exchangers [Chen, 1990], waste water treatment plants [Su, 1991, Su, 1992], catalytic reforming systems in a petroleum refinery [Su, 1992], nonlinear oscillations associated with multi–legged locomotion in biological systems [Venkataraman, 1994], time series [Connor, 1992a], and various artificial nonlinear systems [Chen, 1990, Narendra, 1990, Qin, 1992]. Furthermore, we have previously reported that gradient-descent learning is more effective in NARX networks than in recurrent neural network architectures with "hidden states" when applied to problems including grammatical inference and nonlinear system identification [Giles, 1994, Horne, 1995]. Typically, these networks converge much faster and generalize better than other networks. The results in this paper show the reason why gradient-descent learning is better in NARX networks.

II. VANISHING GRADIENTS AND LONG-TERM DEPENDENCIES

Bengio *et al.*[Bengio, 1994] have analytically explained why learning problems with long–term dependencies is difficult. They argue that for many practical applications the goal of the network must be to *robustly latch information*, i.e., the network must be able to store information for a long period of time in the presence of noise. More specifically, they argue that latching of information is accomplished when the states of the network stay within the vicinity of a hyperbolic attractor, and robustness to noise is accomplished if the states of the network are contained in the *reduced attracting set* that attractor, i.e., if the eigenvalues of the Jacobian are contained within the unit circle. In the Appendix to this chapter, we discuss this definition of robustness in more detail and describe how some of the assumptions associated with it might be loosened.

In this section we briefly describe some of the key aspects of the results in Bengio [1994]. A recurrent neural network can be described in the form

$$\mathbf{x}(t+1) = f(\mathbf{x}(t), \mathbf{u}(t); \mathbf{w}) \tag{1}$$

$$\mathbf{y}(t) = g(\mathbf{x}(t)), \tag{2}$$

where $\mathbf{x}$, $\mathbf{u}$, $\mathbf{y}$ and $\mathbf{w}$ are column vectors representing the states, inputs, outputs, and weights of the network, respectively. Almost any recurrent neural network architecture can be expressed in this form [Nerrand, 1993], where f and g depend on the specific architecture. For example, in simple first–order recurrent neural networks, f would be a sigmoid of a weighted sum of the values $\mathbf{x}(t)$ and $\mathbf{u}(t)$ and g would simply select one of the states as output.

We define $\mathbf{u}_p(t), t = 1...T$ to be an input sequence of length T for the network (for simplicity, we shall assume that all sequences are of the same length), and $\mathbf{y}_p(T)$ to be the output of the network for that input sequence.

In what follows we derive the gradient-descent learning algorithm in a matrix–vector format, which is slightly more compact than deriving it expressly in terms of partial derivatives, and highlight the role of the Jacobian in the derivation.

Gradient-descent learning is typically based on minimizing the sum–of–squared error cost function

$$C = \frac{1}{2} \sum_p \left(\mathbf{y}_p(T) - \mathbf{d}_p\right)' \left(\mathbf{y}_p(T) - \mathbf{d}_p\right), \tag{3}$$

where $\mathbf{d}_p$ is the desired (or target) output for the pth pattern[1] and $\mathbf{y}'$ denotes transposition of a vector $\mathbf{y}$. Gradient-descent is an algorithm which iteratively updates the weights in proportion to the gradient

$$\Delta \mathbf{w} = \eta \nabla_{\mathbf{w}} C, \tag{4}$$

where η is a learning rate, and $\nabla_{\mathbf{w}}$ is the row vector operator

$$\nabla_{\mathbf{w}} = \begin{bmatrix} \frac{\partial}{\partial w_1} & \frac{\partial}{\partial w_2} & \cdots & \frac{\partial}{\partial w_n} \end{bmatrix}. \tag{5}$$

By using the Chain Rule, the gradient can be expanded

$$\nabla_{\mathbf{w}} C = \sum_p \left(\mathbf{y}_p(T) - \mathbf{d}_p\right)' \nabla_{\mathbf{x}(T)} \mathbf{y}_p(T) \nabla_{\mathbf{w}} \mathbf{x}(T). \tag{6}$$

We can expand this further by assuming that the weights at different time indices are independent and computing the partial gradient with respect to these weights,

---

[1] We deal only with problems in which the target output is presented at the *end* of the sequence.

which is the methodology used to derive algorithms such as Backpropagation Through Time (BPTT) [Rumelhart, 1986, Williams, 1995]. The total gradient is then equal to the sum of these partial gradients. Specifically,

$$\nabla_{\mathbf{w}} C = \sum_p (\mathbf{y}_p(T) - \mathbf{d}_p)' \nabla_{\mathbf{x}(T)} y_p(T) \left[\sum_{\tau=1}^{T} \nabla_{\mathbf{w}(\tau)} \mathbf{x}(T) \right] . \qquad (7)$$

Another application of the Chain Rule to Equation 7 gives

$$\nabla_{\mathbf{w}} C = \sum_p (\mathbf{y}_p(T) - \mathbf{d}_p)' \nabla_{\mathbf{x}(T)} y_p(T) \left[\sum_{\tau=1}^{T} J_{\mathbf{x}}(T, T - \tau) \nabla_{\mathbf{w}(\tau)} \mathbf{x}(\tau) \right] , \qquad (8)$$

where $J_{\mathbf{x}}(T, T - \tau) = \nabla_{\mathbf{x}(\tau)} \mathbf{x}(T)$ denotes the Jacobian of (1) expanded over $T - \tau$ time steps.

Bengio et al. [Bengio, 1994] showed that if the network satisfies their definition of robustly latching information, i.e., if the Jacobian at each time step has all of its eigenvalues inside the unit circle, then $J_{\mathbf{x}}(T, n)$ is an exponentially decreasing function of n, so that $\lim_{n \to \infty} J_{\mathbf{x}}(T, n) = 0$. This implies that the portion of $\nabla_{\mathbf{w}} C$ due to information at times $\tau \ll T$ is insignificant compared to the portion at times near T. This effect is called the problem of *vanishing gradient*, or *forgetting behavior* [Frasconi, 1992]. Bengio m et al. claim that the problem of vanishing gradients is the essential reason why gradient-descent methods are not sufficiently powerful to discover a relationship between target outputs and inputs that occur at a much earlier time, which they term the problem of *long–term dependencies*.

III. NARX NETWORKS

An important class of discrete–time nonlinear systems is the Nonlinear AutoRegressive with eXogenous inputs (NARX) model[2] [Chen, 1990, Leontaritis, 1985, Ljunkg, 1987, Su, 1991, Su, 1992]:

$$y(t) = f\left(u(t - D_u), \dots, u(t - 1), u(t), y(t - D_y), \dots, y(t - 1)\right), \qquad (9)$$

where $u(t)$ and $y(t)$ represent input and output of the network at time t, D_u and D_y are the input and output order, and the function f is a nonlinear function. When the function f can be approximated by a Multilayer Perceptron, the resulting system is called a *NARX recurrent neural network* [Chen, 1990, Narendra, 1990].

In this chapter we shall consider NARX networks with zero input order and a one-dimensional output, i.e., those networks which have feedback from the output only. However there is no reason why our results could not be extended to

---

[2]The terminology on how to properly describe this architecture in the literature is conflicting. We chose the term NARX based on previous references.

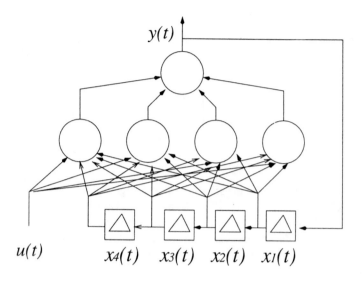

Figure 1. A NARX network with four output delays.

networks with higher input orders. Thus, the operation of NARX networks with zero input order is defined by

$$y(t) = \Psi\left(u(t), y(t-1), \ldots, y(t-D)\right) , \qquad (10)$$

where the function Ψ is the mapping performed by the MLP, as shown in Figure 1. The weight links in the figure can be adjusted or fixed; it depends on the application.

From a system perspective, it is preferrable to put equations into a state space form [Kailath, 1980]. In this form the Jacobian can be examined and derived [Khalil, 1992]. Since the states of a discrete–time dynamical system can always be associated with the unit–delay elements in the realization of the system, we can then describe such a network in the following state space form

$$x_i(t+1) = \begin{cases} \Psi\left(u(t), \mathbf{x}(t)\right) & i = 1 \\ x_{i-1}(t) & i = 2, \ldots, D \end{cases} \qquad (11)$$

and

$$y(t) = x_1(t+1) . \qquad (12)$$

137

NARX networks are not immune to the problem of long–term dependencies. The Jacobian of the state space map (11) is given by

$$J_{\mathbf{x}}(t+1,1) = \nabla_{\mathbf{x}(t)}\mathbf{x}(t+1) = \begin{bmatrix} \frac{\partial \Psi(t)}{\partial x_1(t)} & \frac{\partial \Psi(t)}{\partial x_2(t)} & \cdots & \frac{\partial \Psi(t)}{\partial x_{D-1}(t)} & \frac{\partial \Psi(t)}{\partial x_D(t)} \\ 1 & 0 & \cdots & 0 & 0 \\ 0 & 1 & \cdots & 0 & 0 \\ \vdots & \vdots & \ddots & \vdots & \vdots \\ 0 & 0 & \cdots & 1 & 0 \end{bmatrix}$$

(13)

If the Jacobian at each time step has all of its eigenvalues inside the unit circle, then the states of the network will be in the reduced attracting set of some hyperbolic attractor, and thus the system will be robustly latched at that time. As with any other recurrent neural network, this implies that $\lim_{n \to \infty} J_{\mathbf{x}}(t, n) = 0$. Thus, NARX networks will also suffer from vanishing gradients and the long–term dependencies problem.

IV.   AN INTUITIVE EXPLANATION OF NARX NETWORK BEHAVIOR

In the previous section we saw that NARX networks also suffer from the problem of vanishing gradients, and thus are also prone to the problem of long-term dependencies. However, we find in the simulation results that follow that NARX networks are often much better at discovering long-term dependencies than conventional recurrent neural networks.

An intuitive reason why output delays can help long-term dependencies can be found by considering how gradients are calculated using the backpropagation-through-time (BPTT) algorithm. BPTT involves two phases: unfolding the network in time and backpropagating the error through the unfolded network. When a NARX network is unfolded in time, the output delays will appear as jump-ahead connections in the unfolded network. Intuitively, these jump-ahead connections provide a shorter path for propagating gradient information, thus reducing the sensitivity of the network to long-term dependencies. However, one must keep in mind that this intuitive reasoning is only valid if the total gradient through these jump-ahead pathways is greater than the gradient through the layer-to-layer pathways.

Another intuitive explanation is that since the delays are cascaded together, the propagation of information does not necessarily have to pass through a non-linearity at each time step, and thus the gradient is not modified by the derivative of the nonlinearity, which is often less than one in magnitude.

It is possible to derive analytical results for some simple toy problems to show that NARX networks are indeed less sensitive to long-term dependencies. Here we give one such example, which is based upon the latching problem described in [Bengio, 1994].

Consider the simple one node autonomous recurrent network described by,

$$x(t) = \tanh(wx(t-1)), \qquad (14)$$

where $w = 1.25$, which has two stable fixed points at ± 0.710 and one unstable fixed point at zero. The following one node, autonomous NARX network (no internal inputs)

$$x(t) = \tanh\left(w_1 x(t-1) + w_2 x(t-2) + \ldots + w_D x(t-D)\right) \qquad (15)$$

with D output delays has the same fixed points as long as $\sum_{i=1}^{D} w_i = w$.

Assume the state of the network has reached equilibrium at the positive stable fixed point. In this case we can derive the exact gradient. For simplicity, we consider only the Jacobian $J(t,n) = \frac{\partial x(t)}{\partial x(t-n)}$, which will be a component of the gradient $\nabla_{\mathbf{w}} C$. Figure 2 shows plots of $J(t,n)$ with respect to n for $D = 1$, $D = 3$, and $D = 6$ with $w_i = w/D$. These plots show that the effect of output delays is to flatten out the curves and place more emphasis on the gradient due to terms farther in the past. Note that the gradient contribution due to short term dependencies is deemphasized. In Figure 3 we show plots of the ratio

$$\frac{J(t,n)}{\sum_{\tau=1}^{n} J(t,\tau)}, \qquad (16)$$

which illustrates the percentage of the total gradient that can be attributed to information n time steps in the past. These plots show that this percentage is larger for the network with output delays, and thus one would expect that these networks would be able to more effectively deal with long–term dependencies.

V. EXPERIMENTAL RESULTS

Simulations were performed to compare the performance of learning long–term dependencies on networks with different number of feedback delays. We tried two different problems: the latching problem and a grammatical inference problem.

A. THE LATCHING PROBLEM

We explored a slight modification on the latching problem described in [Bengio, 1994]. This problem is a minimal task designed as a test that must necessarily be passed in order for a network to latch information robustly. Bengio et al. describe the task as one in which "the input values are to be learned." Here we give an alternative description of the problem, which allows us to reexpress the problem as one in which only weights are to be learned.

In this task there are three inputs $u_1(t)$, $u_2(t)$, and a noise input $e(t)$, and a single output $y(t)$. Both $u_1(t)$ and $u_2(t)$ are zero for all times $t > 1$. At time $t = 1$, $u_1(1) = 1$ and $u_2(1) = 0$ for samples from class 1, and $u_1(1) = 0$ and

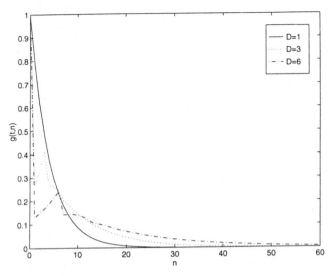

Figure 2: Plots of $J(t, n)$ (the Jacobian expanded over n time steps) as a function of n for different number of output delays ($D = 1$, $D = 3$, and $D = 6$). Although all of these curves can be bounded above by a function that decays exponentially, the values of $J(t, n)$ decay at a slower rate as D becomes larger.

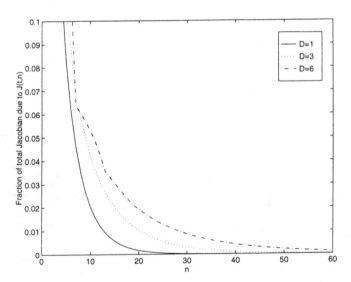

Figure 3: Plots of the ratio $\frac{J(t,n)}{\sum_{\tau=1}^{n} J(t,\tau)}$ as a function of n for different number of output delays ($D = 1$, $D = 3$, and $D = 6$). These curves show that the portion of the gradient due to information n time steps in the past is a greater fraction of the overall gradient as D becomes larger.

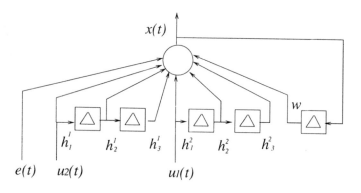

Figure 4. The network used for the latching problem.

$u_2(1) = 1$ for samples from class 2. The noise input $e(t)$ is given by

$$e(t) = \begin{cases} 0 & t \leq L \\ U(-b, b) & L < t \leq T \end{cases} \tag{17}$$

where $U(-b, b)$ are samples drawn uniformly from $[-b, b]$.

This network used to solve this problem is a **NARX** network consisting of a single neuron,

$$s(t) =$$

$$\tanh\left(wx(t-1) + h_1^1 u_1(t) + \ldots + h_L^1 u_1(t) + h_1^2 u_2(t) + \ldots + h_L^2 u_2(t) + e(t)\right) \tag{18}$$

where the parameters h_i^j are adjustable and the recurrent weight w is fixed. In our simulations, we used $L = 3$. The network is shown in Figure 4.

Note that the problem as stated is identical to the problem stated by Bengio *et al.* except that here we are using uniform instead of Gaussian random noise. In our formulation the values h_i^j are weights which are connected to tapped delay lines on the input of the network, while Bengio m et al. describe them as learnable input values.

In our simulation, we fixed the recurrent feedback weight to $w = 1.25$, which gives the autonomous network two stable fixed points at ± 0.710 and one unstable fixed point at zero, as described in Section 4. It can be shown [Frasconi, 1995] that the network is robust to perturbations in the range $[-0.155, 0.155]$. Thus, the uniform noise in $e(t)$ was restricted to this range. Note that if Gaussian random noise is used, then there is some non–zero probability that the error would be outside of this range regardless of the variance, and thus it is possible for the network to fail to correctly classify all training values due to Gaussian noise. We felt that such effects should be avoided in order to exclusively test the sensitivity of the network to long–term dependencies, and so we chose to use uniform noise instead.

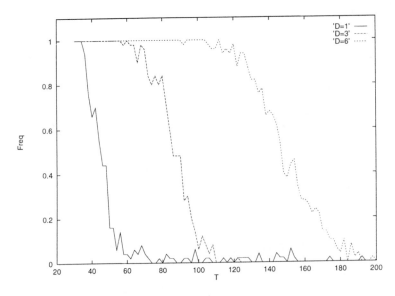

Figure 5: Plots of percentage of successful simulations as a function of T, the length of the input strings, for different numbers of output delays ($D = 1$, $D = 3$, and $D = 6$).

For each simulation, we generated 30 strings from each class, each with a different $e(t)$. The initial values of h_i^j for each simulation were also chosen from the same distribution that defines $e(t)$. For strings from class one, a target value of 0.8 was chosen, for class two -0.8 was chosen.

The network was run using a simple BPTT algorithm with a learning rate of 0.1 for a maximum of 100 epochs. (We found that the network converged to some solution consistently within a few dozen epochs.) If the absolute error between the output of the network and the target value was less than 0.6 on all strings, the simulation was terminated and determined successful. If the simulation exceeded 100 epochs and did not correctly classify all strings then the simulation was ruled a failure.

We varied T from 20 to 200 in increments of 2. For each value of T, we ran 50 simulations. We then modified the architecture to include output delays of order $D = 3$ and $D = 6$, with all of the recurrent weights $w_i = w/D$. Figure 5 shows a plot of the percentage of those runs that were successful for each case. It is clear from these plots that the NARX networks become increasingly less sensitive to long–term dependencies as the output order is increased.

B. AN AUTOMATON PROBLEM

In the previous problem, the inputs to the network consisted of a noise term whose magnitude was restricted in such a way that the network was guaranteed to remain within the basin of attraction of the fixed points for a single node. Here we explore two extensions to that problem. First, we consider larger networks and, second, we consider inputs which are not as restrictive. In particular, we consider learning an automata problem in which the inputs are boolean valued. In contrast to the previous problem, all signals are fed into the same single input channel.

In this example, the class of a string is completely determined by its input symbol at some prespecified time t. For example, Figure 6 shows a five-state automaton, in which the class of each string is determined by the third input symbol. When that symbol is "1," the string is accepted; otherwise, it is rejected. By increasing the length of the strings to be learned, we will be able to create a problem with long term dependencies, in which the output will depend on input values far in the past.

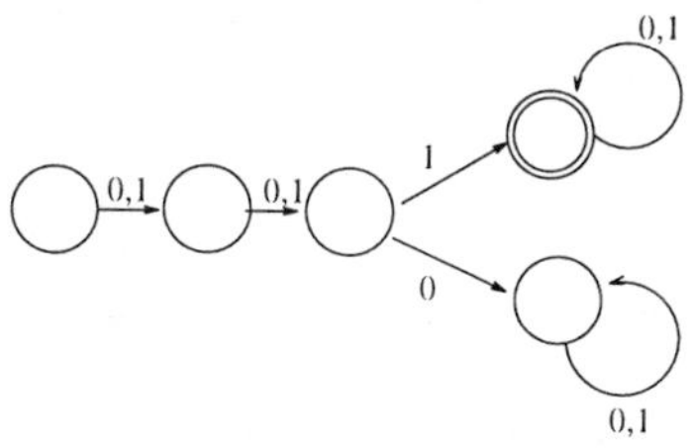

Figure 6. A five-state tree automaton.

In this experiment we compared Elman's Simple Recurrent Network [Elman, 1990a] against NARX networks. Each network had six hidden nodes. Since the output of each hidden node in an Elman network is fed back, there were six delay elements (states) in the network. The NARX network had six feedback delays from the output node. Thus, the two architectures have the exact same number of weights, hidden nodes, and states. The initial weights were randomly distributed in the range $[-0.5, 0.5]$.

For each simulation, we randomly generated a training set and an independent testing set, each consisting of 500 strings of length T such that there were an equal number of positive and negative strings. We varied T from 10 to 30. For the accepted strings, a target value of 0.8 was chosen, for the rejected strings -0.8 was chosen.

The network was trained using a simple BPTT algorithm with a learning rate 0.01 for a maximum of 200 epochs. If the simulation exceeded 200 epochs and did not correctly classify all strings in the training set, then the simulation was ruled a failure. We found that when the network learned the training set perfectly, then it consistently performed perfectly on the testing set as well. For each value of T, we ran 80 simulations.

Figure 7 shows a plot of the percentage of the runs that were successful in each case. It is clear from this plot that the NARX network performs far better than the Elman network at learning long-term dependencies.

We also wanted to see how the performance varied due to different numbers of output delays. We chose three different networks in which the size of the output tapped delay line was chosen to be either 2, 4, or 6. To make the total number of trainable weights comparable, the networks had 11, 8, and 6 hidden nodes

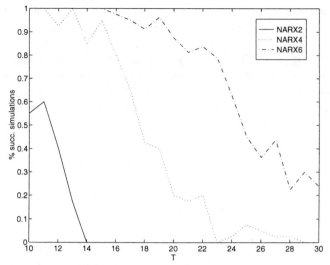

Figure 7: Plots of percentage of successful simulations as a function of T, the length of input strings, for the Elman networks vs. NARX networks.

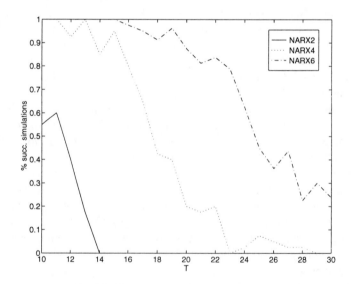

Figure 8: Plots of percentage of successful simulations as a function of T, the length of the input strings, for NARX networks with different numbers of output delays ($D = 2$, $D = 4$, $D = 6$).

respectively, giving 56, 57, and 55 weights.

Figure 8 shows the result of the experiment. It is clear that the sensitivity to the long-term dependencies decreases as the number of output delays increases.

VI. CONCLUSION

In this paper we considered an architectural approach to dealing with the problem of learning long–term dependencies, i.e., when the desired output depends on inputs presented at times far in the past, which has been shown to be a difficult problem to learn for gradient-based algorithms. We explored the ability of a class of architectures called NARX recurrent neural networks to solve such problems. We found that although NARX networks do not circumvent this problem, it is easier to discover long–term dependencies with gradient-descent in these architectures than in architectures without output delays. This has been observed previously, in the sense that gradient-descent learning appeared to be more effective in NARX networks than in recurrent neural network architectures that have "hidden states" on problems including grammatical inference and nonlinear system identification [Giles, 1994, Horne, 1995].

The intuitive explanation for this behavior is that the output delays are manifested as jump–ahead connections in the unfolded network that is often used to describe algorithms like backpropagation through time. Another explanation is that the states do not necessarily need to propagate through nonlinearities at every time step, which may avoid a degradation in gradient due to the partial derivative of the nonlinearity.

We presented an analytical example that showed that the gradients do not vanish as quickly in NARX networks as they do in networks without multiple delays when the network is contained in a fixed point. We also presented two experimental problems which show that NARX networks can outperform networks with single delays on some simple problems involving long–term dependencies.

We speculate that similar results could be obtained for other networks. In particular we hypothesize that any network that uses tapped delay feedback [Back, 1991, Leighton, 1991] would demonstrate improved performance on problems involving long–term dependencies. It may also be possible to obtain similar results for the architectures proposed in de Vries [1992], Frasconi [1992], Poddar [1991], and Wan [1994].

ACKNOWLEDGMENTS

We would like to acknowledge Andrew Back, Yoshua Bengio, and Juergen Schmidhuber for useful discussions and suggestions. We would also like to thank the anonymous reviewers for helpful suggestions that greatly improved this manuscript.

APPENDIX: A CLOSER LOOK AT ROBUST INFORMATION LATCHING

In this section we make a critical examination of the definition of robust latching given by Bengio et al.[Bengio, 1994]. Specifically, they assume that if a network is to be robust to noise, then the states must always be in the reduced attracting set of the hyperbolic attractor. While such a condition is sufficient to latch information robustly, it is not necessary. In this section we show how robustness may be redefined to be both necessary and sufficient.

First, Bengio et al. assume the existence of a "class–determining" subsystem that computes information about the class of an input sequence v. If, say, only the first L values in the input sequence (to be classified) are relevant for determining the class of v, the output of the subsystem is some valuable signal of length L, coding the class, whereas the outputs at times greater than L are unimportant and can be considered minor fluctuations. In their experiments, the fluctuations are modeled as a zero–mean Gaussian noise with a small variance.

The outputs $u(t)$ of the class–determining subsystem feed a latching subsystem,

$$S: \quad \tilde{\mathbf{x}}(t) = M(\tilde{\mathbf{x}}(t - 1)) + u(t) . \tag{19}$$

It will be useful to consider the corresponding autonomous dynamical system

$$S_A: \quad \mathbf{x}(t) = M(\mathbf{x}(t - 1)) . \tag{20}$$

The key role in latching the class information of $\{\tilde{\mathbf{x}}(t)\}$ in S is played by the hyperbolic attractors of $\{\mathbf{x}(t)\}$ in S_A. It is assumed that the important class information is coded in the first L time steps of $u(t)$; inputs at times $t > L$ are unimportant and can be considered as noise. Note that this is the key reason why Bengio et al. needed to assume the existence of a class–determining subsystem, which will somehow "highlight" the important information at times $t \leq L$, but suppress the information in the succeeding times steps.

The important inputs at times $t \leq L$, cause the states $\tilde{\mathbf{x}}(t)$ to move to the "vicinity" of a hyperbolic attractor X of S_A. If the values of $u(t)$ for $t > L$ are sufficiently small, then the states of S will not move away from X, thus latching the information coded in $u(1), \dots, u(L)$ for an arbitrary long time.

Having established this scenario for latching information of possibly long input sequences, Bengio et al. discuss what it means for the system to be robust. Specifically, they allow the input to be noisy but bounded, i.e., $\|u(t)\| < b(t)$ such that the latching system S initiated in a state from $\Gamma(X)$, receiving additive inputs bounded by $b(t)$, will stay in a vicinity of X.

They conclude that $\Gamma(X)$ is a subset of the basin of attraction $\beta(X)$ of X (in S_A), such that for all $\mathbf{x} \in \Gamma(X)$ and $l \geq 1$, the eigenvalues of $J_{\mathbf{x}}(t, l)$ are contained within the unit circle. Such a set is called "the reduced attracting set of X." Specific bounds of $b(t)$ are given so that $\tilde{\mathbf{x}}(t)$ is asymptotically guaranteed to stay within a prescribed neighborhood of X.

They point out that if the network is to latch information robustly, then it must necessarily suffer from the problem of vanishing gradients, i.e., $\mathbf{x}(t) \in \Gamma(X)$ implies $\|J_\mathbf{x}(\tau, 1)\| = \|\nabla_{\mathbf{x}(\tau)}\mathbf{x}(\tau + 1)\| < 1$, for $t \le \tau < T$ and therefore when $t \ll T$, we have $\|\nabla_{\mathbf{x}(t)}\mathbf{x}(T)\| \to 0$.

While their analysis is valuable for pointing out problems associated with learning long–term dependencies using gradient-descent methods, their definition of robustness is too strong. In the remainder of this section we discuss conditions that are both necessary and sufficient for the network to be robust to noise.

Bengio *et al.* require that $\Gamma(X)$ be the reduced attracting set of X, but it is sufficient to find a set of possible states in the basin of attraction of X such that the system $\mathcal{S}$, fed with sufficiently small inputs $u(t)$, does not diverge from X.

A useful formalization of this idea in dynamical systems' theory is stated in terms of the *shadowing lemma* [Coven, 1988, Garzon, 1994]. Given a number $b > 0$, a b–pseudo–orbit of the system $\mathcal{S}_A$ is a sequence $\{\tilde{\mathbf{x}}(t)\}$ such that $\|M(\tilde{\mathbf{x}}(t)) - \tilde{\mathbf{x}}(t + 1)\| < b$, for all $t \ge 0$. Pseudo–orbits arise as trajectories of the autonomous system $\mathcal{S}_A$ contaminated by a noise bounded by b. One may ask to what extent such "corrupted" state trajectories $\{\tilde{\mathbf{x}}(t)\}$ are informative about the "real" trajectories $\{\mathbf{x}(t)\}$ of the autonomous system $\mathcal{S}_A$. It turns out that in systems having the so-called *shadowing property*, corrupted state trajectories are "shadowed" by real trajectories within a distance depending on the level of the input noise. Bigger noise implies looser shadowing of the corrupted trajectory by an uncorrupted one. Formally, system $\mathcal{S}_A$ has a shadowing property if for every $\epsilon > 0$, there exists a $b > 0$, such that any b–pseudo–orbit $\{\tilde{\mathbf{x}}(t)\}$ is ϵ–approximated by an actual orbit of $\mathcal{S}_A$ initiated in some state $\mathbf{x}(0)$, i.e., $\|\tilde{\mathbf{x}}(t) - M^t(\mathbf{x}(0))\| < \epsilon$, where M^t means the composition of M with itself t times, and M^0 is the identity map.

It is proved in Garzon [1994] that, except possibly for small exceptional sets, discrete–time analog neural networks do have the shadowing property. In particular, they show that that the shadowing property holds for networks with sigmoidal (i.e., strictly increasing, bounded form above and below, and continuously differentiable) activation functions.

As long as $\mathcal{S}_A$ has the shadowing property, it is sufficient to pick arbitrary small $\epsilon > 0$ and start in a point $\tilde{\mathbf{x}}(0) \in \beta(X)$ whose distance from the border of $\beta(X)$ is at least ϵ. Then there exists a bound b on additive noise $u(t)$ such that a "corrupted" trajectory $\{\tilde{\mathbf{x}}(t)\}$ of $\mathcal{S}_A$ (i.e., a trajectory of $\mathcal{S}$) will be "shadowed" by a real trajectory $\{\mathbf{x}(t)\}$ of $\mathcal{S}_A$ originating in some $\mathbf{x}(0)$ from the ϵ–neighborhood of $\tilde{\mathbf{x}}(0)$. Since $\mathbf{x}(0) \in \beta(X)$, $\{\mathbf{x}(t)\}$ converges to X and so $\tilde{\mathbf{x}}(t)$ will not move away from X. Smaller ϵ results in tighter bounds b.

Hence, to achieve a "robust" latch of an information to an attractor X, it is not strictly necessary for the states to be in the reduced attracting set of X. In fact, for every state $\tilde{\mathbf{x}}(0)$ from the basin of attraction $\beta(X)$ of X, there exists a bound on additive inputs $u(t)$ such that $\{\tilde{\mathbf{x}}(t)\}$ will asymptotically stay in an ϵ–neighborhood of X.

REFERENCES

Back, A. D., Tsoi, A. C., FIR and IIR synapses, a new neural network architecture for time series modeling, *Neural Computation*, 3(3), 375, 1991.

Bengio, Y., Simard, P., Frasconi, P., Learning long-term dependencies with gradient is difficult, *IEEE Transactions on Neural Networks*, 5(2), 157, 1994.

Chen, S., Billings, S. A., Grant, P. M., Non-linear system identification using neural networks, *International Journal of Control*, 51(6), 1191, 1990.

Connor, J., Atlas, L. E., Martin, D. R., Recurrent networks and NARMA modeling. In Moody, J. E., Hanson, S. J., Lippmann, R. P., editors, *Advances in Neural Information Processing Systems*, 4, 301, 1992.

Coven, E., Kan, I., Yorke, J., Pseudo-orbit shadowing in the family of tent maps, *Transactions AMS*, 308, 227, 1988.

de Vries, B., Principe, J. C., The gamma model — A new neural model for temporal processing, *Neural Networks*, 5, 565, 1992.

Elman, J. L., Finding structure in time, *Cognitive Science*, 14, 179, 1990.

Frasconi, P., Gori, M., Maggini, M., Soda, G., Unified integration of explicit rules and learning by example in recurrent networks, *IEEE Transactions on Knowledge and Data Engineering*, 7(2), 340, 1995.

Frasconi, P., Gori, M., Soda, G., Local feedback multilayered networks, *Neural Computation*, 4, 120, 1992.

Garzon, M. F., Botelho, F., Observability of neural network behavior. In Cowen, J. D., Tesauro, G., Alspector, J., editors, *Advances in Neural Information Processing Systems*, 6, 455, Morgan Kaufmann, 1994.

Giles, C. L., Horne, B. G., Representation and learning in recurrent neural network architectures, in *Proceedings of the Eighth Yale Workshop on Adaptive and Learning Systems*, 128, 1994.

Gori, M., Maggini, M., Soda, G., Scheduling of modular architectures for inductive inference of regular grammars, in *ECAI'94 Workshop on Combining Symbolic and Connectionist Processing, Amsterdam*, 78, Wiley, 1994.

Hihi, S., Bengio, Y., Hierarchical recurrent neural networks for long-term dependencies. *Advances in Neural Information Processing Systems*, 8, MIT Press, 1996.

Hochreiter, S., Schmidhuber, J., Long short term memory. Forschungsberichte Künstliche Intelligenz FKI-207-95, Institut für Informatik, Technische Universität München, 1995.

Horne, B. G., Giles, C. L., An experimental comparison of recurrent neural networks. In *Advances in Neural Information Processing Systems 7*, 697, MIT Press, 1995.

Kailath, T., *Linear Systems*, Prentice Hall, Englewood Cliffs, NJ, 1980.

Khalil, Hassan K, *Nonlinear Systems*, Macmillan Publishing Company, New York, 1992.

Leighton, R. R., Conrath, B. C., The autoregressive backpropagation algorithm, *Proceedings of the International Joint Conference on Neural Networks*, 2, 369, 1991.

Leontaritis, I. J., Billings, S. A., Input-output parametric models for non-linear systems: Part I: Deterministic non-linear systems, *International Journal of Control*, 41(2), 303, 1985.

Ljung, L., *System Identification: Theory for the User*, Prentice-Hall, Englewood Cliffs, NJ, 1987.

Mozer, M. C., Induction of multiscale temporal structure. In Moody, J. E., Hanson, S. J., Lippmann, R. P., editors, *Advances in Neural Information Processing Systems*, 4, 275, Morgan Kaufmann, 1992.

Narendra, K. S., Parthasarathy, K., Identification and control of dynamical systems using neural networks, *IEEE Transactions on Neural Networks*, 1, 4, 1990.

Nerrand, O., Roussel-Ragot, P., Personnaz, L., Dreyfus, G., Marcos, S., Neural networks and nonlinear adaptive filtering: Unifying concepts and new algorithms, *Neural Computation*, 5(2), 165, 1993.

Poddar, P., Unnikrishnan, K. P., Non–linear prediction of speech signals using memory neuron networks. In Juang, B., H., Kung, S., Y., Kamm, C., A., editors, *Neural Networks for Signal Processing: Proceedings of the 1991 IEEE Workshop*, 1, IEEE Press, 1991.

Puskorius, G. V., Feldkamp, L. A., Neurocontrol of nonlinear dynamical systems with Kalman filter-trained recurrent networks, *IEEE Transactions on Neural Networks*, 5(2), 279, 1994.

Qin, S.-Z., Su, H.-T., McAvoy, T. J., Comparison of four neural net learning methods for dynamic system identification, *IEEE Transactions on Neural Networks*, 3(1), 122, 1992.

Rumelhart, D. E., Hinton, G. E., Williams, R. J., Learning internal representations by error propagation. In Rumelhart, D. E., McClelland, J. L., editors, *Parallel Distributed Processing: Explorations in the Microstructure of Cognition*, 318, MIT Press, 1986.

Schmidhuber, J., Learning complex, extended sequences using the principle of history compression, *Neural Computation*, 4(2), 234, 1992.

Schmidhuber, J., Learning unambiguous reduced sequence descriptions. In Moody, J. E., Hanson, S. J., Lippman, R. P., editors, *Advances in Neural Information Processing Systems*, 4, 291, Morgan Kaufmann, 1992.

Seidl, D. R., Lorenz, D., A structure by which a recurrent neural network can approximate a nonlinear dynamic system. In *Proceedings of the International Joint Conference on Neural Networks*, 2, 709, 1991.

Siegelmann, H. T., Horne, B. G., Giles, C. L., Computational capabilities of recurrent NARX neural networks, *IEEE Transactions on Systems, Man and Cybernetics*, Accepted. Also, Technical report UMIACS-TR-95-78 and CS-TR-3500, University of Maryland, College Park, MD, 1996.

Siegelmann, H. T., Sontag, E. D., On the computational power of neural networks, *Journal of Computer and System Science*, 50(1), 132, 1995.

Sontag., E. D., Systems combining linearity and saturations and relations to neural networks, Technical Report SYCON–92–01, Rutgers Center for Systems and Control, 1992.

Su, H. T., McAvoy, T. J., Identification of chemical processes using recurrent networks, *Proceedings of the American Controls Conference*, 3, 2314, 1991.

Su, H.-T.,McAvoy, T. J., Werbos, P., Long–term predictions of chemical processes using recurrent neural networks: A parallel training approach, *Industrial Engineering and Chemical Research*, 31, 1338, 1992.

Venkataraman, S. T., On encoding nonlinear oscillations in neural networks for locomotion. In *Proceedings of the Eighth Yale Workshop on Adaptive and Learning Systems*, 14, 1994.

Wan, E. A., Time series prediction by using a connectionist network with internal delay lines. In A.S. Weigend and N.A. Gershenfeld, editors, *Time Series Prediction*, 195, Addison–Wesley, 1994.

Williams R. J., Zipser, D., Gradient-based learning algorithms for recurrent networks and their computational complexity. In Y. Chauvin and D. E. Rumelhart, editors, *Back-propagation: Theory, Architectures and Applications*, 433, Lawrence Erlbaum Publishers, 1995.

Chapter 7

OSCILLATION RESPONSES IN A CHAOTIC RECURRENT NETWORK

Judith E. Dayhoff

Complexity Research Solutions, Inc.
Silver Spring, MD

Peter J. Palmadesso

Plasma Physics Division
Naval Research Laboratory
Washington, D.C.

Fred Richards

Dynamic Software Solutions
Alexandria, VA

I. INTRODUCTION

Dynamic neural networks are capable of prolonged self-sustained activity patterns, in which each neuron has an activation level that can change over time, and different neurons can be at different levels, with different changes over time. An enormous repertoire of self-sustained activity patterns is possible, due to the wide variety of oscillations that networks can engage in. Oscillations include n-state oscillations (repeating finite sequences of states), limit cycles (quasiperiodic), and chaos. An infinitude of different oscillations is possible for each type. The resulting set of possible oscillations and activity patterns has potential for increasing the capacity and capability of neural networks for computational purposes. Whereas feedforward neural networks have extensive applications in recognition and control, with many highly successful performances in applications, their output is a fixed vector. Single-layer networks, such as those studied by Hopfield, have fixed vectors (stable states) as output. In contrast, dynamic networks can produce a wide variety of oscillations as output, and enhanced computational properties are expected to be realized by dynamic neural networks that oscillate.

Recently, neurobiological investigators have suggested that the brain may use chaotic behavior and oscillatory states to store and recognize patterns, and that chaotic states are "waiting" states, whereas simpler oscillators are recognition and response states [Yao and Freeman, 1990, Yao et al, 1991, Freeman et al., 1988]. Theoretical investigations have shown a tremendous variety of oscillatory states possible, and systematic ways to produce chaos in a network, along with a progression of oscillatory states moving a network from a fixed point to chaos [Sompolinsky et al., 1988, Doyon et al., 1993, Palmadesso and Dayhoff, 1994]. Some investigators have researched computations that use limit cycles, strange attractors, chaos, or transient behaviors in associative memory or information processing models [Kumagai et al. , 1996, Yao, 1991, Chapeau-Blondeau, 1993, Moreira and Auto, 1993, Dmitriev et al., 1993, Dmitriev and Kuminov, 1994, Hjelmfelt and Ross, 1994, Wang, 1996, Lin et al., 1995, Dayhoff et al., 1998]. These studies make it natural to suggest that new paradigms using oscillations as final states are likely to enhance the development of powerful methods for information processing with artificial neural networks. This prospect has received increasing research interest recently and requires more characterization of dynamic network activities.

Here we study chaotic neural networks that can be used to produce pattern-to-oscillation maps. First, chaotic behavior is developed in a sparsely connected neural network with random weights, as described by Doyon [Doyon et al., 1993], [Doyon et al., 1994]. To the chaotic network, an external pattern is applied and the network usually locks into a simpler dynamic attractor, consisting of a limit cycle or simple n-state oscillator. A range of intensity for the applied pattern has been considered, and the resulting attractor changes as the intensity is increased. An increase in intensity eventually results in a stable fixed-point attractor. When different patterns are applied with the same intensity, they evoke different oscillations and differing dynamic activities. Adjusting the pattern intensity helps to produce a pattern-to-oscillation map. This approach has promise for developing paradigms in which the evoked attractor represents a memory, pattern class, or optimization result. The neural network model used in this chapter differs from that of other investigators cited above, except for previous work by Samuelides and coworkers [Cessac, 1994, Cessac et al., 1994, Cessac, 1995, Cessac and Quoy, 1995, Doyon et al., 1993, Quoy et al., 1995], who have presented a variety of theoretical results for the network's dynamics without an applied external pattern, and have found positive results on Hebbian weight adjustment in the presence of applied external patterns. Here we present results on the effects of variations in pattern strengths, the adaptation of the pattern strength variable, and the responses of the network to noisy patterns.

In Section 2, we illustrate a progression to chaos in a network with no stimulus patterns [Doyon et al., 1993]. A series of different attractors is obtained. Different initial states usually do not evoke different attractors. The application of external patterns to the network is addressed in Section 3. Effects of increasing pattern strengths are shown, and capacity and uniqueness of evoked oscillations is illustrated. Some resilience to pattern noise is attained. Dynamic adjustment of pattern strength is described in Section 4, which results in a pattern-to-oscillation map that is unique and results in a low complexity oscillator in response to each pattern. Further characteristics of the pattern-to-oscillation map, including resilience to pattern noise, are discussed in Section 5. The impact of this type of approach is discussed in Section 6.

II. PROGRESSION TO CHAOS

Dynamic attractors can be developed in a random neural network, and a progression from a single fixed-point stable state to a chaotic oscillation can be obtained. The construction of the network is as follows. A random network with full or sparse interconnections is configured as a single layer of neurons, where closed-loop connections are allowed and weights are set at random. A multiplier g can be applied to all of the weights at the same time, and, when g is increased sufficiently, chaotic behavior occurs [Sompolinsky et al., 1988, Doyon et al., 1993]. Thus the network can be modulated into a chaotic state. The neural units are simple biologically inspired units, performing a weighted sum.

$$a_j(t+1) = f\left(\sum_{i=1}^{N} gw_{ji} a_i(t) \right) \tag{1}$$

where $a_j(t)$ = activation of unit j at time t, w_{ji} = weight to unit j from unit i, N = the number of processing units, g a multiplier, and f a nonlinear squashing function. The squashing function used in our experiments was

$$f(x) = \left[\frac{1}{1 + e^{-x}} - 0.5 \right] * 2 \tag{2}$$

Reciprocal connections did not have to be the same (e.g., $w_{ij} \neq w_{ji}$), and self-loops were suppressed in our experiments as a simplification. The activation values could vary from -1.0 to 1.0, and the parameter g is a multiplier for all weights and can be set at any value greater than zero. The interconnections and weights were chosen at random. Networks were denoted as (N, K), where N was the total number of processing units, and K the number of incoming interconnections for each unit. The K units that sent interconnections to each unit were selected at random, and the values of the weights were selected from a uniform random distribution [-1,1], with the random variable divided by K, as specified in Doyon et al., [1993]. With this model, we have examined a variety of paths from single fixed-point attractors to chaos.

The parameter g is a multiplier for all weights. Thus, the original set of weights becomes amplified or de-amplified depending on whether g>1 or g<1. A stronger set of driving forces is then presented to each neuron as g increases above 1. The incoming sum for neuron j is

$$S_j = \sum gw_{ji} a_i \tag{3}$$

and the modulated weight is gw_{ji}. The neuron then performs the squashing function to determine its next activation value:

$$a_j(t+1) = f(S_j) \qquad (4)$$

The parameter g can also be considered as a scaling of the x-axis in the squashing function. Organizing equation (1) differently, we get

$$R_j = \sum_{i=1}^{N} w_{ij} a_i(t) \qquad (5)$$

where R_j is now the incoming sum for unit j, and

$$a_j(t+1) = f_g R_j \qquad (6)$$

where $f_g = f(gx)$, a sigmoid squashing function with a re-scaled horizontal axis. Here the weight is not modulated by g, but the horizontal scale of the sigmoid is modulated by g. In both contexts, g is key to producing chaos.

Figure 1 shows the symmetric sigmoid function, with the x=y line. Figure 2 shows the function f_{10}, which compresses the horizontal direction of the squashing function so that two pockets form, bounded in part by the x=y line. This curvature in turn causes there to be two absorbing states, at the upper and lower intersections, for the single neuron case [Dayhoff, 1998]. It is thus not surprising that dynamic attractors - oscillations and chaos - develop at increased values of g.

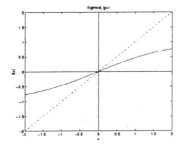

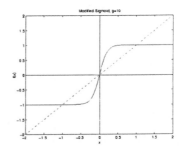

Figure 1. Symetric sigmoid function, with the x=y line

Figure 2. Modified sigmoid function with g=10

A network with 64 units, each with 16 incoming connections, was constructed with random initial weights. Transitions from fixed-point attractors to chaotic attractors were observed as g was increased starting from numbers below 1.0. Figure 3 illustrates such a progression, from a fixed point attractor to a chaotic attractor, with average activation a(t+1) graphed as a function of a(t), to form a map of the dynamics. Use of the average activation in the plot was chosen to project the many dimensions (64 activation levels) to a single measured observation over time.

For low values of g (e.g., g=0.9), a single fixed-point attractor was observed, shown in Figure 3(a), which has a single point at (0,0). When g was increased to 1.0, a limit cycle appeared (Figure 3(b)), consisting of a dense set of points along a closed loop. When g was increased to 1.1, the four corners of the closed loop became pointed, and the span of the graph increased from +/- 0.025 to +/- 0.04 (Figure 3(c)). When g was increased to 1.2, the limit cycle took on a new shape along the x=y diagonal, with an expansion in range to within +/- 0.08 (Figure 3(d)). In Figure 3(e), g was increased to 1.3, and the limit cycle developed several wiggles, and expanded in range to +/- 0.1. When g=1.4 (Figure3 (f)), the wiggles appear deeper, and the span increases to within +/- 0.15. When g was increased to 1.5, the previously observed closed loop appears to have changed to a figure that roughly outlines the previous loop several times, with different variations each time, and gives the appearance of scribbling (Figure 3(g)). When g=1.6, a locking occurs into a finite-state oscillator (Figure 3(h)). When g=1.7 (Figure 3(i)), chaotic or irregular behavior occurs. This type of progression shows the tremendous range and complexity of dynamic attractors and the ability to exert some control over their appearance, through varying the single parameter g. Figure 3 illustrates a progression for one network of 64 neurons; Doyon and colleagues [Doyon et al., 1993] have characterized four types of paths to chaos in networks of 128 neurons. In some cases, increasing the number of iterations calculated allowed activity that appeared chaotic to resolve into a limit cycle. Sometimes the number of transients in these cases would be too large to be practical to implement in a computational application. Thus, for practical use to be made of dynamic neural networks, a "chaotic" response would be considered to be behavior that appeared to be chaotic in a limited predefined time frame

A. ACTIVITY MEASUREMENTS

We have experimented with measurements that reflect the type of activity observed in the maps drawn in Figure 3. An activity measurement was computed by an algorithm that uses the average activation over the entire network over a period of time, usually 1000 iterations of Equation (1). The range of the graph of a(t) versus a(t+1), as in Figure 3, is defined to cover the points generated by the n iterations used. The graph is then divided into a 10 by 10 grid, with evenly spaced lines. The percentage of non-empty grid squares is the grid coverage. Grid coverage tends to reflect the types of activity shown in Figure 3, and thus can be used as an appropriate measurement or reflection of the network's activity.

Chaotic behavior such as in Figure 3(i) tends to have coverage values in the range >73. Limit cycles tend to be in the range 43-57, and n-state oscillations, such as Figure 3(h) are in a range >2, usually small. The coverage measurement can be used in the method shown next for adjusting the pattern strengths in the pattern-to-oscillation map. Other measurements of activity could be substituted for grid coverage. Ideally, the best activity measurement would be always high when chaotic, irregular behavior occurs and progressively lower as the network dynamics progresses to a fixed point. Although the grid coverage usually adheres to this pattern, there are exceptions.

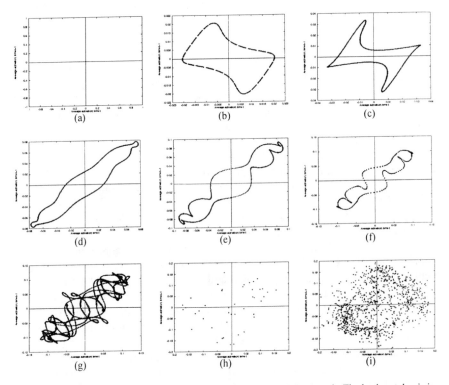

Figure 3. Progession from fixed point to chaos in a random (64, 16) network. The horizontal axis is average activation at time t+1, a(t-1) and the vertical axis is average activation at time t, a(t). (a) g=0.9, (b) g= 1.0, (c) g=1.1, (d) g=1.2, (e) g=1.3, (f) g=1.4, (g) g =1.5, (h) g=1.6, (i) g=1.7

Figure 4 shows the coverage measurement graphed versus the value of the multiplier g, for two different networks. The coverage measurement is 1 for small values of g, and then increases until the coverage value is consistently at a high level, generally above about 70. Usually, once a high level of coverage is attained, reflecting irregular activity or chaos, higher values of g continue to evoke high coverage levels. The lowest value of g for which a high coverage level is attained is an indicator that the network is at the "edge of chaos".

B. DIFFERENT INITIAL STATES

It is computationally interesting to find a paradigm whereby a pattern-to-oscillation map can be produced, because then the initial state of the network could be set from a pattern vector, and the evoked oscillation could represent a pattern class or other computational answer evoked by the initial pattern. We first explored whether different initial states of the network would produce different attractors in the random networks described above, but were not satisfied with the potential of this approach, as described next.

We generated a series of random networks with a (64,16) configuration, as described in Section 2. A series of random pattern vectors were used as initial states to the network. The resulting attractor was then observed. In most cases, only one attractor was observed, which was reached from a wide variety of initial states. The initial states in this experiment were generated at random from a [-1,1] uniform distribution. Sometimes there were two attractors (limit cycles or n-state oscillations), reached from different initial states, but they were symmetric with one another, having a 180 degree rotational symmetry about the origin. Figure 5 illustrates such an example. About half of the initial states (taken at random) evoked each attractor. Although different initial conditions could evoke different (but symmetric) limit cycles in this case, this scenario does not offer enough flexibility to discriminate patterns by the limit cycles they evoke.

Occasionally, different attractors were observed from different initial states during our simulations of networks with random weights. This circumstance was very rare among our observations, and in these cases the parameter g was first tuned to be very near a bifurcation point. Figure 6 shows such an example. Figure 6(a) shows an 8-state oscillator. This occurs at g=1.72 in a (64,16) random network. Figure 6(b) shows the same network except that a different initial state was selected at random. The 8 points appear to have bifurcated into 8 rings, which are asymmetric about the origin. A third random initial state evoked the limit cycle in 6 (c), which is symmetric to that in 6 (b). It was also possible to evoke an oscillator symmetric to that of 6(a) with other initial states. Although different initial conditions evoke different attractors in this case, this scenario also does not offer enough flexibility to discriminate many patterns by the limit cycles they evoke. However, this does not rule out the possibility of creating intricate and desired distinctions between different types of initial states according to which attractor is evoked if suitable weight adjustments are made.

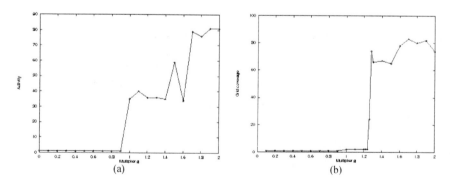

(a)   (b)

Figure 4. Activity level – in this case, coverage level – as a function of g, for two different networks. (a) For this network, a bifurcation was exhibited when g = 0.9, to generate an oscillation instead of a fixed point. The map appeared chaotic when g reached 1.7, and for higher values of g. (b) For this network, a rapid set of bifurcations occurred to generate oscillations at g = 1.26 and the coverage of the map was above 60 until g = 1.6, where chaotic behavior occurred. Both networks were (64,16) with randomly assigned weights as described in Section A.

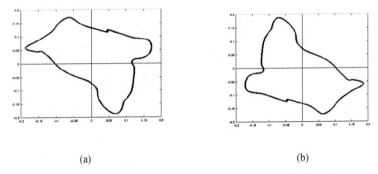

(a)   (b)

Figure 5. Symmetric attractors evoked by different initial states in the same network. The initial state of the network was set so that neuron activation levels matched a random pattern vector E ($a_i(0) \leftarrow e_i$).

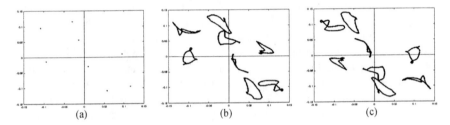

(a)   (b)   (c)

Figure 6. A case where different initial states lead to different attractors, from a random (64,16) network. (a) An 8-state oscillator (b) A limit cycle with 8 closed loops (c) A limit cycle symmetric to part (a).

III. EXTERNAL PATTERNS

Next, we treat a pattern vector as an external stimulus, to overcome the limitations in flexibility encountered when patterns are applied as initial states. To include an external stimulus, the updating equation for the neurons (1) can be modified as follows:

$$a_j(t+1) = f\left(\sum_{i=1}^{N} gw_{ji} a_i(t) + \alpha e_i \right) \tag{7}$$

where $E=(e_1,e_2,...,e_n)$ is the external input pattern. The input E is then applied at every time step, and its strength is modulated by the multiplier α. The vector E can then be assigned as a pattern to be classified, and a pattern-to-oscillation map can be generated.

The network is initially put in a chaotic oscillation. The chaotic net does not have an external stimulus, and updates by (1). To produce the chaotic network, the parameter g is increased until the network reaches chaotic behavior. Typically, we do not increase g more than is necessary to produce chaotic behavior, so the network can be said to be at the "edge of chaos". An external input E is then applied to the chaotic net, and the network uses (7) to update. The externally applied input usually "locks" the chaotic network into a simpler attractor, often a limit cycle. This scenario can thus be called "attractor locking".

The attractor that results depends on the characteristics of the externally applied pattern (for the same network) and the weights and configuration of the network. A chaotic network was updated for varying amounts of time without an external input, and regardless of when E was applied, the same dynamic attractor was observed. Figure 7 shows the results when a chaotic behaving network receives an external stimulus pattern. The graph of Figure 7(a) shows activity of the chaotic network, without any applied pattern. The other graphs show the results of applying different external patterns. The patterns were generated at random from a uniform distribution [-1,1].

A. PROGRESSION FROM CHAOS TO A FIXED POINT

Each pattern has a strength, α, as shown in equation (7). As the pattern strength α is increased, the dynamics of the network's activity moves through a progression to a fixed point. In all cases examined, a sufficiently high α produced a fixed point. Figure 8 shows the progression of a network's dynamics as a function of α ((a)-(i)), from chaos (a) to a fixed point (i). One external pattern, at increasing strengths, was applied to the same chaotic network.

Figure 9(a) shows activity measurements as a function of α for the same network. Figure 9(b) is based on another random network, with a different random pattern. The activity measurement always starts high (generally >73), which is indicative of chaotic oscillation. When α is increased, there is a point at which the activity measurement enters a mode that has limit cycles or finite state oscillations (usually activity values of about 2-57). At sufficiently high α, the activity becomes a fixed point. These transitions happen at different values for α for the two examples shown in Figure 9.

B. QUICK RESPONSE

Figure 10 shows the results of applying an external pattern to a network, including transients before a limit cycle is obtained. All points were plotted after application of the external pattern. The transients were included in the figure to illustrate that sometimes very few transients occur after the external pattern is applied and before the limit cycle is attained. The possibility for fast classification to occur when a network is initially in a chaotic state has been suggested by Freeman [Yao and Freeman, 1990], in reference to olfactory neural models that wait for stimuli in a chaotic state and lock into a simpler oscillation after a stimulus is received. Because such fast classification of patterns with chaotic networks is of interest, we explored the relationship between the number of transients and the value of the pattern strength, using the (64,16) networks described in Section 2.

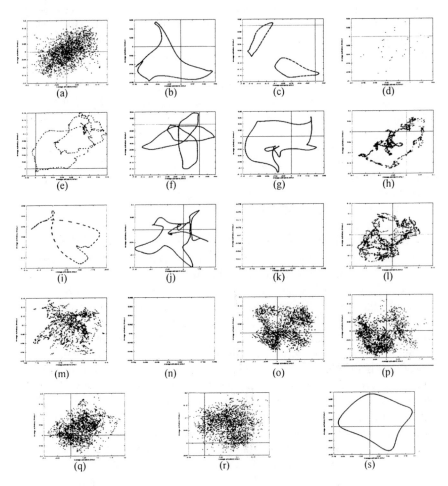

Figure 7. A chaotic network has 18 different patterns applied, with different results on the dynamics. (a) Activity of the chaotic network, before an external pattern is applied. Multiple g is set just above the value where chaotic activity occurs. (b-s) Activity of the network after 18 different patterns were applied. Evoked dynamics is highly unique. Most graphs show recognizable low-order dynamics – limit cycles and n-state oscillations – but some show chaotic (irregular) behavior and others show fixed points only. Graphs have the horizontal axis as average activation at time $t + 1$, $a(t - 1)$, and the vertical axis as average activation at time t, $a(t)$. The patterns were generated from a uniform random distribution [-1, 1].

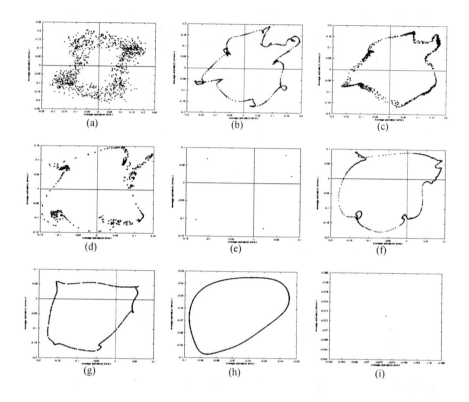

Figure 8. Progression of maps for the same pattern applied to the same chaotic network, at increasing pattern strengths.

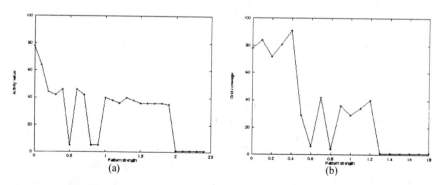

Figure 9. Activity measurement (grid coverage) as a function of pattern strength for two different patterns, applied to two different chaotic networks.

Figure 11 shows results on a random (64,16) network, where the number of observed transients is graphed as a function of pattern strength. The decrease in the number of transients above $\alpha=1.4$ correlates with a limit cycle (ring) that shrinks into a fixed point as the pattern strength increases further. In the region where $\alpha < 1.4$, there is a path from the first limit cycle, obtained at high strength, to chaos, which undergoes several transitions. Figure 11 shows a graph of number of transients as a function of α. In Figure 11, there is a peak at $\alpha=1.4$ and a decrease to $\alpha=1.2$. This observation leads to the hypothesis that there are specific conditions under which the number of transients before an attractor is reached is low, leading to fast responses and/or fast recognition.

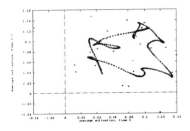

Figure 10. Results of applying an external pattern to the network

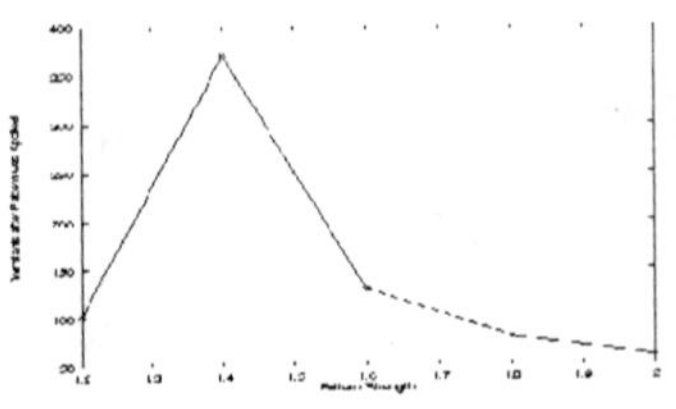

Figure 11. Observed transients as function of pattern strengths

IV. DYNAMIC ADJUSTMENT OF PATTERN STRENGTH

Our goal was to produce a pattern-to-oscillation map in which the evoked oscillation satisfies a criterion that indicated it is a relatively simple oscillation. We define a Criterion A as follows.

Criterion A:
-- A repeating sequence of states, e.g., a finite n-state oscillation $(n>1)$.
OR
-- A limit cycle (quasi-periodic).

In Figure 7, most of the evoked attractors satisfied this criterion. Several did not, and remained chaotic in appearance (Figures 7(l)(m)(o)(p)(q)(r)). It is also possible to evoke a fixed point (Figure 7(n)). Here there is no *a priori* knowledge of the best choice for α. To produce the map, a chaotic network is used. Thus, the initial parameters are (1) the network weights, randomly assigned, and (2) the connection configuration. A value of g_c for the multiplier in (1) was set just above the transition to chaotic behavior. A set of external patterns is then applied to the network, one at a time. Initially, a value for the pattern strength α_b is chosen. External patterns are then applied, each with strength α_b, as in Equation (3), with results similar to Figure 7.

The value of α_b can be chosen so that a set of random test patterns usually evokes oscillations that meet Criterion A above. Any evoked oscillation that fits criterion A is considered to be the result of the pattern-to-oscillation map.

For patterns that evoke oscillations that do not fit Criterion A, we do not yet have a suitable oscillation for the pattern-to-oscillation map. So, a procedure is used to adjust the pattern strength until an oscillation that fits Criterion A is evoked. In the end, each pattern has its own strength parameter, and each oscillation evoked fits criterion A.

The adjustment procedure is constructed based on the following observations about an activity value as a function of α

Values a, b, c, d can be set so that

1. If activity $\leq d$ then α is too high.
2. If activity $\geq c$ (chaotic), then α is too low.
3. If activity is between a and b, then a limit cycle or n-state oscillation is assumed present.

If the activity of the network is represented by the coverage value, then good cutoff values are at d=1, and approximately c=73, a=42, and b=53. If coverage value is used for the activity measurement, then Observation 3 is usually correct, and the limit cycle or n=state oscillation is assumed present.

1.	Choose α_{init}. Try to choose a value so that most typical patterns evoke limit cycles or n-state oscillations.
2.	Set δ to a small value > 0 and $\ll \alpha_{init}$
3.	Set a and b so that [a,b] is the desired window for activity measurements.

For each pattern i, do the following

4. Set $\alpha_i(1) \leftarrow \alpha_{init}$
5. Set $i_{hi} = i_{low} = 0$
6. Set k=0, iteration number
7. Increment k:= k+1
8. Measure the activity m(k) when the pattern i is applied at strength $\alpha_i(k)$. If a $\leq$ m(k) $\leq$ b, then done with pattern i
9. If m(k) < a then i_{low} = k
10. If m(k) > b then i_{hi} = k
11. If $i_{low} > 0$ and $i_{hi} > 0$ then

$$\alpha_i(k+1) = \frac{\alpha_i(i_{low}) + \alpha_i(i_{hi})}{2}$$

12. If m(k) > b and $i_{low} = 0$ then
$$\alpha_i(k+1) \leftarrow \alpha_i(k) + \delta$$
13. If m(k) < a and $I_{hi} = 0$ then
$$\alpha_i(k+1) \leftarrow \alpha_i(k) - \delta$$
14. Go to 7 for next iteration

Figure 12. Strength Adjustment Algorithm

An algorithm for pattern strength adjustment is given in Figure 12. This algorithm only uses parameters a and b, and targets [a,b] as the window for desired activity. If the activity measurement is initially too large or too small, the pattern strength is changed and a new activity measurement is taken. If this does not fall into the desired range [a,b], then the amount of change is adjusted appropriately to eventually reach the desired range.

V. CHARACTERISTICS OF THE PATTERN-TO-OSCILLATION MAP

Resilience to pattern noise has been observed in oscillations evoked by external patterns. A set of specific patterns was simulated and used as base patterns. To each base pattern, ten noisy patterns were generated by adding small random numbers to each entry. The resulting oscillation was then observed, to see how the evoked oscillations compared among the noisy versions of the same base pattern.

Figure 13 shows the result for one base pattern. The base pattern was simulated at random and applied with a strength of 1.6. The same α was used for the noisy versions of the base pattern. Figure 14 shows the same results but with a different form of display, in which successive points generated by the network are connected. Figure 14 thus reflects more of the dynamic action of the network over a progression of times. These plots were generated to see whether the building of each figure was with the same type of sequence of points, and in all cases show that the figure, roughly triangular, was constructed by sampling three points over each 360 degree traversed. Figure 14(f) in which a triangular-shaped limit cycle has split into two triangles, has the same sampling pattern of three points per 360 degrees.

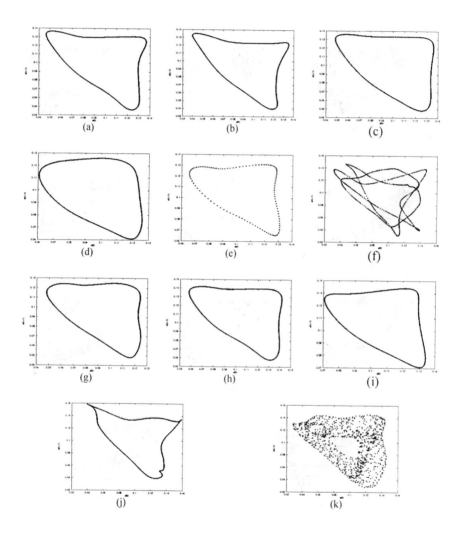

Figure 13. A chaotic network has different external patterns applied, each at strength $\alpha = 1.6$. (a) The base pattern, with 64 entries, each from a uniform random distribution (-1:1). (b-k) The base pattern with 5% noise added, to make 10 different variations of the pattern.

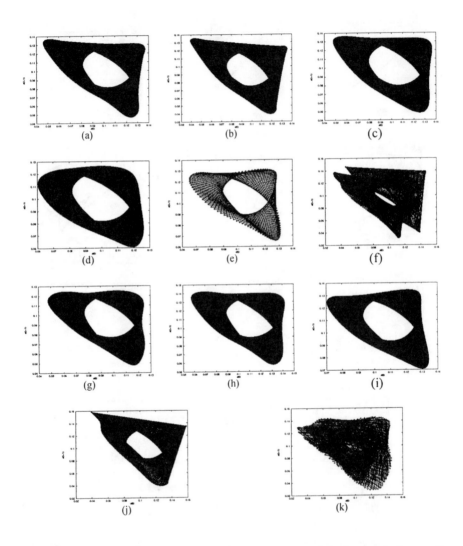

Figure 14. A chaotic network has different external patterns applied. The map is drawn with successively generated points interconnected. (a) The base pattern, with 64 entries, each from a uniform random distribution (-1:1). (b-k) The base pattern with 5% noise added, ten times to generate ten variations of the base pattern. The pattern strength $\alpha = 1.6$, and the attractors are the same as in Figure 13.

Figure 15 shows the base pattern and its ten variations, plotted together. Successive entries of the pattern vector are marked on the horizontal axis, with values in the vertical axis. The pattern entries were generated at random from a [-1,1] distribution, and the added noise was generated from a uniform random distribution [-0.05,0.05], adding 5% noise.

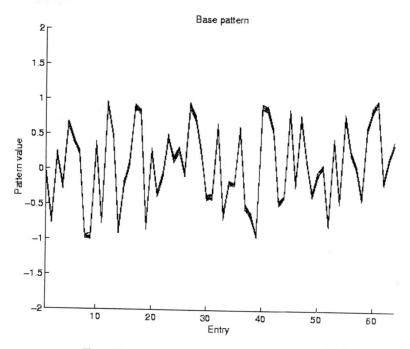

Figure 15. The base pattern and its ten variations, plotted together.

Figures 16, 17, and 18 show applications of the same base pattern as in Figures 13 and 14, with the same ten variations, to the same network, with varied pattern strengths. In Figure 16, a pattern strength of 1.4 was used, which is weaker than that in Figure 13. There is an increase in the variation among the evoked attractors in Figure 16 compared with Figure 13.

In Figure 17, a pattern strength of 1.8 was used, which is stronger than that in Figure 13. The variation in the evoked attractors was less. In Figure 18, a considerably weaker strength (1.2) was used, resulting in large amounts of variation. These preliminary results suggest that different values for the pattern strength change the map's resilience to noise, and that the oscillations show less variation at a stronger pattern strength than at weaker pattern strengths. For these figures (Figures 13-14, 16-18), the pattern strength evoked a limit cycle which was the result of the last bifurcation from the final fixed point, as in Figure 8(h).

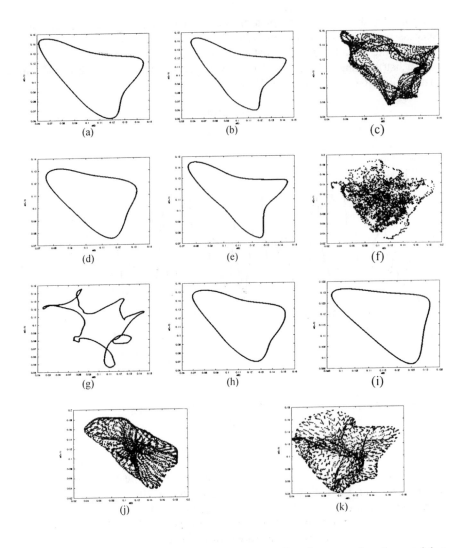

Figure 16. The base pattern (a) and its ten variations (b-k). Here the pattern strength α was 1.4, a decrease compared with Figure 13.

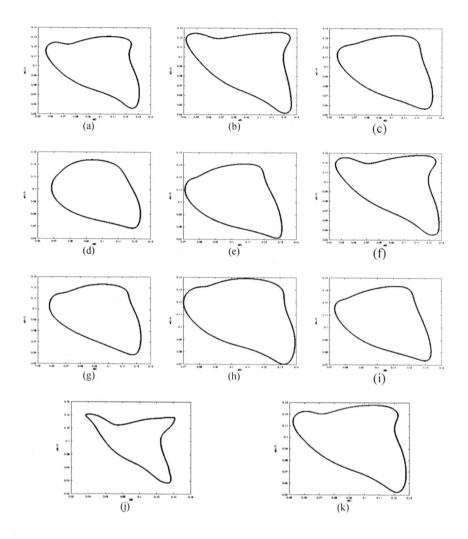

Figure 17. The base pattern (a) and its ten variations (b-k). Here the patterns strength α was 1.8, an increase compared with Figure 14. The variations between the evoked attractors is less compared with Figure 14, where α was 1.6.

171

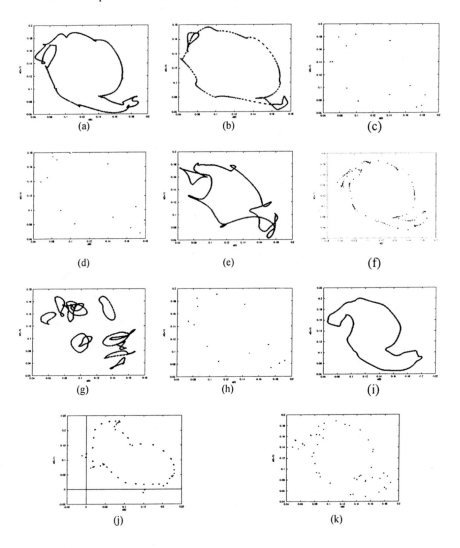

Figure 18. The base pattern (a) and its ten variations (b-k). Here the pattern strength α was 1.2, a large decrease compared with Figure 14. The variations between the evoked attractors is considerably higher compared with Figure 14, where α was 1.6.

VI. DISCUSSION

The use of an evoked oscillation when an external pattern is applied to a chaotic network forms the groundwork for a potentially powerful approach to associative memory, recognition, and other potential computational applications. A wide range of different pattern inputs can evoke unique dynamic attractors, and the entry into the attractor often occurs quite rapidly. Thus there is the potential for performing useful computations, such as pattern classification, where the attractor that is evoked would represent the pattern class, associated memory, or other computational result.

Capacity is high with the model shown here, in the sense that many different patterns can each evoke a different attractor. Whereas the Hopfield network showed a capacity of about $0.15n$ attractors (memories) for n neurons, the number of oscillation attractors that could be used in our approach far exceeds n.

A previous study has applied a Hebbian-like learning approach to reduce the dynamics from chaos to quasi-periodic attractors in the presence of an external pattern. The network's chaos is reduced during the learning of a pattern to gain a specific response of a limit cycle to the pattern [Quoy et al., 1995]. Capacity, however, was found to be seriously limited in this study, although changes in neural architecture are hoped to increase capacity. We propose here that the adjustment of α, along with Hebbian-like training, could possibly increase the capacity of such a training paradigm. Higher pattern strength α tends to evoke simpler periodic or quasi-periodic attractors. Noise resilience is demonstrated through Figures 13-18. The same pattern, with added noise, evokes similar attractors. Higher values of pattern strength α can cause the attractors to be even more similar, whereas lower values of pattern strength tend to disperse the similarities. Quantitative analysis of attractor similarity has been introduced, but the graphical presentation shown here (Figures 13-14, 16-18) was chosen to show a more complete comparison of the attractors that are evoked.

Recognition of attractors is a problem for which feedforward time-delay networks would be naturally appropriate. Previous study has shown that different closed trajectories can be learned, recognized and generated by TDNNs and ATNNs [Lin et al., 1995]. Generalization capabilities would reflect the ability of the network to recognize the boundary between one class of applied pattern and another, when new external patterns are applied. This could be tested in a combined system with a TDNN or ATNN recognizer as a post-processor.

Previous investigations have addressed the activity of the chaotic networks with a mean theory approach [Sompolinsky et al., 1988]. The result of using a fixed external pattern (a "bias") with a fixed strength, and varying the multiplier g, has been analyzed [Cessac, 1994a,b]. It is found that the distance from the highest g that evokes a fixed point to the lowest g that evokes chaos is surprisingly small, and diminishes as the number of neurons n grows, with fully connected random networks. The evolution of the neurons is a white noise in the thermodynamic limit [Cessac, 1995].

Cessac [Cessac, 1994a] shows an absolute stability criterion for discrete time neural networks. In the thermodynamic limit, critical lines were found to divide planar graphs of the average bias of the external pattern versus g into areas with one fixed point, two stable points, one fixed and one strange attractor, and one strange attractor. In finite size systems, the line of destabilization and the appearance of chaos are not identical: there is an intermediate periodic and quasi-periodic regime corresponding to the quasi-periodic route to chaos observed in finite neural networks. Doyon and colleagues [Doyon et al., 1993] show a quasi-periodic route to chaos in a class of finite random networks. We have illustrated one route for a 64-neuron network in this chapter (Figure 3).

Research on dynamic neural networks is highly motivated because there is potential for gaining superior generalization and pattern classification. Dynamical systems can have complex basin boundaries, including fractal boundaries [Ott, 1993], and the dynamic neural networks presented here are examples of such dynamic systems. Fractal basin boundaries and other complicated boundaries could enable a recognition scheme to place arbitrarily complex boundaries between different pattern classes, with a tremendous amount of fine structure. The tailoring of basin boundaries to fit the solution of a recognition problem has so far been considered only for limited cases with a different neural network paradigm [Hao et al., 1994, Venkatesh et al., 1990, Dayhoff and Palmadesso, 1998] and fractal boundaries were not taken into account.

Dynamic neural networks have an extensive armamentarium of behaviors, including dynamic attractors - finite-state oscillations, limit cycles, and chaos - as well as fixed-point attractors (stable states) and the transients that arise between attractor states. In our experiments, this tremendous spectrum of differing activities develops naturally as a result of the network's processing units, asymmetric weights, and closed-loop interconnections. Components that could oscillate or individually produce chaos did not have to be built into the network to insure the presence of dynamics. The resulting networks are enormously flexible, capable of prolonged self-sustained activity, and able to undergo progressions of oscillations that are controlled by modulating parameters and applied patterns.

Although the neural architectures studied here are artificial, they are inspired by biological structures. Furthermore, the ability for self-sustained activity is clear in biology, as neurons in the brain have recorded "spontaneous" activity, and animals can maintain ongoing awareness, consciousness, and mental activity. The extent to which a capability for self-sustained activity and changing oscillations contributes to these biological and behavioral abilities is as yet unknown. We propose that underlying oscillations, changes in oscillation complexity, and modulated progressions of oscillations may contribute to biological activities such as awareness, mental transitions, mental representations, consciousness, and high-level tasks. If so, this chapter shows a simplified and abstracted model that represents such neural oscillations, their modulation by externally applied patterns, and progressions between simple fixed states, more complex oscillations, and chaos.

ACKNOWLEDGMENTS

J. Dayhoff was supported by the Naval Research Laboratory (N00014-93-K-2019), the National Science Foundation (CDR-88-03012 and BIR9309169), the AFOSR Summer Faculty Research Program, AFOSR SREP contract 97-0850, ITT contract 1400256, and the Office of Naval Research. P. Palmadesso and F. Richards acknowledge support from the Office of Naval Research.

REFERENCES

Cessac, B., Doyon, B., Quoy, M., Samuelides, M., Mean-field equations, bifurcation map and chaos in discrete time neural networks, *Physica D*, 74, 24, 1994.

Cessac, B., Absolute stability criterion for discrete time neural networks, *Journal of Physics A*, 27, L297, 1994.

Cessac, B., Occurrence of chaos and at line in random neural networks, *Europhysics Letters*, 26(8), 577, 1994.

Cessac, B., Increase in complexity in random neural networks, *Journal de Physique I*, 5, 409, 1995.

Cessac, B., Quoy, M., Influence of learning in chaotic neural networks, Technical Report 713/12/95, Universitat Bielefeld Postfach 10 01 31 33501 Bielefeld, BiBos at PHYSIK.UNI-Biefeld.DE, 1995.

Chapeau-Blondeau, F., *Chaos Solitons Fractals*, 3(2), 133, 1993.

Dayhoff, J. E., Palmadesso, P. J., Capacity for basin flexibility in dynamic binary networks, *Proceedings of World Congress on Neural Networks* (WCNN), 1, 365, 1995.

Dayhoff, J. E., Palmadesso, P. J., Richards, F., Lin, D.-T., Patterns of dynamic activity and timing in neural network processing, *Neural Networks and Pattern Recognition*, Omidvar and Dayhoff, Eds., Academic Press, Boston, 1998.

Dmitirev, A. S., Kuminov, D., Chaotic scanning and recognition of images in neural-like systems with learning, *J. Commun. Technol. Electron.*, 39(8), 118, 1994.

Dmitriev, A. S. et al, The simple neural-like system with chaos, *Proc. Int. Conf. Noise in Physical Syst. and 1/f Fluctuations*, Kyoto, Japan, 501, 1993.

Doyon, B., Cessac, B., Quoy, M., Samuelides, M., Control of the transition of chaos in neural networks with random connectivity, *International Journal of Bifurcation and Chaos*, 3(2), 279, 1993.

Doyon, B., Cessac, B., Quoy, M., Samuelides, M., On bifurcation and chaos in random neural networks, *Acta Biotheoretica*, 42, 215, 1994.

Freeman, W. J., Yao, Y., Burke, B., Central pattern generating and recognizing in olfactory bulb: a correlation learning rule, *Neural Networks*, 1, 277, 1988.

Hao, J., Tan, S., Vandewalle, J., A new approach to the design of discrete Hopfield associative memories, *Journal of Artificial Neural Networks*, 1(2), 247, 1994.

Hjelmfelt, A., Ross, J., Pattern Recognition, chaos, and multiplicity in neural networks and excitable system, *Proc. Nat. Academy Sci.*, USA, 91, 63, 1994.

Kumagai, T., Hashimoto, R., Wada, M., Learning of limit cycles in discrete-time neural network, *Neurocomputing*, 13, 1, 1996.

Lin, D.-T., Dayhoff, J. E., Ligomenides, P. A., Trajectory production with the adaptive time-delay neural network, *Neural Networks*, 8, (3): 447-461, 1995.

Moreira, J. E., Auto, D. M., Intermittency in a neural network with variable threshold, *Europhys. Lett.*, 21(6), 639, 1993.

Ott, E., *Chaos in Dynamical Systems*, Cambridge University Press, Cambridge, 1993.

Palmadesso, P. J., Dayhoff, J. E., Attractor locking in a chaotic neural network: stimulus patterns evoke limit cycles, *Proceedings of the World Congress on Neural Networks (WCNN)*, 1:254-257, 1995.

Quoy, M., Doyon, B., Samuelides, M., Dimension reduction by learning in a discrete time chaotic neural network, *Proceedings of World Congress on Neural Networks* (WCNN), 1:300-303, 1995.

Samuelides, M., Doyon, B., Cessac, B., Quoy, M., Spontaneous dynamics and associative learning in an asymmetric recurrent random neural network, *Annals of Mathematics and Artificial Intelligence*.

Sompolinsky, H., Crisanti, A., Sommers, H. J., Chaos in random neural networks, *Phys. Rev. Let.*, 61(3), 259, 1988.

Venkatesh, S. S., Pancha, G., Psaltis, D., Sirat, G., Shaping attraction basins in neural networks, *Neural Networks*, 3:613-623, 1990.

Wang, L., Oscillatory and chaotic dynamics in neural networks under varying operating conditions, *IEEE Trans. on Neural Networks*, 7(6), 1382, 1996.

Yao, Y., Freeman, Model of biological pattern recognition with spatially chaotic dynamics, *Neural Networks*, 3(2), 153,1990.

Yao, Y., Freeman, W. J., Burke, B., Yang, Q., Pattern recognition by a distributed neural network: an industrial application, *Neural Networks*, 4, 103, 1991.

Chapter 8

LESSONS FROM LANGUAGE LEARNING

Stefan C. Kremer

**Guelph Natural Computation Group
Dept. of Computing and Information Science
University of Guelph**

I. INTRODUCTION

Recurrent networks can be categorized into two classes, those that are presented with a constant or one-time input signal and are designed to enter an interesting stable state, and those that are presented with time-varying inputs and are designed to render outputs at various points in time. This chapter concerns the latter which are called dynamical recurrent networks [Kolen]. In this case, the operation of the network can be described by a function mapping an input sequence to an output value, or a sequence of output values. The input and output values are continuous and multi-dimensional, resulting in vector representations. Specifically, we define the behaviour of a network by

$$f : X^t \to Y^t, \tag{1}$$

where $X = \Re^n$ and $Y = \Re^m$ and n and m represent the dimensionalities of the input and output vectors, respectively. t represents the length of the sequence which is usually given a temporal interpretation.

A. LANGUAGE LEARNING

A special case of this type of operation which is often used in many recurrent networks is the assumption that

- $X = \{0, 1\}^n$ and $Y = \{0, 1\}^m$ for a logistic transfer function

  or

- $X = \{-1, 1\}^n$ and $Y = \{-1, 1\}^m$ for a logistic transfer function

In this situation, the input and output values are discrete. This approach is used in any problem where inputs are selected from a discrete alphabet of valid values and output values fall into discrete categories.

The problem of dealing with input sequences in which each item is selected from an input alphabet can also be cast as a formal language problem. A formal language is defined:

Definition 1 *Formal Language: a set of strings of symbols from some alphabet.*

179

Typically Σ is used to represent the alphabet, and the input language L is the power-set of Σ:

$$L = 2^{\Sigma}. \tag{2}$$

One of the most simple functions that has a language as its domain is that of identifying a particular subset of this input language. That is, we consider a language

$$L_1 \subseteq L \tag{3}$$

and we define $f_{L_1} : L \to \{\text{accept}, \text{reject}\}$ as:

$$f_{L_1}(s) = \begin{cases} \text{accept} & \text{if } s \in L_1 \\ \text{reject} & \text{otherwise} \end{cases} \tag{4}$$

This is the classical problem solved by a formal computing machine (such as a finite state automaton, pushdown automaton, or Turing machine) which is said to accept the language L_1.

A recurrent network can be applied to this type of problem as well, and many have studied these networks in this context (see this Chapter's references for detailed list). With a recurrent network, one typically would like the system to learn to make this type of categorization (though there have been numerous papers on the representational powers of these networks independent of their ability to learn to identify member strings; e.g., Horne [1994], Siegelmann [1995].

B. CLASSICAL GRAMMAR INDUCTION

Now, when one talks of learning to make this categorization, one could equivalently talk about learning the language L_1. Yet, if the language L_1 is infinite in size, then to learn L_1 one has to represent it in some finite form. We define this finite form as a grammar:

Definition 2 *Formal Grammar: a finite characterization of a potentially infinite language.*

The classical approach to representing grammars is to use a 4-tuple, $G = (V, T, P, S)$. Here, V represents a set of symbols, known as variables, which are used as intermediate results in the derivation of member strings. Similarly, T represents a set of symbols, called terminals, which defines the alphabet of the language represented by the grammar (i.e., $T = \Sigma$). P is a finite set of rules, called productions, defining how strings of variables and terminals can be rewritten as other strings of variables and terminals in the process of deriving a member string. Specifically, productions take the form $\alpha \to \beta$, where α and β are strings of symbols from the Kleene closure of the union of variables and terminals: $(V \cup T)^*$. Lastly, S is a special variable called the start symbol.

The process of deriving a legal string for a given grammar can be formalized as follows: First, the current string is initialized to be the start symbol. Second, strings of symbols within the current string that match the left-hand side of one of the productions are replaced by the right-hand side of the production. The second step is repeated until only terminal symbols remain in the current string, at which point, the current string represents a legal string. Formally, we define the rewrite operator, $\Rightarrow$, by asserting that $\gamma\alpha\delta \Rightarrow \gamma\beta\delta$ if and only if the production $\alpha \rightarrow \beta$ is a member of P. This operator represents one application of step two in the process above. Multiple applications can then be represented by the reflexive-transitive rewrite operator, $\overset{*}{\Rightarrow}$, which is defined as the reflexive and transitive closure of $\Rightarrow$. Applying the latter operator to the start symbol, S, the language described by the grammar, G, is defined as

$$L_G = \{s | s \in T^* \text{and} S \overset{*}{\Rightarrow} w\} \tag{5}$$

C. GRAMMATICAL INDUCTION

This representation of a language by a grammar has lead the field of language learning to be known as *grammatical induction*. This field has been studied extensively in the purely symbolic paradigm for over 30 years. In those 30 years, much knowledge has been acquired and some of this knowledge can be parlayed into techniques for improvement of learning in recurrent networks. This is the focus of this chapter.

D. GRAMMARS IN RECURRENT NETWORKS

Another finite representation of potentially infinite languages is in the form of a weight matrix W in a recurrent network. In this scenario, string acceptance is determined by presenting vector encodings of the input symbols to the network, one at a time. Activations are propagated through the network for multiple cycles, until all input symbols have been presented. At that time, the output units are examined and a decision on membership is made. Because recurrent networks can store information about previous input symbols in the activation values transmitted through their recurrent connections, these networks can render decisions on strings presented one symbol at a time. The decisions made for the input strings will be defined by the weight matrix of the network. Thus, the weights define the set of strings that will be accepted and hence the language. In this sense, the weight matrix is a grammar according to our definition.

Although the representations in the connectionist paradigm are very different from those used in the classical symbolic approach, the problem faced by the two approaches is exactly the same. This means that it may be possible to transfer some insights on the problem of grammar induction from symbolic techniques to recurrent networks.

Clearly, the problem of language learning defined above is only one special case of the kinds of problems that recurrent networks can address. It does not cover situations in which input sequences consist of continuous real-values, nor on problems involving more sophisticated outputs beyond simple accept/reject decisions. Nonetheless, we will discover in what follows that it is an informative case that offers insights into approaching the problem of training recurrent networks in general.

E. OUTLINE

The chapter is organized along the lines of four lessons based on results from the work in symbolic grammar induction. After this introductory section, Lesson 1 shows that the problem of language learning is a surprisingly difficult one. This motivates the remaining sections which focus on how one can simplify the problem of language learning and also other types of recurrent network problems. Lesson 2 focuses on restricting the kinds of languages and other problems which can be learned. Lesson 3 describes techniques for ordering the search for problem solutions to speed the learning time. Lesson 4 explains how ordering training data during the training process helps narrow down the solution possibilities. A conclusions section at the end of the chapter summarizes our results.

II. LESSON 1: LANGUAGE LEARNING IS HARD

We begin by considering two variations on grammar learning. Gold [Gold, 1967] has identified two basic methods of presenting strings to a language learner: "text" and "informant." A text is a sequence of legal strings containing every string of the language at least once. Typically, texts are presented one symbol after another, one string after another. Since most interesting languages have an infinite number of strings, the process of string presentation never terminates.

An informant is a device which can tell the learner whether any particular string is in the language. Typically the informant presents one symbol at a time, and upon a string's termination supplies a grammaticality judgment.

Gold [Gold, 1967] investigated the problem of language identification in the limit. He asked the question: Which classes of languages are learnable with respect to a particular method of information presentation? A class of languages is learnable if there exists an algorithm which repeatedly guesses languages from the class in response to example strings, and "Given any language of the class, there is some finite time after which the guesses will all be the same and will all be correct" [Gold, 1967]. The algorithm does not keep guessing forever or, more precisely, it settles on a particular language and that language is correct.

Gold showed that this is a surprisingly difficult task. For example, if the method of information presentation is a text, then only finite cardinality languages can be learned. Finite cardinality languages consist of a finite number of legal strings, and are a small subset of the regular sets (the smallest set in the Chomsky hierarchy). In other words, none of the language classes typically studied in language theory are text learnable.

The situation is only slightly more promising if both positive and negative examples from the language are available. Under informant learning, only two kinds of language are identifiable in the limit. These are regular sets (which are those languages having only transition rules of the form $A \to wB$, where A and B are variables and w is a (possibly empty) string of terminals), and context-free languages (which are those languages having only transition rules of the form $A \to \beta$, where A is a single variable). Other languages, however, like the recursively enumerable languages (those having transition rules, $\alpha \to \beta$, where α and

β are arbitrary strings of terminals and non-terminals) remain unlearnable.

The fact that regular sets and context-free languages are learnable under the informant learning paradigm by no means implies that such learning is practical. Pinker points out that "in considering all the finite state grammars that use seven terminal symbols and seven auxiliary symbols (states), which the learner must do before going on to more complex grammars, he must test over a googol (10^{100}) candidates" [Pinker, 1979]. This reveals that even for tiny computational machines (seven states) the language learning problem is often intractable if no *a priori* knowledge is available to remove some of the machines from consideration.

The conclusion which must be drawn from Gold's and Pinker's observations is that grammatical induction is an exceptionally complex task. So complex, in fact, that it cannot be solved as originally posed by Gold. In the following sections, we shall present a number of modifications to the original problem which overcome the inherent difficulties implied by Gold's and Pinker's conclusions and thus allow the problem to be solved.

Even though Gold and Pinker worked in a symbolic paradigm for language learning, they made no assumptions particular to this approach. The same conclusions can be applied to the problem of learning languages by connectionist networks. This means that if recurrent networks are to solve language learning problems or even more complicated problems, we must modify our approach to learning in order to overcome the intractability and extreme slowness inherent in language learning tasks.

III.   LESSON 2: WHEN POSSIBLE, SEARCH A SMALLER SPACE

The difficulty of any search depends on the number of candidate solutions that must be considered, called the hypothesis space.

A.   AN EXAMPLE: WHERE DID I LEAVE MY KEYS?

We begin by considering a simple example: Suppose you are unable to find your car keys. We shall assume that the keys are somewhere in the house. A simple search algorithm might involve searching the house from top to bottom starting on the upper floor and moving down to the basement. This represents an exhaustive brute-force search like the scenario suggested by Pinker when he described considering all grammars with seven terminal and seven non-terminal symbols.

Now suppose you know for a fact that you have not been upstairs or downstairs since you last used the keys. In this case, it would be sensible to reduce the search space from the entire house to just the ground floor. This would no doubt lead to a more efficient search and you would expect to find your keys sooner. Thus, reducing the search space increases search efficiency.

Of course, there is a drawback to a reduced search space. Suppose you had forgotten that you had in fact traveled upstairs and left the keys there. Now your search of only the ground floor would be guaranteed to fail. A reduced hypothesis space is useful only if it does not exclude the goal.

B. REDUCING AND ORDERING IN GRAMMATICAL IN-DUCTION

Naturally, the techniques of hypothesis space reduction and ordering described in the previous example are applicable to search in general-not just car key searches. As such, they can be used to make the task of grammatical induction solvable or tractable. The notion of hypothesis space reduction in the context of grammatical induction refers to searching for a grammar consistent with the training data in a class which is smaller than the class of unrestricted (Chomsky type-0) grammars.

Symbolic grammar induction systems have used the class of context-free grammars (Chomsky type-2) and the class of regular grammars (Chomsky type-3) as reduced hypothesis spaces. However, the fact that Gold showed that even the smallest of these classes is not learnable based solely on text training data, combined with the fact that most interesting grammars belong to the larger classes, have made these restrictions unpopular techniques for hypothesis space reduction.

A more useful technique is to devise a class of grammars which lies tangential to Chomsky's hierarchy. Such a tangential class contains some grammars which are not regular and some grammars which are not context-free but contains only a subset of the unrestricted grammars. By using a class tangential to the Chomsky hierarchy as one's hypothesis space it will be possible to represent some of the grammars which only fall into the unrestricted class, while at the same time reducing the size of the hypothesis space so as to identify members of the space based on input data more rapidly. Of course, as with the car key example, it is critical to choose a hypothesis space that contains those grammars which are to be learnable.

This type of hypothesis restriction was first suggested by Chomsky [Chomsky, 1965]. While working on the problem of human language acquisition, he proposed that only those grammars possessing the basic properties of natural languages should be considered as candidates for grammatical induction. By weighting the naturalness of languages based on a specific set of properties, he proposed an induction algorithm which considered only those languages which were consistent with the training sample and had a sufficiently high weight.

Another popular technique for restricting the space is to employ the *universal base hypothesis*. Under this hypothesis, different grammars are defined by means of a two-step process. First, a universal base grammar which all different grammars use is defined. Then, a restricted class of rewrite rules are employed to translate from the symbols of the universal base grammar to a variety of derived grammars. The grammars derived in this fashion form a reduced hypothesis space which can then be used to define a grammatical induction algorithm. This approach is fundamental to Wexler and Culicover's [Wexler, 1980] model of human language learning.

C. RESTRICTED HYPOTHESIS SPACES IN CONNECTIONIST NETWORKS

Restricted hypothesis spaces in symbolic grammatical induction systems are typically described in terms of restrictions on the type of grammar rules they employ. In recurrent networks, the languages that the network recognizes are determined by three factors: (1) the network topology (sometimes called architecture), (2) the number of hidden units, and (3) the connection weights in the network. Thus, we can restrict the kinds of languages (or equivalently grammars) that can be learned by adjusting network topologies, number of hidden units and/or weights.

D. LESSON 2.1: CHOOSE AN APPROPRIATE NETWORK TOPOLOGY

The computational power of a number of topologies, given appropriate weights, has been studied. While some topologies are potentially as powerful as Turing machines, others are much more restricted in their computational power. Initially, one might be tempted to select the most powerful network for all applications, but the arguments above reveal that it may be wiser to select a more restricted architecture in order to make the learning algorithm tractable, especially if one knows that a solution to the current problem can be found by the computationally weaker architecture.

One of the first architectures suggested for processing time-sequence data was the window in time network used in the classic NETtalk [Sejnowski, 1986]. It has also been used by a variety of other authors including Lang et al. [Lang, 1990], Lapedes and Farber [Lapedes, 1987], and Waibel et al. [Waibel, 1989]. The topology of this network consists of a feedforward network which is presented with a finite history of input patterns called an input window (Figure 1). Since this window is of finite length, there will always be inputs which fall outside of this window (i.e., are too old). This means that there will always be certain kinds of strings that this network cannot correctly classify, namely strings who's categorization depends on symbols that fall outside the window. More specifically, Giles, Horne, and Lin [Giles, 1995] were first to recognize that Kohavi [Kohavi, 1978] had previously called this subclass of finite state automata "definite machines." Kremer [Kremer, 1995a] also developed a grammatical formulation in the form of a 4-tuple for this language.

The preceding architecture is not a recurrent network though it can be used in applications where recurrent networks are used (which explains why we discussed it here). A variation on the Window-in-Time topology is to use two temporal windows: One window on the input symbols (as in WIT memories) and a second on the output symbols produced by the network (Figure 2). In this network, output values are fed back into the network as inputs. Because of its similarity to infinite impulse response filters (IIRs), this type of topology has been called neural network IIR. Narendra and Parthasarathy [Narendra, 1990] have used this type of short-term memory.

Locally recurrent [Frasconi, 1995] networks use a different kind of recurrence. In these networks the activation values of hidden nodes are computed according to the formula

$$a_j(t) = f(net_j(t)),$$ (6)

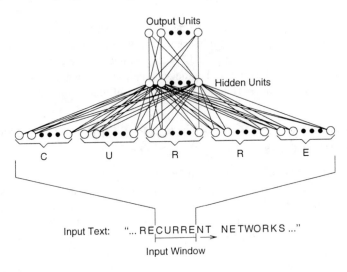

Figure 1. Window-in-time Network.

where

$$net_j(t) = \sum_i w_{ji} \cdot a_i(t) + w_{jj} a_j(t - 1).\qquad(7)$$

Here, w_{jj} represents a recurrent, time-delay connection from the unit to itself (Figure 3). A potential advantage of this type of network over the previous networks discussed is that it can adapt its internal representation. Whereas the previous networks had their memory fixed by the network's inputs or target outputs, this type of network can adapt their internal representations to the given task and it is these internal representations that are fed through the recurrent connections. Despite this, these networks are still limited in their representational capacity [Frasconi, 96]. In Kremer [1999], some specific problems that these networks cannot represent are identified.

Another approach, which has been widely used, is based on computing the network's internal state using a single-layer first-order feedforward network [Rumelhart, 1986] which uses the previous state (also called context) and the current input symbol as input (Figure 4). This approach is used in Elman's [Elman, 1991a, Elman, 1990] Simple Recurrent Networks (SRN), Pollack's [Pollack, 1989, Pollack, 1990] Recurrent Auto-Associative Memory (RAAM), Maskara and Noetzel's [Maskara, 1992] Auto-Associative Recurrent Network (AARN), and Williams and Zipser's [Williams, 1989] Real Time Recurrent Learning (RTRL) networks. Unlike locally recurrent networks, where the only time-delayed connection that a unit receives is from itself, in these networks time-delayed connections can come from any of the network's internal units. This gives this topology the computational power of finite state automata [Kremer, 1995], or if infinite precision units are used, the computational power of Turing machines [Siegelmann, 1991, Siegel-

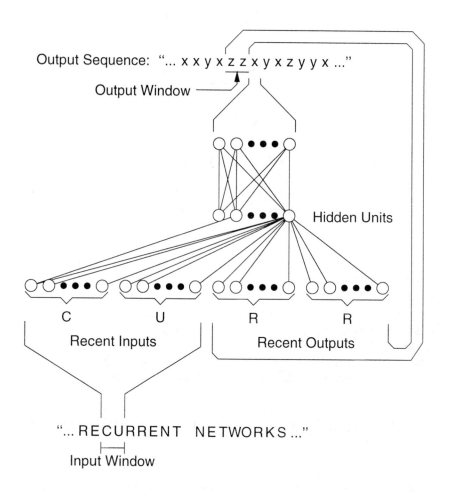

Figure 2. Neural Network IIR.

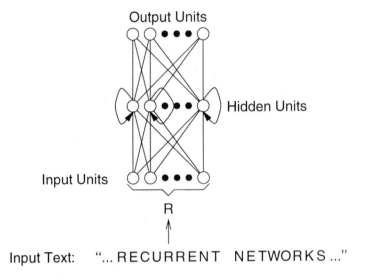

Figure 3. Example of a Locally Recurrent Network.

mann, 1992]. A variation on this approach has also been developed that uses second order connections between input and previous hidden and current hidden unit activations [Giles, 1990].

These four different network topologies have different representational capacities. It is important when selecting a topology to choose one which has the representational power to solve the task at hand, but not more representational power than necessary, because this will extend the search space of potential solutions which can make learning take much longer or make it intractable altogether.

E.   LESSON 2.2: CHOOSE A LIMITED NUMBER OF HIDDEN UNITS

Another way, to limit the power of recurrent networks, is to limit the number of hidden units, which obviously constrains the kinds of computations the network can perform. It is fairly obvious that the types of constraints imposed by limiting hidden units in recurrent networks will not fall along the lines of the classical Chomsky hierarchy of languages. Instead, in recurrent networks, a hierarchy based on decision regions in the geometry of the input and internal representation spaces will form. These types of network-based hierarchies may even fall along lines which more closely resemble the distinctions between natural and artificial languages since the network-hierarchies are a consequence of a parallel processing architecture which may be considered more brain-like than the grammatical rules which distinguish symbolic language hierarchies.

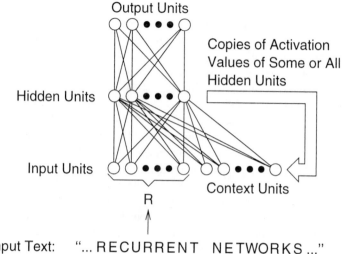

Figure 4. Example of a Network that Uses Old Hidden Unit Activations to Compute New Activations.

F. LESSON 2.3: FIX SOME WEIGHTS

Choosing a limited number of hidden units also effectively reduces the number of weights in the network. Since it is the weights which determine the computation performed, this will naturally constrain these computations. An alternative to limiting the number of weights is to fix the values of some of the weights in the network. This effectively reduces the degrees of freedom in the system, reducing the search space for the learning algorithm and thus offering a potential speed-up to learning. Of course, in order to be of use in solving a given problem, the fixed weights in the network should incorporate some *a priori* knowledge about the problem to be solved.

Fixing weights, however, cannot guarantee that the supplied *a priori* knowledge will actually be incorporated in the grammar induced by a recurrent network, because the trained weights in the network can overpower or nullify the contributions of the fixed weights. Suppose that the trained weights of the connections leading into node i in some recurrent network are much larger than the fixed weights leading into the same node. Since the signals transmitted through each connection are multiplied by the connection's weight and then summed together by node i, the effect of the fixed weights will be negligible compared to the effects of the larger trained weights. In this situation, the trained weights overpower the fixed weights.

Now suppose that all the connections leading out of node j are trained and have a very small weight after the training process. In this case any fixed weights leading into node j will affect the activation value of the node, but this activation value will be ignored by the rest of the network due to the small outgoing weights. In this sense, the trained weights nullify the effect of the fixed weights.

Of course, a network which ignores *a priori* knowledge in either of these two ways will further limit its representational capacity. That is, a recurrent network with n nodes will be able to represent a large class of languages. A recurrent network of the same size which has some fixed weights and uses those fixed weights to compute its behaviour will be able to represent a smaller class of languages. Finally, a recurrent network with n nodes which has some fixed weights but does not use these weights in its computation (either because they are overpowered or because they are nullified) will be able to represent the smallest class of languages.

Frasconi, Gori, Maggini, and Soda [Frasconi, 1995] have explored fixing network weights based on *a priori* knowledge about an isolated word recognition task to be solved. Specifically, they develop a network consisting of two separate networks with a common 1-Layer output function. One of the networks (called "K") consists entirely of fixed weights whose values are assigned based on the available knowledge. The other network (called "L") has adaptive weights whose values are learned based on training data. By using this modular approach, these authors are able to prevent the trained weights from overpowering the fixed weights. However, the output layer can still ignore the values of the state nodes in K by setting all weights originating from the K-memory to small values. We defer the discussion of the type of *a priori* knowledge used by the authors and how this knowledge is encoded into connection weights to the original papers [Frasconi, 1991, Frasconi, 1995].

Frasconi et. al.'s networks are able to achieve a recognition rate as high as 92.3% in empirical performance tests. The authors indicate that this is a significant achievement due to the fact that the task of isolated word recognition is complicated by the fact that the words used are composed only of vowel and nasal sounds. They further argue that their approach is more efficient than ones which do not use *a priori* knowledge. Unfortunately, the authors do not provide any empirical data comparing networks with *a priori* data to networks without *a priori* data.

From these considerations and empirical results, we can conclude that it is advisable to consider incorporation any knowledge of the kinds of solutions that we want our network to find into the connection weights of the network. A number of such encoding techniques have been developed for different kinds of networks, and the reader is referred to [Frasconi, 1991, Frasconi, 1995, Giles, 1992b, Giles, 1993] for detailed discussions of encoding.

G. LESSON 2.4: SET INITIAL WEIGHTS

While it is obvious that fixing weights in a recurrent network restricts the hypothesis space, it is less apparent that initial weights can also restrict the space. To recognize the latter fact, we must realize that the search of the hypothesis space in recurrent networks is usually governed by a gradient-descent algorithm. This implies that each candidate grammar considered during the search must have a smaller error value than the previous. But, since the initial weights of a network define a grammar and since that grammar is assigned an error value, it must be the case that all grammars with higher error values than the initial grammar are omitted from the search. Thus, the initialization of weights can serve to restrict the hypothesis space by causing all grammars with higher error values to be rejected outright. Figure 5 illustrates an initial set of weights (i.e., a point in weight space), a fictional error function, and those grammars which are not explored during the search algorithm (shaded grey).

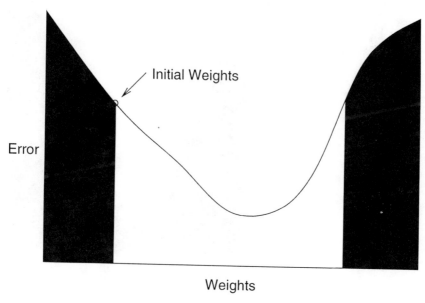

Figure 5. Initializing Weights to Limit Space.

It is interesting to note that "good" *a priori* knowledge will tend to significantly reduce the hypothesis space, while "bad" knowledge tends not to reduce the hypothesis space as much, because good *a priori* knowledge will tend to result in a network having a small error value. Since only those networks and grammars with even smaller error values are explored, the hypothesis space will tend to be greatly reduced. Conversely, bad *a priori* knowledge will tend to result in a network with a large error value. In this case there will be many recurrent networks and grammars having smaller error values and hence the hypothesis space will tend to remain large. This is an extremely useful property since it implies that good information will tend to have a large (positive) effect while bad information will tend to have very little effect.

There is, however, one serious drawback in choosing initial weights to restrict the hypothesis space: local minima in the error function. If the function mapping weight values to network error is non-monotonic, then it may be the case that to get to a smaller error value one must first travel though a region (in weight space) of larger error. Since the gradient descent algorithm travels only down the error gradient, such smaller error values can never be achieved. That is, the initial weights do not limit the hypothesis space to all networks with smaller error values, but rather only to those recurrent networks lying within the current basin of attraction. If the attractor at the bottom of this basin represents a local minimum (as opposed to a global minimum), then the hypothesis space will be unduly restricted to exclude the best solutions. This is illustrated in Figure 6.

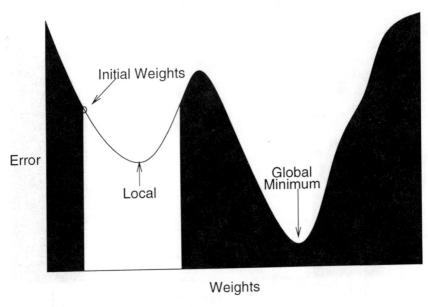

Figure 6. How initial weights can reduce the hypothesis space to exclude optimal solutions.

We can conclude that setting initial weights to an approximation of the solution is almost always desirable and one approach to overcoming the learning difficulties suggested by Gold and Pinker.

IV.   LESSON 3: SEARCH THE MOST LIKELY PLACES FIRST

Another way to speed search (in general) is to order or bias the hypothesis space based on some heuristic. Suppose you are a habitual car key loser and that you keep track of where your keys turn up after each search. The results of such record keeping might be something like: coat pocket: 53%, hallway shelf: 27%, kitchen table: 16%, beside telephone: 3%, in refrigerator: 1%. If you know that most of the time the missing key has been located in your coat pocket, then it makes sense to begin your search there. That is, it is logical to order your hypothesis space and bias it in favour of the coat pocket. But just like a bad hypothesis space reduction can hinder search, a bad ordering can also impede an effective search. For example, using the hypothesis ordering designed for your car keys to find a pitcher of orange juice would clearly be very inefficient.

Just as hypothesis space restriction can be used to simplify the search for a grammar, hypothesis space ordering has also been applied to grammatical induction within the symbolic paradigm. In this case, a working hypothesis about the grammar (from the hypothesis space) is used as a starting point. Then, as new evidence about the grammar is presented in the form of training data, a change to the hypothesis is made. The nature of this change is defined by some heuristic. That is, certain types of hypothesis changes will be favored over other changes even if both are consistent with the training data. The chosen hypothesis change results in a new working hypothesis, and the process is repeated. Typically all of the possible hypothesis changes are evaluated and the resulting hypotheses are evaluated according to some weighting scheme. Then only the highest valued new hypothesis is selected as the new working hypothesis. This is analogous to a best-first search algorithm.

A weighting scheme could be based on complexity, for example, by assigning a weight inversely proportional to the number of auxiliary symbols (states) used by each grammar. This weighted selection process effectively orders the grammars of the hypothesis space. While searching for a grammar which is consistent with the training data, this ordering favors certain solutions over others. Ideally, good solutions to the problem to which the grammatical induction system is applied would be considered first and, thus, learning would be speeded.

While we have seen in the previous section that setting initial weights can restrict a hypothesis space, it is perhaps even more natural to think of setting initial weights as a technique for ordering the exploration of that remaining space. Obviously the initial weights define the first potential grammar which is explored by the induction algorithm. The exploration of subsequent grammars is governed by the learning algorithm. When the learning rate used by the gradient-descent algorithm is small, each grammar considered will lie close to the previous candidate grammar in the recurrent networks weight space. Since the output and state of a recurrent network are governed by functions continuous in the connection weights of the network, a small change in a connection weight will tend to result in a small change in output and state. This means that the exploration of the hypothesis space will proceed via similar grammars.

One advantage of using an ordering technique as opposed to a hypothesis space restriction technique is that there is often some uncertainty associated with *a priori* knowledge about a task. This implies that an irreversible decision, like eliminating certain grammars from consideration, is less desirable than an approach which can eventually ignore incorrect information. Setting the initial weights of a network can operate in this fashion, since even if the first weights are wrong and the network updates weights in small steps, the network will still be able to eventually explore other regions of the hypothesis space. This conclusion has been empirically verified by Giles and Omlin [Giles, 1993]. They initialized the weights of recurrent networks to implement one automaton, A, and then trained the recurrent networks to represent another (different) automaton, B. Despite the fact that this imposed an ordering on the hypothesis space which caused the network to explore automaton A first, the network was still able to eventually find and learn automaton B.

Specifically, Giles and Omlin [Giles, 1993] trained a recurrent network to implement a randomly generated 10-state finite-state automaton. Then, they initialized the weights of the automaton to encode a different randomly generated 10-state automaton. The authors discovered that, so long as the assigned weight values assigned were not too large (> 2), the networks were able to learn the correct automaton in spite of the "malicious" information provided by weight initialization. Of course, the authors also found that learning times were significantly longer for "malicious" information than for correct information. Giles and Omlin's results indicate that even if *a priori* knowledge is incorrect, an ordering scheme such as initializing weights can sometimes still find the correct solution.

V. LESSON 4: ORDER YOUR TRAINING DATA

The previous two sections discussed methods that could be used to speed the learning process before network training begins. This section describes a technique to provide information to the network during training. In the traditional grammar induction paradigm, the learner is required to identify a grammar based on a set of positive (and optionally a set of negative) example strings. Under input ordering, the data available to the learner consists not of a set of strings, but of a sequence of strings. That is, there is an order associated with the input data. If input strings are presented in a non-random order, then the position of a string within the sequence can represent an additional source of information about the grammar to be induced.

For an input ordering to be advantageous, two criteria must be met: (1) The presentation of a string s at time t must encode some information other than the mere fact that the string is a member (or not a member) of the language. (2) The learning system must be informed of the import of this encoded information and use it to limit or order the exploration of the remaining search space. Only when both of these criteria are met can a computational advantage be realized.

A. CLASSICAL RESULTS

We begin our discussion of input ordering by examining how input ordering works and what it can achieve. Gold [Gold, 1967] proposed a type of input string orderings which can improve the classes of grammars that can be induced using only positive input strings (text learning). This ordering scheme uses indirect negative information to learn languages which cannot be learned from positive information alone. This is done by using the absence of a string at a particular point in a sequence to infer that the string is illegal.

Suppose an order on all possible strings (grammatical and ungrammatical) is known to the learning system and this order defines how the environment provides the input data (e.g., alphabetical order). Note that there is an important distinction between knowing the order in which a sequence of strings is presented and the actual sequence of strings. An ordering defines a relation between all possible strings for a given alphabet, i.e., Σ^*, and thus defines where each string should belong (if it were legal), whereas the input sequence generally consists of only a subset of Σ^* and defines the actual set of legal strings.

Now assume that the induction environment presents all the grammatical strings to the learner according to the given order. Then, by omitting a string at the appropriate time, the environment essentially informs the learning mechanism that the given string is ungrammatical. Since this implies that the training set effectively contains both grammatical and ungrammatical strings, it is equivalent to informant learning as defined by Gold. Since Gold has already shown that primitive recursive languages are identifiable in the limit under informant learning, this class of languages must also be learnable under ordered text learning. While this strict sense of ordering is obviously an unrealistic idealization for practical grammar induction systems, Gold's work does point out the power that an ordering scheme can provide.

A less stringent ordering scheme has been proposed by Feldman [Feldman, 1972]. He showed that even an effective approximate ordering of the input strings could be used to convey indirect negative information. If there exists a point in time by which every grammatical sentence of a given length or less has appeared in the sample, then a learner capable of computing this point in time can also compute which sentences are not in the language (this could be the case in human language learning if children were spoken to in short sentences). Once again this is equivalent to a learner's being provided with both grammatical and non-grammatical strings, appropriately labeled.

The common thread to both of these techniques is the fact that the learner reacts differently to the same set of strings presented in differing orders. More specifically, strings which are presented early cause the learner to make certain assumptions about remaining strings which affects the order in which potential grammars are considered, or the size of the hypothesis space which is explored. More efficient and tractable learning can be accomplished by tailoring the learning algorithm and the input sequence to each other.

B. INPUT ORDERING USED IN RECURRENT NETWORKS

A simple ordering scheme which can be placed on strings is to sort them in order of increasing length. Das et al. [Das, 1993] have used a recurrent network training scheme whereby short simple strings are presented first, and progressively longer strings are presented as learning proceeds. They contend that "incremental learning is very useful when (a) the data presented contains structure, and (b) the strings learned earlier embody simpler versions of the task being learned" [Das, 1993], a well-known concept in machine learning theory. In this situation, the fact that short strings are presented early, together with the fact that these strings embody simple versions of later strings, implies that it is possible to use the strings which have already been presented to make certain implicit logical inferences about strings which have not yet been presented. A grammar induction system can be designed to use these inferences to dynamically reduce or re-order the space grammars it can induce.

For example, when a string of length n is presented as input to Das et al.'s system, it is possible to conclude that all strings which are shorter than n and have not yet been presented must be ungrammatical. This implies that these shorter strings will not be presented at a later point in time. In this sense, additional information about future strings (i.e., that they will not contain certain short strings) is transmitted by the ordered data. We will see shortly how a network learning system could function in this fashion.

Giles et al. [Giles, 1991, Giles, 1992, Giles, 1992a] and Miller and Giles [Miller, 1993] have used another simple ordering scheme: alphabetical ordering. If input strings are presented in strict lexicographic order, then the presentation of a string, s, implies that all lexicographically preceding strings which have not been presented must be ungrammatical, in the case of text learning, and must be of irrelevant (don't care) grammaticality, in the case of information learning. In this sense, an alphabetical presentation order can convey additional information (regarding the grammaticality of unpresented strings). Once again, a learning system which is tuned to this type of ordering in the sense that it restricts or orders the space of inducible grammars dynamically could perform better than a system in which input is not ordered. (Empirical data describing Giles et al.'s and Miller and Giles' results is described in the papers listed above.)

Both lengthening and alphabetical input orderings are very restrictive in the sense that they precisely prescribe the order of presented strings. For practical applications, it is often more desirable to use a less stringent ordering. Consider a case where input strings are presented in phases. In the first phase, all short strings, and only short strings, are presented. In later phases other strings are presented. We shall refer to this type of partial ordering as multi-phase uniform complete since the strings presented in the first phase are uniformly short and completely represented. A multi-phase uniform complete input ordering can provide additional information in the same sense that a lengthening input ordering does, with the exception that assumptions about strings which have not been presented can only be made at the end of a phase, as opposed to after each string. Giles et al. [Giles, 1990] have used a multi-phase uniform complete ordering to train recurrent networks. A similar ordering technique has been used by Elman [Elman, 1991a, Elman, 1991] who used a form of ordering to train his networks.

C. HOW RECURRENT NETWORKS PAY ATTENTION TO ORDER

We have now seen that the training environments used for recurrent networks sometimes contain additional implicit information (beyond the grammaticality of individual strings) in the form of string ordering. This represents one of the two components required for a more efficient learning system. The second component is a learner that uses the additional information. In this section we examine how input ordering affects the solutions explored and found by recurrent networks, thereby addressing this second component. Specifically, we examine two types of order sensitivity: engineered sensitivity and natural sensitivity.

One way of ensuring that a learning system makes use of input ordering is to specifically design an induction algorithm around an ordering scheme. Since every symbolic algorithm "is equivalent to and can be 'simulated' by some neural net" [Minsky, 1967], it is not at all surprising that it is possible to realize such a hand-crafted algorithm in the form of a connectionist network. As an example, Porat and Feldman [Porat, 1991] have designed a connectionist network which implements an algorithm which induces FSA based on alphabetically-presented input strings. In order to implement the algorithm, however, the connectionist network requires an extremely complex control structure (compared to typical connectionist networks) and has both hardwired and mutable connections. Thus, the resulting learning system seems more like a connectionist-iterative learning hybrid than a purely connectionist architecture.

An alternative to designing the learning system to accommodate a particular input order is to design the input order to accommodate the learning system. This is typically done in recurrent networks, where network design is based on principles such as simplicity, homogeneity, and local processing. Having designed the network according to these principles, the researcher can only ensure cooperation between input order and learner by adjusting the input order to suit the network's own natural sensitivities to this order. In a sense, the researcher has assumed part of the burden of learning the language. It turns out that the order of pattern presentation affects recurrent network (and other network) learning greatly, because initial weight changes in a network can draw solutions toward a certain local minimum from which the recurrent cannot later escape. This occurs because recurrent networks do not perform true gradient descent.

Recall that, in order to efficiently approximate the gradient, weight adjustments, $\Delta w_{ji}(t)$, are made piecewise over time. This implies that the component of the gradient caused by a pattern presented at time t is computed after the weight adjustment caused by the pattern at time $t - 1$ has been made. This, in turn, means that successive weight adjustments are not commutative. To better understand the implications of this fact, we consider a simple example. Suppose we have a language consisting of only two training strings. Suppose also that the network error, for each of these two strings is given in Figure 7a and b, and the total error for both strings is given in Figure 7c). Now suppose that the network's initial weights and corresponding errors are represented by the point labeled "B" in all three graphs. Clearly if the network is first trained only on the string whose error function is depicted in (a), then the network's weights will move to the point labeled "C." Subsequent training with the second string will keep the network's weights at "C" since it represents a local minimum in the second string's error space. By contrast, if the network is first trained using only the second string, (b), then the network will converge to point "A." Again, subsequent training will not change the weights in the network. Thus, it is clear that the order of string presentation during training limits the hypothesis space (range of weights) which is considered in searching for an error minimizing solution during later string presentations.

While it is easy to see that input ordering affects hypothesis space search during learning, it is much more difficult to identify the ideal ordering scheme for a

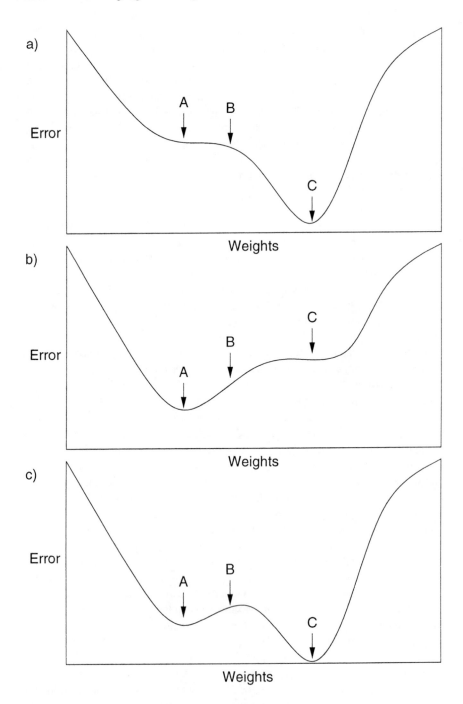

Figure 7. Why Input Order Matters.

recurrent network. In the example above, presenting the string (a) before string (b) will restrict the range of weights to include the global minimum of the error space. By contrast, presenting string (b) prior to string (a) also restricts the range of weights, but the restricted range does not include the global minimum of the error space. Thus, in this simple example, it is important to present string (a) first.

In more general terms, it is always best to present strings whose error functions have local minima at the same points in weights space as the total error function has global minima. Since the presentation of a string adjusts the weights of the network so that the string's error is reduced, the network's weights will approach a local minimum in the presented string's error function. Ideally, this local minimum in the string's error function will correspond (or lie close to) a global minimum in the total error. Since the specific strings satisfying this condition depend entirely on the language to be learned by the recurrent network, we cannot identify a general ideal ordering scheme. Instead we turn to the empirical evidence to show that the ordering schemes described above do in fact correspond to the natural sensitivities to input order in recurrent networks.

Das et al. [Das, 1993] compared training recurrent networks with a lengthening input ordering to training the same recurrent networks with a random ordering of strings. They observed a 50% reduction in training time for the lengthening ordering scheme. Giles et al. [Giles, 1992a] also observed an improvement in training times when they presented strings in alphabetical order and concluded that "the sequence of strings presented during training is very important and certainly gives a bias in learning" [Giles, 1992a] and that "training with alphabetical order . . . is much faster and converges more often than random order presentation" [Giles, 1992a].

While the performance improvements realized by the ordering schemes of Das et al. [Das, 1993] and Giles et al. [Giles, 1992a] took the form of accelerated learning, Elman [Elman, 1991a, Elman, 1991] used ordering to learn an otherwise unlearnable grammar. In two learning experiments, Elman's multi-phase consistent complete ordering approach was used after previous attempts to train the network on the entire data set (complex and simple sentences) failed. In both cases, Elman found that, "when the network was permitted to focus on the simpler data first, it was able to learn the task quickly and then move on successfully to more complex patterns" [Elman, 1991a]. This evidence clearly shows that input ordering can be used in the connectionist domain (just as it has in the symbolic paradigm) to improve learning efficiency and tractability.

VI. SUMMARY

In this chapter, we have examined the problem of language learning as a special case of training recurrent networks. By examining results from the field of grammatical induction from the past 30 years, we have discovered 4 useful lessons that can be applied to training recurrent networks. The first lesson is that learning languages is hard regardless of paradigm used. Since language learning is one of the simplest cases of the kinds of learning that recurrent networks are tasked with, we must infer that learning in recurrent networks is difficult in general. From this first lesson, we turn our attention to making learning easier.

The second lesson revealed that, while it is tempting to select the most representationally powerful computational tool possible for language learning tasks, this is a dangerous choice since the representational power is inversely related to the effectiveness of learning. Thus, we will often want to select a smaller search space. There are 4 ways of accomplishing this in recurrent networks: (1) selecting an appropriate network topology, (2) selecting an appropriate number of internal units, (3) fixing some weights with appropriate values, and (4) setting the initial weights to restrict the search space.

The third lesson showed that ordering the exploration of the hypothesis space can also be very advantageous. This can be accomplished by setting initial weights. Empirical evidence revealed that this is a very effective technique to speed learning which does not doom the training process even if malicious incorrect data is used.

The fourth lesson focussed on the effect of ordering training data. This technique represents a method for indirectly providing information about which strings are not in the language. A simple example revealed that recurrent network based language learners are capable of using string ordering to effect the learning process.

While language learning is only one potential application of recurrent networks, it is an informative one. These examinations have revealed effective techniques for language learning derived from previous research. In most cases, these techniques have already been implemented as heuristics for improving the training of recurrent networks with significant success. This chapter serves to ground these techniques in a formal theory, thereby giving insights into why they work and why, how, and when they should be applied. An extended version of this work can be found in Kremer [1996a].

REFERENCES

Chomsky, N., *Aspects of the Theory of Syntax*, MIT Press, Cambridge, 1965.

Das, S., Giles, C. L., Sun, G.-Z., Using prior knowledge in a NNPDA to learn context-free languages. In *Advances in Neural Information Processing Systems*, Hanson, S. J., Cowan, J. D., Giles C. L., Eds., Morgan Kaufmann Publishers, 5, 65, 1993.

Elman, J., Finding structure in time, *Cognitive Science*, 14, 179, 1990.

Elman, J., Incremental learning, or the importance of starting small, Tech. Rep. CRL Tech Report 9101, Center for Research in Language, University of California at San Diego, La Jolla, CA, 1991.

Elman, J. L., Distributed representations, simple recurrent networks and grammatical structure, *Machine Learning*, 7(2/3), 195, 1991.

Feldman, J., Some decidability results on grammatical inference and complexity, *Information and Control*, 20, 244, 1972.

Frasconi, P., Gori, M., Computational capabilities of local-feedback recurrent networks acting as finite-state machines, *IEEE Transactions on Neural Networks*, 7(6), 1521, 1996.

Frasconi, P., Gori, M., Maggini, M., Soda, G., A unified approach for integrating explicit knowledge and learning by example in recurrent networks, In *1991 IEEE INNS International Joint Conference on Neural Networks – Seattle,* 1, IEEE Press, 811, 1991.

Frasconi, P., Gori, M., Maggini, M., Soda, G., Unified integration of explicit rules and learning by example in recurrent networks, *IEEE Transactions on Knowledge and Data Engineering*, 7(2), 340, 1995.

Giles, C., Miller, C., Chen, D., Chen, H., Sun, G., Lee, Y., Learning and extracting finite state automata with second-order recurrent neural networks, *Neural Computation*, 4(3), 393, 1992.

Giles, C., Sun, G., Chen, H., Lee, Y., Chen, D., Higher order recurrent networks & grammatical inference. In *Advances in Neural Information Processing Systems,* 2, Touretzky, D. S., Ed., Morgan Kaufmann Publishers, 380, 1990.

Giles, C. L., Chen, D., Miller, C., Chen, H., Sun, G., Lee, Y., Second-order recurrent neural networks for grammatical inference. In *1991 IEEE INNS International Joint Conference on Neural Net works – Seattle*, 2, IEEE Press, 281, 1991.

Giles, C. L., Horne, B., Lin, T., Learning a class of large finite state machines with a recurrent neural network, *Neural Networks*, 8(9), 1359, 1995.

Giles, C. L., Miller, C. B., Chen, D., Sun, G. Z., Chen, H. H., Lee, Y. C., Extracting and learning an unknown grammar with recurrent neural networks. In *Advances in Neural Information Processing Systems*, 4, Moody, J. E., Hanson, S. J., Lippmann, R. P., Eds., Morgan Kaufmann Publishers, Inc., 317, 1992.

Giles, C. L., Omlin, C., Inserting rules into recurrent neural networks. In *Neural Networks for Signal Processing II, Proceedings of The 1992 IEEE Workshop* Kung, S., Fallside, F., Sorenson, J. A., Kamm, C., Eds., IEEE Press, 13, 1992.

Giles, C. L., Omlin, C., Extraction, insertion and refinement of symbolic rules in dynamically-driven recurrent neural networks, *Connection Science*, 5(3,4), 307, 1993. Special Issue on Architectures for Integrating Symbolic and Neural Processes.

Gold, E. M., Language identification in the limit. *Information and Control*, 10, 447, 1967.

Horne, B. G., Hush, D. R., Bounds on the complexity of recurrent neural network implementations of finite state machines. In *Advances in Neural Information Processing Systems*, 6, Cowan, J. D., Tesauro, G., Alspector, J., Eds., Morgan Kaufmann Publishers, Inc., 359, 1994.

Kohavi, Z., *Switching and Finite Automata Theory*, second ed., McGraw-Hill, Inc., New York, 1978.

Kolen, J. F., Kremer, S. C.,, Eds. *A Field Guide to Dynamical Recurrent Networks*, IEEE Press, To Appear.

Kremer, S. C., On the computational power of Elman-style recurrent networks, *IEEE Transactions on Neural Networks*, 6(4), 1000, 1995.

Kremer, S. C., *A Theory of Grammatical Induction in the Connectionist Paradigm*, PhD thesis, University of Alberta, 1995a.

Kremer, S. C., Identification of a specific limitation on local-feedback recurrent networks acting as Mealy/Moore machines, *IEEE Transactions on Neural Networks*, 10(2), 433, 1999.

Lang, K. J., Waibel, A. H., Hinton, G., A time-delay neural network architecture for isolated word recognition, *Neural Networks*, 3(1), 23, 1990.

Lapedes, A., Farber, R., Nonlinear signal processing using neural networks prediction and system modelling, Tech. Rep. LA-UR-262 or LA-UR87-2662, Los Alamos National Laboratory, Los Alamos, 1987.

Maskara, A., Noetzel, A., Forced learning in simple recurrent neural networks. In *Proceedings of the Fifth Conference on Neural Networks and Parallel Distributed Processing*, 107, 1992.

Miller, C., Giles, C. L., Experimental comparison of the effect of order in recurrent neural networks, *International Journal of Pattern Recognition and Artificial Intelligence*, 7(4), 849, 1993. Special Issue on Neural Networks and Pattern Recognition.

Minsky, M., *Computation: Finite and Infinite Machines*, Prentice-Hall, Inc., Englewood Cliffs, NJ, 1967.

Narendra, K. S., Parthasarathy, K., Identification and control of dynamical systems using neural networks, *IEEE Transactions on Neural Networks*, 1(1), 4, 1990.

Pinker, S., Formal models of language learning, *Cognition*, 7, 217, 1979.

Pollack, J., Implications of recursive distributed representations. In *Advances in Neural Information Processing Systems*, 1, Touretzky, D., Ed., Morgan Kaufmann, 527, 1989.

Pollack, J. B., Recursive distributed representations, *Artificial Intelligence*, 46, 77, 1990.

Porat, S., Feldman, J., Learning automata from ordered examples, *Machine Learning*, 7(2-3), 109, 1991.

Rumerlhart, D., Hinton, G., Williams, R., Learning internal representation by error propagation, In *Parallel Distributed Processing: Explorations in the Microstructure of Cognition*, McClelland, J. L., Rumelhart, D., and the P.D.P. Group, Eds., 1: Foundations. MIT Press, Cambridge, MA, 1986.

Sejnowski, T. J., Rosenberg, C. R., NETtalk: a parallel network that learns to read aloud, Tech. Rep. JHU/EECS-86/01, John Hopkins University Electrical Engineering and Computer Science, 1986.

Siegelmann, H., Sontag, E., Turing computability with neural nets, *Applied Mathematics Letters*, 4(6), 77, 1991.

Siegelmann, H., Sontag, E., On the computational power of neural nets, In *Proceedings of the Fifth ACM Workshop on Computational Learning Theory*, ACM, 440, 1992.

Siegelmann, H., Sontag, E., On the computational power of neural nets, *Journal of Computer and System Sciences*, 50(1), 132, 1995.

Waibel, A., Hanazawa, T., Hinton, G., Shikano, K., Lang, K., Phoneme recognition using time-delay neural networks, *IEEE Transactions on Acoustics, Speech and Signal Processing*, 37(3), 328, 1989.

Wexler, K., Culicover, P., *Formal Principles of Language Acquisition*, MIT Press, Cambridge, MA, 1980.

Williams, R. J., Zipser, D., A learning algorithm for continually running fully recurrent neural networks, *Neural Computation*, 1(2), 270, 1989.

Chapter 9

RECURRENT AUTOASSOCIATIVE NETWORKS: DEVELOPING DISTRIBUTED REPRESENTATIONS OF HIERARCHICALLY STRUCTURED SEQUENCES BY AUTOASSOCIATION

Ivelin Stoianov

Department Alfa-Informatica
University of Groningen
The Netherlands

I. INTRODUCTION

In spite of the growing research on connectionist Natural Language Processing (NLP), there are still a number of challenges to be solved, for example, the development of proper linguistic representations. Natural language is a dynamic system with underlying hierarchical structure and sequential external appearance. Therefore, NLP systems need an adequate hierarchical system of linguistic representations. What we roughly distinguish as letters, words, sentences, etc., needs to be encoded in a proper and systematic manner, permitting direct, "*holistic*" operations over the resultant abstract representations rather than over external sequential forms [Chalmers, 1990, Blank, 1992, Hammerton, 1998]. Those representations should be static, unique characterizations of the original objects, which is necessary for reproducing them back into their sequential form. They should allow holistic transformations and associations to representations from other modalities – visual, effectual, etc. Natural language is not the only structured process where static representations at different levels are necessary for modeling: consider composite actions, dynamic visual processes and so on. We find other examples also outside of cognitive modeling, such as modeling economic processes and physical phenomena.

A widely used practice in connectionist natural language modeling is localistic and handcrafted feature based encoding [Seidenberg, 1989, Elman 1990, Plaut, 1996, Henderson, 1998], which restricts the capacity of the processing system. It would be preferable that those representations evolve in the course of experiencing the language in its external sequential form, which is in accordance with our capacity to learn any language without any prior knowledge of it. A first attempt to build such representations was suggested by Pollack, [1990]. He extended the static Multilayered Perceptron [Rumelhart,

1986] to the Recursive Auto Associative Memory (RAAM) model, which develops compact distributed representations of the static input patterns through an autoassociation. RAAM was further extended to a Sequential RAAM (SRAAM) for sequential processing. Different implementations of the latter model had variable success even when applied to trivial data [Chalmers, 1990, Blank, 1992, Blair, 1997, Kwasny, 1995, Hammerton, 1998].

The development of global-memory recurrent neural networks, such as the Jordan Recurrent Networks [Jordan, 1986] and the Simple Recurrent Networks (SRN) by Elman [Elman, 1990] stimulated the development of models that gradually build representations of their sequential input in this global memory. The Sentence Gestalt Model [St. John, 1990] gradually encodes the input words into a *gestalt* and questions it further for roles with another static network. Similar architecture under the name "Movie Description Network" was presented by Cottrell, Bartell, and Haupt [Cottrell, 1990] which was trained to gather representations of the sequential visual input (a movie) and describe it with some simple language. A more recent implementation of SRAAM by Kwasny and Kalman [Kwasny, 1995] employs SRNs in order to build representations of the sequential input.

In this chapter, I propose a novel connectionist architecture designed to build and process a hierarchical system of static distributed representations of complex sequential data. It follows upon the idea of building complex static representations of the input sequence, but has been extended with the ability to reproduce these static representations in their original form, by building unique representations for every input sequence. The model consists of sequential autoassociative modules – Recurrent Autoassociative Networks (RANs). Each of these modules learns to reproduce input sequences and, as a side effect, develops static distributed representations of the sequences. If requested, these modules unpack static representations into their original sequential form. The complete architecture for processing sequentially represented hierarchical input data consists of a cascade of RANs. The input tokens of a RAN module from any but the lowest level in this cascade scheme are the static representations that the RAN module from the lower level has produced. The input data of the lowest level RAN module are percepts from the external world. The output of a module from the lowest level can be associated with an effector. Then, given a static representation set to the RAN hidden layer, this effector would receive commands sequentially during the unpacking process.

RAN is a recurrent neural network which conforms to the dynamics of natural languages. Also, RANs produce representations of sequences and interpret them by unpacking back to their sequential form. The more extended architecture – a cascade of RANs – resembles the hierarchy in natural languages. Furthermore, given representative training environment, this architecture has the capacity to develop the distributed representations in a *systematic* way. The question whether connectionist models can develop systematic representations has been discussed ever since the challenge put by Fodor and Pylyshin [Fodor, 1988] that only classical symbolic systems can guarantee systematicity (see Aydede [1997] for review). Connectionist systems claimed to meet this challenge are the

RAAM and SRAAMs, and the Smolensky's tensor products [Smolensky, 1990] among others. Later in this chapter I will argue that RANs provide an account of systematicity, too. Therefore, I believe that the RAN and the RAN cascade can participate in a more global cognitive model, where the distributed representations they produce are extensively transformed and associated.

This chapter continues with a discussion of the hierarchy in dynamic data in the next section. A review of connectionist sequential processing is given, after which the RAN model is presented in detail in section four. In the same section a small RAN example is presented for developing representations of syllables. The cascade model is given in section five, where a two-level representation of words is presented too. Next, I discuss some cognitive aspects related to RAN and how this architecture might provide some answers for cognitive modeling. After a discussion of RAN capacities and the representations it develops in section seven, the chapter will finish with a conclusion.

II. SEQUENCES, HIERARCHY, AND REPRESENTATIONS

Static objects and dynamic processes are mutually interconnected. On one hand, dynamic processes are ultimately composed of sequences of static objects but, on another hand, the same dynamic processes are generated by single objects and might be represented by these objects. This is more explicit in discrete dynamic objects, such as sequences composed of discrete data. The sequences are entities by themselves and consist of strings of tokens, but these sequences might build even more complex sequences. Therefore, sequential data might have some underlying structure more complex than linear: that is, there might be some hierarchy within a long sequence composed of basic tokens. For example, in natural languages, there are basic tokens – phonemes or letters; next, there are words consisting of sequences of letters or phonemes, sentences consisting of sequences of words, and so on (1). That is, in natural language, dynamic objects are part of other, more complex dynamic objects. Hierarchical objects naturally evolved during evolution are better suited to represent, process, and transmit information, than linear objects. Another advantage of this hierarchy is the redundancy among the linguistic objects, which makes the transmission of the information content in this sequence more reliable.

$$((John)(loves)(Ma-ry)) \qquad (1)$$

Sequential data that have such composite structure might have very long external representations, that is, representations consisting of rows of lowest level tokens. For example, in natural languages average sentences have some 50 characters and the current chapter has more than 15,000 characters. This data is difficult to represent and process in this external form. It has structure and I believe we organize and remember the language we experience in accordance with this structure. In the natural languages, for example, there are mechanisms for referring to some substructures – e.g., definite markers and pronouns. When it comes to processing those structures as single entities, we prefer to use internal representations of those structures rather than their external forms. Definite noun phrases and pronouns are just the external expressions of those internal representations and we use them very often. Single internal representations are much more economical to use when associating linguistic expressions to visual objects, actions, etc. Those associations are made between the internal representations of those complex objects rather than between their external representations. Therefore, if we want to model a cognitive system dealing with such a variety of data, it should properly organize a system of such representations.

Similar systems of representations naturally occur in symbolic approaches when modeling cognition: the external *terminal* tokens are organized by a system of rules with the help of internal *non-terminal* nodes, which in turn are similar to the internal static representations discussed. People still argue that because of this organization of the symbolic approach and its unlimited representational capacity, cognitive modeling should be based on the classical "language of thoughts" [Fodor, 1988], meaning the use of syntactically structured representations and rules defined over those representations. Connectionists object to this approach, mainly because of the so-called *symbol grounding problem* – the problem of explaining the relations between representations (symbols) and objects in the environment where a cognitive agent exists [Searle, 1984, Dorffner, 1991]. Connectionist architectures are particularly good at associating low level data – percepts or effectors – to higher level processing systems. Another problem concerning the symbolic approach is related to the "hardness" of its rule-based logical computations [Smolensky, 1991]. Models should accommodate the "softness" of cognition, as connectionism does, by processing data in a more fuzzy, stochastic manner.

Nevertheless, connectionism is still looking for an answer to the question of how to organize the information coming from the external sensors. Some of the available connectionist solutions are still not satisfactory. Although the implementation of the sequential RAAM proposed by Kwasny and Kalman [Kwasny, 1995] was promised to provide a better solution than the standard sequential RAAM, Hammerton [Hammerton, 1998] found that in practice this model did not learn even trivial data well. Therefore, the door is still open for other more optimal solutions and, in section four of this chapter, I propose another model: a cascade of Recurrent Autoassociation Neural Network to build a system of such representations.

In the next section I will present some details about a few connectionist architectures for sequence processing, but before that, I will outline more explicitly some features that connectionist systems and distributed representations must meet.

First, these representations should develop *emergently*, in the course of experiencing the external training data. Different levels of representations should develop *consequently*, one after another, possibly refining the representations from the lower levels. The lowest level of representations should be *perceptual* in case of dealing with sensors or *effectual* when producing actions. This gradual representation development, together with latter associations to representations from other modalities, solves the *symbol grounding problem*. Multi-modal associations should develop in simultaneously processing different modalities, for example, linguistic and visual.

Next, in order to meet the cognitive modeling requirements [Fodor, 1988], these representations should have a kind of *structure* allowing a combinatorial syntax, not necessarily explicit as in the classical symbolic systems, but understandable for other connectionist modules. This requirement is necessary for emergence of *systematicity* among those representations and for *holistic* computations [Hammerton, 1998, Smolensky, 1991]. The latter are structural operators acting upon the whole complex static representations, rather than on the token parts of the structure (sequence). Systematicity is the key to higher-order cognitive processes.

A failure to accommodate these features, when modeling language, results in models with limited capacities and no lasting implications, which is typical for many of the experiments reported that feature, for example, static language processing and hand-coded data encoding. Neither of those two popular approaches is in accordance with the spirit of natural language. We acquire language sequentially, hearing sounds and building or recognizing gradually a number of objects or temporal structures, such as, words, phrases and sentences. Similarly, when thinking, we produce and articulate language sequentially (possibly silently) by translating those structures back into temporal events, finishing this process by executing motor commands. The number of those structures is enormous and a designer's hardwired encoding does not seem plausible at all. Also, the number of existing languages and our competence to learn any of them implies that those objects should develop constantly during the communication process, from the early childhood.

III. NEURAL NETWORKS AND SEQUENTIAL PROCESSING

A. ARCHITECTURES

For more that a decade, neural network research has been considered important not only because it makes efforts toward explaining our intelligence, but also because it provides effective working models for solving a wide range of practical problems. Numerous researchers (e.g., [Rumelhart, 1986, Grossberg, 1982, Kohonen, 1984, and Hopfield, 1982]) established the theoretical background in this field. The models they have developed – the Multilayer Perceptron trained with supervised Backpropagation learning algorithm, the ART & ART-Map, the self-organizing Kohonen Maps and the Hopfield Networks, correspondingly – were theoretically [Hornik, 1989] and experimentally [Lawrence, 1995] proven to be capable of solving many static tasks. Although the response of some of these models to the input pattern depends on their internal dynamics (Hopfield and Grossberg Neural Network models), they are not endowed with the capacity to process dynamic or sequential patterns. Hopfield NNs are designed to search iteratively for one of the encoded attractors. ART models develop localistically represented categories, which restricts their capacity when processing large variety of sequences, even with some special encoding schemes.

Problems such as language processing and robot control, which are essentially dynamic, pushed the connectionist investigations toward searching for NN models capable of handling such dynamic data. The first NN models were still static, encoding limited dynamics by means of a window, shifting over sequential data. The NETtalk model [Sejnowski, 1987] was trained to produce phonetic representations of words, where the context required to map the current letter was encoded within a shifting window of size seven – three letters on the left and three letters on the right side of the letter to be pronounced. This is an example of the so-called *Finite Input Response* filter, where the system response to a given input is limited to a predefined number of steps.

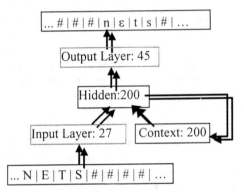

Figure 1. Simple Recurrent Network that "reads" words, that is, maps orthographic to phonologic lexical representations.

The first real recurrent models were extensions of the Multilayer Perceptron with recurrent connections. They implement another type of dynamics – *Infinite Input Response* – where the input at a certain time influences the system response until the dynamics are externally reset. Several recurrent versions of the MLP were developed. In one of them [Jordan, 1986], the network state at any point at a time is a function of the input at the current time step, plus the state of the output units at the previous step. In another recurrent model proposed by Elman [Elman, 1990] – Simple Recurrent Networks (SRNs) – the network's current state depends on the current input and its own internal state, which is represented by the activation of the hidden units in the previous moment – see Fig.1. This internal state is considered as a context that provides information for the past. The SRNs were successfully employed for many linguistic and other tasks where the objects have sequential nature [Reilly, 1995, Wilson, 1996, Cairns, 1997, Stoianov, 1998, Stoianov, 1999]. Simple Recurrent Networks were initially trained by Elman with the standard backpropagation (BP) learning algorithm, in which errors are computed and weights are updated at each time step. While more biologically motivated because of the local-in-time weight adjustments, the BP is not as effective as the backpropagation through time (BPTT) learning algorithm, in which error signal is propagated back through time and temporal dependencies are learned better. A detailed technical description of the SRNs and the BPTT algorithm is presented in section four.

The static self-organizing Kohonen Map neural network was extended with recurrent connections too, which made the network responses dependent on both the current input and the last neural map activations. Models following this idea are the Temporal Kohonen Map (TKM) by Chappell and Taylor [Chappell, 1993] and the Self-Organizing Feature Map for Sequences (SARDNET) by James and Miikkulainen [James, 1995], among others. There are still other connectionist architectures able to process dynamic data, usually by inducing dynamics in existing static models with recurrent connections among neurons (*global memory*) or implementing dynamics in neurons (*local memory*). The latter types of architectures vary with regard to the place of the dynamics – in the weights, in the activation function, or both [Lawrence, 1995, Tsoi, 1994].

A common restriction on most of the recurrent models is that the input data they process has to be linear in the temporal dimension. These networks are able to recognize and classify the temporal sequences they have been trained on (SRNs and Jordan Networks) or they have clustered during the self-organization process (TKM and SARDNET), but they can not extract more complex temporal features or substructures. In addition, as the length of the sequences becomes greater, the performance worsens. This problem has been recognized by a number of authors. Bengio, Simard, and Frasconi [Bengio, 1994] showed that earning long-distance dependencies is difficult even for very simple tasks (long strings of a few basic symbols). Miikkulainen and Dyer [Miikkulainen, 1991] emphasized that the required network size, the number of training examples, and the training time become intractable as the sequence temporal complexity grows.

B. REPRESENTING NATURAL LANGUAGE

As I discussed earlier in the previous section, an important moment when dealing with sequences is the ability to develop a hierarchical structure of representations of the processed sequences. This question is especially apparent in natural language modeling. In earlier connectionist models, the lexemes were represented in a static manner with some artificial and not always effective encoding schemes (e.g., in Seidenberg [1989] and Plaut [1996]), and sentences consisted of some artificial and very limited in number words [Elman, 1990, Miikkulainen, 1991, Tabor, 1997]. When modeling some other problems, for example learning lexical phonotactics [Stoianov, 1998, Stoianov, 1999] or learning the mapping from orthographic to phonetic representations for certain language [Stoianov, 1999], one does not really need static representations of words, but in other cases, such as holistic computations or static associations, this is obligatory. To my knowledge, there are no approaches that model people's full capacity to deal with structured dynamic data using connectionism.[1] People associate the sounds they hear with visual patterns or actions. Similarly, they associate actions with words and sentences. All of these objects are realized as sequences of small parts, spanning time. In order to treat them as single entities, we shall enclose them and represent them statically. This naturally leads to a search for methods packing sequences into static representations and unfolding them back into their sequential form.

High-level connectionist language modeling has focused on small illustrative problems: as the learning is restricted to simple grammars and a very limited number of words [Elman, 1990, Tabor, 1997] or word TAGs [Henderson, 1998]. I attribute this not to the connectionist models' inability to learn complex dependencies, but rather to the absence of adequate concepts of how to develop high-level distributed representations. Thus far, representations have been designed mostly by hand, either feature based or even simpler – localistically. This works well at the bottom stages of language processing, where a very limited number of characters and phonemes constitute words, but not at higher linguistic levels, where large number of words, phrases, sentences build more complex structures. The variety at those levels is enormous. How can representations be developed for such objects? Hand-crafting here simply does not work. Some cognitive scientists suggest "tensor products" [Smolensky, 1990], which expand with the increase of the data complexity. Others suggest syntactic structures to be represented both in time and space (Temporal Synchrony Variable Binding [Henderson, 1998], but these solutions do not produce fixed-sized static representations for input objects of variable complexity. Therefore, others support the more plausible idea of static, fixed-size, emergently developed connectionist "symbols." But how can such representations be developed?

A significant attempt toward a more systematic way of representing structures and sequences was the development of the Recursive Auto-Associative Memory (RAAM) by Jordan Pollack [Pollack, 1990]. This architecture is another simple extension of MLP. The RAAMs auto-associate the input data, which is a concatenation of two patterns, and use the activations of the hidden layer neurons to represent this concatenation (Fig. 2a). This is equivalent to the learning of a simple symbolic rule. When applied recursively, that is, when using the developed representations as an input for another compression, RAAM can learn a grammar and develop representations for the non-terminal symbols in this grammar. This makes RAAM a connectionist implementation of a symbolic processor. However, theoretical problems arise from connectionist point of view, due to the need for an external symbolic mechanism to store representations. Also, the training process is immensely difficult due to the recursive reuse of the ever changing representations in the course of the training [Kwasny, 1995].

RAAMs were theoretically extended to model a stack, which made the model capable of learning and representing sequences – Sequential RAAM (SRAAM). However, this model needs an external stack during the training, which is a step

---

[1] See the following discussion on the (S)RAAM connectionist models.

back from connectionism, as commented earlier. It is difficult for SRAAM to learn even trivial structures and sequences, which makes it an impractical model. Also, RAAM produces representations at every time step, to be reused as inputs, while dynamic objects with uniform structure need single static representations. In that respect, producing single representations of a whole object is more economical – representations at certain level should be produced only if there is a necessity of using them. In natural language, producing static representations of items such as syllables, words and sentences is more useful than producing representations of arbitrary combinations of letters, words, etc. Syllables are involved in morphological transformations. Words are associated with visual patterns and actions; sentences have more concrete semantic meanings. We know that those linguistic objects are distinguished because they have certain functions, and we make use of them. On the contrary, producing representations of arbitrary combination of mixed items is not so useful.

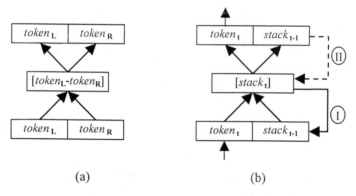

(a)   (b)

Figure 2. (a) RAAM: left and right input tokens are autoassociated, which results in a single compact representation of the input tokens at the hidden layer. (b) SRAAM: based on RAAM and SRN. (I) *Compression*: tokens apply one at a time to the input and they are autoassociated, together with the previous state of the context. This results in ever more compact representation of the input sequence at the hidden layer. (II) *Decompression*: a compact representation applies to the hidden layer and produces the last token from the encoded sequence and the previous state of the stack, which in turn is applied again to the hidden layer.

Another implementation of the sequential RAAM was presented by Kwasny and Kalman [Kwasny, 1995]. Their SRAAM combines the architecture of the Simple Recurrent Networks and the RAAM idea for autoassociation (Fig. 2b). The stack that the RAAM requires during the learning is encoded in the contextual memory of the SRN. This makes the training faster and easier. Further, Kwasny and Kalman suggested a variation of the mean square error function that boosts small differences between the targeted and resulted neuron activations. When combined with a modified conjugate gradient training algorithm, this reportedly improved the learning. And still another important contribution in this work was a method for representing recursive structures – by means of symbolic transformation of any tree structure into a binary tree, which can easily be transformed to a sequence. Those two operations are reversible, which allows reconstructing the original structures from their sequential representations.

Exploring holistic computations, Hammerton [Hammerton, 1998] attempted to recreate the Chalmers [Chalmers, 1990] experiments using the Kwasny and Kalman SRAAMs, which was promised to learn faster and more reliably. For this purpose, he used the corpus from Chalmers, [1990] – a small corpus containing 250 sequences built out of 13 distinct items. Standard backpropagation learning algorithm and two variations of the Kwasny and Kalman training algorithm were utilized. Hammerton reported that, with the best learning algorithm (the noted earlier modified error function and the conjugate gradient training), the network encoded and decoded up to 85% of the 130 training and 87.5% of the remaining 120 unseen testing sequences (Hammerton, p. 43), which departs from the reported perfect learning by Kwasny and Kalman (with SRAAM on a more complex task) and Chalmers (with RAAM on the same task). Therefore, Hammerton concluded that "the SRAAM is not as effective a vehicle for holistic symbol processing as it initially appeared."

Also, there are two other problems when those models are used to develop sequential representations. First, as I said earlier, they produce static representations at every time step, which is more useful for representing recursive structures than sequential data. Next, due to the stack-based memory organization, the input sequences are reproduced inversely. Therefore, one would need another external mechanism to reverse those sequences. The solution I propose in the next section is based on an autoassociation and SRN, too, but it implements a *queue* rather than a *stack* mechanism, which leads to reproducing the sequences in the right order.

The first attempt to employ recurrent architectures for producing a 'gestalt' or a single static representation of a sequence of words (statically represented) was made by St. John and McClelland [St. John, 1990] – the Story Gestalt Model. This model comprises two networks – a Jordan Recurrent Network which gradually processes the input sentence and uses the activations of the output layer to represent the sequence presented as input thus far. This compact representation was called *gestalt*. The second NN is a static MLP, trained to extract some information of interest for a sequence represented with its gestalt as input to the MLP (Fig. 3). Another similar model, the Movie Description Network by Cottrell, Bartell, and Haupt [Cottrell, 1990] uses the Simple Recurrent Networks to develop representations of simple movies presented as input to the SRN. A second SRN produces a verbal description of the input movie. These are specific, rather than universal, models; they produce representations which are not necessarily unique and can not be involved in a hierarchical system of representations of composite data.

The capacity of SRN to process sequential data was exploited in another approach, aimed at obtaining static representations of syllables [Gasser, 1992]. In this model, one recurrent network was trained on a sequential mapping – an input train of phones to an output train of patterns, which are concatenations of

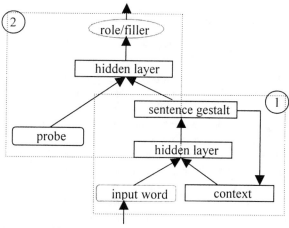

Figure 3. Story Gestalt Model by St. John. In this architecture, a Jordan recurrent network (1) gradually produces representations of the input sequence. Next, a MLP (2) extracts from these representations some of the constituents of the sentence.

the same phones and a static lexical representation of the word the phones belong to. The recurrent layer activations at the end of each syllable were recorded and used by a second network that was trained to unpack these representations to their original sequential form. Having originally the task of word recognition, this scheme requires that both phones and lexical representations be offered during training. Static syllable representations are resulted as a side effect. This approach takes a direction which is opposite to the gradual building of language representations. Instead of building word representation, it does the opposite – it produces syllable representations in the course of word recognition.

The approach presented here takes another direction, consistent with the principle of gradual language evolution and learning, by processing and evolving language items of increasing complexity. Another problem with the solution presented by Gasser is that because the packing and unpacking processes are split, this method requires the training sequences during both learning tasks, which is less plausible and increases the learning time. The sequential autoassociative task in my approach requires only a short-term memory to keep the sequence to be presented for a second time at the output layer and the system only has to perceive the input the environment provides throughout the learning (which may last indefinitely: we can keep the learning going non-stop).

IV. RECURRENT AUTOASSOCIATIVE NETWORKS

In this section I will present an architecture designed to develop and make use of static, implicitly structured, interpretable representations of sequences. The proposed model is an extension of the Simple Recurrent Networks [Elman, 1990]. Recall that SRN is a recurrent neural network architecture based on the feedforward Multi Layered Perceptron with a global context memory storing the recent activation of the SRN hidden layer,[2] which is fed back as an additional input to the hidden layer itself (Fig. 1). The context layer has the capacity to encode all the information for the input provided to the network, since the beginning of the sequence. Hence, if we reset the context layer and apply a sequence, at every moment the hidden layer and the context layer (after a short delay) will contain static distributed information for this sequence, which as we will see later is not necessarily a representation of the input sequence, but rather depends on the learning task.

There are different possibilities to obtain static representations of the input sequence. One of them is just to use the context layer activation after the whole sequence has been processed in an item prediction task – similarly to the *gestalt* models by St. John and McClelland [St. John, 1990] and Cottrell, Bartell, and Haupt [Cottrell, 1990]. The networks there were trained to predict the next input token, which forces the networks to learn information specific to this particular task, but is insufficient for developing complete representations of the input sequences. We need an organization or a learning task that guarantees that the distributed representations developed by the network (1) contain all information about the sequence, (2) are unique for each sequence, and (3) contain enough information to reproduce the sequence, which is a consequence of (1) and (2).

Representations satisfying the above requirements evolve naturally, if we train the network on an autoassociation task, that is, to reproduce the input sequence. But then, there is another problem – the timing, when to present the input and the output patterns. One can try to reproduce the current input pattern immediately, but this will not produce any useful hidden layer representations – there will be no need of a context for this task. A delay of one step, or two, or some other fixed number of steps would train the network to develop information specific for the prediction task, but the representations would still not necessarily satisfy the conditions 1 – 3. In order to produce such representations, the network has to be trained on an autoassociative task in which the input sequence starts to be reproduced after the whole input sequence has been represented to the input, followed by a unique pattern, a *trigger*, indicating the end of the sequence. This way, if the training set contains sequences, which in turn contain another sequence in the training corpus as an initial sub-sequence, then the network will still produce distinct representations for both sequences. The static representation of the sequence will be just the

---

[2] The term "layer activation" denotes a numerical vector with the activations of all neurons in that layer.

216

hidden layer activations at the moment when the trigger has been applied and processed by the network (Fig. 4).

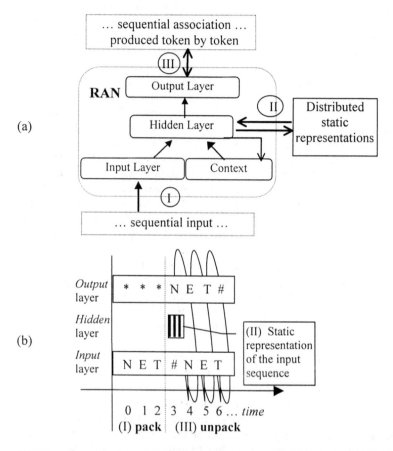

Figure 4. Recurrent Autoassociative Network: (a) architecture and (b) functional temporal unfolding. Operations: (I) input sequence packing (time steps 0–3), (II) obtaining or setting a static representation (time step 3), and (III) unpacking the static representation to its sequential form (time steps 3-6).

There are some other details to be specified, namely the input pattern after the trigger has been applied to the input layer, the target output pattern before that and the target output pattern after the sequence has been reproduced. The target output pattern after the reproduction of the whole input sequence is another special pattern, labeled *end-of-sequence*, which will signal that the whole sequence has been produced. The input patterns after the trigger might be either the same trigger, repeatedly provided until the network produces the end-of-sequence pattern, or, what I found more helpful to the network in learning this difficult task, the last ouput pattern provided to the inner larger. The latter approach provides guiding information about how far the network has progressed in reproducing the sequences, and experiments have demonstrated that, indeed, it is easier for the network to learn the task with this approach.

With regard to the output target patterns at the time when the sequence is still being provided to the input, the learning algorithm used – backpropagation through time [Haykin, 1994] – does not necessarily need target patterns at the earlier moments, provided that an error signal is being propagated back through time. Indeed, the sequential autoassociative task provides such an error, which originates in the second phase of the autoassociation (Fig. 4, step III).

Another possibility is to train the network at the same time on a prediction task. First the network produces its anticipations about the coming patterns. Next, it reproduces the whole sequence using no external input, but only what the network has encoded at the context layer, perhaps reusing the produced output pattern as input. The latter approach is more plausible considering what each of us has observed when listening to a speech in a noisy environment, that we use anticipations in interpreting that speech. In such a noisy environment, having received some initial context, the network can produce the most probable sequence for this left context and next to produce the static representation for this sequence by presenting the triggering pattern. Both approaches were tested, but in the latter case the performance was worse, which I attribute to the higher computational complexity of this joint task. The network in the second approach has to learn two tasks, which makes the learning harder. When using the first approach, the network learns the autoassociative task faster and with fewer errors. The first approach satisfies the above outlined requirements, concerning the representations produced, and therefore it was used in the experiments reported on here.

In summary, by training a recurrent neural network on an autoassociation task as described above with a training corpus containing a set of sequences, the network learns to produce static distributed representations of these sequences. The hidden layer activations, at the moment the triggering pattern is applied to the input and processed by the network, are used for this purpose. The static representations for each input sequence are unique due to the specific setting of the autoassociative task. After successful training, a RAN network has two functions: firstly, to generate the static representation of a given input sequence (Fig. 4: steps I and II) and secondly, to reproduce the original sequential form of a static representation, when the hidden layer is set to the static representations (Fig. 4: steps II, III).

A. TRAINING RAN WITH THE BACKPROPOGATION THROUGH TIME LEARNING ALGORITHM

The RAN (Fig. 4) and the SRN (Fig. 1) models have the same architecture and share similar feedforward processing steps and learning algorithms. However, when SRNs are trained on prediction task they can also be trained with the standard error backpropagation algorithm, while RANs can only be trained with backpropagation through time learning algorithm (Haykin 1994), because in the first feedforward processing phase (Fig. 4, phase I), there is no error signal originating at the output layer and backpropagated through the network, but only error signal computed in the second phase (Fig.4, phase III) and backpropagated through time. With regard to this, any other learning algorithm that backpropagates error signal through time can be used, too. What is important, when using BPTT to train RANs, is to set properly the sequence of input-output training data, according to the scheme outlined earlier in this section. The BPTT learning algorithm is generally known to the potential readership, but for completeness, it will be described in this subsection.

SRNs have two working regimens – a utilization of a trained network and network training. The first one is simply applying a forward pass, where the current input signal is propagated forward throughout the network and the current context layer activation is used. After each forward step, the hidden layer activation is copied to the context layer, to be used later. The network utilization is the same as the forward step in the BPTT, which in turn is described in the next section. The BPTT learning algorithm itself is more complicated. It includes: firstly, a forward pass (2-5) for all input tokens, keeping the network activations in a stack; secondly, a backward through time pass (6-9), where the errors are computed at the output layer and backpropagated through the network layers and through time, and thirdly, updating the weights with the accumulated weight-updating values (10). During the second step, at each time moment but the last one, a *future error* is used, processed and backpropagated further through time.

1. Forward Pass

In the following description, $|IL|$, $|HL|$, $|CL|$, $|OL|$ stand for the size of the input, hidden, context and output layers, correspondingly. The input signals provided to the hidden layer neurons and output layer neurons are noted as $net^H_i(t)$ and $net^O_i(t)$. Next, $in_j(t)$, $cn_k(t)$, $hn_i(t)$ and $on_l(t)$ stand for the activations of the j-th input, k-th context, i-th hidden and l-th output neurons at time t. And finally, w^H_{ij}, w^H_{ik}, and w^O_{li} are the weights of the connections between j-th input neuron and i-th hidden neuron, k-th context neuron and i-th hidden neuron, and i-th hidden neuron and l-th output neuron, respectively. For convenience, the bias for all layers is encoded as an extra input neuron ($j=0$; $i=0$) with constant activation 1. The activation function $f(.)$ is of sigmoidal type – the logistic function or the hyperbolic tangent function.

The items of the training/testing sequence $S=[c_1c_2...c_{|S|}]$ are referenced with an index t, set to zero in the beginning of the sequence processing. Also, before applying a new sequence, the context layer is reset by setting all context neurons $cn_k(t=0)$ to zero ($k=1...|CL|$). The sequences are presented to the network one token c_t at a time. For each token, a forward pass is processed. Firstly, the hidden layer is activated in accordance with (2) and (3):

$$net^H_i(t) = \Sigma_{j=0...|IL|}\, w^H_{ij}\, in_j(t) \ + \Sigma_{k=1...|CL|}\, w^H_{ik}\, cn_k(t) \qquad (2)$$
$$hn_i(t) = f(net^H_i(t)) \qquad (3)$$

After the activation of the hidden neurons, their activation values are copied to the context neurons. Next, the signal is propagated further to the output layer, by activating all neurons at the output layer: (4,5).

$$net^O_l(t) = \Sigma_{i=0...|HL|} \, w^O_{li} \, hn_i(t) \tag{4}$$
$$on_l(t) = f(net^O_l(t)) \tag{5}$$

Specifically for the RANs, if the forward pass is a part of the BPTT learning algorithm, a training sequence S of input/output patterns according the scheme in Fig. 4b is built. On another hand, if the network is used for packing only, the static distributed representation of a sequence being applied to the input layer is the activation of the hidden layer at the moment when the delimiter pattern has been processed. In turn, in order to unpack (decode) the static representation of a sequence, it is applied to the hidden layer and propagated forward; the resulted output pattern is the first element of the sequence. Next, this output pattern is provided as an input to the network and propagated forward, by using the last hidden layer activation as a context. This process is repeated until a pattern recognized as a delimiter pattern is produced at the output layer.

2. Backward Through Time Pass

The second step of the BPTT learning algorithm for a given training sequence is propagating the error signal back through the network and time. We suppose that the forward steps for each token in the sequence are already done, keeping the activations and the target patterns in a stack. Next, error and weight updating values are computed in an earlier time cycle, that is, starting from the last token. Firstly, error deltas at the output layer and the updates of the weights connecting the hidden layer to output layer are computed with (6) and (7). Note, that S stands for the whole training sequence (the original sequence presented at the input layer and targeted later at the output layer). Also, τ denotes a global time index and $\Delta w(\tau)$ stands for the accumulated $\Delta w(t)$ for all items from the current sequence.

$$\delta^O_l(t) = f'(net^O_l(t)) \, (C_l(t) - on_l(t) \,) \tag{6}$$
$$\Delta w^O_{li}(\tau) = \eta. \, \Sigma_{t=1 \, ... \, |S|} \, \delta^O_l(t) \, hn_i(t) \tag{7}$$

In (6), $C_l(t)$ denotes the desired activation of the l-th output neuron ($l=1...|OL|$) at time t. Provided that the activation function $f(x)$ is the logistic function $f(x) = (1+e(-x))^{-1}$, the derivative of $f(x)$ is $f'(x) = x(1-x)$. Next, deltas and updating values of the weights connecting the hidden layer to the input and the context layers are computed in accordance to (8) and (9):

$$\delta^H_i(t) = f'(net^H_i(t)) \, [\, \Sigma_{l=1...|OL|} w^O_{li} \delta^O_l(t) + \Sigma_{k=1...|CL|} w^H_{ik} \delta^H_k(t+1) \,] \tag{8}$$
$$\Delta w^H_{ij}(\tau) = \eta \, \Sigma_{t=1...|S|} \, \delta^H_i(t) \, n_j(t-1) \tag{9}$$

where $i = 1 \, ... \, |HL|$, $j = 0 \, ... \, (|IL| + |CL|)$ and $n(t)$ is a joined vector containing both $in(t)$ and $cn(t)$. The second sum in (8) represents the context layer delta-term $\delta_k^C(t)$, computed by backpropagating the delta $\delta^H_i(t+1)$ through the weights connecting the context neurons to the hidden neurons. And finally, all weights are updated according to (10) with the accumulated weight-updating values, computed with (7) and (9).

$$w(\tau) = w(\tau - 1) + \Delta w(\tau) \tag{10}$$

Error Back propagation learning algorithms are known for the possibility of getting stocked in a local minima on the error surface. There are number of techniques designed to overcome this problem. The most useful technique is to apply a momentum term α to (10), as is done in (11). The momentum term keeps the movement over the weight error space for some time, even if the network has fallen into a local minimum. Usually, $\alpha = 0.7$.

$$\Delta w'(\tau) = \alpha \, \Delta w(\tau - 1) + (1 - \alpha) \, \Delta w(\tau) \tag{11}$$

Another technique that has similar effect is to apply initially a higher learning coefficient η and, next, to decrease it gradually. This implements a quicker rough search for the region where the global minimum is located. Later, the exact location of the error minimum is searched with smaller steps. Usually, the initial $\eta = 0.2$ and the decrease might be exponential with a very small step (e.g., 0.9995). For further reading about SRN, BP, and BPTT and other recurrent learning algorithms, one can refer to Haykin [1994].

B. EXPERIMENTING WITH RANs: LEARNING SYLLABLES

The idea of using RAN to develop static representations of sequences was tested on natural language data. A set of 140 distinct syllables was collected from a list of 100 polysyllabic Dutch words. The syllables were represented as sequences of Latin characters. The mean length of the syllables was 4.1 ± 1.12 σ. The characters were represented orthogonally, in a vector of length 27, that is, for every symbol there was a correspondent neuron which was set active any time this symbol was encoded. The 27th position was activated when the special triggering pattern for the input layer and the end-of-sequence pattern for the output layer were presented or targeted. In order to speed up the training, the *non-active* and *active* neuron states were set to 0.1 and 0.9 respectively, which set the working regimen of the neuron activation functions within an almost linear range rather than around the extremes zero and one, where the sigmoid derivatives approach zero. The size of the hidden layer was set to 30. The learning algorithm was backpropagation through time. The training was organized in epochs, in which all patterns were presented randomly, according to their frequency of occurrence in the corpus. The words were taken from the

CELEX[3] lexical data base. The network error was measured after each training epoch as percent character and syllable misprediction. During the training process, the network error followed the standard pattern of quick initial error drop and subsequent slow rate of decrease. After approximately 50 epochs, the network error was reduced to 1%. Further training would reduce the error even more, but it would take much more time.

From an implemental point of view, it was interesting to test different strategies for representing the trigger and end-of-sequence patterns, for instance, whether it is possible to use only the neurons used for encoding the standard input and output patterns, or whether an extra neuron is necessary. Tests were conducted with patterns such as all neurons active, non-active, or taking a value of 0.5. In all three cases, the performance was worse than the approach with an extra, switching neuron. Therefore, the later approach was used in the following experiments. It has the additional advantage of always allowing the encoding of a distinct switching pattern, even if the above patterns are used to represent data.

This first experiment suggests that SRNs can learn such a task. Now, it is interesting to see what kind of static representations the network has developed after the training. A simple observation of those vectors does not say much (Fig. 5, top), because the network has organized those representations just to accomplish its task, not to make them readable by humans, which is the case in the high-level symbolic systems. It is more important that the network itself can 'read' those representations, that is, it can reproduce the original sequential form. Yet, some analysis might be useful in order to persuade the reader that those representations are worth something. For this purpose, a Kohonen Map neural network was trained to organize those representations. The Kohonen Map is known as very useful for clustering such a data. The resultant map and a minimal spanning tree are given in Figure 5, at the bottom.

As expected, syllables with same front parts are located at similar positions (e.g., *ant, ann, aus, am, aan, a*), but also, syllables with similar ends are placed at close positions (e.g., *pol - rol*; *tra - dra*). The RAN very clearly has captured the common external features among the training sequences: similar sequences are mapped into close positions; that is, their distributed representations are close. This raised expectations that the network would generalize, that is, reproduce unseen input sequences (and produce their static representations). This hypothesis was tested and the results demonstrated that RAN did generalize, although very modestly. Among the tested sequences, unseen during the training, only 15 syllables were successfully reproduced at the output, that is, about 10% generalization. But the network was trained on a very small number of sequences, therefore, I predicted that if the network were trained on a larger data set, the percent of the generalization would be even larger. The second experiment in section five confirmed this hypothesis.

---

[3] The CELEX lexical database contains lexical data for Dutch, German, and English languages. Address: Center for Lexical Information, POBox 310, 6500 AH Hijmegen, The Netherlands, http://www.kun.nl/celex/ Email: celex@mpi.nl

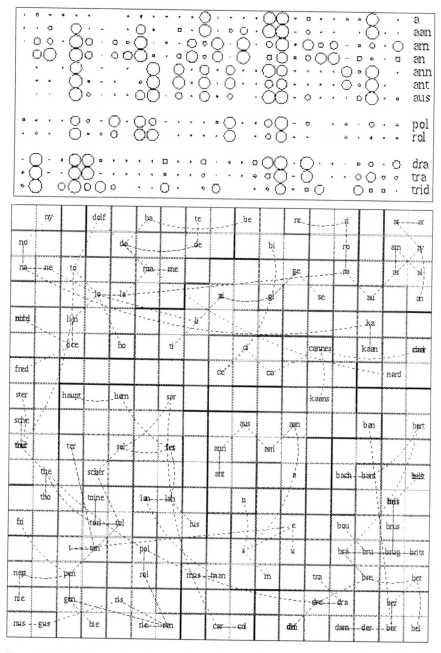

Figure 5. (top): Representations developed by the RAN. Each line stands for one vector. Each circle represents one value in the representation. The larger the circles, the greater the correspondent values. (bottom): A Kohonen Map neural network trained to cluster those representations (see text). The network maps similar syllables into close positions, meaning that those representations are close to each other. The lines connecting cells represent a minimal spanning tree.

223

V. A CASCADE OF RANs

The main goal of this work, as stated earlier in the chapter, is to build a connectionist model that develops static distributed representations of a set of hierarchically structured sequences. Single Recurrent Autoassociative Networks produce single-level static representations only. A natural development of RANs to cope with hierarchically structured sequential data is to build a cascade of RANs, in which each RAN deals with subsequences of the external patterns at certain level. That is, the RANs from each level are fed with sequences of patterns developed at lower-level RAN, produce static representations of those sequences, and provide them as input patterns to the following-level RANs. Also, whenever they are requested, those RAN modules will decode (unpack) representations, for example, if the following-level RAN module needs to decode some object into its sequential representation (Fig. 6).

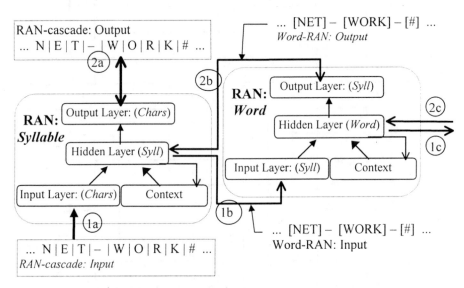

Figure 6. RANs and the mechanism of multi-level sequence processing. Stream of chars is presented to the input of the *syllable*-RAN (1a), which builds *syllable*-representations and provides them to the *word*-RAN (1b), which, in turn, builds *word*-representations and exports them further (1c). Similarly, if *word*-RAN is presented with a *word*-representation (2c), it will unpack it to train of *syllable*-representations and will provide them to the *syllable*-RAN (2b), which in turn will unpack them to train of chars (2a).

Following the representations developed from the lowest to the higher level RAN, note that this cascade model gradually transforms the temporal-dimension complexity into a spatial-dimension complexity, that is, long sequences of patterns of simple elements will be transformed into shorter sequences of complex static representations, distributed among an increasing number of neurons. This way, trains of percepts that implicitly contain high-level, sequentially represented concepts will be transformed into static representations of those concepts and these representations will also be reconstructed back to their external sequential form. This is important, as we will see in the next section, for solving the *symbol grounding* problem. RANs also provide an account of another important property – *systematicity* among the representations built. The more sequences learned at a certain level, the larger the network generalization will be; that is, after exploring many combinatorial possibilities among the input data, the RAN modules will build static representations in a systematic manner.

Still, there are some questions to be answered. For instance, why do we need such hierarchical structure, when a single RAN can be trained to produce the same highest-level static distributed representations and to output sequential associations? There are two points which speak in favor of the cascade structure. First, it is difficult for one homogeneous network to learn long-distance relationships [Miikkulainen, 1991] for discussion [Christiansen, 1999]. BPTT learning algorithm propagates back error, but the more steps it propagates back, the smaller the influence of those errors is to the earlier steps. Studying different patterns of recursion, Christiansen and Chater found that the depth of embedding (or recursion) SRNs can handle well is in the range 3 – 5 steps. Hence, learning sequences longer than 5 tokens would be more difficult. Even if one uses some techniques to improve the learning, the general tendency to perform worse on longer sequences remains.

Another advantage of the hierarchical system of representations is the possibility to access intermediate representations of the input train of simple elements (e.g., words), if we need to apply holistic operations or to interpret them. In natural languages, when we hear a sentence, we have an access to its constituents, each of which has some relations with other objects. Only a hierarchical system can handle such intermediate representations and a RAN cascade automatically develops such static representations.

This cascade structure has one important limitation – that the cascade should be designed in advance and remain fixed throughout its life. This raises two design questions – how to determine the data structure and how to determine the size of the RAN hidden layers, that is, the size of the representations at each level. Also, there should be a segmentation mechanism that signals the end of the sub-sequences for every cascade level.

Different levels may be selected according to the natural hierarchy in the input data. For example, when learning natural language, one might favor learning representations of syllables, words, sentences and so on. The input sequence might be split into sub-sequences either by use of some external markers – syllabic delimiter, space between words, full-stop (or even larger pause) – or by learning phonotactics and word order and segmenting at proper points, where low-frequency combinations are about to be formed. Cairns, Shillcock, Chater, and Levy [Cairns, 1997] have connectionist experiments on this matter. Likewise, if we use the approach in which RAN both predicts the following pattern and reproduces the sequence (see the previous section), then RAN itself could be used to segment the input sequences.

With regard to the structures that such a cascade architecture can represent, this model imposes a few restrictions. First, one cascade may develop representations of fixed-depth trees, where RANs at each cascade-level process one tree-level. As a consequence, true recursive structures can not be fully represented. Still, recursive structures can be approximated up to a certain depth. Next, leaves (terminal patterns) may occur only at the bottom level of these trees. For example, sequence (12a) with internal structure (12b) is illegal in a two-level cascade because the token 'd' is at the second level rather than at the bottom level. The allowed structures of this sequence are given in (12c). This limitation corresponds to the gradual way of information entrance and processing in the cognitive systems, starting from the bottom, perceptual level.

$$a\,b\,c\,d \hspace{7cm} (12a)$$
$$(\,(abc)\,d\,) \hspace{6.5cm} (12b)$$
$$(\,(a)\,(bcd)\,) \qquad (\,(ab)\,(cd)\,) \qquad (\,(abc)\,(d)\,) \qquad (abcd) \qquad (12c)$$

In case we need to develop representations of any tree structures, such as (12b), those tree structures can be transformed into plain sequences as in Kwasny, [1995]. However, this method needs an external symbolic device that transforms structures in both directions. Another solution might involve marking the distributed representations with level-labels and providing them to the correspondent RANs. This solution needs a supervisor that distributes the patterns, and it is biologically more plausible than the first solution.

Sequences with complex structure, such as sentences in natural language, may be processed with one RAN-level, too. The sentence structure that is known as syntax may simply evolve among the distributed representations, instead of being taught explicitly. Similarly, Elman [Elman, 1990] trained the SRNs on a prediction task and later found that the developed context layer representations correspond at each time step to the syntactic category of the sequence processed thus far.

The size h of the hidden layers at each level should be based on the informational content of the sequences the correspondent RAN is going to pack. Parameters in this measure are the number of distinct tokens $|C|$, the number of possible sequences $|S|$, the maximal length of the sequences to be represented k, and the number of neuron states b.

First, let us enumerate the maximal number of distinct patterns P_{max} that the RAN should encode in the hidden layer. The maximal number of strings composed of up to k tokens is $[(|C|^{k+1} - 1) / (|C| - 1) - 1]$, which is the total number of permutations with repetition of 1, 2, 3, ... k items selected from $|C|$ items. In the same way, the actual number of training strings is $|S|$. We should count the maximal number of strings, because the network is expected to generalize after the training, that is, to reproduce combinations of items, unseen during training. Next, the number of distinct patterns that RANs need to reproduce a sequence of k items is $2k+1$, which is the number of context states when autoassociating the input sequence (see section 4). Therefore, the maximal number P_{max} of distinct patterns necessary to produce unique representations of strings composed of up to k tokens is $[(|C|^{k+1} - 1) / (|C| - 1) - 1](2k + 1)$. The actual number of necessary distinct patterns P satisfies condition (13).

$$|S| (2k+1) \leq P \leq [(|C|^{k+1} - 1) / (|C| - 1) - 1] (2k+1) \tag{13}$$

Next, the number N of patterns that h neurons can represent, each of which having b distinct states is $N=b^h$. That is, the number of neurons necessary to represent N patterns is $h=log_b(N)$. Therefore, the number of hidden neurons necessary to encode P distinct patterns is

$$log_b(|S| (2k+1)) \leq h \leq log_b([(|C|^{k+1} - 1) / (|C| - 1) - 1] (2k+1)) \tag{14}$$

from which we derive :

$$log_b(|S|)+log_b (2k+1) \leq h < (k+1)log_b(|C|) - log_b(|C|-1)+log_b (2k+1) \tag{15}$$

Formula (15) estimates the minimal number of neurons that is necessary to represent a certain number of sequences with RAN. As mentioned earlier, the right-hand side number should be used in order to achieve better generalization. However, formula (15) does not guarantee that this number of hidden neurons is enough for the network to perform the autoassociation task for all strings and develop their distributed representations. In a recurrent neural network, hidden layer neurons also have other functions, related to the network processing. In addition, given the enormous complexity of the learning problem, it is very difficult for the learning algorithm to find proper weights producing these particular representations. Usually more neurons are necessary to learn a particular task than the theoretical estimations. Therefore, a scaling coefficient $\gamma > 1$ will be applied to (15) that will account for these and other factors related to the network processing mechanisms. This will give to the learning algorithm more freedom to find a proper weight set solving the training problem.

Now, let us find an estimation of the necessary RAN hidden layer size in the previous example by using (15). The base b will be set to 2 states and the coefficient γ to 5.0. The experiment was learning 140 syllables ($|S|$=140) built out of 26 distinct letters ($|C|$=26). The maximal string length was 4 (k=4). Then according to (15), $50 < h_{syll \ RAN} < 110$. In the reported experiments, 30 hidden neurons were enough to encode almost all training sequences.

Finally, let me discuss the strategy of the order in which the networks should be trained at the different levels, and what training regime to select. This includes the question of whether to train the different RAN levels gradually and then keep them fixed, or to keep training them, while training the higher-level networks simultaneously. We can also refine them in a later stage of the training of the higher-level network, because initially the current network will generate too large an error, which might destroy the developed representations. Another completely different strategy for training the whole cascade is to train all RANs simultaneously. However, this is a very complicated learning task and it is doubtful whether the network cascade would get to the solution in reasonable time. Instead, building the lower levels first and leaving a small amount of freedom for later change is preferred. A behavior close to this strategy appears to work with humans – initially people learn to produce simple syllables, next more complex syllables, then words, small phrases, and so on. Which strategy is better is a question of a lot of experiments. In the rest of the experiments, the gradual development strategy was chosen – training the networks gradually, starting from the lowest level and keeping them fixed later.

A. SIMULATION WITH A CASCADE OF RANs: REPRESENTING POLYSYLLABIC WORDS.

A step toward building a hierarchical model of natural language according to the hierarchical design presented earlier is a cascade model producing representations of natural language polysyllabic words. This model involves two RAN modules: a syllable-RAN, which builds static representations of syllables, and a word-RAN, which builds static representations of words. In this subsection I will present an experiment which is a natural extension of the experiment described in the previous section. The syllable-RAN is be the same as before – with 27 input and output neurons and 30 hidden neurons. This means that the word-RAN input and output layers have to have 31 neurons, the last one standing for representing the trigger and end-of-word patterns. The size of the hidden layer is again 30, which is determined by the complexity of the concrete learning task – there are only 100 sequences to be learned, consisting of some 140 possible syllables, with average length of the input sequence 4 syllables. In a more complicated case, we would need many more hidden neurons (see the previous subsection).

The network training (BPTT) is organized as follows: First, a training word is selected from the training corpus, containing pre-syllabified words. Next, for each syllable in the selected word, the syllable-RAN produces the correspondent static representation, which in turn is provided to the word-RAN input layer. The static representations of the syllables belonging to the current word are kept in a buffer until the learning procedure for the current word is finished. When all the syllabic patterns are presented to the input of the second RAN, a triggering pattern is provided to the word-RAN and the processed syllabic patterns are presented as target patterns to the output layer, one at a time, and error is calculated. The same targeting patterns, with one step delay, are presented to the input layer again (see the previous section and Fig. 4 for details). Next, during the second phase of BPTT learning algorithm, the accumulated error is propagated back through time, till the beginning of the sequence. Finally, the weights are updated with the accumulated weight-updating values.

The cascade is tested by encoding the training or testing words and decoding (unfolding) the developed static representations of those words back to sequential forms (string of letters), and comparing the resulting strings with the expected strings. The RAN error is measured as the percent of erroneous predictions of letters, syllables, and words. Syllables are considered to be predicted correctly if all the correspondent letters are reproduced correctly.

Similarly, words are learned if all corresponded syllables are reproduced correctly. The performance of the word-RAN after 100 training epochs was as follows: 1.8% character error, 4% syllable error, and 6% word error.

B. A MORE REALISTIC EXPERIMENT: LOOKING FOR SYSTEMATICITY

In this subsection a more realistic experiment will be presented – building the representations of some 850 polysyllabic Dutch words, consisting of about 600 distinct syllables. The reason less complex examples were presented in the earlier sections was, firstly for the reader to get an idea of the developed static representations (Fig. 5) and, more importantly, to show that generalization increases by increasing the number of combinations learned by the networks.

We will use again (15) to estimate the necessary hidden layer size. For the syllable-RAN, $|C|=26$, $|S|=600$, $k=5$. Then $70 < h_{syll\ RAN} < 150$. Similarly, for the word-RAN, $|C|=600$, $|S|=850$, $k=5$. Then, $100 < h_{word\ RAN} < 300$.

The cascade consists again of two RANs – a syllable RAN and a word RAN. The syllable-RAN has 100 hidden neurons. The word-RAN is set to 350 hidden neurons. All other conditions are the same as in the first experiment. The training of the syllable-RAN resulted in 0.6% erroneous letter prediction and 2.5% erroneous syllable prediction, that is, some 15 syllables were not entirely learned. Further error analysis showed that there was one mispredicted letter among those syllables, which means that those syllables were produced almost correctly (3/4). The word-RAN did not reach the success of the syllable-RAN, with 2.7% letter misprediction, 5.0% syllable misprediction and 14.1% word misprediction.

In order to examine the influence of the hidden layer size to the performance, similar experiments were conducted with smaller hidden layers. The syllable-RAN was tested with 50 and 30 hidden neurons. Word-RANs were tested with 300 and 250 hidden neurons, using the earlier reported syllable-RAN with 100 hidden neurons as syllabic pattern builder. With decreasing the hidden layer size, the performance of both networks gradually dropped. The syllable-RANs learned 70% and 28% training syllables, correspondingly (Table 1). The word-RAN performance decreased too: 80.8% and 76.9% of the words were entirely learned (Table 2). The performance measured at item-level decreased more gradually. For the word-RAN, fewer syllables were erroneously reproduced and even less letters were mistaken.

Table 1. The performance of the *Syllable*-RAN trained on 600 distinct syllables, when varying the hidden layer size.

Syllable RAN	Error (%)	Hidden layer size		
		30	50	100
Mispre-dicted	Syllables	72	30	2.9
	Chars	18	7.2	1.1

Those experiments support to some extent formula (15) that is based on the information content of the hidden layer and number of data to be encoded. With decreasing the number of hidden neurons below the suggested size, the performance deteriorates. Nevertheless, there is another reason for this. The error backpropagation learning algorithm more easily finds escape routes from local minima when there are more weights – if some set of the weights are trapped into a valley on the multi-dimensional error surface, other weights would let the network drive out of this point. Therefore, the more complex the task, the more neurons are necessary. If the number of the neurons seems very large, consider the brain, where billions of neurons participate in different cognitive tasks. Practically, with the ever increasing computational power, this will not be a question in a few more years.

Table 2. Performance of the *word*-RAN trained on 850 polysyllabic words with input vector size 100, when varying the hidden layer size.

Word RAN	Error (%)	Hidden layer size		
		250	300	350
Mispre-dicted	Words	23.1	19.2	14.1
	Syllables	7.8	6.8	5.0
	Chars	4.2	3.6	2.7

The more interesting question now concerns the generalization of the syllable-RAN and the word-RANs. Tested on a larger corpus with 9,000 words and 2,320 distinct syllables, the syllable-RAN successfully reproduced, that is, generated unique representations of another 1150 syllables, which is more than 190% generalization as opposed to the first example with only 10% generalization. This result shows that a network trained with more combinatorial possibilities generalizes better. In turn, this shows the RAN capacity to produce static distributed representations *systematically* (see section 7 for discussion).

The word-RAN generalized well too, with successful reproduction of 1,500 words unseen during the training, which is about 180% generalization. It is interesting to note that the word-RAN generalized as well as the syllable-RAN after learning fewer combinatorial possibilities than the syllable-RAN did (850 words made out of 600 distinct syllables, while the 600 syllables are made out of 26 distinct letters). I attribute this to the nature of the input data of those two RANs. On one hand, the syllable-RAN is provided with localistically encoded letters, which gives no prior information about the similarity among the classes they represent. On the other hand, the word-RAN is supplied with much more "meaningful" distributed representations, systematically produced by the syllable-RAN. This also suggests that if the letters were represented with features (consonant/vowel, voiced, place, manner, etc.), perhaps the syllable-RAN would learn the task even more easily, with fewer hidden neurons, and would generalize better.

VI. GOING FURTHER TO A COGNITIVE MODEL

Once we have a method to represent the complex structured data that we experience externally in some dynamic (sequential) form, we can go further and learn some relations between representations coming from different modalities. For example, the auditory modality would produce representations of linguistic objects, just as we discussed earlier in the chapter; visual modality is a source for even more complex objects. In addition to those sensory modalities, there are effector modalities – muscles, glands, and so on. Having representations of objects of those modalities, we can make associations between them. And those associations are the sources for representation *grounding* – multi-modal associations.

Complex multi-modal mappings can be effected with any static connectionist model – self-organizing or trained by a teacher. And both would be biologically motivated, because those associations can be made whenever two representations occur in the same time and there is a will or attention to learn those coincidences. Neural Network models that might be used for this purpose are the supervised Multilayered Perceptron, the ART-Map network by Carpenter and Grossberg [Carpenter, 1992] or the autoassociative memory by John Hopfield [Hopfield, 1982], among other connectionist models.

In the framework of RAN cascades, sequential patterns from each modality have to be divided into different conceptual levels and correspondent RANs have to be trained to produce static representations. Next, static associations (mappings) between patterns from different modalities have to be learned with static neural networks (Fig. 7). Then, when a sequence is applied as input to a learned modality, that is, to its corresponding lowest-level RANs, higher level representations will be produced. This in turn will activate corresponding patterns in other modalities, which might be expanded to lower level sequences. Activation of a high-level representation might also cause expansion to the corresponding lowest-level sequence, as well as producing sequences of other modalities.

Yet another possible extension toward a more global cognitive model would be a composite input pattern for certain RANs in the cascade. This composite pattern might be the concatenation of representations from different modalities (Fig. 8). The reason for such a concatenation will be presented with an example from natural language. Word representations developed on the basis of the external form of the words which would capture systematic dependencies related to combinations of letters (phonemes) into words, but not categorical or semantic information, which might be necessary when processing sentences. Therefore, the input to a sentence-RAN might consist of the developed lexical static representations and the associated patterns from visual modalities. This would let the sentence-RAN develop sentence representations that properly reflect the meanings of the words, not only their external auditory or visual form. This makes the picture more difficult to implement, but the brain we are trying to model is not less complex.

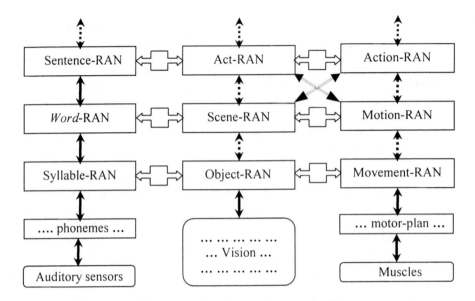

Figure 7. Cognitive model based on a network of RAN cascades. Each RAN-cascade (a column) stands for different modality. The RANs in each cascade represent different conceptual levels. The horizontal and diagonal bi-directional arrows represent static associations between different modalities. In addition to this picture, there should be a central attentive system that directs the flow of activations.

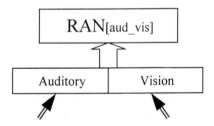

Figure 8. RAN developing static representations of multi-modal sequential data (auditory and visual). The distributed representations developed would feature multi-modal systematicity.

Using these complex schema, we can model complex associations we encounter in our life. Still, there are a lot of other questions to be answered – synchronization, more optimal learning, etc. This huge net of associations needs some central supervisor directing the spread of activations. Modeling cognitive processes such as attention, awareness, etc. maybe would resolve some of those questions.

VII. DISCUSSION

The basic question addressed in this chapter is how to build static representations of complex sequential data with connectionist models, concerning primarily natural language. Dynamic data exist in any cognitive modality, and it is important to have a mechanism that compresses (and uncompresses) dynamic objects into the more convenient static representations. Also, it would be useful if those representations were produced in a systematic way. This would allow further complex processing (holistic computations), e.g., asking questions, change of tense, or even mathematical operations.

Association is one of the basic forms of learning. Repetition, or auto-association, provides a powerful mechanism for cognitive development, too. We can observe this mechanism throughout the animal species. Baby animals develop initial behavior without being taught, but just by attempting to imitate their parents. Humans develop language in a similar way: infants initially start to repeat sounds (babbling), next they repeat simple words, small phrases and so on, until they develop full-scale language capacity [Jusczyk, 1997]. Infants left out of language environment simply can not develop language or have great difficulties developing language later. Similar motivations drove me to use autoassociation in a connectionist model for developing representations of the external world.

Regarding the connectionist models that can process dynamic data, recurrent neural networks are such connectionist models that allow us to process sequential data. The more specific simple recurrent network is a powerful universal model which I have exploited for this purpose, by setting an autoassociation task and arranging the data to develop the desired static representations. The suggested architecture is called recurrent autoassociative network. The model was extended further to a cascade of RANs, aiming at developing static representations of hierarchically structured sequential data. In this cascade, RAN modules at each level are designated to develop static representations of different level of complexity (or different conceptual levels) – words, sentences, and so on.

What is the importance of this model? To what extent does it increase the capacity of connectionist modeling? The discussion in section two on the representations of sequences that one needs when modeling natural languages and the capacities of the connectionist models presented in section three clearly demonstrate that the question of how to develop distributed representations of composite dynamic data is still open. Local encoding is restricted, random representations lack systematicity, and the feature-based representations are limited and rather artificial. All those representations keep NNs away from real data. In order to get closer to our cognitive capacity, we need a mechanism that builds representations, starting from the bottom and gradually building ever more complex representations.

The idea of building a *gestalt* representing input data was promising, but it was not elaborated further. The RAN model has something in common with the earlier works on gestalt: they all develop representations of the sequential input data in the network global memory. They differ in the learning task they set to the SRN and in the way they use this context. The gestalt models use the context developed for information retrieval at every moment, which causes uncertainties, while the RANs develop unique static representations of the input sequences by a special attack on the learning task, which makes the same RANs able to reproduce the input sequence and which is not the case with the gestalt models. The gestalt model needs a second network trained to extract information from the context of the first network.

The other similar and important architectures: RAAM and SRAAM were initially reported to work well on sequential and recursive data, but other experiments did not confirms the expected performance (Hammerton 1998). Also, the RAAMs need an external stack and boot RAAM and SRAAM reproduce the sequences in inverse order. This might cause interpretational problem when processing longer sequences – it would require an external stack to invert them back to the normal order. Still, the idea of RAN clearly owes the idea of autoassociation as a source of developing compact representations to the RAAM models.

The experiments in section five on modeling sequences with a cascade of RAN modules demonstrate that RANs handle reasonably well both locally encoded low-level data (we can assume that this is a kind of perceptual data) and continuous distributed data. The network learned to autoassociate in both cases, although there were more difficulties in learning the latter types of patterns. I attribute this to insufficient computational resources, because the larger the hidden layer is, the better the performance is (see Table 2). On the other hand, word-RAN generalized very well given the small number of training syllabic combinations, which is due to the truly distributed syllabic patterns, as opposed to the localistically encoding input for the syllable-RAN.

With regard to the hidden layer size that is required for a RAN to learn a particular task, it is difficult to find a theoretical measure because the representations are continuous and, theoretically speaking, even one real value number can encode any sequence. However, limitations from the limited effective working range of the sigmoidal activation functions apply and by enumerating the maximal number of distinct patterns to be encoded in the hidden layer, an estimation of the required hidden layer size was derived (15). Still, more theoretical and systematic experimental research is necessary in order to determine other factors related to the hidden layer size, such as factors related to the way the data is processed and encoded in the neural networks, especially in recurrent models.

Neural Networks were reproached by Fodor and Pylyshyn [1988] for not being able to produce systematic representations. The ongoing debate on this challenge inspired the development of a number of architectures that more or less meet the requirements characterizing systematicity [Smolensky, 1990, Smolensky, 1991, Aydede, 1997]. In this subsection I will explain how the distributed representations developed by RAN account for systematicity. The debate on this human cognitive property is important because it explains our capacity to think. A classical example for systematicity is that if we can think of

"Mary loves John," then we can think of "John loves Mary" too. With this simple example, one can distinguish a few descriptive characteristics of systematicity: *compositionality* (atoms constitute thoughts), *generalization* (the atoms "John" and "Mary" are semantically similar and therefore interchangeable) and exploration of *combinatorial* possibilities (similar atoms might apply at same position).

The Fodor's classical "Language of Thoughts" respects fully the first and the third characteristics and partially the second. The hard logic rules, which underlie symbolism – the background of the classical cognitive explanation – can not account for similarities across all items because they do not make use of continuous metrics to compute such similarities. Therefore, in the symbolic systems, similarities across items do not give rise to generalization unless a system of artificially developed features characterizing the items is applied.

On the contrary, an important property of connectionism is generalization, but some connectionist representations do not feature the other characteristics, with the localistic representations being such a very strong example. Feature-based encoding comprises compositionality and allows combinatorial possibilities, but it is rather artificial and symbolic in spirit. Other distributed representations, such as those produced by the RAAM and the SRAAM models, show that neural networks can produce distributed representations that have compositional structure, although in an implicit manner [Chalmers, 1990, Blank,1992, Hammerton, 1998].

Similarly to the RAAM and symbolic models, RAN models produce composite representations too. Of course, RANs are not aimed at producing distributed representations understandable by humans. This is reserved for symbolism. The representations that RANs produce are designed to be understandable, firstly, by the RANs themselves and, secondly, by other computational models able numerically to analyze data and eventually extract useful features from this data. RANs can unpack representations to the original row of tokens – this is part of the autoassociative task. With regard to the other models, the Kohonen Map that was trained in section 4.2 to cluster the distributed representations of syllables clearly demonstrates that other models can "understand" those representations, too (Fig. 5). In this case, the Kohonen Map was just an instrument to persuade the reader that those representations are organized in a systematic way. In addition, similarly to the ability of RAN to decode the distributed representations, other connectionist models should also be able to extract information for the encoded items, that is, to do holistic computations. Experiments with distributed representations produced by RAAM and SRAAM show that this is possible [Chalmers, 1990, Hammerton, 1998] and RANs produce distributed representations following the same principles as SRAAM; only the order of reproducing the sequences is different. The (S)RAAM models implement a stack, while the RANs implement a queue. Therefore, I expect holistic computations will be able to apply on the distributed representations developed by the RAN, too.

With regard to the explorations of combinatorial possibilities, the models should not only have the capacity to explore different combinations, but the training environment should provide them to the networks, too. Similarly, symbolic learning algorithms can extract rules only if the learning data provide different examples. This is the same with humans, too. We start to combine words properly after having had enough experience in a language environment. Another example is related to algebra. Students learn to add and subtract first by example, and then they realize the nature of the operators "add" and "subtract." With regard to the capacity to explore such combinations, RANs have this capacity, by allowing tokens to take any position in the input sequence. Similarly to Deacon, [1997] I hypothesize that a systematic organization *emerges* in RANs after exploring a great number of possible combinations of patterns and starting to use and rely on some common features among the representations rather than on particular patterns, which Deacon characterizes also as example "forgetting."

VIII. CONCLUSIONS

Sequential processing is recognized as a difficult problem, especially when sequential complexity, in terms of length and internal structure, increases. In the present chapter I proposed a framework for processing structured sequential data, as found in natural languages, movies, actions, and so on. The approach is based on the idea that by sequential autoassociation, a single recurrent NN – recurrent autoassociative network – can develop static representations of sequences composed of uniform items. A hierarchical set, or cascade of such networks, develops static distributed representations of ever more complex sequences, where each structural level in the data is processed by one RAN module, and the input sequences for the upper levels are developed by the lower level RAN. For this purpose, recurrent networks are trained on autoassociative tasks (RAN modules), and they develop unique static representations of the input sequences at their hidden layers (Fig. 4). Those static representations are used as interface patterns for the next level RAN (Fig. 6). The static representations at the highest level RAN are the distributed representations of the most complex data or whole input sequence, e.g., sentences or stories. In section five, an example was given of how this model might work for developing representations of Dutch polysyllabic words. Further, in section six, it was suggested how the cascade model might be extended to a more global cognitive model, where the static representations at each level were suggested to be associated with other static representations (of sequence of other modalities) via static mappings. Such a net of multi-modal associations, I believe, would be an implementation of natural language *grounding* and a base for *semantics*.

Although I claim that this model will be able to solve the problem of developing representations of hierarchically structured sequences, there are still some questions that remain open, especially if we want to develop an autonomous cognitive model. For instance, the learning processes and flow of activations should be driven by a supervisor, similar to the attentive system. Also, the learning algorithm can be replaced with a more effective one. Next, instead of using SRN-based autoassociators, one might use other, more effective or more neurobiologically motivated learning algorithms and neural network models, for example, recurrent self-organization networks and the other models presented in this book. Nevertheless, I believe the suggested model is an important step in connectionist modeling, and I strongly encourage the reader to experiment with the RAN cascade on different problems, especially to investigate holistic computations with the distributed representations developed by RANs.

ACKNOWLEDGMENTS

I am grateful to my supervisor, Prof. Dr. John Nerbonne for his useful advice and comments on this work, and to James Hammerton for his important remarks and suggestions on (S)RAAMs and *holistic* computations. Also, I am thankful to Dr. Larry Medsker for his cooperation in the course of writing this chapter. The Kohonen Map tool for data analysis and visualization was provided by Peter Kleiweg. The work is supported by a grant from the Behavioral and Cognitive Neuroscience School at Groningen University, The Netherlands.

REFERENCES

Aydede, M., Language of thought: the connectionist contribution, *Minds and Machines* (7), 57, 1997.

Altman, G. T. M., *Cognitive Models of Speech Processing*, MIT Press, Cambridge, 1990.

Bengio, Y., Simard, P., and Frasconi, P. Learning long-term dependencies with gradient descent is difficult, *IEEE Transactions on Neural Networks*, 5(2), 157, 1994.

Blank, D. S., Meeden, and L., Marsgall, J., Exploring the symbolic/subsymbolic continuum: a case study of RAAM, in *Closing the Gap: Symbolism vs. Connectionism*, Dinsmore, J., Ed., Lawrence Erlbaum Associuates, 1992.

Blair, A. D., Scaling-up RAAMs, *Tech. Report CS-97-192*, University of Brandeis, 1997.

Cairns, P., Shillcock, R., Chater, N., and Levy, J., Bootstrapping word boundaries: a bottom-up corpus-based approach to speech segmentations, *Cognitive Psychology*, 32(2), 111, 1997.

Carpenter, G. and Grossberg, S., A self-organising neural network for supervised learning, recognition and prediction, *IEEE Communication Magazine*, 38, 1992.

Chalmers, D. J., Syntactic transformations on distributed representations, *Connection Science*, 2(1,2), 53, 1990.

Chappell, C. J. and Taylor, J. G., The temporal Kohonen map, *Neural Networks*, 6, 441, 1993.

Christiansen, M. H. and Chater, N., Toward a connectionist model of recursion in human linguistic performance, *Cognitive Science*, (in press), 1999.

Clark, A., Systematicity, structured representations and cognitive architecture: a reply to Fodor and Pylyshyn, in *Connectionism and the Philosophy of Mind*, Horgan, T. and Tienson, J., Eds., Kluwer Academic Publishers, Dordrecht, 198, 1991.

Cleeremans, A., Servan-Schreiber, D., and McClelland, J. L., Finite state automata and simple recurrent networks, *Neural Computation*, 1, 372, 1989.

Cottrell, G. W., Bartell, B., and Haupt, C., Grounding meaning in perception, *German Workshop on Artificial Intelligence*, 1990.

Deacon, T. W., *The Symbolic Species*, W. W. Norton & Co. Inc, New York, 1997.

Dorffner, G., "Radical" connectionism for natural language processing, *Proceedings of Spring Symposium on Connectionism*, NLP, Standford, 95, 1991.

Elman, J. L., Finding structure in time, *Cognitive Science*, 14, 179, 1990.

Elman, J. L., Bates, E., Johnson, M. H., Karmiloff-Smith, A., Parisi, D., and Plunket, K., *Rethinking Innates*, MIT Press, Cambridge, MA, 1996.

Fodor, J. and Pylyshyn, Z., Connectionism and cognitive architecture: a critical analysis, *Cognition*, 28, 3, 1988.

Fodor, J. and McLaughlin, B., Connectionism and the problem of systematicity: why Smolensky's solution doesn't work, in *Connectionism and the Philosophy of Mind*, Horgan, T. and Tienson, J., Eds., Kluwer Academic Publishers, The Netherlands, 1991.

Gasser, M., Learning distributed representations for syllables, *Proceedings of the 14th Annual Conference of the Cognitive Science Society*, 396, 1992.

Grossberg, S., *Studies of Mind and Brain*, Kluwer Academic Publishers, Boston, 1982.

Hammerton, J. A., Exploiting holistic computations: an evaluation of the sequential RAAM, Ph.D. thesis, University of Birmingham, UK, 1998.

Haykin, S., *Neural Networks*, Macmillan College Pub., 1994.

Henderson, J. Connectionist architecture with inherent systematicity, *Proceedings of the 18th Conference of the Cognitive Science Society*, La Jolla, CA, 1996.

Henderson, J. and Lane, P., A connectionist architecture for learning to parse. *Proceedings of COLING-ACL Conference*, Montreal, 531, 1998.

Hirshman, E. and Jackson, E., Distinctive perceptual processing and memory, *Journal of Memory and Language*, 36, 2, 1997.

Hornik, K., Stinchcombe, M., and White, H., Multilayer feedforward networks are universal approximators, *Neural Networks*, 2, 359, 1989.

Hopfield, J. J., Neural networks and physical systems with emergent collective computational abilities, *Proceedings of the National Academy of Sciences*, USA, 79, 2554, 1982.

James, D. L. and Miikkulainen, R., SARDNET: a self-organising feature map for sequences, in *Advances in Neural Processing Systems*, Tesauro, Touretzky, and Leen, Eds., 7, 1995.

Jordan, M. I., Attractor dynamics and parallelism in a connectionist sequential machine, *Proceedings of the 8th Annual Conference of the Cognitive Science Society*, Amherst, MA, 531, 1986.

Jusczyk, P. W., *The Discovery of Spoken Language*, MIT Press, Cambridge, MA, 1997.

Kohonen, T., *Self-Organisation and Associative Memory*. Springer-Verlag, New York, 1984.

Kwasny, S. C. and Kalman, B. L., Tail-recursive distributed representations and simple recurrent networks, *Connectionist Science*, 7(1), 61, 1995.

Lawrence S., Giles, C. L., and Fong, S., On the applicability of neural networks and machine learning methodologies to natural language processing, *Technical Report UMIACS-TR-95-64 and CS-TR-3479*, University of Maryland, 1995.

Miikkulainen, R. and Dyer, M., Natural language processing with modular PDP networks and distributed representations, *Cognitive Science*, 15(3), 343, 1991.

Plate, T. A., Distributed representations and nested compositional structure, Ph.D. thesis, University of Toronto, 1994.

Plaut, D. C., McClelland, J., and Seidenberg, M., Connectionist models of memory and language, in Levy, J., Bairaktaris, D., Bullinaria, J., Cairns, P., Eds., UCL Press Ltd., London, 1995.

Plaut, D. C., McClelland, J., Seidenberg, M., and Patterson, K., Understanding normal and impaired word reading: computational principles in quasi-regular domains, *Psychological Review*, 103, 56, 1996.

Pollack, J. B., Recursive distributed representation, *Artificial Intelligence*, 46, 77, 1990.

Reilly, R. G., Sandy ideas and coloured days: some computational implications of embodiment, *Artificial Intelligence Review*, 9, 305, 1995.

Rumelhart, D. E., Hinton, G. E., and Williams, R. J., *Parallel Distributed Processes*, 1&2, MIT Press, Cambridge, MA, 1986.

Searle, J. R., *Minds, Brains and Science*, Harvard University Press, Cambridge, MA, 1984.

Seidenberg, M. S. and McClelland, J. L., A distributed, developmental model of word recognition & naming, *Psychological Review*, 96, 523, 1989.

Sejnowski, T. J. and Rosenberg, C. R., Parallel networks that learn to pronounce English text, *Complex Systems*, 1, 145, 1987.

Servan-Schreiber, D., Cleeremans, A., and McClelland, J. L., Graded state machines: the representation of temporal contingencies in simple recurrent networks, *Machine Learning*, 7, 161, 1991.

Smolensky, P., Tensor product variable binding and the representation of symbolic structures in connectionist systems, *Artificial Intelligence*, 46, 159, 1990.

Smolensky, P., The constituent structure of mental states: a reply to Fodor and Pylyshyn, in *Connectionism and the Philosophy of Mind*, Horgan, T. and Tienson, J., Eds., Kluwer Academic Publishers, Dordrecht, 281, 1991.

Sperduti, A., On the computational power of recurrent neural networks for structures, *Neural Networks*, 10(3), 395, 1997.

St. John, M. F. and McClelland, J. L., Learning and applying contextual constraints in sentence comprehension, *Artificial Intelligence*, 46, 217, 1990.

Stoianov, I. P., Recurrent autoassociative networks and sequential processing, *Proceedings of the International Joint Conference on Neural Networks*, Washington, DC, 1999.

Stoianov, I. P., Nerbonne, J., and Bouma, H., Modelling the phonotactic structure of natural language words with simple recurrent networks, in *Computational Linguistics in the Netherlands*, Coppen, P.-A., van Halteren, H., and Teunissen, L., Eds., Rodopi, Amsterdam, 77, 1997.

Stoianov, I. P., Stowe, L., and Nerbonne, J., Connectionist learning to read aloud and correlation to human data, *21st Annual Conference of the Cognitive Science Society*, Vancouver, 1999.

Tabor W., Juliano, C., and Tanenhaus, M. K, Parsing in an dynamical system: an attractor-based account of the interaction of lexical structural constraints and sentence processing, *Language and Cognitive Processing*, 1997.

Tsoi, A.C. and Back, A. D., Locally recurrent globally feedforward networks: a critical review of architectures, *IEEE Transactions on Neural Networks*, 5, 229, 1994.

Wilson, W. H., Tower networks and letter prediction, *Cognitive Modelling Workshop of the 7th Australian Conference on Neural Networks*, http://psych.psy.uq.oz.au/workshop.html, 1996.

Chapter 10

COMPARISON OF RECURRENT NETWORKS FOR TRAJECTORY GENERATION

David G. Hagner

Product Development Division
Ford Motor Company

Mohamad H. Hassoun

Department of Electrical and Computer Engineering
Wayne State University

Paul B. Watta

Department of Electrical and Computer Engineering
University of Michigan-Dearborn

I. INTRODUCTION

Recurrent neural networks are universal approximations of dynamic systems and hense can be used to model the behavior of a wide range of practical systems which can be described by ordinary differential equations [Funashi and Nakamura, 1993]. The ability to model such systems is an important task for non linear control systems design, system identification, and testing.

An interesting feature of recurrent neural networks is their ability to "learn" a trajectory from training data. Under certain conditions, these networks can also generalize [Hassoun, 1995, Hagner, 1999] from the training data to produce smooth and consistent dynamic behavior for entirely new inputs or new regions of state space (i.e., inputs or regions of state space not encountered during training).

In this chapter, we discuss the use of single- and multilayer recurrent neural networks for the approximations of two famous 2-dimentional limit cycles: the circle and the figure-eight. We will give a qualitative and quantitative analysis of the neural net approximations of these autonomous systems for various network architectures (internally and externally recurrent), learning rules (incremental and conjugate gradient descent, and three variations of the extended Kalman filter), and initial conditions (previous states on the trajectory and previous states set near the origin).

A variety of approaches and architectures has been proposed in the literature for approximating such trajectories, including discrete-time, feedforward networks with tapped delay line external recurrence [Tsung and Cottrell, 1995]; discrete-time, feedforward networks with adaptable time delays [Lin, Dayhoff, and Ligomenides, 1995]; discrete-time, single-layer, recurrent networks with adaptable time constants [Sundareshan and Condarcure, 1998]; continuous time, single-layer recurrent networks with adaptable time constants [Toomarian and Barhen, 1992; Pearlmutter, 1995]; and continuous time, single-layer recurrent networks with adaptable time constants and adaptable time delays [Cohen, Saad, and Marom, 1997].

Previous studies of two-dimensional limit cycle trajectories have involved simulations of one architecture and one learning algorithm, and used only one set of initial conditions. Several studies also investigated only the circle trajectory, which proved to be relatively easy for any architecture/algorithm combination to learn, and thus does not provide a test able to delineate the differences in performance. Recurrent network architectures have been experimentally compared [Horne and Giles, 1995], though not on autonomous network applications like those considered here. Additionally, recurrent network learning algorithms have been compared [Logar, Corwin, and Oldham, 1993; Williams and Zipser, 1995], though with a focus on algorithm speed, and not on architecture and performance (defined here as the ability of the network to accurately match the desired training data).

The remainder of this chapter is organized as follows. Section 2 reviews the structure of recurrent neural network architectures and gives definitions of internal and external recurrence. Section 3 discusses how the training sets for the circle and the figure-eight are generated. Section 4 presents the quantitative error measures and performance metrics which are used to assess the quality of the network dynamics during the playback phase. Section 5 briefly reviews the five training algorithms which are simulated. Section 6 describes the simulations performed in this work and the results of these simulations, and provides comparative analyses of network architecture and training algorithm performances and properties. Section 7 presents the conclusions reached concerning the capabilities and limitations of the network architectures and training algorithms when applied to learning the limit cycle trajectories, and a discussion of possible future extensions of this work.

II. ARCHITECTURE

Feedforward neural networks can model static mappings, but do not have the capability to generate dynamic behavior. By adding recurrent connections, though, a feedforward network can be transformed into a recurrent network which can be used to model dynamic systems. For the recurrent networks described here, we will start with a multilayer feedforward neural net, where neurons are grouped into layers and layers are cascaded one after the next. We will assume full interconnectivity between layers, but each layer will be connected to the layer which immediately follows. For example, in a 3-layer network, layer 1 will be fully connected to layer 2, and layer 2 fully connected to layer 3, but no direct feedforward connections will be present between layer 1 and layer 3.

Once the feedforward structure of the network is fixed, recurrent connections can be added by using two main types of recurrence: internal and external. *Internal recurrence* is defined here as the connection of outputs of units of a given layer to the inputs of units in that same layer. *External recurrence* is defined as the connection of outputs of the final (output) layer of a network to the inputs of units in the first (input) layer. This type of network that has both feedforward and recurrent layers has been termed a recurrent multilayer perceptron (RMLP) network [Puskorius and Feldkamp, 1994], and combines the instantaneous mapping capabilities of multilayer feedforward networks (often referred to as multilayer perceptron, or MLP, networks) with the system state memory, or dynamics, of recurrent networks.

Each unit in the recurrent network has inputs from other units, as well as a single output to other units (and possibly the external environment). The output y of a unit at time step $n+1$ is given by its describing function

$$y(n + 1) = f\left[\sum_{j = 1}^{J} x_j(n)w_j(n) \right]$$

Here, $x_1(n)$, $x_2(n)$, . . ., $x_J(n)$ are the inputs to the neuron at (discrete) time step n. Note that in general, the total input vector $\mathbf{x}$ is composed of outputs of other units, bias inputs, and external inputs, though for the autonomous networks considered here, there will be no external inputs. Associated with each input is a weight $w_1(n)$, $w_2(n)$, . . ., $w_J(n)$, which, during the training phase, also evolves in time. In this chapter, the discussion will focus on activation functions which are either linear: $f(x) = x$, or sigmoidal: $f(x) = \tanh(x)$.

An example of a 3-layer recurrent network is shown in Figure 1. This network has three feedforward units in layer 1, two recurrent units in layer 2, and two feedforward units in layer 3. In addition, this network has external recurrence with two unit time delays. We will use the notation $3 \times 2_R \times 2(2)$ to represent this structure. The subscript R indicates that the layer has recurrent connections (output of the layer is fed back into the input of that layer). The 2 in parenthesis at the end indicates that the network has external recurrence with two delays.

Various architectures were tested initially to determine the advantages and disadvantages of the different architecture types, and to determine which subset of the many possible architectures would be used for the final comparison analysis with the different training algorithms. The variations studied were 1) linear vs. sigmoidal unit activation functions, 2) single recurrent layer vs. hidden recurrent layers with a two-unit feedforward output layer, 3) single vs. multiple hidden feedforward layers with a two-unit feedforward output layer, 4) recurrent layer networks with and without external recurrence, and 5) up to five unit delays used for external recurrence.

During initial network simulation analysis, it was found that if a network contained a single layer, the units required sigmoidal activation functions to learn the trajectories, and if the network employed an output layer with feedforward linear units, the hidden layer (recurrent or feedforward) similarly required sigmoidal units. This is as expected for this application of learning nonlinear trajectories where a linear combination of unit values is not sufficient.

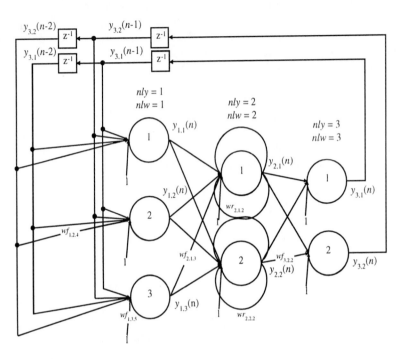

Figure 1. A 3-layer $3 \times 2_R \times 2(2)$ network with three units in layer 1, two recurrent units in layer 2, and 2 units in layer 3. This network has external feedback with 2 unit delays.

For a feedforward output layer with or without external recurrence, only two units are required, as any additional units' outputs would not be connected. For a feedforward output layer, linear units provided faster convergence, but the solutions exhibited inferior off-trajectory performance compared to feedforward output layers with sigmoidal units. These trajectories were similar to the *center*, or *vortex* trajectories generated by two-dimensional linear systems with a purely imaginary conjugate pair of eigenvalues (for a description of phase-plane analysis of linear and non-linear systems, see Van De Vegte [1986] and Dickinson [1991], indicating that the network was not exploiting the nonlinearities of the hidden units). Additionally, feedforward output layers with sigmoidal units were more robust during training, whereas linear unit learning often diverged during training. Thus sigmoidal activation functions were used for all units in both hidden and output layers.

It was found that single recurrent layer networks performed well, and the addition of hidden recurrent layers did not provide any noticeable benefits. Coupling these findings with the fact that the addition of external recurrence to a single layer recurrent network would be redundant, the only recurrent unit architecture to be tested in the final analysis was a single layer of recurrent units with sigmoidal activation functions.

Externally recurrent networks with one hidden layer generally performed as well as networks with multiple hidden layers. Additionally, externally recurrent networks with a recurrent hidden layer provided no noticeable benefit over networks with a single recurrent layer, or compared to externally recurrent networks with a single feedforward hidden layer.

As indicated above, the only two architectures that both provided good performance and were also different enough to warrant further comparison were the single layer recurrent n_R and single hidden layer feedforward with external recurrence $n \times L(D)$.

Initial experimentation with the number of units and the number of delays determined that the minimum network sizes for the circle trajectory were 2_R and $2 \times 2(1)$ for internal and external recurrence, respectively. One larger network (for each architecture) was then chosen to provide a significant increase in the number of parameters (weights), without increasing the network size such that it became computationally prohibitive. These network sizes were 4_R and $4 \times 2(1)$. Thus the total number of architecture/algorithm combinations to be compared for the circle trajectory was 4 networks x 5 algorithms =20.

Similar experimentation for the figure-eight trajectory led to the determination that the minimum network sizes were 4_R and $4 \times 2(4)$ for internal and external recurrence, respectively. Two additional, larger networks (for each architecture) were chosen for the figure-eight trajectory to be 6_R, 8_R, $6 \times 2(4)$, and $8 \times 2(4)$. Thus the total number of architecture/algorithm combinations to be compared for the figure-eight trajectory was 6 networks x 5 algorithms = 30.

III. TRAINING SET

The training set for the circle and the figure-eight consists of 2-dimensional samples of the trajectory, as shown in Figures 2a and b.

For both trajectories, $M = 100$ samples are used because this value offered a balance between a smaller M that provided more distinction between data points (beneficial because incremental training algorithms tend to optimize for the current region if that region presents little new information) and a larger M that provided a smoother, more accurate representation of the continuous-time trajectory.

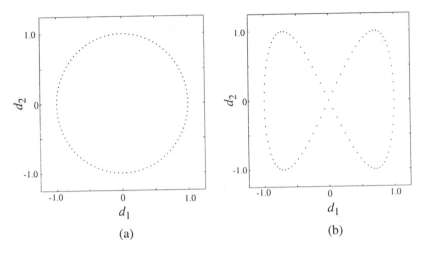

Figure 2. (a) The circle and (b) figure-eight training sets; both contain $M = 100$ samples.

In the case of the circle, the target vector $\mathbf{d}$ at time step n is given by

$$\mathbf{d}(n) = \begin{bmatrix} d_1(n) & d_2(n) \end{bmatrix} = \begin{bmatrix} \sin\left(\dfrac{2\pi n}{100} + \dfrac{\pi}{2}\right) & \sin\left(\dfrac{2\pi n}{100}\right) \end{bmatrix}$$

and for the figure-eight trajectory, the target vector is given by

$$\mathbf{d}(n) = \begin{bmatrix} d_1(n) & d_2(n) \end{bmatrix} = \begin{bmatrix} \sin\left(\dfrac{2\pi n}{100} + \dfrac{\pi}{2}\right) & \sin\left(\dfrac{4\pi n}{100}\right) \end{bmatrix}$$

To train the network to learn the limit cycle trajectories, the target values, $d(n)$, were taken as the coordinates of the subsequent point on the trajectory, and the target value for the final, Mth point was the first point, to train the network to oscillate around the trajectory.

IV. ERROR FUNCTION AND PERFORMANCE METRIC

One way to assess network performance is by formulating an error function which measures the difference between the neural net approximation and the desired trajectory. A common measure is the standard sum of squared errors defined by

$$E(\mathbf{w}) = \frac{1}{2} \sum_{n=1}^{M} \sum_{l=1}^{L} [d_l(n) - y_l(n)]^2 \tag{1}$$

where $d_l(n)$ is the target value and $y_l(n)$ is the actual output of output unit l at time step n. The error function given here is called the *batch error*, because it contains the sum of the errors over the entire training set; that is, the error over all M time steps. Some training algorithms make use of this error function, and others make use of the *instantaneous error*,

$$E(\mathbf{w}, n) = \frac{1}{2} \sum_{l=1}^{L} [d_l(n) - y_l(n)]^2 \qquad (2)$$

where the errors are summed only over the L output units, and not over time, and thus may be written as $E(\mathbf{w}, n)$. Both definitions of the error function will be used in the discussion of training algorithms in the next section, as this work considers both incremental and batch training algorithms.

In training mode, as the network output is computed for each step and the error vector calculated, a technique called *teacher forcing* may be employed, which substitutes the previous target values for the past network output values after the computation of the error and prior to computing the next step. This has been shown to be an effective technique for maintaining training algorithm stability [Puskorius and Feldkamp, 1994; Williams, 1992; Hagner, 1999]. In full teacher forcing, the previous target value is substituted; for partial teacher forcing, a weighted sum of the previous target value and the network output value is used [Hagner, 1999].

Besides the use of error functions, network performance may also be qualitatively assessed by visual comparison of the network trajectory to the target trajectory. The network trajectory is generated in the *recall*, or *playback* mode, after the *training* mode is finished. In playback mode, a set of initial conditions is provided, and the network output is computed for the first time step. These results are then used to generate the network output for the second time step, etc., until the desired number of steps is taken. Because it is desired that the trajectory be a limit cycle trajectory (i.e., once the network output approaches the target trajectory, it remains on that trajectory) and there may be transient effects due to initial conditions, the network will be run through $10M$ steps, with all steps plotted, providing both the transient and steady-state portions of the trajectory.

A network's performance may be measured quantitatively by the error function and qualitatively by visual inspection of the network trajectory. These two measures often do not correlate well, as the error function calculated using teacher forcing may be quite different from the error function calculated during playback (which represents a network's true performance), when teacher forcing is not used. Additionally, the trajectory generated during playback may become unstable after a certain number of steps, indicating that the network has not generated a true limit cycle, and thus a measurement of trajectory stability is also desirable.

A network's performance generally improves as the error decreases during training, but the relationship is often not smooth, as shown in Figure 3, and may vary by large amounts in only a few training cycles. For example, during a training run on the figure-eight trajectory, the value of the training error (calculated with teacher forcing) might decrease rapidly while the network trajectory is confined near a single point, and thus the trajectory error (calculated without teacher forcing) is large. As training continues and the training error decreases more slowly as a minimum is approached, a sudden improvement in performance may be seen as the network begins oscillation, or the trajectory changes abruptly from an elliptical oscillation to a figure-eight. Sometimes the error decreases quickly during these performance improvements, as the algorithm leaves a local minimum or a long, flat valley, and sometimes it changes little. At other points in training, a network's performance may be fairly good for a period of time (the algorithm may be in a plateau), and then may deteriorate rapidly as the algorithm enters a new region of weight space, even though the training error decreases continuously.

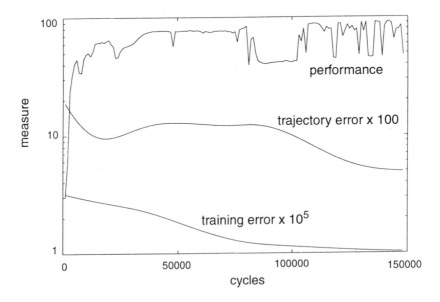

Figure 3. Performance and error vs. training cycles for an $8 \times 2(4)$ network trained with incremental gradient descent to learn the figure-eight trajectory.

Figure 3 shows the dependence of training error, trajectory error (with initial conditions on the trajectory), and performance (quantitatively given below in Equation 3) for one simulation of the incremental gradient descent algorithm on the figure-eight trajectory. Note the large variation in the performance metric for smoothly decreasing training and trajectory errors after 100,000 cycles, and also the variation in the trajectory error for smoothly decreasing training error around 25,000 cycles.

The trajectory without teacher forcing, made during playback, may be quantitatively measured. The straightforward method of calculating the value of the error function during playback provides a measure of the performance, but it is calculated over the first "loop" of M steps, and thus may contain transient characteristics of the playback, and may not represent the quality of the steady-state trajectory. Thus a measure of the error function is needed for the steady-state trajectory (as stated previously, 10 "loops" were sufficient for the networks to reach steady-state conditions, and thus the performance metric is defined over the last loop, or last M steps of the playback trajectory). The errors during the transients typically cause the trajectory to "fall behind" the target trajectory, because the network trajectory typically starts at a point off the target trajectory and eventually is attracted to it, though when this happens the points are not synchronized. A network trajectory that is on the target trajectory but unsynchronized, or out of phase with respect to the target trajectory, is defined here to be perfectly good; the network has learned the limit cycle trajectory, and because there is no external input to serve as a clock signal, the fact that the trajectories overlap is sufficient.

A measure of the amount of trajectory "overlap" is thus required; the standard error function will not provide a relevant result, because it relies on the synchronization of the trajectory points and would provide a poor result for an exact trajectory match that is out of phase. The measure of trajectory overlap is accomplished by performing a convolution of the last M steps of the network trajectory and the target trajectory. The value of the error function is calculated for the target trajectory and the network trajectory M times, where for each instance the starting point of the network trajectory is shifted 1 step. The minimal value of the convolution occurs for the shifted trajectory that provides the minimum error; this value is used as the measure of overlap. The error minimum obtained from the convolution is then used to calculate a performance measure, on the scale from 0 to 100, where 100 indicates an almost perfect overlap of trajectories.

The steady-state performance measure is given by

$$P_{ss}(\mathbf{w}) = \frac{1}{2}[100e^{-\alpha_p E_{ss1}(\mathbf{w})} + 100e^{-\alpha_p E_{ss2}(\mathbf{w})}] \tag{3}$$

where α_p is a constant chosen for the specific figure or trajectory such that visually "fair" steady-state trajectories achieved performance measures between 80 and 90, "very good" trajectories achieved performance measures between 90 and 95, and "excellent" trajectories achieved performance measures between 95 and 100, $E_{ss1}(\mathbf{w})$ is the value of the error function that provided the minimum during the convolution procedure for the first set of initial conditions (on-trajectory), and $E_{ss2}(\mathbf{w})$ is the value of the error function that provided the minimum during the convolution procedure for the second set of initial conditions (off-trajectory). The network's overall performance measure was thus the average of the individual performance measures for the two steady-state trajectories resulting from the two sets of initial conditions. For a network to achieve an "excellent" overall performance measure of 95 to 100, both steady-state trajectories must achieve "excellent" performance measures (e.g., if the on-trajectory performance measure was 95 and the off-trajectory performance measure was 11, the resulting overall performance measure would be 53, indicating "poor" performance).

V. TRAINING ALGORITHMS

There are several training algorithms that have been developed and applied to training recurrent neural networks, the principal ones being the real-time recurrent learning (RTRL) algorithm [Williams and Zipser, 1989a], backpropagation-through-time (BPTT) [Rumelhart, Hinton, and Williams, 1986; Werbos, 1990], and the extended Kalman filter [Williams, 1992; Puskorius and Feldkamp, 1994]. These algorithms all make use of the gradient of the error function with respect to the weights to perform the weight updates (the specific method in which gradient is incorporated into the weight updates distinguishes the different methods). RTRL computes the gradient information by integrating forward in time as the network runs, while BPTT integrates backwards in time after the network takes a single step forward (other variations of the BPPT algorithm use various quantities for the number of forward steps and the number of backward integration steps [Williams and Zipser, 1995]). BPTT and RTRL are considered gradient-descent algorithms. The extended Kalman filter algorithm uses the gradient in the linearization of the system, such that the method of Kalman filtering may be applied, and is not a gradient-descent algorithm. All three algorithms have been implemented as incremental algorithms, though BPTT has also been modified for use in batch mode [Williams and Zipser, 1995].

The incremental versions of BPTT and RTRL are relatively slow, due primarily to the fact that small learning rates are typically used in order to keep the algorithms stable during training. The batch version of BPTT is faster, as it performs the backwards error integration every M steps, and it can provide the same gradient information as RTRL in a more efficient manner [Williams and Zipser, 1995]. Batch versions also have the attractive quality that they may be used with second-order gradient techniques which generally converge to a minimum in fewer cycles than first-order, incremental algorithms. The extended Kalman filter algorithm has also been shown to converge to a solution in relatively fewer steps [Singhal and Wu, 1989; Shah and Palmieri, 1990; Puskorius and Feldkamp, 1994], and may be implemented with gradient information obtained similarly to RTRL. Therefore, to commonize the development of the algorithms for this analysis, the RTRL method of obtaining gradient information was used and applied to all the algorithms tested here: incremental gradient descent, conjugate gradient descent, and the extended Kalman filter. Note that a faster conjugate gradient algorithm would have used the batch version of BPTT, but RTRL provided the same gradient information and was also applicable in its incremental form for all the other algorithms.

The following sections briefly review gradient-descent-based and Kalman filter-based training algorithms. A more complete discussion can be found in Hagner [1999].

A. GRADIENT DESCENT AND CONJUGATE GRADIENT DESCENT

In gradient descent, the parameters (in this case the weights) of the system are adjusted at each step in the direction of steepest descent, or in the direction of the negative of the gradient vector of the error function. For batch mode, the weights are thus updated according to

$$\mathbf{w}(k + 1) = \mathbf{w}(k) - \eta \nabla_w E(\mathbf{w})$$

where η is a positive *learning rate* parameter, and $\nabla_w E(\mathbf{w})$ is the gradient of the error function with respect to the weight vector.

If the instantaneous, or incremental, error function is used instead of the batch error function, the resulting algorithm will not follow the true gradient, but rather an approximation to it. The weights generated by this algorithm will thus have a component of randomness, and therefore this incremental algorithm is termed *stochastic gradient descent*. It is also referred to as the *least mean squares* (LMS) algorithm [Haykin, 1994; Hassoun, 1995] or *incremental gradient descent*. The weight updates are made every step, based on the incremental error of Equation 2.

Gradient descent methods that use second-order information about the error surface to determine (and thus vary) η during training offer improved performance, especially if the error function is a quadratic function of the weights (or close to quadratic). Newton's method [Haykin, 1994; Hassoun, 1995] uses the Hessian matrix $\nabla_w^2 E(\mathbf{w})$ along with the current gradient $\nabla_w E(\mathbf{w})$ to generate the weight updates according to

$$\mathbf{w}(k + 1) = \mathbf{w}(k) - [\nabla_w^2 E(\mathbf{w})]^{-1} \nabla_w E(\mathbf{w})$$

This method has the serious drawback that the inverse of the Hessian matrix of the error function (with respect to the weights) is prohibitively time-consuming to calculate for most networks with more than a few weights (the size of the Hessian is the square of the number of weights), and is thus impractical. Additionally, and possibly more importantly, the inverse of the Hessian is required, and there is no guarantee that this matrix is nonsingular at each step.

A more useful method that also employs the Hessian matrix is the conjugate gradient algorithm [Press et al., 1992; Haykin, 1994; Hassoun, 1995], which uses the Hessian matrix implicitly in its calculation of weight updates. It uses the previous gradient and the last step direction to compute a new direction that is conjugate to both, and it does so iteratively without requiring the calculation of either the Hessian or its inverse. The direction vector is calculated in terms of the previous direction vector as

$$\mathbf{v}(k+1) = -\nabla_w E(\mathbf{w}) + \alpha(k)\mathbf{v}(k)$$

where the scalar $\alpha(k)$ is here taken from the *Polak-Ribiere conjugate gradient* formulation [Press et al., 1992; Haykin, 1994] given by

$$\alpha(k) = \frac{[\nabla_w E(\mathbf{w}, k) - \nabla_w E(\mathbf{w}, k-1)] \cdot \nabla_w E(\mathbf{w}, k)}{\nabla_w E(\mathbf{w}, k-1) \cdot \nabla_w E(\mathbf{w}, k-1)}$$

Here all the weights of the network have been collected in a single vector $\mathbf{w}$, and the gradient components have also been arranged in a vector. A line-minimization routine is employed to search in the direction $\mathbf{v}$ to find where the error function takes on its smallest value (along the vector $\mathbf{v}$). The step size which results in this minimal value is η_{opt} for this update. The update to the weight vector is then

$$\mathbf{w}(k+1) = \mathbf{w}(k) + \eta_{opt}\mathbf{v}(k+1)$$

The conjugate gradient method provides determination of η_{opt}, as well as a greatly increased convergence rate compared to incremental or batch gradient descent. A reduction in the number of training cycles required for convergence of one to two orders of magnitude was typical for simulations conducted here. The conjugate gradient algorithm has been applied to the training of feedforward neural networks [Makram-Ebeid, Sirat, and Viala, 1989; van der Smagt, 1994]. The conjugate gradient algorithm applied here to the RTRL dynamic derivatives has exhibited very large learning rates at times during the training process, but this does not seem to hamper its performance (it has been reported in Williams and Zipser [1989a] that small learning rates are required for stable algorithm performance).

The conjugate gradient algorithm is by definition a batch algorithm, and as such is not suited for on-line training, where the size of the training data set is not known a priori. However, for the application of trajectory learning here, this was not an issue.

B. RECURSIVE LEAST SQUARES AND THE KALMAN FILTER

The formulation of the least squares algorithm that computes parameter updates based on past parameter estimates is termed the *recursive least squares* (RLS) *filter* and is a special case of the more general *Kalman filter*. For a complete derivation of both, see Haykin [1996]. Both algorithms generate an estimate of an optimal parameter vector that minimizes an error measure (typically the sum of squared error) for a linear system and therefore are applicable to the training of neural networks.

In the case of a single unit, and taking the activation function to be linear such that the unit response is given by $y = \mathbf{w}^T\mathbf{x}$, the method of linear least squares filtering may be employed to find a set of weights that minimizes the weighted sum of squared error given by

$$E(\mathbf{w}) = \sum_{i=1}^{n} \lambda^{n-i} e^2(i)$$

where $e(i) = d(i) - y(i)$, $d(i)$ is the target value at time i, and λ^{n-i} is an exponential *forgetting factor*, $0 < \lambda < 1$, used to decrease the effect of past data and permit the algorithm to track variations in data.

The RLS algorithm may be adapted for the case of a network that contains hidden units as well as visible output units, and for the case of units that have nonlinear activation functions (the least squares method and the Kalman filter are methods directly applicable to *linear* systems). This algorithm is called the extended RLS, the *extended Kalman filter* (EKF), or equivalently the *global extended Kalman filter* (GEKF); *global* because the algorithm is applied to the network as a whole, *extended* because the linear RLS has been extended to the nonlinear case, and *Kalman filter* because RLS is a special case of the Kalman filter.

The learning equations [Haykin, 1996] which result from the Kalman filter approach are given below in Equations (4) - (7). Further discussion and analysis of these equations can be found in Hagner [1999].

$$\mathbf{K}(n) = \lambda^{-1}\mathbf{P}(n-1)\mathbf{H}(n)[\mathbf{I} + \lambda^{-1}\mathbf{H}^T(n)\mathbf{P}(n-1)\mathbf{H}(n)]^{-1} \qquad (4)$$

$$\mathbf{e}(n) = \mathbf{d}(n) - \mathbf{y}(n) \qquad (5)$$

$$\mathbf{w}(n) = \mathbf{w}(n-1) + \mathbf{K}(n)\mathbf{e}(n) \qquad (6)$$

$$\mathbf{P}(n) = \lambda^{-1}\mathbf{P}(n-1) - \lambda^{-1}\mathbf{K}(n)\mathbf{H}^T(n)\mathbf{P}(n-1) + \mathbf{Q}(n) \qquad (7)$$

Here, $\mathbf{H}(n)$ is a matrix of derivatives of the network unit outputs with respect to the network weights, $\mathbf{K}(n)$ is the Kalman gain matrix, $\mathbf{P}(n)$ is the conditional error covariance matrix, and $\mathbf{Q}(n)$ is a diagonal covariance matrix which introduces artificial process noise.

It should be noted that the GEKF algorithm formulation given in Equations (4) - (7) has been derived from the RLS algorithm with exponential forgetting. The forgetting factor λ is not employed (or, equivalently, set to unity) in the EKF formulation of Singhal and Wu [1989] and the GEKF formulations of Puskorious and Feldkamp [1994], and thus the GEKF algorithm presented here is slightly different. A variable scalar learning rate, $\eta(n)$, is used in Puskorious and Feldkamp [1994] which results in a formula for the Kalman gain, $\boldsymbol{K}(n)$, different from (4), given by

$$\mathbf{K}(n) = \mathbf{P}(n-1)\mathbf{H}(n)[\eta^{-1}(n)\mathbf{I} + \mathbf{H}^{T}(n)\mathbf{P}(n-1)\mathbf{H}(n)]^{-1}$$

where $\eta(n)$ is typically set to a value less than unity at the start of training and increases to unity as training progresses.

The GEKF algorithm is computationally intensive due primarily to the update calculations for the approximate (due to the linear system approximation) conditional error covariance matrix $\mathbf{P}(n)$, which scales as the square of the number of weights in the network. A modification to the GEKF algorithm that assumes certain interactions between weights are negligible is the *decoupled extended Kalman filter* (DEKF) algorithm [Puskorius and Feldkamp, 1994]. The negligible weight interactions are accounted for as zeros in the $\mathbf{P}(n)$ matrix, and if the weights are grouped such that there are assumed to be no interactions between weights in different groups, the $\mathbf{P}(n)$ matrix can be arranged in block-diagonal form. If the groups are chosen such that weights feeding a unit make up a group, then the decoupling is termed *node-decoupled*, and the algorithm is called *node-decoupled* EKF, or NDEKF [Puskorius and Feldkamp, 1994].

The derivation of the DEKF (or NDEKF) algorithm proceeds similarly to that for the GEKF algorithm, except that the block-diagonal form of $\mathbf{P}(n)$ is exploited to reduce the computational complexity. For the case of g groups of weights, there will now be g weight vectors $\mathbf{w}(n)$, as well as g $\mathbf{H}(n)$, $\mathbf{P}(n)$, and $\mathbf{K}(n)$ matrices, which are subsets of their full, GEKF counterparts.

A variation of the single-unit RLS algorithm that employs linearization of the nonlinear unit activation function (similarly to the EKF algorithms described above), and an approximation to the estimation error, $e(n)$, has been developed and termed the *multiple extended Kalman algorithm* (MEKA) [Shah and Palmieri, 1990], and is applicable to multi-layered networks. This algorithm in effect applies an RLS optimization separately to the individual units of the network, whereas the NDEKF algorithm, which includes only weight interactions in a unit's weight group, carries out a global filtering (estimation) operation.

Various EKF algorithms have been successfully applied to the training of both feedforward (MLP) [Shah and Palmieri, 1990] and recurrent [Singhal and

Wu, 1989; Williams, 1992; Puskorius and Feldkamp, 1994] networks. GEKF is computationally intensive, and the modifications (DEKF and MEKA) to the standard algorithm have provided substantial reduction in the computations required, resulting in faster algorithms that retain much of the power of GEKF. These applications of EKF algorithms have been shown to provide convergence in relatively few training iterations, offset partially by an increase in computations over gradient-based algorithms.

VI. SIMULATIONS

A. ALGORITHM SPEED

Comparisons have been made among the speeds of training algorithms for recurrent networks [Logar, Corwin, and Oldham, 1993; Williams and Zipser, 1995]. The focus of this work is on the effects of recurrence on network performance and the efficacy of various training algorithms for architectures with recurrence, and thus the analysis here has been limited to only five training algorithms in a primary effort to find the common effects of recurrence, and secondarily to compare the algorithms' performances on the applications considered here (the ability of the algorithm to converge to a good solution was analyzed in more detail than its pure computational complexity).

All of the algorithms obtained the gradient information from the identical RTRL calculation, which has a computational complexity of $O(n^2)$, where n is the number of weights. The optimization algorithms had complexities of $O(n)$ for the incremental and conjugate gradient descent algorithms; $O\left[\sum_{i=1}^{g} n_i^2\right]$ where n_i is the number of weights for a given unit, and g is the total number of units in the network for the MEKA and NDEKF algorithms; and $O(n^2)$ for the GEKF algorithm. Therefore, the overall training algorithm speed was dominated by the common RTRL calculation.

The RTRL type of calculation for obtaining the gradient, $\nabla_w E(\mathbf{w})$, that includes dependence on past values of the gradient, is required for internally recurrent networks and for externally recurrent networks that use less than full teacher forcing. If an externally recurrent network uses full teacher forcing, then the current gradient does not depend on past values, because the output units had their values set to the target values before each step, and these target values are constants and have no dependence on the weights. This permits a straightforward backpropagation of the error to obtain the gradient, with only partial derivatives and no total derivatives used, which has a computational complexity of $O(n)$. This would have been applicable to all the externally recurrent networks using full teacher forcing, resulting in increased training speed for all the algorithms, but especially for the incremental and conjugate gradient-descent algorithms, which would have had a *total* computational complexity of $O(n)$. RLS algorithms' speed would have then been dominated by the RLS complexity of $O\left[\sum_{i=1}^{g} n_i^2\right]$ for the

for the MEKA and NDEKF algorithms, and $O(n^2)$ for the GEKF algorithm.

The resulting algorithm computational complexities were measured for a fixed number of iterations, and calculated in units of seconds/cycle, where each cycle involved one pass through the M data points. These values were then plotted versus the square of the number of weights, as shown in Figure 4, to check the overall $O(n^2)$ dependence expected.

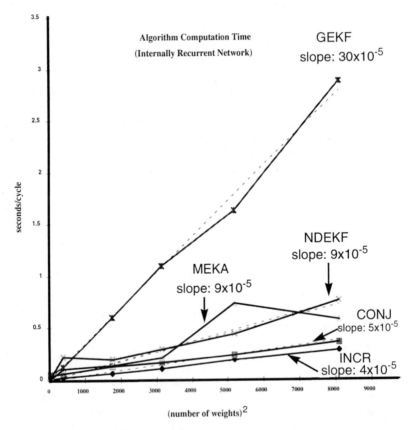

Figure 4. Training algorithm computation time (for internally recurrent networks) in seconds per training cycle vs. the square of the number of network weights (using a 200 MHz Pentium CPU). Approximate slopes of linear trend lines are shown.

The approximately linear dependence on n^2 is evident for all the algorithms, and the slopes of the linear trend lines may be compared to give the relative speeds of the training algorithms. Normalizing the speed of the slowest algorithm

(GEKF) to 1, the relative speeds of the other algorithms are approximately 3.3 for the MEKA and NDEKF algorithms, 6.0 for the conjugate gradient, and 7.5 for the incremental gradient-descent algorithm. This gives approximate confirmation to the speed-up expected for the MEKA and NDEKF algorithms over the GEKF algorithm (e.g., for a network with 6 units, $n = 42$, $n^2 = 1764$, and $\sum_{i=1}^{6} 7^2 = 294$, the expected order of speed-up is $1764/294 = 6$, which is relatively close to the 3.3 obtained experimentally). Additionally, both the incremental and conjugate gradient algorithms are faster than the RLS algorithms, as expected, with the conjugate gradient algorithm being somewhat slower than the incremental gradient algorithm, due to the computational burden of performing the conjugate direction calculation, minimum bracketing, and line minimization routines.

Algorithm computation times for externally recurrent networks are not shown in Figure 4, due to the lack of validity of comparison with internally recurrent networks. In fact, because of the use of the RTRL algorithm to obtain gradient information instead of using standard backpropogation for the externally recurrent networks with full teacher forcing, all the algorithms ran more slowly on these networks than on the internally recurrent networks, due to the additional computations for multiple layers and delays (standard backpropogation would have enabled externally recurrent networks to train more quickly than internally recurrent networks). So, while the externally recurrent networks could have been faster, they were approximately twice as slow in experimental computation time measurements.

B. CIRCLE RESULTS

To learn the circle trajectory, all algorithms used full teacher forcing, as it generally provided the fastest and most robust learning. Partial teacher forcing sometimes resulted in very fast convergence, but was not a robust technique; learning often diverged as the algorithms became unstable.

The network weights for all the architectures and algorithms were obtained from a uniform random distribution from -0.1 to +0.1.

The incremental gradient descent algorithm for the circle trajectory employed learning rates for the feedforward weights and recurrent weights of 0.002. Larger learning rates decreased the number of cycles required for convergence, but resulted in solutions with lower performance due to the algorithm taking relatively large steps around the vicinity of the minimum. The value used here provided a good trade-off between performance and convergence speed. The figure-eight trajectory simulations used learning rates for the feedforward weights of between 0.1 and 0.2 for the externally recurrent architectures, and a feedforward weight learning rate of .01 and recurrent weight learning rate of 0.2 for the internally recurrent architectures. The learning rates for the figure-eight trajectory were larger than those for the circle trajectory because of the large number of iterations needed to approach convergence; the largest rates possible that permitted stable algorithm performance were used. It was found that for the internally recurrent architectures, a feedforward weight learning rate that was smaller than the recurrent weight learning rate by at least a factor of ten ensured algorithm stability.

The RLS algorithms (GEKF, NDEKF, MEKA) were "tuned" for the different algorithm/architecture combinations, though the parameters that were varied were within the following typical ranges. The process noise matrix, Q, was diagonal with elements typically set to 10^{-4}. The forgetting factor, λ, was typically set to the schedule of 0.999 - 0.9999, increasing by 4.5×10^{-6} each step.

Two sets of initial conditions were tested for the results presented here, the first providing the output units with initial condition values **on** the trajectory, and the second with values **off** the trajectory. Note that for externally recurrent networks it is possible to obtain initial conditions that place the network exactly on the desired trajectory, because the initial unit output values have no effect (the network output is a function of only the input and the weights). However, for the internally recurrent networks this exact placement is not possible, because the initial unit output values do contribute to the network output, and these unit values are not known. In these simulations, a "best" estimate for the internally recurrent network initial unit output values was used, which was the actual unit output values at the last or Mth step during training. Thus as the internally recurrent network training error was reduced, the initial conditions of the hidden unit outputs more closely matched those required to be on the target trajectory.

A typical simulation result is shown in Figure 5, which shows a network's output for 10 "loops" (one loop is defined as taking M steps, where M is the number of training points, 100 in these simulations) starting from the two different initial conditions on and off the desired trajectory. The result shown is for an internally recurrent network with 2_R architecture, trained with the conjugate gradient algorithm for 7 cycles.

The first step that the network takes from these initial conditions is indicated on the plots by the small circle indicating the first trajectory point. The trajectory with initial conditions off-trajectory provides some measure of a solution's *basin of attraction*, and the degree to which the limit cycle trajectory is an attractor. The trajectory shown in Figure 5 is a stable attractor, with the off-trajectory initial condition resulting in a trajectory that spirals outward from the origin in a few loops to converge to the limit cycle oscillation of the desired trajectory. Note that all 10 loops are shown in both plots, indicating both the degree to which the trajectory is stable, and the closeness to which it follows the desired trajectory (the target trajectory is indicated by the dotted line).

A limit cycle will exhibit convergence from both sides of the trajectory, and this characteristic is able to be seen in Figure 6. The results are for the same network as in Figure 5, though with two different initial conditions, one inside and one outside of the trajectory, obtained by setting the initial unit values to 0.07 and 0.27, respectively.

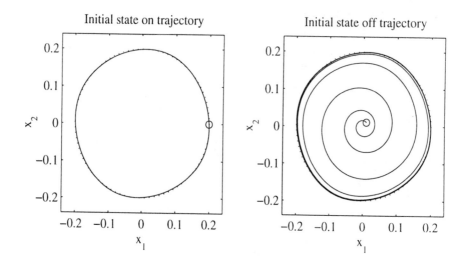

Figure 5. Circle trajectory generated by 2_R network trained with the conjugate gradient algorithm for 7 cycles (performance measurement: 99.7).

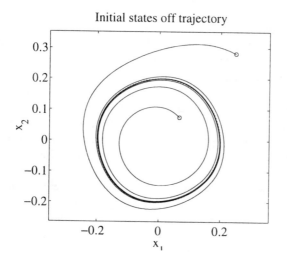

Figure 6. Two convergence regions for the same 2_R network as in Figure 5.

Figure 7 shows the resulting trajectories for the larger, $4 \times 2(1)$ network, trained with the GEKF algorithm for 300 cycles. In general, the faster trajectory convergence shown here, compared to that for the smaller, 2_R network (shown in Figure 5), was typical for the larger networks, possibly because the smaller networks required the units to operate further in their nonlinear regions to achieve

261

the nonlinear trajectories, and possibly due simply to the convergence dynamics resulting from a larger number of units.

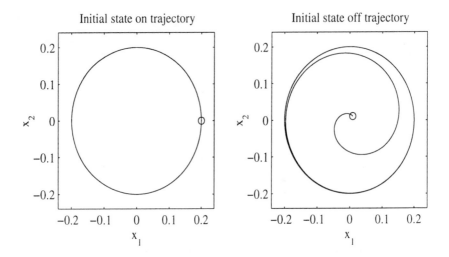

Figure 7. Circle trajectory generated by $4 \times 2(1)$ network trained with the GEKF algorithm for 300 cycles (performance measurement: 100).

All 20 architecture/algorithm combinations learned the circle trajectory and provided excellent performance for the 100 simulations, as shown in Table 1. Each architecture/algorithm was trained 5 times with different initial weight values to provide some measure of the learning performance repeatability, and the initial weight values were identical for all algorithms and a given architecture.

A performance was counted as successful if it provided stable, limit cycle oscillation for both on- and off-trajectory initial conditions (this stability was determined by visual inspection). The table row labeled "Success" gives the number of stable solutions out of 5 runs total. The row labeled "Ave Performance" gives the average performance value of those solutions that were stable. The row labeled "Ave Cycles" gives the average number of cycles required during learning to achieve the given performance for the stable solutions. The row labeled "Training Time" is an estimate of the total training time, in minutes, for the algorithm to iterate through the "Ave Cycles" given, calculated from the algorithms' computation times given by the linear trend lines in Figure 4.

As expected, the conjugate gradient, GEKF, NDEKF, and MEKA algorithms in general converged to solutions in far fewer cycles than the incremental gradient algorithm (on the order of 100 times fewer cycles for the internally recurrent architecture, and approximately 5 times fewer cycles, on average, for the externally recurrent architecture). The one notable exception was the performance of the NDEKF algorithm on the $2 \times 2(1)$ architecture: this algorithm required a relatively large number (14400 on average) of cycles and time to converge, possibly due to the effect of neglecting the coupling of weights in the conditional error covariance matrix, $P(n)$.

Training Algorithm	Metric	Architecture			
		Single Layer		Tap Delay Net	
		2_R	4_R	2x2(1)	4x2(1)
Incremental Gradient Descent	Success	5	5	5	5
	Ave Performance	99.7	99.6	99.1	99.1
	Ave Cycles	3000	3000	6400	4000
	Training Time (min)	0.1	0.8	12.3	2.6
Conjugate Gradient Descent	Success	5	5	5	5
	Ave Performance	99.7	99.5	99.8	99.9
	Ave Cycles	7	11	1100	1440
	Training Time (min)	0.0002	0.004	0.3	1.2
GEKF	Success	5	5	5	5
	Ave Performance	99.4	99.6	100	100
	Ave Cycles	19	31	680	720
	Training Time (min)	0.003	0.1	1.0	3.5
NDEFK	Success	5	5	5	5
	Ave Performance	99.4	99.4	97.4	98.6
	Ave Cycles	17	34	144000	1200
	Training Time (min)	0.001	0.02	6.2	1.7
MEKA	Success	5	5	5	5
	Ave Performance	99.4	99.3	99.5	99.5
	Ave Cycles	20	22	360	340
	Training Time (min)	0.001	0.01	0.2	0.5

Table 1. Circle trajectory simulation results.

There was no performance improvement for the larger networks compared to their smaller counterpart [4_R vs. 2_R and $4 \times 2(1)$ vs. $2 \times 2(1)$], indicating that the smaller networks were adequate to learn the circle trajectory and were not affecting network or algorithm performances (except for convergence dynamics, as noted earlier).

The primary conclusion drawn from the above experimental analysis is that the speed of convergence of the conjugate gradient, GEKF, NDEKF, and MEKA algorithms for the internally recurrent architectures was much greater than for the externally recurrent architectures. The internally recurrent networks converged in at least 10 times fewer (and often 100 times fewer) cycles, and in at least 50 times less (and often 200 times less) time.

It is also notable that for this trajectory, the very simple algorithm of incremental gradient descent provided solutions with performances comparable to those for the more complex algorithms, indicating that for certain trajectories, incremental gradient descent is adequate. And though incremental gradient descent required many more training cycles, it had the smallest cycle computation time, resulting in total training times comparable to the other algorithms.

C. FIGURE-EIGHT RESULTS

The initial weights, teacher forcing, and algorithm parameters were set to values similar to those used for the circle trajectory. It was found that full teacher forcing again provided the best learning performance.

The resulting figure-eight trajectories for the different successful (stable attractor) solutions were dissimilar for the different simulations, unlike the circle results, which were almost identical. The trajectories shown in Figures 8 and 9 show the results of solutions for the 4_R architecture trained with GEKF for 2000 cycles, and the 8_R architecture trained with GEKF for 500 cycles, respectively. Both trajectories are stable attractors and the basins of attraction exhibit quite different dynamics prior to convergence to the final trajectory. As for the circle trajectory, it was found that, in general, the larger the network, the smoother the convergence from the off-trajectory starting point to the final trajectory, consistent with the results shown in Figures 8 and 9.

The results for the 150 simulations of the single layer architectures are given in Table 2, and the results for the tap delay networks are given in Table 3. Again, the numbers in the tables represent the results of 5 different runs.

The figure-eight was, in general, far more difficult to learn for all the networks and training algorithms than the circle. This is most likely because the trajectory crosses itself in output-unit (phase-plane) space, so that the network must store not only the past state of the trajectory, but also information about *multiple* previous states (e.g., storing the direction, or derivative of the trajectory).

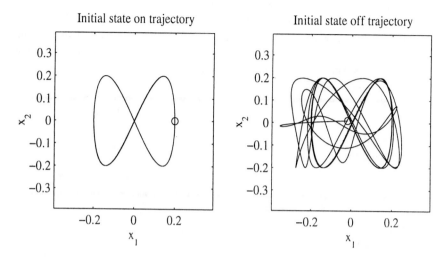

Figure 8. Figure-eight trajectory generated by 4_R network trained with the GEKF algorithm for 2000 cycles (performance measurement: 100).

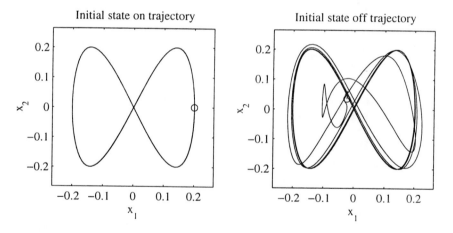

Figure 9. Figure-eight trajectory generated by 8_R network trained with the GEKF algorithm for 500 cycles (performance measurement: 99.9).

As with the circle trajectory, the conjugate gradient, GEKF, NDEKF, and MEKA algorithms converged to solutions in far fewer cycles than the incremental gradient algorithm (on the order of 15 times fewer cycles for the internally recurrent architecture and approximately 150 times fewer cycles, on average, for the externally recurrent architecture).

The incremental gradient descent and MEKA algorithms exhibited some performance improvement for the larger internally recurrent networks compared to their smaller counterparts, as did the conjugate gradient algorithm for the externally recurrent architecture. This does not, however, indicate that the smaller networks were inadequate to learn the figure-eight trajectory, because the excellent performances of the networks trained by the GEKF algorithm show that all the networks contained ample representational capability.

Training Algorithm	Metric	Single Layer Architecture		
		4_R	6_R	8_R
Incremental Gradient Descent	Success	1	1	2
	Ave Performance	91.7	95.5	97.1
	Ave Cycles	48000	14000	29000
	Training Time (min)	12.8	16.5	100.2
Conjugate Gradient Descent	Success	0	0	0
	Ave Performance	-	-	-
	Ave Cycles	-	-	-
	Training Time (min)	-	-	-
GEKF	Success	3	3	3
	Ave Performance	99.3	99.6	99.8
	Ave Cycles	1470	900	770
	Training Time (min)	2.94	7.9	20.0
NDEFK	Success	2	2	4
	Ave Performance	98.1	98.6	98.6
	Ave Cycles	2900	2050	475
	Training Time (min)	1.74	5.4	3.7
MEKA	Success	1	2	4
	Ave Performance	85.1	98.4	97.9
	Ave Cycles	1200	2100	2050
	Training Time (min)	0.72	5.6	15.9

Table 2. Figure-eight trajectory simulation results.

Training Algorithm	Metric	Tap Delay Net Architecture		
		4x2(4)	6x2(4)	8x2(4)
Incremental Gradient Descent	Success	0	0	0
	Ave Performance	-	-	-
	Ave Cycles	-	-	-
	Training Time (min)	-	-	-
Conjugate Gradient Descent	Success	2	1	2
	Ave Performance	95.3	97.6	99.4
	Ave Cycles	4500	9000	10000
	Training Time (min)	15.9	69.4	135.0
GEKF	Success	1	4	3
	Ave Performance	98.6	99.6	99.2
	Ave Cycles	800	730	600
	Training Time (min)	16.9	33.8	48.6
NDEFK	Success	0	0	0
	Ave Performance	-	-	-
	Ave Cycles	-	-	-
	Training Time (min)	-	-	-
MEKA	Success	0	0	1
	Ave Performance	-	-	89.5
	Ave Cycles	-	-	450
	Training Time (min)	-	-	10.9

Table 3. Figure-eight trajectory simulation results.

The primary conclusion drawn from the figure-eight trajectory simulations is that 4 out of the 5 training algorithms were able to converge to good solutions for the internally recurrent network, and only 2 out of the 5 were able to do so for the externally recurrent architectures, indicating that for this limit cycle trajectory, the internally recurrent architecture is the better choice.

The internally recurrent architecture did, however, pose difficulty for the conjugate gradient algorithm, which became quickly trapped in poor local minima for all of the 15 simulations. This may indicate that internal recurrence results in more local minima than external recurrence, and that the 4 incremental algorithms are robust enough to escape these minima but the conjugate gradient algorithm is not.

The other notable conclusion is that the GEKF learning algorithm was far superior to the other 4 algorithms for this trajectory. The GEKF algorithm reached good solutions 57% of the time (17 out of 30 simulations), and converged to good solutions for all 6 of the architectures. None of the other algorithms was able to reach good solutions for all the architectures or both types of recurrence, as indicated by the blank entries in Tables 2 and 3. Of course, it is possible that the other algorithms might have reached good solutions for these architectures if additional simulations had been run. Additionally, the performances of the solutions obtained with the GEKF algorithm were in all simulations superior to those obtained by the other algorithms. This excellent performance indicates that the capability of the algorithm more than made up for its relatively high computational complexity, with the result that it is the preferred algorithm for learning this figure-eight trajectory.

D. ALGORITHM ANALYSIS

Incremental gradient descent. This algorithm was relatively slow, as expected, compared to the other, second-order algorithms. This was not a large problem for networks learning the circle trajectory, as this algorithm found minima that provided excellent performance results very similar to the other algorithms. This was most likely due to the shape of the error cost function in weight space, which appeared to contain very few, if any, local minima. This shape of the error surface permitted all the algorithms to find minima with good solutions (in fact, very often the different algorithms running with different initial weight values converged to the *same* minimum, identified by the nearly identical final weight vector).

When this algorithm was applied to the figure-eight trajectory, however, it performed poorly. The algorithm converged very slowly, requiring tens of thousands of training cycles to approach a minimum, which was often one that provided poor performance. Gradient descent was so slow that it was impractical for use with the figure-eight trajectory, compared to the superior convergence properties of the second-order algorithms. (Gradient descent required almost 2 hours to reach a good (though poorer than the other 4 algorithms) solution for the 8_R network, and almost 24 hours for the $8 \times 2(4)$ network; note that the solutions for the $8 \times 2(4)$ network were not counted as stable, as the performance metric never became consistent). An advantage of this algorithm is that it was very robust (given small enough learning rates), requiring no heuristics to keep the algorithm from diverging or to optimize performance.

Conjugate gradient descent. This algorithm converged in relatively few iterations, compared to the incremental gradient-descent algorithm, as expected. It performed very well on the circle trajectory, but less well on the figure-eight. This algorithm, due to its inherent line minimization routine, was susceptible to becoming trapped in local minima, which was evident for the internally recurrent architecture learning the figure-eight trajectory. It performed better with the externally recurrent architecture on the figure-eight, though its convergence rate was inferior to those of the RLS algorithms. As was the case for the incremental gradient-descent algorithm, this method was very robust, requiring no heuristic adjustments to algorithm parameters to ensure stable convergence characteristics.

Recursive least squares. These algorithms also converged in far fewer iterations than did the incremental gradient-descent algorithm. In addition, as a group they performed better than the incremental and conjugate gradient-descent methods. They did, however, require the appropriate setting of algorithm parameters to optimize performance, which required additional "set-up" time not necessary for the gradient-descent algorithms. It was necessary to set two primary parameters, the process noise matrix Q and the forgetting factor λ, to values appropriate for the application.

Values for Q in the range of 10^{-2} to 10^{-6} were best, and typically 10^{-4} was used in the simulations. While the inclusion of the process noise matrix is not included in the standard RLS algorithm derivation, it is a standard part of the Kalman filter algorithm. Because of the similarity of these algorithms, the process noise matrix was tested with the RLS algorithms, found to be very beneficial in increasing the convergence rate, and was thus used in all the simulations.

The use of forgetting factor λ, (a positive number less than unity called the *exponential forgetting factor* [Åström and Wittenmark, 1989]), provides an ability for the estimator to track variation in the input or, equivalently, to discount old data by weighting it less. Values less than unity also had the effect of increasing the rate of convergence quite substantially, most likely due to the fact that the forgetting of old information when the actual trajectory was far from the desired trajectory was beneficial. Initial λ values smaller than final values provided even faster convergence, and the typical schedule was 0.999 - 0.9999, increasing by 4.5×10^{-6} each step (this implied reaching the final value in 200 steps, or 2 training cycles, for the 100-point data sets used here). Forgetting factor values less than unity did, however, cause the RLS algorithms to become unstable during periods when the updates to the weights were small, as will be discussed in the following section.

E. ALGORITHM STABILITY

The conjugate gradient-descent algorithm was the most stable of the five tested here. It never diverged during training, and required no tuning of parameters to ensure this stability. However, this stability sometimes came at the cost of the algorithm becoming trapped in local minima. The incremental gradient descent algorithm was also very stable. The algorithm diverged only when too large a learning rate was chosen. This was easily remedied by decreasing the learning rate through trial-and-error to find the largest value that was stable.

The RLS algorithms were not as stable as the other two algorithms just discussed. There were two sources of instability: the process noise matrix Q and the forgetting factor λ.

If Q was too large, the algorithm would not converge, in effect attempting to estimate the noise rather than learning the trajectory. This problem was addressed by the trial-and-error method to choose the largest element values for Q that permitted smooth error reduction during training.

The forgetting factor λ was typically chosen, as previously indicated, to vary over the range of 0.999 to 0.9999, incrementing by 4.5 x 10^{-6} each step. If values much smaller than 0.999 were used for the *initial* value, the algorithm was unstable during the period in which λ was small. If values much smaller than 0.9995 were used for the *final* value, the algorithm reduced error rapidly but sometimes became unstable before reaching a minimum. A final value of 1.0 was stable, but resulted in very slow reduction of error.

As indicated above, the use of *exponential forgetting* provides an ability for the RLS estimator to track variation in the input and discount old data. When the algorithm enters a region where the updates to the weights are very small, then the inputs to the estimator are fairly constant, and there is little new information provided by each step. $P(n)$ increases exponentially, leading to what is termed *estimator windup* [Åström and Wittenmark, 1989].

Exponential forgetting is thus sensitive to the degree to which the system is persistently excited, or the amount of new information that is provided at each step. Unfortunately in the problems considered here, where there is no external input (excitation), the input will not be (sufficiently) persistently excited during all phases of training, and methods to ensure sufficient excitation that are useful on certain system identification problems, such as injecting extra perturbation signals, are not applicable here, as perturbation would cause the system to learn a response different from the desired limit cycle oscillation.

Other methods to avoid estimator windup are to keep $P(n)$ bounded, to stop weight updates when the estimator error is small, and to adjust the forgetting factor automatically [Haykin, 1996] or by a schedule such as setting λ to 1.0 after a predetermined number of cycles or at a certain level of estimator error. Methods for ensuring $P(n)$ remains bounded, such as by keeping the trace of the $P(n)$ matrix constant at each iteration or selectively forgetting information only in the direction generating new information, are given in [Haykin, 1996].

The problem of estimator windup was evident in all three RLS algorithms after they had reached points at which the weight updates were very small, but had a more deleterious effect on both the MEKA and NDEKF algorithms, as indicated in Tables 2 and 3 by their relatively poor performances on the figure-eight trajectory for internally recurrent architectures and the lack of stable solutions found for the externally recurrent architectures. These algorithms often diverged before the error had been reduced to values small enough to result in good performances. In this respect, these versions of the RLS algorithm were more susceptible to estimator windup than the GEKF algorithm, which did exhibit divergence, though after the algorithm had advanced sufficiently close to minima providing good performance. It is unknown if these algorithms could have efficiently reduced the error further, and if this would have resulted in solutions with better performance, though the ability of the conjugate gradient descent algorithm to do so for the externally recurrent networks suggests that this is the case. It is thus likely that the MEKA and NDEKF algorithms could benefit significantly from the use of the stabilizing heuristics mentioned above for avoiding estimator windup, or from the use of different variations of the RLS algorithm such as the square-root adaptive filter [Söderström and Stoica, 1989; Haykin, 1996].

It should be noted that the instability caused by estimator windup is due to the exponential forgetting employed in the RLS derivation. It is not a problem for the slightly different EKF algorithms that are derived using Kalman filter methods [Singhal and Wu, 1989; Puskorius and Feldkamp, 1994], and thus these formulations may provide more stable operation than those derived here using RLS methods. It is not known, however, how the benefits of the learning rate heuristic used in Puskorius and Feldkamp [1994] for the GEKF and NDEKF algorithms compare to those exhibited by the exponential forgetting in the RLS-derived GEKF and NDEKF algorithms given here.

F. CONVERGENCE CRITERIA

The learning algorithms occasionally generated network weights that provided good results *prior* to convergence, and poor results once convergence was attained. These good solutions were not due to weights that constituted a minimum in the error surface, and thus the algorithms passed through these regions of weight space on the way to a minimum.

Training was stopped for the simulations in this work if convergence was reached (for the conjugate gradient and RLS algorithms, this was fairly evident by the fact that the reduction of training error at successive iterations became negligible), or if the reduction in training error was small and the performance value for successive iterations remained within a band, typically ±2 units of the performance metric used here, given in Equation 3.

The good solutions obtained in the middle of training did not usually meet these convergence criteria, and thus were not accepted as valid. This did not greatly affect the number of good solutions found by the architecture/algorithm combinations because algorithms tended to converge later to minima with solutions of equal or higher performance. However, for some simulations, especially for incremental gradient descent, convergence resulted in poor results, indicating that the algorithm was beginning to overfit the data and had passed the point where the network generalizes well. In these instances, it would have been possible to employ a form of *early stopping* [Hassoun, 1995] to stop training in a region of weight space that provided good performance, though prior to convergence. For example, the early stopping technique could have been used during the simulation depicted in Figure 3, where the training had relatively short periods where the performance was good, prior to and after convergence.

G. TRAJECTORY STABILITY AND CONVERGENCE DYNAMICS

The basin of attraction that a trained network exhibits is one measure of the stability of the network, or its robustness with respect to initial conditions. To study this property, the networks were tested with starting points far from the trajectory. As stated above, for the circle trajectory the initial condition values were 0.0001 and for the figure-eight 0.01.

All 100 of the circle simulations resulted in a similar basin of attraction for the initial condition off the trajectory, as shown in Figure 5. The trajectory spiraled out from the origin, taking several "loops" to converge to the desired circle trajectory. Ten loops of network trajectory are shown in the plot, indicating that the remaining loops were coincident, and therefore had converged to a stable trajectory. Thus the trajectory was a stable attractor.

As seen in Tables 2 and 3, only 38 out of 150 (or 25%) of the simulations for the figure-eight resulted in networks that produced stable attractors. Many of the simulations did produce sustained oscillators (the on-trajectory initial conditions resulted in a trajectory following the target trajectory), but not attractors (the off-trajectory initial conditions resulted in a trajectory that failed to converge to the desired trajectory within $10M$ steps). In some simulations this may have been due to the trajectories being similar to the *center*, or *vortex*, trajectories generated by two-dimensional *linear* systems with a purely imaginary conjugate pair of eigenvalues, indicating that the network was not exploiting the nonlinearities of the hidden units. The statistics were not kept for this subset of results, as the interest was is generating stable attractor trajectories.

In some of the figure-eight simulations, when the algorithms were near convergence to a minimum, the performance would sometimes switch between excellent (values in the high 90's) and poor (values in the high 40's) as the off-trajectory result changed from converging to the desired trajectory to not converging (not an attractor), as shown in Figure 3. Because the on-trajectory result was still good (the trajectory was stable) and the contribution of the off-trajectory result was zero, the total performance measure was reduced by a factor of two. This indicated that the off-trajectory performance was very sensitive to the initial conditions. If only small changes in the weights could cause the trajectory to switch between converging and not converging, it is most likely that changes to the values of the off-trajectory initial conditions would also have a dramatic effect on the trajectory convergence characteristics.

Note that in the simulations presented above, the neural nets were trained only with data on the trajectory itself, and not with noisy data, or data from a basin of attraction around the trajectory. Although not explicitly trained to learn an attractor limit cycle, the simulation results show that the networks do, in fact, produce such asymptotically stable attractors. This inherent stability was evident for both the internally and externally recurrent networks and has been previously reported [Williams and Zipser, 1989b; Pearlmutter, 1995; Tsung and Cottrell, 1995; Cohen, Saad, and Marom, 1997]. The basins of attraction for these types of figures were studied in Tsung and Cottrell [1995] and Sundareshan and Condarcure [1998], but in Tsung and Cottrell [1995] the training data were chosen specifically to produce desired basins of attraction, and in Sundareshan and Condarcure [1998] the desired trajectory data included the initial, transient trajectory from the origin out to the final circle trajectory and thus was explicitly trained.

Why recurrent neural nets, trained only with data on the trajectory, are able to produce stable attractor limit cycles is not clear. Further, the use of full teacher forcing in effect trains the network to step to a point close to the trajectory, starting from a point on the trajectory, as discussed in Tsung and Cottrell [1995]. This is the opposite of what is required for a limit cycle, for which the network needs to step to a point on the trajectory, starting from a point off the trajectory (as is done when no teacher forcing is used). Thus the limit cycle properties observed in these simulations are inherent characteristics of the resultant network dynamics.

VII. CONCLUSIONS

Internally recurrent hidden layers did not increase network performance over single-layer internally recurrent networks, and multiple feedforward hidden layers did not improve the performance of feedforward, externally recurrent networks, for the limit cycle trajectories considered in this work.

All the architecture/algorithm combinations were able to learn the circle trajectory, with the internally recurrent architectures providing convergence in far fewer cycles than the externally recurrent architectures, especially for the conjugate gradient and RLS algorithms.

The figure-eight trajectory proved to be much more difficult to learn than the circle, presumably due to the trajectory's crossing itself. In this case, two different points on the trajectory require the network to produce identical output values. The internally recurrent architectures permitted convergence to good solutions more often than did the externally recurrent architectures (28 vs. 14 good solutions out of 75 simulations each for the internally and externally recurrent networks, respectively). The GEKF algorithm proved to be the superior training algorithm for this trajectory, providing the most good solutions and the solutions with the best performances. The GEKF algorithm found limit cycle solutions for 17 of the 30 possible (compared to 8, 8, 5, and 4 for the NDEKF, MEKA, conjugate gradient, and incremental gradient algorithms, respectively).

GEKF was able to repeatedly find good solutions for both the internally and externally recurrent network architectures, an ability that was not achieved by any of the other algorithms. It appears that the excellent performance of the GEKF algorithm was due to its ability to converge to minima with very low values of error, and it did so in relatively few training cycles. While initial experimentation on nonlinear single input-single output system identification shows agreement with the above findings, further analysis is needed to determine if these results are applicable to problems of nonlinear dynamic system modeling.

The incremental and conjugate gradient-descent algorithms are quite stable, while the RLS algorithms suffer from instability due to estimator windup near convergence, though this was less of a problem for the GEKF algorithm.

The networks were, in general, able to learn to generate limit cycle trajectories, with basins of attraction in which trajectories converged to final, steady-state trajectories. This convergence property was inherent in the resulting network dynamics, and not explicitly part of the training method.

In retrospect, it would have been beneficial to separate the performances for the two initial conditions tested, and thus have distinct metrics for the network's performance as a sustained oscillator and as an oscillator that was an attractor. Also, testing trained networks with multiple off-trajectory initial conditions (rather than only one) would have provided more information about the basin of attraction for the trajectories. Cursory testing of the figure-eight trajectories with multiple initial conditions indicates that these trajectories had complex attractor characteristics, where some initial conditions resulted in convergence to limit cycles, some converged to fixed points, and some produced chaotic trajectories that did not appear to either converge or diverge.

A possibility for future work would be to continue the initial analysis on identification of nonlinear systems, and extend this by studying the performances of the recurrent network architectures and training algorithms for identification of real physical systems with experimentally collected data sets. This would indicate if the findings here were applicable to a broader class of systems, and facilitate analysis of the capabilities of the networks and learning algorithms to model systems when presented with noisy, real data.

REFERENCES

Åström, K. J. and Wittenmark, B., *Adaptive Control*. Reading, MA: Addison-Wesley Publishing Company, 1989.

Cohen, B. C., Saad, D., and Marom, E., "Efficient training of recurrent neural network with time delays," *Neural Networks*, 10(1), 51, 1997.

Dickinson, B. W., *Systems: Analysis, Design, and Computation*. Englewood Cliffs, NJ: Prentice-Hall, 1991.

Funashi K.-I. and Nakamura, Y., "Approximation of dynamical systems by continuous time recurrent neural networks," *Neural Networks*, 6, 801, 1993.

Hagner, D. G., *Experimental Comparison of Recurrent Neural Network Architectures and Training Algorithms for Trajectory Generation*, Master's Thesis, Department of Electrical and Computer Engineering, Wayne State University, Detroit, 1999.

Hassoun, M. H., *Fundamentals of Artificial Neural Networks*. Cambridge, MA: MIT Press, 1995.

Haykin, S., *Neural Networks: A Comprehensive Foundation*. Upper Saddle River, NJ: Prentice Hall, 1994.

Haykin, S., *Adaptive Filter Theory*. Upper Saddle River, NJ: Prentice Hall, 1996.

Horne, B. G. and Giles, C. L., "An experimental comparison of recurrent neural networks," in *Advances in Neural Information Processing Systems* 7, 1994, Tesauro, G., Touretzky, D., and Leen, T., Eds. Cambridge, MA: MIT Press, 697, 1995.

Lin, D.-T., Dayhoff, J. E., and Ligomenides, P. A., "Trajectory production with the adaptive time-delay neural network," *Neural Networks*, 8(3), 447, 1995.

Logar, A. M., Corwin, E. M., and Oldham, W. J. B., "A comparison of recurrent neural network learning algorithms," in *International Joint Conference on Neural Networks*, San Francisco, 1129, 1993.

Makram-Ebeid, S., Sirat, J.-A., and Viala, J.-R., "A rationalized error back-propagation learning algorithm," in *International Joint Conference on Neural Networks*, Washington, 2, 373, 1989.

Pearlmutter, B. A., "Gradient calculations for dynamic recurrent neural networks: a survey," *IEEE Trans. Neural Networks*, 6(5), 1212, 1995.

Press, W. H., Teukolsky, S. A., Vetterling, W. T., and Flannery, B. P., *Numerical Recipes in C, The Second Edition*. Cambridge, UK: Cambridge University Press, 1992.

Puskorius, G. V. and Feldkamp, L. E., "Neurocontrol of nonlinear dynamical systems with Kalman filter trained recurrent networks," *IEEE Trans. Neural Networks*, 5(2), 279, 1994.

Rumelhart, D. E., Hinton, G. E., and Williams, R. J., "Learning internal representations by error propagation," in *Parallel Distributed Processing: Explorations in the Microstructure of Cognition*, Rumelhart, D. E. and McClelland, J. L., Eds., Vol. 1. Foundations, Cambridge, MA: MIT Press, 319, 1986.

Shah, S. and Palmieri, F. , "MEKA—a fast, local algorithm for training feedforward neural networks," in *International Joint Conference on Neural Networks*, San Diego, Vol. 3, 41, June 17-21, 1990.

Singhal, S. and Wu, L., "Training multilayer perceptrons with the extended Kalman algorithm," in *Advances in Neural Information Processing Systems 1*, Denver, 1988, Touretzky, D. S., Ed. San Mateo, CA: Morgan Kaufmann, 133, 1989.

Söderström, T. and Stoica, P., *System Identification*. New York: Prentice Hall, 1989.

Sundareshan, M. K. and Condarcure, T. A., "Recurrent neural-network training by a learning automaton approach for trajectory learning and control system design," *IEEE Trans. Neural Networks*, 9(3), 354, 1998.

Toomarian, N. B. and Barhen, J., "Learning a trajectory using adjoint functions and teacher forcing," *Neural Networks*, 5, 473, 1992.

Tsung, F.-S. and Cottrell, G. W., "Phase—space learning," in *Advances in Neural Information Processing Systems 7*, Tesauro, G., Touretzky, D., and Leen, T., Eds. Cambridge, MA: MIT Press, 481, 1995.

Werbos, P. J., "Backpropagation through time: what it does and how to do it", *Proceedings of the IEEE*, 78(10), 1550, Oct., 1990.

Williams, R. J., "Training recurrent networks using the extended Kalman filter," in *International Joint Conference on Neural Networks*, Baltimore, Vol. 4, 241, 1992.

(a) Williams, R. J. and Zipser, D., "A learning algorithm for continually running fully recurrent neural networks," *Neural Computation*, 1, 270, 1989.

(b) Williams, R. J. and Zipser, D., "Experimental analysis of the real-time recurrent learning algorithm," *Connection Science*, 1(1), 1989.

Williams, R. J. and Zipser, D., "Gradient-based learning algorithms for recurrent networks and their computational complexity," in *Backpropogation: Theory, Architectures, and Applications*, Chauvin, Y. and Rumelhart, D. E., Eds., Hillsdale, NJ: Lawrence Erlbaum Associates, 433, 1995.

van der Smagt, P. P., "Minimization methods for training feedforward neural networks," *Neural Networks*, 7(1), 1, 1994.

Van De Vegte, J., *Feedback Control Systems*. Englewood Cliffs, NJ: Prentice-Hall, 1986.

Chapter 11

TRAINING ALGORITHMS FOR RECURRENT NEURAL NETS THAT ELIMINATE THE NEED FOR COMPUTATION OF ERROR GRADIENTS WITH APPLICATION TO TRAJECTORY PRODUCTION PROBLEM

Malur K. Sundareshan, Yee Chin Wong and Thomas Condarcure

Department of Electrical and Computer Engineering University of Arizona, Tucson, AZ 85721-0104

I. INTRODUCTION

The most fundamental characteristic that enables a neural network to serve as a useful computational device is its learning capability. The implementation of an appropriately tailored learning algorithm, *i.e.*, a rule for adaptive adjustment of the network parameters such as the interconnection weights and gains of nonlinear characteristics, can endow the network with the capability for evolving into a structure that performs a desired computation. Designing a computationally efficient and yet simply implemented learning algorithm is hence at the core of successful neural network implementations for practical problems. Although interest in general learning theory and development of systematic training schemes has enjoyed a resurgence in recent times in the context of neural networks applications, they have a much longer history, tracing their origins to machine learning [Nilsson, 1965] and to adaptive learning control systems [Mendel, 1970].

When one narrows the discussion down to the specific context of neural network training, there are two general guiding principles on which many popular algorithms are based. These are Hebbian learning and gradient-descent learning. While Hebbian learning derived its following from the parallels that exist in biological systems, gradient-descent methods have attained a greater importance more recently in spite of the lack of conclusive evidence of whether biological systems employ such a mechanism for global learning of complex behaviors. The reason why gradient-descent methods have become popular is the optimization framework they facilitate not only to tailor specific training algorithms but also to provide estimates of the convergence behavior under these algorithms. A specific approach that has attained a considerable degree of popularity in recent times is the backpropagation rule [Rumelhart, 1986], which employs a gradient descent scheme to adjust the interconnection weights of a multilayer neural net in order to minimize a measure of the deviation between the actual network output and a reference entity. Alternate ways of specifying this measure, or the "error norm," can be used to develop different algorithms that perform supervised training.

Gradient descent-learning is conceptually very simple. However, in practical implementations it may lead to several problems related to the need for precise computation of gradients of the error function with respect to the network parameters being adjusted for the algorithm to succeed, and the possibility of being trapped at local minima of the error function that prevents the training error to be minimized to its global minimum value. The problems are further exacerbated when recurrent neural networks are attempted to be trained by this approach due to the complexity of implementing the needed updating equations.

Neural networks with recurrent connections and dynamical processing elements are finding increasing applications in diverse areas. While feedforward networks have been recognized to perform excellent pattern recognition even with very complex nonlinear decision surfaces, they are limited to processing stationary patterns (i.e., patterns that are invariant with time). It requires the power of dynamical networks, such as networks with recurrent and feedback connections, to handle the challenges posed in the storage of spatiotemporal patterns and sequences.

The recognition of the importance of training recurrent neural networks has prompted a host of researchers to investigate devising schemes by which gradient methods, and in particular backpropagation learning, could be extended to these networks. Several notable schemes have been developed with some early contributions made by numerous researchers. The backpropagation-through-time approach of Werbos [Werbos, 1990] attempts to approximate the time evolution of a recurrent net in terms of a sequence of static networks to which gradient methods are applied. Lapedes and Farber [Lapedes, 1986] propose a master slave formulation where deployment of a second neural network (master net) is made to perform the required computations in programming the attractors of the original dynamical network (slave net) to be trained. Similarly, Pineda [Pineda, 1987] and Almeida [Almeida, 1987] propose a second neural network, of the same dimension as the original one, for implementing the backward propagation equation in order to avoid a more complex matrix inversion in the weight adjustment process. A direct differentiation of the neural activation dynamics to calculate the error gradients is proposed by Williams and Zipser [Williams, 1989], which, although it provides some benefits of reducing the storage capacity needed, is still computationally very cumbersome and scales poorly to large networks (i.e.,networks with large numbers of dynamical processing elements and a large set of adjustable parameters). The algorithm proposed by Sato [Sato, 1990] is based on Lagrange multipliers, while Pearlmutter [Pearlmutter, 1989] gives a variational method that involves solving a set of "adjoint equations". A detailed survey of the various attempts to extend backpropagation learning to recurrent networks is also given by Pearlmutter [Pearlmutter, 1995].

A major problem with the backpropagation approach used for recurrent network training is the computational intensity. For illustration, in the specific formulation given by Pearlmutter [Pearlmutter, 1989] that utilizes variational arguments, the complexity arises in the form of the need to solve a set of differential equations backwards in time and the need to store variables for recall later when the forward solution is implemented. Although this is not a drawback unique to backpropagation methods and is shared by many optimal control methods (such as dynamic programming [Bertsekas, 1987]), it certainly limits the attractiveness of the training scheme. Also limiting the usefulness for practical implementations is the fact that such gradient-based approaches do not scale well for large-sized networks. For a typical trajectory learning problem that involves training a continuous trajectory, defined over a time interval divided into L time steps, to a network with N neurons, some estimates [Toomarian, 1992] indicate that the total number of multiplications and additions required for the implementation of the required updating scales as $O(N^4 L)$. This clearly imposes a significant computational burden and is practically infeasible even for medium-sized networks. For overcoming the computational demands and ensuring a relatively manageable implementation, one is usually forced to making simplifying approximations, such as coarser gradient evaluations and heuristic selections of high gains in the activation functions (instead of allowing the network to find the optimized parameter values) [Sudharsanan, 1991, Sudharsanan, 1994], which in turn lead to reduced training efficiency. In several precision applications, as for instance those encountered in multijointed robot control [Karakasoglu, 1993] and reliable tracking of target maneuvers in severe clutter and noise environments [Wong, 1998], for which neural network-based solutions are becoming very attractive, making such approximations could pose serious limitations and alternate training procedures that bypass the need for computation of gradients of the error function are clearly useful.

The primary focus in this chapter is the design of supervised training schemes for recurrent neural networks that do not require gradient evaluations. In particular, we describe two distinct approaches, one that employs concepts from the theory of learning automata and the other based on the classical simplex optimization approach. Besides the elimination of the need for evaluation of error gradients, these approaches result in simple training algorithms suitable for implementation on low-end platforms such as personal computers. They also offer the flexibility of tailoring a number of specific training schemes based on the selection of linear and nonlinear reinforcement rules for updating automaton action probabilities and specification of different error norms. For demonstrating the training efficiency with these approaches, the illustrative task of spatiotemporal signal production by a trained neural network will be considered. To underscore the complexity involved in this task compared to learning of isolated fixed points, one may note that while a variety of networks, both static and dynamic, can be used for the fixed point learning problem even on arbitrarily high dimensional spaces, the trajectory learning problem requires exploiting the unique capability of recurrent neural networks for approximating the temporal dynamics. The practical usefulness of this problem can also be appreciated by noting that the ability of a recurrent neural net to be trained to produce desired trajectories and to converge to attractor trajectories from arbitrary starting points can be used effectively in several control applications, particularly where precise repetitive actions are desired to be performed, such as those arising in process control and robotic manipulator control.

The structure of the chapter is as follows. In Section 2, we shall provide a mathematical description of the learning problem in general dynamical systems and specialize this to spatiotemporal training of recurrent neural networks. Some important concepts such as incremental training and teacher forcing that contribute to the efficiency of training are also discussed. In Section 3, some basics on learning automata will be introduced and specific training policies that can be developed utilizing a penalty-reward structure for reinforcement learning will be discussed. Performance of these methods in training a recurrent neural network to produce prespecified periodic trajectory patterns is also established. The use of a nonlinear simplex optimization approach for neural network training will be discussed in Section 4. Some basics on simplex optimization are briefly introduced and a systematic training scheme for recurrent networks is developed. For comparison with the earlier approach, the trajectory production performance resulting from this approach is also established by considering specific benchmark trajectory patterns.

II. DESCRIPTION OF THE LEARNING PROBLEM AND SOME ISSUES IN SPATIOTEMPORAL TRAINING

A. GENERAL FRAMEWORK AND TRAINING GOALS

For a precise description of the learning problem and the training objectives considered in this article, it is useful to adopt the general framework afforded by considering the problem of modifying the behavior of a general nonlinear dynamical system to meet specified objectives. Consider the problem of training an N-dimensional system whose dynamics are described by the nonlinear differential equation

$$\dot{x}(t) = \Im(x, u, \wp) \tag{1}$$

where $x(.): \Re \to \Re^N$ is the N-dimensional vector that describes the evolution of the system state, $u(.): \Re \to \Re^m$ is a vector of external inputs (fixed or time-varying), $\wp \in \Re^M$ is a set of adjustable parameters and $\Im$ is a nonlinear function whose properties can be specified to include different types of dynamical behavior of interest. For instance, one may require $\Im$ to satisfy

Lipschitz conditions in all of its arguments to ensure continuity of system trajectories, or to meet appropriate limiting conditions such as saturation limits and limits on the rise time of the trajectories in order to ensure boundedness and stability properties [Sudharsanan, 1991a]. The problem of interest is to develop an organized procedure for adjusting the parameters in the set $\wp$ such that the dynamical system exhibits desired time-behavior when started at an initial state $x(t_0) = x_0$. The system behavior desired may be specified in different ways depending on the particular application to which the system may be employed, such as: (i) requiring the system to exhibit an "asymptotically stable behavior", i.e., $\|x(t)\|$ bounded for all time $t \geq t_0$ and $\lim_{t \to \infty} x(t) = x_e$, where x_e is a specified equilibrium state of system (1), or (ii) requiring the system to exhibit an acceptable "tracking behavior", i.e., $\|x(t) - x^*(t)\| \leq \varepsilon$ for all $t \geq t_0$, and a specified $\varepsilon > 0$ and a trajectory to be tracked $x^*(t)$.

The specific problem cited above of training the network to ensure stability of the equilibrium points is of importance for fixed point learning, and a variety of applications such as associative memory designs and synthesis of nonlinear input-output mappers can be based on this property. For illustration, in the case of a network which is designed to serve as a reliable associative memory, the information stored corresponds to its stable equilibria. It has been established that by a careful selection of the nonlinear activation functions and of the interconnection weights, the network can be endowed with a number of stable equilibria, each of which corresponds to a to-be-stored memory vector. Furthermore, the size of the basins of attraction for each of these stable equilibria can be tailored in order to ensure desired levels of reliability in the memory recall process. As shown in Sudharsanan [1994], there exists intricate interrelations between the stability properties of the network equilibria and the convergence properties of the training algorithms that can be synthesized for these networks. In particular, one can attempt to utilize analytical stability results for these networks [Sudharsanan, 1991a, Sudharsanan, 1991b] in order to pre-select the shapes of the nonlinear activation functions (selection of the dc gain, for instance), which in turn enables one to develop learning rules that approximate gradient schemes but offer simple implementation possibilities. It must however be appreciated that the *a priori* selection of the nonlinear gains almost always leads to a suboptimal solution to the overall training of the recurrent neural network.

The second problem cited above of training the network to track a specified trajectory $x^*(t)$ is a more complex one. It is well known in the literature on nonlinear dynamical systems [Khalil, 1992] that under certain conditions the tracking problem can be reduced through an appropriate transformation to a corresponding problem of ensuring the stability of an equilibrium point of a transformed system. In particular, by defining the vector $y(t)$ as

$$y(t) = x(t) - x^*(t) \qquad (2)$$

one can transform the nonlinear system described by (1) into an equivalent system

$$\dot{y}(t) = g(y, u) \qquad (3)$$

such that the tracking problem of forcing $x(t)$ to follow $x^*(t)$ in system (1) can be reduced to the problem of ensuring the stability of the equilibrium point $y(t) = 0$ in system (2). However, when the desired objective is one of training system (1) to perform a desired task, *i.e.,* explicitly adjust the parameters in the set $\wp$, such a reformulation of the problem may not be very useful in practice since the transformation given by (2) makes an explicit handling of these parameters almost always impossible. Consequently, any attempts at simplifying training by approximations such as those discussed above for the fixed point learning problem are more difficult to obtain in this case.

It is evident from the above discussion that training a dynamical system to produce state-space trajectories of specified forms constitutes a highly challenging learning problem due to the diversity in the possible spatiotemporal features that may need to be learned. A problem of particular interest is to train the system to exhibit desired limit cycles, which focuses only on the asymptotic behavior of the state-space trajectory to converge to a prespecified periodic temporal behavior. In the context of neural network training, an aspect of particular significance is ensuring the learning of the true spatiotemporal features as opposed to a point-by-point memorization of the terminal trajectory. This capability is provided by training the network to have the desired attractor dynamics such that arbitrary starting motions are forced to converge to the desired terminal periodic behavior. The complexity of implementing gradient-based training methods for these problems makes the development of alternate learning schemes that do not require the evaluation of gradients particularly attractive.

B. RECURRENT NEURAL NETWORK ARCHITECTURES

The training problems described in the previous section are quite general. For the establishment of specific simple rules for parameter adjustment and also to illustrate how well the training objectives are met in practice by different algorithms, it is useful to consider specialized architectures for the nonlinear dynamical system that is being trained. One such model that has been popular with neural network researchers is the continuous-time recurrent network model described by the set of coupled nonlinear differential equations

$$\frac{dv_i}{dt} + \tau_i v_i(t) = \tau_i \tanh\left(g_i \sum_{j=1}^{N} \omega_{ij} v_i(t) \right), \quad i = 1, 2, ..., N \tag{4}$$

where $v_i(\cdot) : \mathfrak{R} \to \mathfrak{R}$ denotes the state of the ith neuron, $\tau_i \in \mathfrak{R}$ is a time constant referred to as the relaxation time, $g_i \in \mathfrak{R}$ is a parameter that controls the slope of the sigmoidal activation function, and $\omega_{ij} \in \mathfrak{R}$ denotes the interconnection weight from the jth neuron to the ith neuron. The inputs to this network come from the initial conditions $v_i(t_0)$ and the outputs are the observations of the behavior of the state trajectories $v_i(t)$, for $t \geq t_0$. The task of training this network to serve as a useful computational device involves the implementation of an algorithm for progressively updating the $N^2 + 2N$ parameters $\{\omega_{ij}, \tau_i \text{ and } g_i\}$ such that when the training is completed, the network trajectories $v_i(t)$ starting from any initial states $v_i(t_0)$ behave in a prescribed manner to perform the desired computation.

In several practical problems, observing only a subset of the state variables may be of particular importance for checking whether the goals of the desired computation are met, and consequently designation of a set ϑ of output neurons (which is a subset of the total set of neurons) may be appropriate. Also, in certain problems where the input-output mapping behavior of the neural network is of interest, the use of externally applied time-dependent forcing signals to alter the activation dynamics of one or more neurons may be necessary. In order to be able to handle such problems, the dynamical framework can be expanded to permit the introduction of external inputs $I_i(t), i = 1, 2, ..., m$, by modifying the dynamical equation (4) into

$$\frac{dv_i}{dt} + \tau_i v_i(t) = \tau_i \tanh\left[g_i \left(\sum_{j=1}^{n} \omega_{ij} v_j(t) + \sum_{j=1}^{m} \widetilde{\omega}_{ij} I_j(t) \right) \right], \quad i = 1, 2, ..., N$$

$$\tag{5}$$

The weights $\widetilde{\omega}_{ij}$, some of which could be zero, serve to fan-out the m input signals I_i into the individual nodes of the network.[1] The number of weight parameters that need to be trained increases in this case to $N^2 + (m+2)N$.

---

[1] To conform this architecture to the more familiar multilayer configurations, the input signals I_i can be considered as the input nodes of the network. These nodes, however, are different from the N dynamical nodes in that they do not have recurrent or feedback connections, but connect to the N dynamical nodes only in the feedforward direction through the weights $\widetilde{\omega}_{ij}$.

Evidently, for $I_j(t) = 0$, (5) reduces to (4). In this chapter, we will exclusively consider the specialized network architecture described by the dynamical equation (4), since for trajectory learning problems that will be considered for illustration here no external inputs are needed. A schematic of the general recurrent network architecture described by (5) is shown in Fig. 1.

C. SOME ISSUES OF INTEREST IN NEURAL NETWORK TRAINING

1. AN OPTIMIZATION FRAMEWORK FOR SPATIOTEMPORAL LEARNING

As noted earlier, a particularly challenging learning problem is that of training a recurrent network to produce a continuous trajectory of a specified form or to ultimately relax to a desired limit cycle behavior. In fact, this is also one of the tasks where the greater capabilities of dynamical networks are brought into a sharp focus. Recurrent network training to learn such trajectories has received some attention in the recent past with the investigation of schemes which use various forms of gradient descent algorithms. These include the real-time recurrent learning (RTRL) scheme of Williams and Zipser [Williams, 1989], the method of directed derivatives of Pearlmutter [Pearlmutter, 1989], and the method of adjoint operators of Toomarian and Barhen [Toomarian, 1992]. These works have shown that a dynamical network can indeed be trained to exhibit desired limit cycle behavior (it may be noted that this behavior is not possible to emulate in a static feedforward network) and have demonstrated the success of their training algorithms by application to the problem of learning certain benchmark trajectories. Some additional refinements to the use of gradient methods for training to produce continuous trajectories have also been made very recently by Lin et. al. [Lin, 1995] and by Ruiz et. al. [Ruiz, 1998]. While the closeness with which the desired trajectory could be generated varies from one algorithm to another, the required computation of gradients and other implementation considerations for error backpropagation impose considerable burden (in fact, the methods cited above differ from one another mainly in the specific procedure employed for implementing the required gradient computations). The application of alternate training procedures that eliminate the need for gradient computations as will be described in this chapter are of particular interest in the context of this problem.

Two specific benchmark trajectories that have received wide attention in performance evaluations are the "circle trajectory" and the "figure-eight trajectory". A recurrent network can be set up to produce these trajectories by requiring two output nodes in the architecture shown in Fig. 1 to generate oscillatory response of a sinusoidal form with a specified frequency. It is easy to see that requiring the two outputs to oscillate according to the relation

$$o_1(t) = A \sin \omega t \quad \text{and} \quad o_2(t) = A \cos \omega t$$

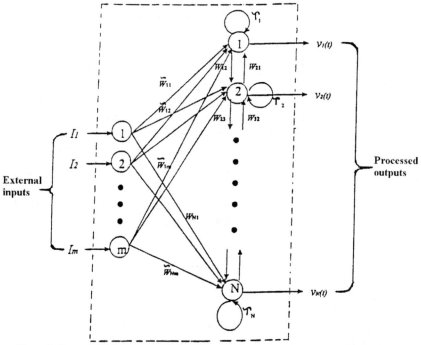

Figure 1. General architecture of an N-node recurrent neural network with m external inputs

with an arbitrary frequency ω would generate a circle with center at the origin and radius A on a two-dimensional plane with $o_1(t)$ and $o_2(t)$ as coordinates, while requiring the two outputs to oscillate according to the relation

$$o_1(t) = A\sin\omega t \quad \text{and} \quad o_2(t) = A\sin 2\omega t$$

would generate a figure-eight pattern passing through the origin of the $(o_1(t), o_2(t))$ plane. It is also easy to see that since the latter trajectory intersects on itself, the training problem is more challenging in this case compared to one of training a non-intersecting trajectory pattern. While these patterns are the ones that have been considered by earlier researchers to demonstrate the training efficiency, more general trajectories can also be formed by specifying the neural network outputs in appropriate forms.

An optimization framework can be developed for such a spatiotemporal learning task extending over a time horizon $\left[t_0, t_f\right]$ by specifying an error functional

$$\varepsilon = \sum_{i\in\vartheta}\int_0^{t_f} f(v_i(t) - v_i^d(t))dt$$

285

where ϑ denotes the set of designated output nodes of the network and $v_i^d(t)$, $i \in \vartheta$, denote the desired output signals. The function $f(.,.)$ can be specified in various ways in terms of the L_1-norm or the L_2-norm of the deviation $v_i(t) - v_i^d(t)$ or any other appropriate measure. The training problem then reduces to minimizing this error functional with respect to the set of adjustable network parameters. An issue of some significance for practical applications is the flexibility available in tailoring an appropriate error functional. It may be noted that conventional gradient-based training procedures typically require an L_2-norm of the error, *i.e.*, selection of $f(v_i, v_i^d) = (v_i - v_i^d)^2$, mainly for simplicity in gradient evaluations. However, when an evaluation of error gradients is not needed, as is the case with the training procedures discussed in this article, we have a greater flexibility in formulating the error functional to be minimized.

2. INCREMENTAL LEARNING

When neural networks are trained in a supervised manner, there is a tendency for the training to proceed rapidly reducing the value of the specified error for some time, until a point is reached where no further training becomes possible. This corresponds to the case when the training has proceeded to a *local minimum.* In the present context, this condition may be visualized by considering the error surface in an N^2+2N+1 space (where the N^2+2N axes correspond to the adjustable parameters of the network and the final dimension corresponds to the error function), which indicates that the error has been reduced with respect to these parameters but has fallen into an energy well, from which a recovery with the type of parameter changes already used is not possible. In the specific application to the trajectory learning problem, which is of particular interest in this chapter, this situation corresponds to the neural network learning to generate a trajectory that reduces the error, but the generated trajectory not having the same shape as the desired trajectory.

In order to reduce the occurrence of becoming trapped in a local minimum, some method of controlling the evolution of trajectories during learning could be used. A simple way of overcoming the problem is by a process of *incremental learning*, which generates a set of intermediate learning goals. Let $\xi_0(t)$ denote the trajectory generated by the neural network at the start of training and $\xi_f(t)$ denote the final trajectory. It is desired to establish M learning goals, where the absolute error between one goal and the next is small. This can be accomplished by defining a sequence of learning goals as

$$\xi_n(t) = \xi_0(t) + n \cdot \Delta\xi(t), \qquad n = 0, 1, ..., M \qquad (6)$$

where $\Delta\xi(t) = [\xi_f(t) - \xi_0(t)]/M$.

For illustration, suppose it is desired to train a dynamic recurrent neural network of the form (1) to output the trajectory

$$v(t) = \sin(\pi t), \quad 0 \le t \le 1.0. \tag{7}$$

Let $v_o(t)$ denote the initial trajectory output of the network for some initial set of parameters and initial states of neurons. An arbitrary number, say 100, of learning targets can be selected as

$$\xi_n(t) = v_0(t) + n \cdot \frac{[\sin(\pi t) - v_0(t)]}{100} \text{ for } 0 \le t \le 1.0, \quad n = 0, 1, ..., 100. \tag{8}$$

When $v_0(t) \approx \xi_i(t)$ within some predetermined error bound, the next learning target becomes $\xi_{i+1}(t)$. Learning progresses through these increments until the final desired target is reached. Fig. 2 shows a succession of these desired trajectories which represent incremental targets.

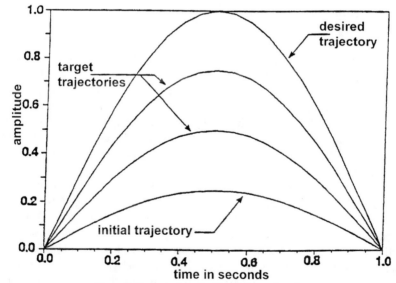

Figure 2. Target trajectories for increment learning

It may be noted that since the neural network being trained is characterized by nonlinear dynamics, the effort in moving from one incremental learning goal to another may not be uniform even when a uniform distance between these learning goals is implicit. This however is of no major consequence insofar as

287

the overall learning performance is concerned since the motivation for modifying the learning goal is to provide a mechanism for perturbation of the error function during the training process, and the objectives of incremental learning are achieved when an appropriately large number of learning goals M is selected for implementation.

3. TEACHER FORCING

In training problems such as trajectory learning, where the desired output is available at every instance of time during the training process, using an appropriate mechanism to directly feed this information to alter the activation dynamics of the neural network provides several benefits. This formalism, referred to as *Teacher Forcing*, has been used by several previous researchers [Williams, 1989, Toomarian, 1992] in one form or another. The idea of including a teaching forcing signal in general supervised learning problems comes from the desire to supply additional instantaneous information from the teacher directly to the activation dynamics during the learning stage. The role of including this signal on the training performance can be understood from the analogy with the use of continuous feedback in reducing the error in closed-loop control systems. A temporal modulation of this signal as learning proceeds is often desirable so that the activation dynamics during learning progressively reduce to the activation dynamics during the recall stage.

In the present work, for improving the trajectory learning performance, a method of teacher forcing similar to the one suggested originally by Williams and Zipser [Williams, 1989] can be employed. In this scheme, the desired network output signals are used in place of the actual network outputs when fed back into the network via the recurrent connections. The actual outputs are still used for computing the error in order to determine whether the parameter updating action at any stage is favorable or not. The teacher forcing drives the network outputs closer to the desired signals as training progresses and the network is trained at each stage as if it were already generating the correct signal. This seems to significantly speed up learning, particularly at the beginning stages.

Upon completion of successful training, *i.e.,* when the error functional becomes zero, the teacher forcing will no longer exist and the network dynamics will revert to the usual dynamics described by (4). As pointed out by Toomarian and Barhen [Toomarian, 1992], there exist training scenarios (particularly arising in trajectory learning problems) where the error functional cannot be reduced to zero and consequently the activation dynamics of the neural network after training is completed, *i.e.,* during the recall phase, will be different from that specified by (4). To avoid this discrepancy, at some point in the training process, when confidence in the shape of generated trajectories is developed, the teacher forcing is disabled and the learning is progressed with the actual outputs of the network. Alternately, a temporally modulated teacher forcing scheme [Toomarian, 1992] that progressively reduces the amount of teacher intervention during the training phase can be employed; a simple mechanism for implementing such modulation is by multiplying the signal by a time-varying gain $\lambda(t) = 1 - e^{\varepsilon(t)/\rho}$, where $\varepsilon(t)$ is the measured error and ρ is an appropriately selected number sufficiently large (a large value of ρ relative to the expected values of error is recommended to prevent $\lambda(t)$ from becoming negative).

III. TRAINING BY METHODS OF LEARNING AUTOMATA

A. SOME BASICS ON LEARNING AUTOMATA

A *learning automaton* interacts adaptively with the environment it is operating in and updates its actions at each stage based on the response of the environment to these actions [Lakshmivarahan, 1981, Narendra, 1989]. Hence an automaton can be defined by the triple (α, β, T) where α denotes the set of actions $\alpha = \{\alpha_1, \alpha_2, ..., \alpha_r\}$ available to the automaton at any stage, $\beta = \{\beta_1, \beta_2, ..., \beta_m\}$ is the set of observed responses from the environment, which are used by the automaton as inputs, and T is an updating algorithm which the automaton uses for selecting a particular action from the set α at any stage. In the present context of neural network training, a specific action at any stage corresponds to the updating of the values of one or more parameters of the network.

For a *stochastic learning automaton*, the updating algorithm specifies a rule for adjusting the probability $p_i(n)$ of choosing a particular action α_i at stage n. Such a rule may be generally described by a functional relation of the form

$$p_i(n+1) = F(p_i(n), \alpha(n), \beta(n)). \tag{9}$$

The learning procedure at each stage hence consists of two sequential steps. In the first step the automaton chooses a specific action $\alpha(n) = \alpha_i$ from the finite set of actions available, and in the second step, the probabilities of choosing the actions are updated depending on the response of the environment to the action in the first step, which influences the choice of future actions.

An alternative way of specifying the updating algorithm is to define a state vector for the automaton and consider the transition of the state due to a certain action, which enables one to state the updating rule in terms of state transition probabilities. This approach has been quite popular in the development of learning automaton theory [Varshavskii, 1963]. For our application to neural network training, however, the action probability updating approach, with the updating algorithms specified in the form of equation (9), provides a simpler and more convenient framework.

For execution of training, the feedback signal from the environment, which triggers the updating of the action probabilities by the automaton, can be given by specifying an appropriate "error" function. The environmental response set $\beta(n)$ at any stage n can then be selected as the binary set $\beta(n) = \{0,1\}$, with $\beta = 1$ indicating that the selected action α_i is not considered satisfactory by the environment and $\beta = 0$ indicating that the action selected is considered satisfactory.[2] For a stochastic automaton with r available actions (*i.e.*, $\alpha = \{\alpha_1, ..., \alpha_r\}$), the updating rules can then be specified in a general form as follows:

For the selected action at the nth stage $\alpha(n) = \alpha_1$, if $\beta(n) = 0$ then

$$p_j(n+1) = p_j(n) - \gamma_j(p(n)) \qquad \text{for } j \neq i$$

$$p_i(n+1) = p_i(n) + \sum_{\substack{j=1 \\ j \neq i}}^{r} \gamma_j(p(n)) \qquad (10)$$

whereas if $\beta(n) = 1$, then

$$p_i(n+1) = p_i(n) - \delta_i(p(n))$$

$$p_j(n+1) = p_j(n) + \frac{1}{(r-1)}\delta_i(p(n)), \qquad j \neq i \qquad (11)$$

The functions $\gamma_j(\cdot)$ and $\delta_i(\cdot)$ are appropriately selected continuous-valued nonnegative functions. The summation $\Sigma\gamma_j$ in (10) and the division by $(r-1)$ in (11) are to ensure preservation of probability measure (*i.e.*, sum of probabilities at $(n+1)$ equals one).

The two sets of equations (10) and (11) specify a *reinforcement learning algorithm*. By tailoring the functions $\gamma_j(\cdot)$ and $\delta_i(\cdot)$ an appropriate degree of reinforcement in the selection of a particular action can be introduced. A scheme where both sets of equations are employed together is termed a *reward-penalty reinforcement scheme*. It is evident that in this scheme an action that is judged favorable is rewarded by having its probability of selection increased while an unfavorable action is penalized by having its probability of selection decreased. Another reinforcement scheme, termed *reward-inaction scheme*, employs the updating only for $\beta(n)=0$, whereas for $\beta(n)=1$ the action probabilities are maintained at the same values as before. These schemes and several other variations of them have been discussed in the literature [Lakshmivarahan, 1981, Narendra 1989]. Due to the stochastic nature of the framework, however, very few analytical results can be developed for these

---

2 In the literature on learning automata [Lakshmivarahan, 1981, Narendra, 1989], this case of β allowed to take two distinct values only is referred to as the *P*-model. More general models where β can take a number of values within an interval have also been discussed.

schemes and studies directed to the evaluation of performance (such as convergence, asymptotic behavior) typically employ simulation experiments.

It should be emphasized that (10) and (11) describe a general framework for tailoring a variety of specific training algorithms useful in particular applications by selecting $\gamma_j(\cdot)$ and $\delta_i(\cdot)$ appropriately as linear or nonlinear functions. In fact, a number of heuristic algorithms where $\gamma_j(\cdot)$ and $\delta_i(\cdot)$ may not have an analytical form can also be considered for realizing improved speed and accuracy in training. In certain applications of neural network training such constructions motivated by intuitive reasoning may indeed prove to be more efficient. An illustrative example of this will be demonstrated in a later section for application to the trajectory learning problem.

B. APPLICATION TO TRAINING RECURRENT NETWORKS

A principal advantage of the learning automaton approach is its ability to determine optimal actions among a set of possible actions and this is particularly useful in neural network training where a number of possible actions exist. For training the neural network described by (4), we will employ the learning configuration schematically shown in Fig. 3. The automaton actions are defined as either an increment or a decrement to any of the network parameters ω_{ij}, τ_i and g_i. For an N-neuron network, this corresponds to a set of $2(N^2 + 2N)$ single parameter updating actions. Multiple parameter actions can also be considered, with the number of possible actions in this case increasing to $2(N^2 + 2N)!$

The environment for this learning configuration comprises the neural network itself together with an appropriately specified error functional ε defined over the time interval $[t_0, t_f]$ as discussed earlier. The feedback signal to the automaton can be defined as

$$\beta = 0 \text{ for action that reduces the error}$$

$$\beta = 1 \text{ for action that does not reduce error.} \tag{12}$$

As noted earlier, function $f(\cdot,\cdot)$ for computing the training error can be specified in various ways; for the examples that will be discussed later, we employed $f(v_i, v_i^d) = |v_i - v_i^d|$ to define the error functional ε. Subsequent to the determination that an action has reduced the error, the corresponding changes to the neural network parameters are retained. However, if the action increases the error, the corresponding parameter changes are not kept. Thus, the only modifications to the neural network structure come from those actions that reduce the value of the specified error.

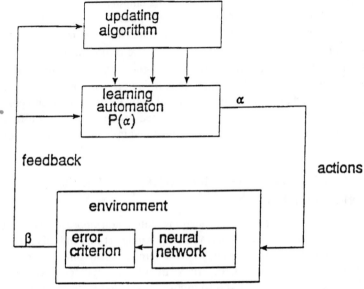

Figure 3. Learning configuration

A probability of selection is initially assigned to each action. Since no *a priori* knowledge generally exists as to which of the network parameters has the greatest influence in reducing the specified error, the entropy in learning is maximum at the beginning of training. Hence, a uniform distribution is used at the beginning for the action probabilities. As learning progresses, the probability associated with each action is changed. This probability determines the relative frequency with which a particular action will be selected. Thus, the more successful a particular action is at reducing the error, the more likely its selection will be in the future stages.

Any available prior knowledge on the qualitative behavior of the network being trained can be utilized in the process of initializing the training algorithm. The network described by (4) is one whose dynamics and equilibrium behavior have been extensively studied in the past [Sudharsanan, 1994, Sudharsanan, 1991a, Sudharsanan, 1991b] and the correlations of these results with the training performance can be exploited for the initial setting of parameter values. For illustration, some past results that underscore the role of high gain sigmoidal nonlinearities in ensuring desirable stability properties for the network equilibria [Sudharsanan, 1991a] and the observed correlation between selection of high gains and improvement in learning rates [Sudharsanan, 1991, Behrens 1991] could be usefully employed in the initial selection of g_i parameters for improving the efficiency of the training process.

In discussing the time-behavior of the training process, two types of convergence come into the picture: convergence of the training error and convergence of the automaton to some optimal action. Convergence of the error is assured by the nature of the learning algorithm. Since changes to the neural network structure come only from those actions that result in a reduction of the error, starting from any finite positive initial error, a monotonic decreasing sequence of positive real numbers is generated. This sequence is bounded and, from the monotone convergence theorem [Bartle, 1992, Condarcure, 1991], is convergent.

Under certain conditions, the learning automaton will converge toward some optimal action depending on the type of reinforcement rule used. By associating with each action a penalty probability, it has been shown in the literature [Narendra, 1989] that if the penalty probabilities are stationary, then the action probabilities will converge to an optimal action. In particular, for the linear reward-inaction scheme (*i.e.*, for $\gamma_j(\cdot)$ a linear function of the argument and $\delta_i(\cdot) = 0$ in the updating rules (10) and (11)), convergence is assured in this sense. It should however be noted that convergence of this type may not be desirable in the present context of neural network training. The penalty probabilities are not known at the start of training and their distribution may not be stationary since the structure of the neural network is constantly changing during the training process. An action that may produce a favorable response at some point in the training process may not yield a favorable response at a later time. Furthermore, the gains g_i and the time constants τ_j are constrained to be nonnegative and hence cannot be continually decremented to take on negative values. Therefore, convergence of the learning automaton to an optimal action is not desirable and will not occur when the reward-penalty reinforcement rules are used (since the probability of any action approaching 1 is not possible with this reinforcement scheme for a nonstationary environment [Narendra, 1989]).

C. TRAJECTORY GENERATION PERFORMANCE

The performance of the training approach described in the last section has been tested in the task of learning continuous trajectories. We shall give the results for a circle trajectory of specified radius 0.5.

Simulation experiments were conducted using a fourth-order Runge-Kutta algorithm for studying the temporal dynamical behavior of the neural network. A time increment of $0.02T$ was selected as the integration time constant, where T is approximately the period of the trajectory to be generated. For implementing the actions of the learning automaton, it is necessary to generate an output function $\alpha(n)$, which maps the stage number n into a selection of the appropriate action to take in a probabilistic fashion. Since these action probabilities are unknown at the start of the experiment, they are initialized to a uniform distribution. Then, as the experiment progresses and successful actions are found, a discrete probability density function is built up, with the probability for a particular action $\alpha_i(n)$ being increased or decreased according to the specific reinforcement in the form of (10) or (11). As the density function is being generated, it is used for the selection of actions by an inverse distribution method. This is done by generating uniformly distributed random numbers (by a standard procedure such as the Lewis-Payne method [Lewis, 1973]) and then summing the numbers in the density function to create a distribution function until the generated random number is greater than the sum. The action is then selected at the point where the sum of the densities is greater than the uniform random number.

A six-node network (*i.e.* $N = 6$) with two nodes designated as the output nodes {$o1$, $o2$} and with no externally applied inputs was trained to generate the desired circle trajectory. In order to attempt to better control the trajectory rise time, rather than try to force the network to generate the circle with an unknown rise time, a parameter η was introduced to modify the desired outputs in the form

$$v_{o1}^d = 0.5(1-e^{-\eta t})\sin \pi t$$
$$v_{o2}^d = 0.5(1-e^{-\eta t})\cos \pi t$$

(13)

For initializing the network, the weights w_{ij} were set to 0.0, the gains g_i were set to 10.0, and the time constants τ_i were set to numbers randomly distributed around 6.0. The initial states of the neurons $v_i(0)$ were chosen to be small random numbers centered around zero. Incremental learning was used with 100 intermediate learning targets established as discussed in Section 2.C.

A brief explanation on the role of parameter η seems useful. Observe that with the selection of $v_{o1}^d(t)$ and $v_{o2}^d(t)$ as in (13), we have

$$v_{o1}^{d^2}(t) + v_{o2}^{d^2}(t) = 0.25 + 0.25(e^{-2\eta t} - 2e^{-2\eta t})$$

and hence as t becomes progressively larger, $v_{o1}^d(t)$ and $v_{o2}^d(t)$ approach the desired signals $0.5\sin(\omega t)$ and $0.5\cos(\omega t)$ respectively for any selection of $\eta > 0$. However, by selection of a sufficiently large η, a scaling of time can be achieved thus accelerating the convergence to desired final values. It may also be noted that the use of $v_{o1}^d(t)$ and $v_{o2}^d(t)$ as in (10) is motivated by our desire to generate the desired circle trajectory from the starting values of $v_{o1}^d(t) = 0$ and $v_{o2}^d(t) = 0$, which corresponds to a more challenging learning task than the case when the initial point is selected to lie on the desired circle. Selection of η hence offers a mechanism for controlling the trajectory rise time which is a highly desirable feature. In the experiments that will be reported later, a representative value of $\eta = 10$ was used.

To test the effects of selecting alternate reinforcement rules and parameter updating actions on the training performance, several experiments [Condarcure, 1991] were conducted. For the sake of brevity, only two illustrative cases will be described in the following.

1. EXPERIMENT 1

In this experiment, a simple linear reward-penalty reinforcement scheme obtained by defining $\gamma_j(\cdot)$ and $\delta_i(\cdot)$ in (10) and (11) as linear functions was used. The reinforcement rules in this case will take the following form:

For an automaton with r available actions, with the selected action at the nth stage $\alpha(n) = \alpha_i$, if $\beta(n) = 0$, then

$$p_j(n+1) = (1-\gamma)p_j(n), \qquad j \neq i$$

and

$$p_i(n+1) = \gamma + (1-\gamma)p_i(n) \qquad (14)$$

whereas if $\beta(n) = 1$, then

$$p_i(n+1) = (1-\delta)p_i(n)$$

and

$$p_j(n+1) = p_j(n) + \frac{\delta}{r-1}(1-\gamma)p_i(n), \qquad j \neq i \qquad (15)$$

In (14) and (15), γ and δ are constants that may be selected appropriately in the ranges $0 < \gamma < 1$ and $0 < \delta < 1$. Also, from (14) it is evident that an action α_i considered favorable will result in a reduction of the probabilities p_j (for $j \neq i$) by a percentage γ while increasing the probability p_i by an amount such that the sum of the probabilities at stage $(n+1)$ is 1. Similarly, when action α_i is unfavorable, the probability p_i is reduced by a percentage δ while the remaining probabilities p_j (for $j \neq i$) are correspondingly increased such that the sum of the probabilities remains at 1, as reflected by the form of the updating rules in (15).

For the numerical simulations we used the values $\gamma = 0.02$ (corresponding to 2% change in the case of a favorable action) and $\delta = 0.01$ (corresponding to 1% change in the case of an unfavorable action); these values were determined from experimentation to give good results.[3] A single parameter action (increment or decrement), defined as an incremental change to one network parameter that is continued until it is no longer successful for a given trial, was employed. The error functional discussed earlier (*viz.* Eq. (5) with $f(v_i, v_i^d) = |v_i - v_i^d|$) was used and it was required that the value of the error be reduced to 0.06 before moving from one learning goal to the next. Teacher forcing was used to help accelerate the learning process at the start and was disabled at the 50th learning

---

[3] In earlier work on learning automata [Lakshmivarahan, 1981, Narendra, 1989], it is observed that a certain degree of asymmetry between the reward and the penalty parameter results in general in a desirable training behavior, *i.e.* rewarding a favorable response more than penalizing an unfavorable response is generally preferable.

increment when the shape of the actual output trajectory was sufficiently close to the desired trajectory.

Fig. 4a depicts the parameter changes or actions that were attempted by the automaton for each learning increment. It may be noted that learning was very easy when teacher forcing was active, which agrees well with intuition. After the 50th step, when teacher forcing was disabled, learning became more difficult, as the network must meet the learning goals on its own. This continued until about step 82, when the automaton developed enough experience in making better selections. The results of this experiment with the network trained for 4 cycles (each cycle corresponding to one period of the sinusoidal waveforms) and then continued to run for another 8 cycles is shown in Fig. 4b, which clearly indicates the stability of the generated limit cycle. It may be noted that only the first three cycles during which the trajectory evolves into the limit cycle are distinguishable while the rest overlap.

2. EXPERIMENT 2

In this experiment the primary goal was to study the effects of allowing multiple parameter actions, *i.e.,* sets of parameters to be updated simultaneously. It is to be noted that since the neural network is nonlinear, the effect of changing more than one parameter at a time is not the same as the combined effect resulting from changing them one after another. For a 6-node network ($N = 6$), the number of possible actions now increases to 48! (*i.e.,* (N^2+2N)!). Consequently, to reduce the memory requirements, two options were exercised. The first is to limit the actions to those that update 10 parameters or less at a time. The second is to store the successful actions in a repertoire for a preferential selection at the later stages. An action is added to the repertoire if it is used successfully to reduce the error, which is the reward. If an action in the repertoire does not successfully reduce the error, it is penalized by being removed from the repertoire. Once all actions existing in the repertoire are used at any stage, new actions are selected randomly from the remaining set of available actions based on a uniform distribution. The following learning reinforcement is also used. When rewarded, the probability for an action in the repertoire stays at its previous value, whereas for a successful action not in the repertoire it is increased from its value in the uniform distribution to a higher value. When penalized, the action probability is reduced to its value in the uniform distribution.

In the framework of the reinforcement rules discussed earlier, the present updating mechanism corresponds to a nonlinear reinforcement scheme, more general than the linear reinforcement rules used in Experiment 1. An analytical modeling of the updating rules is however more difficult to obtain in this case.

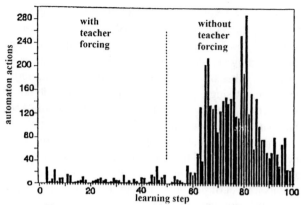

Figure 4a. Automaton actions per learning increment

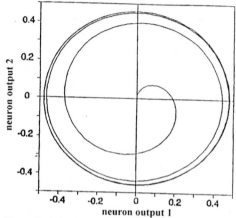

Figure 4b. Neural net output trajectory in Experiment 1

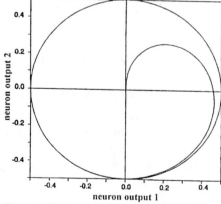

Figure 4c. Trajectory generated in Experiment 2

To provide a greater ease of implementation, in this experiment the activation gains g_i were permanently set to the value 10.0 and learning was restricted to changes in the other parameters (w_{ij} and τ_i). Incremental learning was used as before with 100 learning steps. The result of this experiment is shown in Fig. 4c, which indicates a substantial improvement in the achieved performance over the linear reinforcement-single parameter action case considered in Experiment 1. As can be observed, the trajectory rise time is also significantly reduced in this case (to about 0.2 sec) and the evolution into the final orbit is almost complete within half a cycle. Fig. 4 shows the results of the experiment with the network trained for 4 cycles and then continued to run for another 8 cycles. The remarkable accuracy with which the recall cycles overlap is worthy of emphasis and this represents a level of performance significantly better than that provided by any of the existing training procedures.

As a further note, in the two experiments described above, the training took approximately 2500 attempted actions to reach the final learning goal. It must be emphasized that the computations required at each step are extremely simple (involving updating of probability vectors) and are almost negligible compared to the evaluation of gradients required by existing methods, which makes the present scheme more attractive to implement. Also, comparing the performance depicted in Figs. 4b and 4c with the other available results for the trajectory learning problem, it may be noted that this level of accuracy in generating the circle trajectory could only be achieved in Toomarian [1992] when the learning was started with the initial values of the neuron states adjusted such that the initial point is already on the desired circle (specifically, case 3 in Toomarian [1992]). In contrast, in our case the learning was started with the initial states set at arbitrary small random values. It must also be noted that this level of performance was achieved even when the learning was restricted to only the weights w_{ij} and the time constants τ_i. It is conceivable that even better performance levels can be realized by permitting the activation gains also to be updated, although at the cost of increased memory requirements. What is particularly noteworthy, however, is the significant reduction in computational requirements compared to the conventional gradient-based algorithms.

IV. TRAINING BY SIMPLEX OPTIMIZATION METHOD

A. SOME BASICS ON SIMPLEX OPTIMIZATION

In order to facilitate some understanding on the basics and motivation for the Simplex algorithm, consider the following simple example. Suppose a simple guessing game is being played between a player and a computer. Suppose that the computer has selected an arbitrary nonlinear function, for example $y = f(x)$, and that the player has to guess the value of the variable x that when substituted into the above nonlinear equation (unknown to him) would result in the global minimum of the function. The player can guess the variable value by keying into the computer a number and observing the corresponding function output provided by the computer (if the player somehow manages to guess the correct value of the parameter, the computer would inform him that he has achieved minimality).

There are several ways by which the player can obtain the parameter that would result in the minimum value of the function. First, he can keep guessing the parameter randomly until he found the correct one. This method, however, could take an infinitely long period of time, especially when presented with a highly nonlinear and complex multivariable function (*i.e.*, x becomes a vector variable). Second, he can try to compute the gradient of the function and use it to guide him to the correct parameter. However, with this method if the function is nonlinear, complex, and multivariate, its gradient may be difficult and expensive to compute. Third, he can make use of the knowledge given to him by the computer, *i.e.*, use the returned value of y to strategically locate the desired value of x. Consider the following simplified example. Suppose that the function selected by the computer is as shown in Fig. 5.

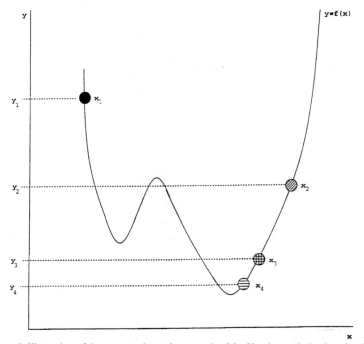

Figure 5. Illustration of the structured search approach of the Simplex optimization algorithm

Also suppose that the first two guesses are x_1 and x_2, and the corresponding results are y_1 and y_2 respectively (see Fig. 5). Further suppose that with the knowledge obtained, *i.e.*, the values of y_1 and y_2, an estimate of the variable x_3 resulting in a lower functional value than those given by x_1 and x_2 can be obtained and that this process can be repeated until some degree of optimality is reached. It is easy to see that if such a structured iterative optimization method can be implemented and applied to this example, the parameter x_4 whose corresponding functional value is the lowest among the four guesses can be obtained. Indeed, the described process is that offered by the Simplex optimization algorithm. Hence the Simplex algorithm may be viewed as a method that strategically searches for the optimal solution based on the information obtained, without needing to know the mathematical expression for the function itself or calculate its gradient at every iteration. The fact that function gradients need not be computed with this method makes it an attractive optimization method especially when applied to complex multivariate functions or to systems such as a recurrent net. Another characteristic of this method that is of significance is its ability to escape the local minima of a function even though it is a simple downhill direct search method. This characteristic is also illustrated in Fig. 5. Before describing the series of steps involved in the simplex iteration, it is appropriate at this point to give a brief discussion on the development of the present algorithm.

A simplex is a geometrical figure consisting of $N+1$ points (or vertices) in an N-dimensional space. In a two-dimensional space, a simplex is a triangle and in a three-dimensional space, it is a tetrahedron. The Simplex algorithm described here is due to Nelder and Mead [Nelder, 1965] and is not to be confused with the Simplex method associated with linear programming. It is a direct downhill search method applicable to any multidimensional problem that requires only function evaluations and not the derivatives. This method, though extremely robust, can be slow in converging especially for problems of high dimensionality. However, in regard to neural network training, the inefficiency of this method, *i.e.,* its slow convergence in high dimensional spaces, can be reduced significantly as will be discussed in a later section. The storage requirement of this method is approximately N^2.

The reason for requiring $N+1$ simplex vertices for an N-dimensional optimization problem can be readily shown. Consider for illustration the one-dimensional function, $y = f(x)$. In order to search a region for x, some sort of boundary must be defined. In the one-dimensional case where the region is bounded by lines or curves, only two points are needed to enclose a region as illustrated in Fig. 6. With these two points the entire region of the function can be searched, if necessary, using the basic operations of expansion and contraction associated with the Simplex algorithm. These are implemented by keeping the better of the two points fixed, and by either expanding or contracting the other point (worse point) with respect to the fixed point the entire region bounded by the lines or curves can be searched if necessary. Similarly, for a two-dimensional function, such as $z = 5x + 3y$, a region (within a plane) can be uniquely defined, enclosed, and searched by three points following the same expansion and contraction operations. Extending the argument to an *N*-dimensional function, it is clear that *N*+1 vertices are required to bound and search a *N*-dimensional region.

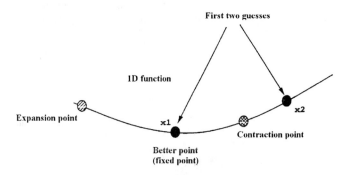

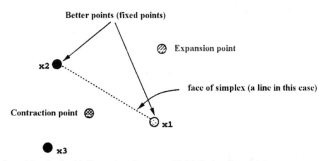

Figure 6. Searching in the N-dimensional space with N+1 simplex points

The simplex algorithm starts with *N*+1 points that can be either arbitrarily chosen or strategically obtained. The algorithm then moves the set of simplex points downhill in the function space, however complex it may be, through a series of steps. Most of the steps executed involve moving the point corresponding to the highest functional value (or lowest functional value in a maximization problem) through the opposite face of the simplex to a point with a lower functional value. This process is illustrated in Fig. 7, which shows 4 simplex points in a 3-dimensional space. In Fig. 7, it can be seen that the simplex point with the highest functional value is moved across the face of the simplex formed by the remaining 3 simplex points, the face being a plane defined by the 3 points in this case, to a location with a lower functional value.

This step is generally called a *reflection* operation. If allowed to do so, the method expands the simplex in steps in one direction or another (a precise mathematical description of the expansion operation will be given in the next section). Contraction of a simplex point occurs when neither the reflection operation nor the expansion operations yield a better simplex point. In the event that neither the contraction, expansion, nor reflection operation yields a lower functional value, the method shrinks itself around the best point.

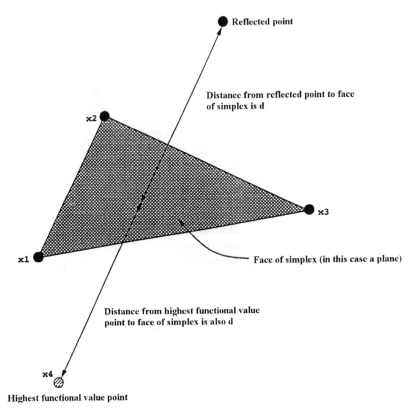

Figure 7. Illustration of reflexion point

The series of steps mentioned above can be mathematically represented by two basic expressions. Let us first define the various parameters that will be needed. Let H_{sp} denote the simplex point with the highest functional value, N_{sp} denote the new simplex point that will replace H_{sp} (that needs to be computed), R_{sp} denote the remaining simplex points (all points excluding H_{sp}), L_{sp} denote the simplex point with the lowest functional value, and S_{sp} denote the simplex point to be shrunk. Also, let α denote the parameter that controls the amount of expansion or contraction, and φ denote the parameter that controls the amount of shrinking. Let N_D denote the dimensionality of the problem (*i.e.,* number of points in the simplex).

The two equations that summarize the various steps encountered in the Simplex algorithm are

$$N_{sp} = \frac{R_{sp}}{N_D}(1-\alpha) + H_{sp}\alpha \tag{16}$$

$$N_{sp} = L_{sp}(1-\varphi) + S_{sp}\varphi \tag{17}$$

Eq. (16) is used for reflecting, expanding, or contracting a simplex point with the parameter α controlling the amount of expansion or contraction. Note that the reflection operation is similar to the expansion operation. The difference between them is the amount by which they are moved across the simplex face. More specifically, in the reflection operation the simplex point is moved to a location across the simplex face that is exactly the same distance away from the face before it is moved; hence the term reflection (see Fig. 7 for clearer illustration). The expansion operation on the other hand moves the simplex point across the face of the simplex to a distance farther away as illustrated in Fig. 8. Since α controls the amount of expansion and contraction, it is clear that α must take on specific values for executing the three operations. Specifically, reflection across the simplex face is achieved with $\alpha = -1$, expansion across the simplex face is achieved by a value of $\alpha < -1$, while contraction is achieved with a value of α satisfying $0 < \alpha < 1$.

The flow of the Simplex algorithm, *i.e.,* the order in which the abovementioned operations are performed, will be discussed in a later section. Although (16) is used for reflecting, expanding, and contracting a simplex point depending on the value of α, the three different operations will be differentiated for clarity from here on. In particular, for reflection operation, (16) is kept unchanged with the parameter α, whereas for the expansion and contraction operations, the parameter α in (16) will be replaced by β and γ, respectively. Note that the fraction R_{sp}/N_D in (16) is a point on the simplex face. In fact, it can be readily shown that R_{sp}/N_D is the center-of-mass of the simplex face and hence is termed the centroid in the later discussion. Eq. (17) is used when neither reflection, expansion, nor contraction of the simplex point yields a lower functional value point. Eq. (17) is in fact a contraction operation around the simplex point with the lowest functional value L_{sp}. The parameter φ in (17) controls the amount of shrinking and can only take on values between 0 and 1. The detailed implementation strategy for neural network training is discussed in the next section.

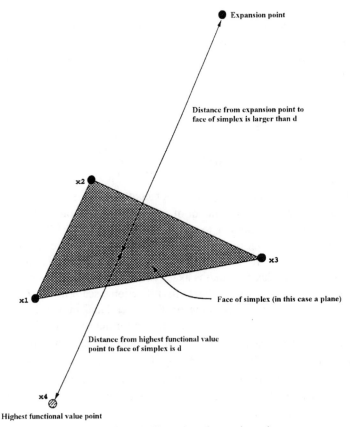

Figure 8. Illustration of expansion point

B. APPLICATION TO TRAINING RECURRENT NETWORKS

The simplex approach is a powerful optimization tool and has been used quite successfully in handling a variety of optimization problems [Wong, 1998, Duan, 1992] with nonlinear objective functions. The motivation for employing this approach in the present work of training a neural network, particularly in preference to the error backpropagation methods (and also to the more general steepest descent optimization approaches), can be explained from the following simple analogy.

The backpropagation approach can be regarded as similar to physically placing a person in a mountainous terrain with his objective being to move to the lowest elevation in that particular terrain (the mountainous terrain symbolizes, in the context of optimization, the peaks and valleys of the object function to be minimized). Having no additional information, other than the knowledge of his own initial elevation, his wisest option is to go down the steepest slope he can find and hope that it will lead him to the lowest elevation. Obviously his ending point will depend on where he starts. If he had been placed right above the global minimum elevation, then he will easily fulfill his objective with the selected strategy. However such a situation could indeed be very rare. Furthermore, how will he know that he has reached the lowest elevation if at all he does? It is more likely that he will stop at the first valley he reaches (a local minimum) and assume that he has found the global lowest elevation when clearly he has not (this illustrates the reason why backpropagation almost always ends up with a sub-optimal solution). Of course if he has enough energy left after the descent, he can always climb out of the valley he has found and try to find a lower elevation (similar to the operations of some modified backpropagation algorithms with a momentum term). However the question still remains unanswered - How will he know that he has indeed reached the global minimum?

With the simplex approach however, it is like randomly placing a group of people, instead of one person, at various selected initial points on the mountainous terrain. Now each person within this group knows his own elevation and spatial position but not the elevations and positions of the others. What would they do to meet the combined objective of finding the lowest elevation point? The wisest thing is to share their information, which is their elevation and spatial position, and have the person with the highest elevation move to a new position calculated from the rest of the group's elevations and positions on the terrain. Once this person has reached his new calculated position he would then report back his new elevation and spatial position to the group and the whole process starts again. With enough iterations, the group must finally converge to a point that will be close to the lowest elevation. One can see that the Simplex algorithm logically and efficiently overcomes settling into a sub-optimal solution as in the backpropagation algorithm. By a repetitive implementation with different sets of initial starting locations, the outcome of the simplex search can be made even more efficient in seeking out the true global minimum elevation. Observe that if the group of people were to record the spatial position and elevation of the point at which they converge, randomly re-position themselves around the terrain, and start the process all over again, they may eventually converge to an elevation that is closer to the true minimum. By repeating this process an arbitrarily large number of times, the group is bound to find the global lowest elevation with probability approaching 1. However the only drawback of this implementation is that if there are too many people in the group, the amount of computation needed to find the new position will increase correspondingly since there is now more information to process.

An implementation of this strategy for a supervised training of the neural network in order to minimize the training error

$$\varepsilon = \frac{1}{K} \sum_{i \in O} \sum_{k=1}^{K} |o_i(k) - \hat{o}_i(k)| \qquad (18)$$

will now be described. In the error criterion formulated above $\hat{o}_i(k)$, $i=1,2,...,n$, denotes the neural network outputs which are the estimates of the desired outputs denoted by $o_i(k)$, $i=1, 2, ..., n$, where n denotes the total number of neural network outputs and K is the total number of training vectors used. The simplex is initialized by selecting an arbitrary set of $N+1$ points in the N-dimensional weight space, where each point corresponds to a selection of weight values (i.e. a vector of dimension N). This selection is made by randomly assigning all weight values within certain chosen bounds W_{max} and W_{min}. With respect to a neural network, the dimension of the weight space, N in this case, is determined by the size of the neural network (i.e. N is the total number of interconnections). Fig. 9 shows an illustrative case of 4 simplex points (for a problem with 3-dimensional weight vectors). The simplex evolution strategy [Nelder, 1965] is then executed, which involves determining the point where ε has the largest value and computing the centroid of the remaining simplex points. ε is a function of the neural network's output $\hat{o}_i(k)$ and the desired output $o_i(k)$ (for $i=1, 2, ..., n$). For a recurrent neural network, such as that shown in Fig. 4, the neural network output is given by

$$\hat{o}_j(n) = \sum_{i=0}^{p} w_{ji}(n) y_{ji}(n) \tag{19}$$

where $w_{ji}(n)$ is the synaptic weight connecting the output of neuron i (in the hidden layer in this case) to the input of neuron j (in the output layer in this case) at iteration n, and $y_{ji}(n)$ - is the output signal of neuron i going into the input of neuron j at iteration n.

Note that there are $p+1$ neurons in the hidden layer as formulated in (19). The centroid of the simplex points, excluding the highest ε, is calculated by averaging the sum of the corresponding elements of each of the simplex points. For example, to illustrate the calculation the centroid of the remaining three simplex points, s_1, s_2, and s_3, in Fig. 9, let the weight values associated with them be

$$s_1 = \begin{bmatrix} w_{11} \\ w_{12} \\ w_{13} \end{bmatrix}, \quad s_2 = \begin{bmatrix} w_{21} \\ w_{22} \\ w_{23} \end{bmatrix}, \quad s_3 = \begin{bmatrix} w_{31} \\ w_{32} \\ w_{33} \end{bmatrix}. \tag{20}$$

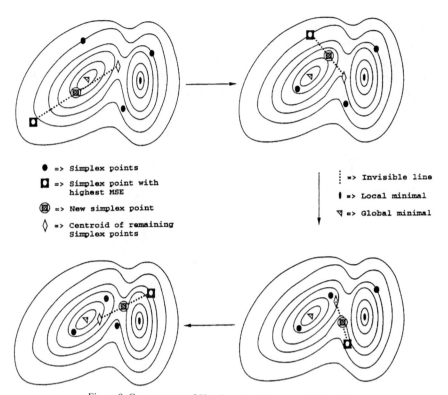

Figure 9. Convergence of Simplex algorithm to a global solution

The centroid, c, is

$$
c = \begin{bmatrix} (w_{11} + w_{21} + w_{31})/3 \\ (w_{12} + w_{22} + w_{32})/3 \\ (w_{13} + w_{23} + w_{33})/3 \end{bmatrix}.
$$
(21)

In general, for an N-dimensional weight space, the centroid may be calculated as

$$
c_i = \frac{1}{N} \sum_{j=1}^{N} w_{ji}, \quad \forall i .
$$
(22)

After the centroid is calculated, a new simplex point is then created by a reflection, expansion, or contraction which involves an operation that consists of joining the centroid computed to the simplex point with the highest ε by an invisible line and locating an expansion point or a contraction point on this line as shown in Fig. 10. The highest ε point is then replaced by the newly

307

generated point to form the new simplex on which the set of operations is repeated. The reflection, expansion, and contraction points are new points obtained using the centroid and the highest ε point via operations similar to extrapolation and interpolation between these two points. First the ε value corresponding to the centroid is found with (18) and (19).

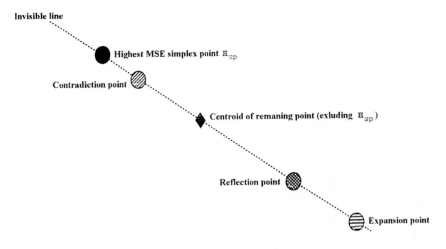

Figure 10. Illustration of reflection, expansion, and contraction operations in the Simplex algorithm

Next, the reflection point along with its ε is calculated. The reflection point is calculated by

$$Rf_{sp} = \frac{R_{sp}}{N}(1-\alpha) + H_{sp}\alpha \tag{23}$$

where Rf_{sp} is the reflection point, H_{sp} is the simplex point with the highest ε, N is the dimension of the weight space (in this case the total number of interconnections in the recurrent network), R_{sp} denotes the remaining simplex points excluding H_{sp}, and α, a parameter that controls the scale of reflection, is selected to be -1 as discussed earlier. If the ε associated with this reflection point is less than the highest ε point, the reflection point is further expanded via the following equation

$$Ex_{sp} = \frac{R_{sp}}{N}(1-\beta) + H_{sp}\beta \tag{24}$$

where Ex_{sp} is the expanded simplex point and β, a parameter that controls the amount of expansion, is selected to be less than -1 (all other parameters in (24) are those defined in (23)). The specific value of β to be selected needs determination through conducting simulation experiments. In the present work, a value of $\beta = -3$ was found to yield the best results. In general β can take other values for different applications. If the expanded point of (24) is still less than the highest ε point, it becomes the new simplex point, else the reflected point found in (23) becomes the new simplex point.

If however ε for the extrapolated point is greater than the highest ε value (*i.e.*, H_{sp}), the centroid becomes the new simplex point. If the ε value corresponding to the centroid is greater than the highest ε value, the contraction point, along with its ε, is calculated via an operation similar to interpolation. That is, the contraction point is calculated by

$$Cn_{sp} = \frac{R_{sp}}{N}(1-\gamma)+H_{sp}\gamma \tag{25}$$

where Cn_{sp} is the contracted simplex point and γ, a parameter that controls the amount of contraction, is selected to be less than 1 (all other parameters in (25) are, again, those defined in (23)). Once again, an appropriate value of γ needs to be determined from experimentation, and it was determined for the present application that 0.5 yielded the best results. If the ε of the contraction point is less than the highest ε point, the contraction point then becomes the new simplex point. If however the ε of the contraction point is higher than the highest ε point, another action would have to be taken. At this point, it is apparent that the set of simplex points is located in an adverse situation. In such scenarios, the simplex points are contracted relative to the best simplex point in all directions thereby shrinking the size of the simplex. Consequently the new set of simplex points is obtained with

$$N_{sp} = L_{sp}(1-\varphi)+S_{sp}\varphi \tag{26}$$

where N_{sp} is the shrunk simplex point, L_{sp} denotes the simplex point with the lowest ε, S_{sp} denotes the simplex point to be shrunk, and φ, a parameter that controls the amount of shrinkage, is selected to be 0.75 (once again after several simulation exercises).

For implementation in the present context, the algorithm can be designed with two distinct stopping criteria. The search for the weights of a specified network structure can be terminated when either the maximum spread of the simplex points is smaller than a prespecified threshold (with the centroid being selected as the optimal one in this case), or the number of iterations performed exceeds a preset threshold. Other criteria can be used to terminate the evolution of the simplex, one such criterion being when the difference in error falls below a preset threshold.

As noted earlier, the only undesirable feature of this training scheme is that as the size of the simplex (number of simplex points) increases, the computational burden correspondingly increases. This however is not unique to the present training scheme since the size of the simplex, *viz.* ($N+1$), depends on the size of the weight vector, which in turn is a function of the total number of interconnections in the neural net, and it is rather well known that the training complexity increases with the size of the neural network. In an attempt to reduce the training complexity, one may place arbitrary limits on the number of interconnections, which however is not attractive. Some reduction in the overall training complexity without arbitrarily limiting the network size can be achieved by partitioning the neural network into a linear and a nonlinear portion, with the nonlinear portion comprising the connections between the input nodes and the hidden nodes while the linear portion consists of the connections between the hidden nodes and the output nodes (an example of which is to have the network outputs formed as a weighted sum of the outputs of the hidden nodes). The simplex optimization is then performed to find the optimal weights in the nonlinear portion, while a linear least squares minimization is used to determine the optimal weights in the linear portion of the network.

A factor of particular significance in the use of the simplex optimization approach to neural network training is the possibility of approaching the true global minimum by a reinitialization of the simplex, as outlined earlier in the discussion of the analogy. It is well known that implementing the simplex algorithm with multiple restart operation (*i.e.*, reinitializing the simplex and executing the algorithm on the new simplex points) has global search property and hence prevents the training procedure from being trapped by local minima of the error function. Furthermore, it is argued in the literature that multiple restarts of the simplex search each time a convergence to a small cluster is attained, has the effect of moving the procedure towards finding a globally optimal solution with probability approaching 1.0. An aspect that deserves some emphasis in regard to practical implementation is that these multiple restarts can be executed in parallel, thus reducing the training time considerably. The flowchart shown in Fig. 11 summarizes the above discussion on the evolution of the simplex points.

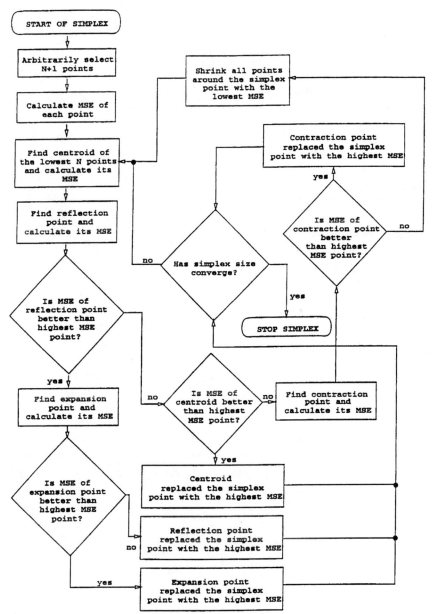

Figure 11. The evolution of the Simplex algorithm

C. TRAJECTORY GENERATION PERFORMANCE

1. EXPERIMENT 1

In this experiment, the recurrent network was trained to generate a circular trajectory centered at (0.5, 0.5) in the Cartesian coordinate space. The x and y components of the trajectory can be mathematically represented as

$$x(t) = A\cos(\omega t) + b \tag{27a}$$
$$y(t) = A\sin(\omega t) + b \tag{27b}$$

where b is introduced to shift the center of the trajectory. In this experiment b in both (27a) and (27b) is set to 0.5 so as to shift trajectory to center at the point (0.5, 0.5). As discussed earlier, parameter A in Eqs. (27a) and (27b) specifies the radius of the circular trajectory and the parameter ω denotes the angular frequency. For this experiment, and also for all the other experiments in this section, A is selected to be 0.2 and ω is selected to be 0.02π.

A recurrent network with the architecture shown in Fig. 4 with five neurons was trained with the Simplex optimization algorithm to produce the desired trajectory. Two of the five neurons were arbitrarily chosen to be the outputs of the recurrent net (giving the x and y components). As with the experiments in the previous section, the recurrent network was driven only by the initial state of its neurons and hence no external input into the system is required. In this experiment, the initial states of the two output neurons were selected to be on the trajectory while the initial states of the other neurons were randomly chosen about zero according to the following distribution, $N(0, 0.00001)$ (*i.e.,* a normal or gaussian distribution with zero mean and a variance of 0.00001).

The training was conducted with teacher forcing, which was maintained until the average absolute errors of the estimates, in both the x and y components, were less than a preset value, δ (δ was chosen to be 0.06 in all of the experiments performed in this section). That is

$$\varepsilon_x = \frac{1}{K}\sum_{i=1}^{K}\left|o_x(i) - \hat{o}_x(i)\right| \tag{28a}$$
$$< \delta$$

$$\varepsilon_y = \frac{1}{K}\sum_{i=1}^{K}\left|o_y(i) - \hat{o}_y(i)\right| \tag{28b}$$
$$< \delta$$

where ε_x and ε_y are the average errors of the x and y components respectively, o_x and o_y are the desired outputs, $\hat{o}_x$ and $\hat{o}_y$ are the network estimated outputs, and K is the length of the training vector presented to the recurrent net. Recall that teacher forcing learning is the process of feeding back, through the output recurrent connections, the desired outputs instead of the actual network outputs. In this manner, the network was trained for one complete cycle of the trajectory. After the training was completed, the network was tested for its ability to produce a stable circular trajectory, given any initial states, when the actual network outputs were fed back.

Interestingly enough, even without removing the teacher forcing during training, the network was able to produce a very stable and roughly circular trajectory. In fact, the recurrent net was run continuously for about 100 cycles and it was found that after some brief period of transient response, the network converged to a single trajectory with only very slight deviations. With this satisfying result, the network was retrained, this time with the teacher forcing slowly removed according to the following equation

$$R_{oj}(i) = \chi A_{oj}(i) + (1 - \chi)D_{oj}(i) \qquad (29)$$

where $j = x, y$ and $i = 1, 2, ..., K$ with A_{oj} and D_{oj} denoting the actual output and desired output, respectively. The parameter χ was incremented from 0 to 1 with a step size of 0.1 each time the average absolute error for each of the components for a specific value of χ reduced to less than 0.06, thus progressively reducing the teacher forcing term.

Figs. 12a-c show the results of one retraining experiment. One may observe that the network converges to a single trajectory that is approximately circular. The generated trajectory can be made more accurate by enforcing a more stringent requirement on the absolute errors before terminating the training (for instance, by requiring the average absolute errors to be less than 0.01).

Of particular interest in this experiment is the sensitivity of the trained neural network to the initial state of neurons. To test this feature, several different simulations were conducted. First, the initial states of the output neurons were set to a point on the trajectory, while the remaining neurons were started at an initial state that is normally distributed around zero according to $N(0, 0.00001)$ (*i.e.*, similar to the initial state conditions of the recurrent net used during training). In all of the simulations conducted with this setup, the network converged to a single circular trajectory after a brief transient period. This is to be expected since this is the manner in which the network was trained. A more challenging scenario would be to set the initial states of all the neurons, including the output neurons, to a value normally distributed around zero with variance 0.00001. The results of several simulations conducted with this set-up also demonstrate that the network converges to a single circular trajectory in all the cases. To further challenge the stability of the recurrent net, several

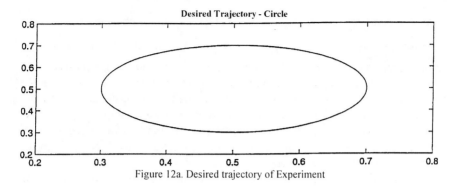

Figure 12a. Desired trajectory of Experiment

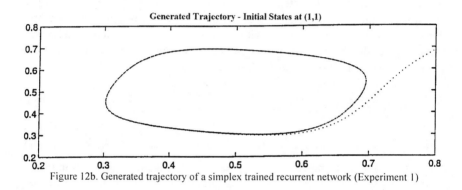

Figure 12b. Generated trajectory of a simplex trained recurrent network (Experiment 1)

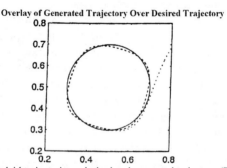

Figure 12c. Overlaid trajectories – desired and generated trajectory (Experiment 1)

simulations with the initial state of all the neurons set randomly according to $N(100,5)$ were conducted. Again, all the results obtained demonstrate convergence of the network to a single circular trajectory. One example of the various simulations is shown in Figs. 12a-c and 13a-b. Figs. 13a and b show the outputs of the two output neurons which demonstrate that the recurrent network has indeed captured the oscillating behavior required to generate the desired circular trajectory. Figs. 12a-c show the desired trajectory, the trajectory produced by the network, and both trajectories overlaid, which confirm that the network has indeed been trained by the Simplex optimization algorithm. The convergence of the recurrent network to produce the same attractor trajectory in all the simulations regardless of the initial states of the neurons illustrates the robustness of the trained network.

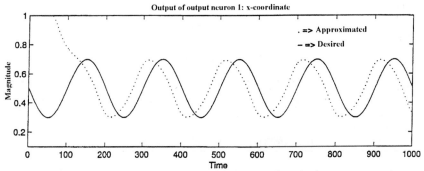

Figure 13a. Desired and generated x-coordinate output of a trained recurrent network
(Experiment 1)

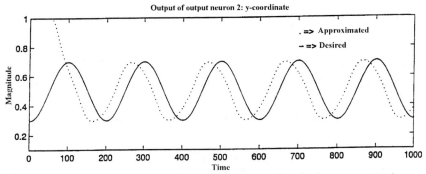

Figure 13b. Desired and generated y-coordinate output of a trained recurrent network
(Experiment 1)

2. EXPERIMENT 2

Although convergence of the recurrent net to the desired trajectory was obtained in all of simulations conducted in Experiment 1, the transient response of the network does not appear to be as smooth and as controllable as desired. A more desirable response of the network is shown in Fig. 14a. As noted, the trajectory of the desired response starts at the center of the trajectory. The trajectory then slowly and smoothly diverges from the center and converges onto the circular attractor pattern. This smoother, more controllable and predictable response is particularly important in control applications where a smooth and predictable transient response is critical to the operation of the control system.

For this experiment, the same five-neuron recurrent net was utilized. The recurrent net was again trained for one complete cycle of the trajectory. The

315

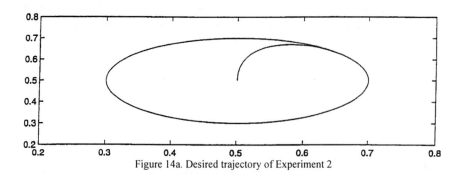

Figure 14a. Desired trajectory of Experiment 2

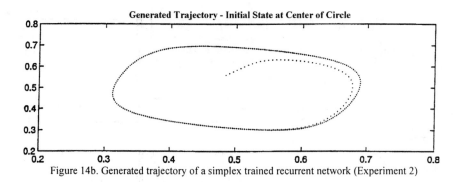

Figure 14b. Generated trajectory of a simplex trained recurrent network (Experiment 2)

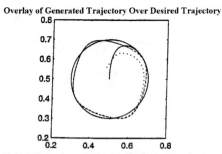

Figure 14c. Overlaid trajectories – desired and generated trajectory (Experiment 2)

equations governing the trajectory were modified slightly to accommodate the smoother and more predictable transient response given by

$$x(t) = (1 - e^{-\partial t}) A \cos(\omega t) + b \qquad (30a)$$

$$y(t) = (1 - e^{-\partial t}) A \sin(\omega t) + b \qquad (30b)$$

(as in Experiment 1, b is set to 0.5). Note that Eqs. (30a) and (30b) differ from (27a) and (27b) with the introduction of the exponential term, $(1 - e^{-\partial t})$. The exponential term is introduced to control the growth of the trajectory from its initial point. The parameter ∂ is preset to achieve the desired trajectory growth.

The training was commenced with teacher forcing learning. The initial states of the output neurons were normally distributed according to $N(0.5, 0.00001)$, while the initial states of the rest of the neurons were selected according to $N(0, 0.00001)$. The training was stopped when the same error criterion as used in Experiment 1 was met (*i.e.*, the average absolute errors in (28a) and (28b) were satisfied with δ chosen to be 0.06). After the training was completed in this manner, several validating simulations were conducted to investigate the response of the network for arbitrary initial states. In the various experiments conducted with the initial states of the network selected according to the specific distributions used in the training process, the network converged to a single circular trajectory in all instances with a much smoother and more predictable transient response. A representative trajectory generated by the network is shown in Fig. 14b. Clearly the transient response of the generated trajectory is similar to the desired transient response illustrated in Fig. 14a (Fig. 14c shows an overlay of the desired trajectory and the trajectory generated by the network). Figs. 15a and b indicate that the network has indeed captured the oscillating behavior required for trajectory generation. An important outcome from this set of experiments is the demonstration that the network can be trained to produce a desired trajectory with specific transient response. As noted before, this characteristic can be exploited in designing control systems with specified trajectory paths.

Also of interest in this experiment was the investigation of how the network would respond when the network was started at initial states different from the one used during training. To test this feature, several simulations were conducted with the initial states of the network selected randomly outside the area enclosed by the trajectory. It is interesting to note that the network failed to converge to the desired trajectory in all instances. Hence it seems that in training the network to produce a smoother and more predictable transient response, the robustness of the network demonstrated in Experiment 1 is lost. In other words, the network trained in this manner is sensitive to the initial states of its neurons. It may be noted, in conclusion, that a more desirable result, *i.e.*, a smoother and more circular trajectory, can be achieved by retraining the network with the teacher forcing term slowly removed according to (29), and enforcing a more stringent stopping requirement (*i.e.*, by requiring the average absolute errors to be less than 0.01 for example).

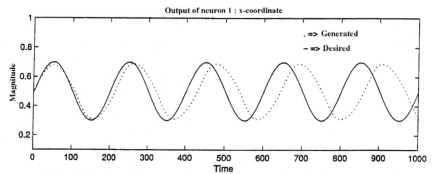

Figure 15a. Desired and generated x-coordinate output of a trained recurrent network
(Experiment 2)

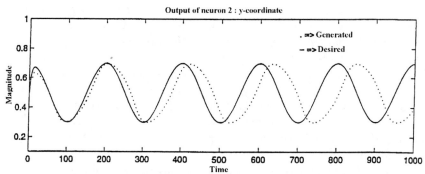

Figure 15b. Desired and generated y-coordinate output of a trained recurrent network
(Experiment 2)

3. EXPERIMENT 3

To further examine the optimization prowess of the Simplex algorithm, an attempt is made to train a recurrent network to generate an even more complex trajectory - the figure-eight pattern. As noted earlier, the figure eight trajectory can be produced by requiring the neural network outputs to converge to the periodic signals

$$x(t) = A\sin(\omega t) + b \tag{31a}$$
$$y(t) = A\sin(2\omega t) + b. \tag{31b}$$

The parameters A, b, and ω were selected to be the same as in the earlier experiments. All the training conditions, including the selection of the initial states, were maintained similar to Experiment 1. Initially a five-neuron network was utilized for this purpose. However, with the selected structure, the network training, with teacher forcing learning implemented, failed to converge to the desired trajectory. Hence, the network size was increased from five neurons to ten neurons. The training was repeated and this time, after a longer period of training than that required for the simpler trajectory - circular pattern, the network converged to the desired trajectory. The results of this experiment are shown in Figs. 16a-b and 17a-d. These results indicate that the network has indeed been trained to generate autonomously the desired trajectory. It should however be mentioned that unlike in the earlier experiments, the network does not demonstrate convergence to a single trajectory. Instead it converges to a series of trajectories.

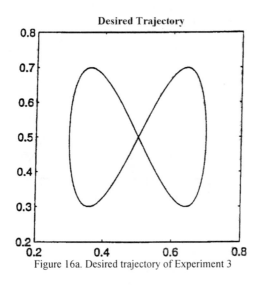

Figure 16a. Desired trajectory of Experiment 3

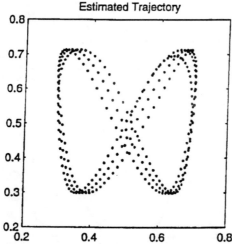

Figure 16b. Generated trajectory of a simplex trained recurrent network (Experiment 3)

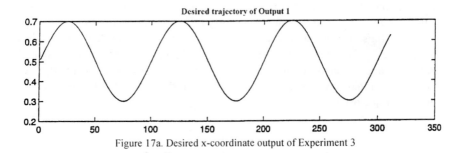

Figure 17a. Desired x-coordinate output of Experiment 3

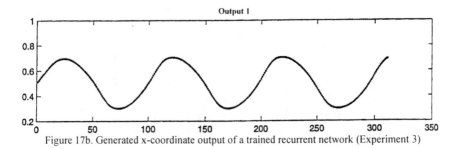

Figure 17b. Generated x-coordinate output of a trained recurrent network (Experiment 3)

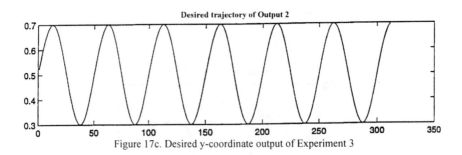

Figure 17c. Desired y-coordinate output of Experiment 3

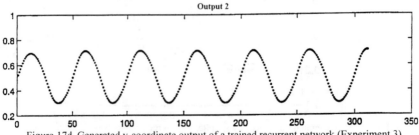

Figure 17d. Generated y-coordinate output of a trained recurrent network (Experiment 3)

V. CONCLUSIONS

Two distinct methods for training recurrent neural networks that eliminate the need for the computation of error gradients were presented in this article. Since gradient computation constitutes the major part of the overall training complexity in the use of gradient-based methods such as backpropagation learning, the methods discussed in this article provide attractive alternatives to the training of neural networks in general and recurrent networks in particular. One of these methods based on the theory of learning automata utilizes the concepts of reinforcement learning and employs use of penalty-reward methods for tailoring specific training policies. The other method utilizes the nonlinear simplex optimization approach and provides a systematic procedure for the adjustment of neural network parameters. The training performance resulting from the two approaches was demonstrated by application to a complex spatiotemporal learning problem of designing a dynamical neural network that outputs a prescribed attractor trajectory pattern. Simulation experiments conducted here with specific benchmark trajectory patterns confirm the efficacy of the learning automata approach and the simplex optimization approach for a simple and efficient training of recurrent nets.

REFERENCES

Almeida, L. B. A learning rule for asynchronous perceptrons with feedback in a combinatorial environment, *Proc. of the IEEE 1st Annual Intl. Conf. on Neural Networks*, 609, San Diego, 1987.

Bartle, R. and Sherbet, D., *Introduction to Real Analysis*. Wiley: New York, 1992.

Behrens, H., Gawronska, D., Hollatz, J. and Schurmann, B., Recurrent and feedforward backpropagation for time-independent pattern recognition, in *Proc. 1991 Intl. Joint Conf. on Neural Networks (IJCNN)*, Seattle, July 1991.

Bertsekas, D. P., *Dynamic Programming,* Prentice-Hall: Englewood Cliffs, NJ, 1987.

Condarcure, T., *A learning automaton approach to trajectory learning and control system design using dynamic recurrent neural networks*, M.S. Thesis, ECE Department, The University of Arizona, 1991.

Duan, Q., Gupta, H. V., and Sorooshian, S., Effective and efficient global optimization for conceptual rainfall-runoff models, *Water Resources Research*, 28, 1015, 1992.

Karakasoglu, A., Sudharsanan, S. I., and Sundareshan, M. K., Identification and decentralized adaptive control using dynamical neural networks with application to robotic manipulators, *IEEE Trans. on Neural Networks*, 4, 919, 1993.

Khalil, H. K., *Nonlinear Systems*, Macmillan: New York, 1992.

Lakshmivarahan, S., *Learning Algorithms: Theory and Applications*. New York: Springer-Verlag, 1981.

Lapedes, A. and Farber, R., Programming a massively parallel computation universal system: static behavior, in *Neural Networks for Computing*, Denker, J. S., Ed., AIP Conference Proceedings, 151, 283, 1986.

Lewis, T. and Payne, W. H., Generalized feedback shift register pseudorandom number algorithm, *Journal of the Association for Computing Machinery*, 20 (3), 456, 1973.

Lin, D. T., Dayhoff, J. E., and Ligomenides, P. A., Trajectory production with the adaptive time-delay neural network, *Neural Networks*, 8, 447, 1995.

Mendel, J. M. and Fu, K. S., Eds., *Adaptive, Learning and Pattern Recognition Systems*, Academic: New York, 1970.

Narendra, K. S. and Thathachan, M. A. L. *Learning Automata, an Introduction*, Addison Wesley, Reading, MA, 1989.

Nelder, A. J. and Mead, R., A simplex method for function minization, *Comput. Journal*, 7, 308, 1965.

Nilsson, N. J., *Learning Machines: Foundations of Trainable Pattern Classifying Systems*, McGraw-Hill: New York, 1965.

Pearlmutter, B. Learning state space trajectories in recurrent neural networks, *Neural Computation*, 1, 263, 1989.

Pearlmutter, B. Gradient calculations for dynamic recurrent neural networks: a survey, *IEEE Trans. on Neural Networks*, 6, 1212, 1995.

Pineda, F. J. Generalization of backpropagation in recurrent neural networks, *Physical Review Letters*, 59 (19), 2229, 1987.

Ruiz, A., Owens, D. H., and Townley, S., Existence, learning, and replication of periodic motions in recurrent neural networks, *IEEE Trans. on Neural Networks*, 9, 651, 1998.

Rumelhart, D. E., Hinton, G. E., and Williams, R. J., Learning internal representations by error propagation, in *Parallel Distributed Processing: Explorations in the Microstructure of Cognition*, Rumelhart, D. E. and McClelland, J. L., Eds., MIT Press: Cambridge, 45, 1986.

Sato, M. A real time running algorithm for recurrent neural networks, *Biological Cybernetics*, 62, 237, 1990.

Sudharsanan, S. I. and Sundareshan, M. K., Training of a three layer recurrent neural network for nonlinear input-output mapping, *Proc. 1991 Intl. Joint Conf. on Neural Networks* (IJCNN-91), Seattle, 1991.

Sudharsanan, S. I. and Sundareshan, M. K., Supervised training of dynamical neural networks for associative memory design and identification of nonlinear maps, *Intl. J. of Neural Systems*, 5, 165, September 1994.

Sudharsanan, S. I. and Sundareshan, M. K., Equilibrium characterization of dynamical neural networks and a systematic synthesis procedure for associative memories, *IEEE Trans. on Neural Networks*, 2, 509, September 1991a.

Sudharsanan, S. I. and Sundareshan, M. K., Exponential stability and a systematic synthesis of a neural network for quadratic minimization, *Neural Networks*, 4, 599, 1991b.

Toomarian, N. and Barhen, J., Learning a trajectory using adjoint functions and teacher forcing, *Neural Networks*, 5, 473, 1992.

Varshavskii, V. I. and Vorontsova, I. P., On the behavior of stochastic automata with variable structure, *Automat. Remote Contr.*, 24, 327, 1963.

Werbos, P., Backpropagation through time: what it does and how to do it, *Proc. of the IEEE*, 78, 1550, 1990.

Williams, R. and Zipser, D., A learning algorithm for continually running fully recurrent neural networks, *Neural Computation*, 1, 270, 1989.

Wong, Y. C. and Sundareshan, M. K., A simplex trained neural network architecture for sensor fusion and tracking of target maneuvers, *Kybernetika*, No. 4-5, 1999.

Chapter 12

TRAINING RECURRENT NETWORKS FOR FILTERING AND CONTROL

Martin T. Hagan, Orlando De Jesús, Roger Schultz

School of Electrical and Computer Engineering
Oklahoma State University, Stillwater, Oklahoma

I. INTRODUCTION

Neural networks can be classified into recurrent and nonrecurrent categories. Nonrecurrent (feedforward) networks have no feedback elements; the output is calculated directly from the input through feedforward connections. In recurrent networks the output depends not only on the current input to the network, but also on the current or previous outputs or states of the network. For this reason, recurrent networks are more powerful than nonrecurrent networks and have important uses in control and signal processing applications.

This chapter introduces the Layered Digital Recurrent Network (LDRN), develops a general training algorithm for this network, and demonstrates the application of the LDRN to problems in controls and signal processing. In Section II we present the notation necessary to represent the LDRN. Section III contains a discussion of the dynamic backpropagation algorithms that are required to compute training gradients for recurrent networks. The concepts underlying the backpropagation-through-time and forward perturbation algorithms are presented in a unified framework and are demonstrated for a simple, single-loop recurrent network. In Section IV we describe a general forward perturbation algorithm for computing training gradients for the LDRN. Two application sections follow the discussion of dynamic backpropagation: neurocontrol and nonlinear filtering. These sections demonstrate the implementation of the general dynamic backpropagation algorithm. The control section (Section V) applies a neurocontrol architecture to the automatic equalization of an acoustic transmitter. The nonlinear filtering section (Section VI) demonstrates the application of a recurrent filtering network to a noise-cancellation application.

II. PRELIMINARIES

In this section we want to introduce the types of neural networks that are discussed in the remainder of this chapter. We also present the notation that we use to represent these networks. The networks we use are Layered Digital Recurrent Networks (LDRN). They are a generalization of the Layered Feedforward Network (LFFN), which has been modified to include feedback connections and delays. We begin here with a description of the LFFN and then show how it can be generalized to obtain the LDRN.

A. LAYERED FEEDFORWARD NETWORK

Figure 1 is an example of a layered feedforward network (two layers in this case). (See Demuth *et al.* [1998] for a full description of the notation used here.) The input vector to the network is represented by $\mathbf{p}^1$, which has R^1 elements. The superscript represents the input number, since it is possible to have more than one input vector. The input is connected to Layer 1 through the input weight $\mathbf{IW}^{1,1}$, where the first superscript represents the layer number and the second superscript represents the input number. The bias for the first layer is represented by $\mathbf{b}^1$. The net input to Layer 1 is denoted by $\mathbf{n}^1$, and is computed as

$$\mathbf{n}^1 = \mathbf{IW}^{1,1}\mathbf{p}^1 + \mathbf{b}^1 \tag{1}$$

The output of Layer 1, $\mathbf{a}^1$, is computed by passing the net input through a transfer function, according to $\mathbf{a}^1 = \mathbf{f}^1(\mathbf{n}^1)$. The output has S^1 elements. The output of the first layer is input to the second layer through the layer weight $\mathbf{LW}^{2,1}$. The overall output of the network is labeled $\mathbf{y}$. This is typically chosen to be the output of the last layer in the network, as it is in Figure 1, although it could be the output of any layer in the network.

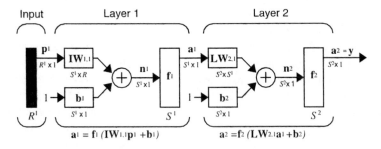

Figure 1. Example of a Layered Feedforward Network

Each layer in the LFFN is made up of 1) a set of weight matrices that come into that layer (which may connect from other layers or from external inputs), 2) a bias vector, 3) a summing junction, and 4) a transfer function. (In the LDRN, a set of tapped delay lines may also be included in a layer, as we will see later.) In the example given in Figure 1, there is only one weight matrix associated with each layer, but it is possible to have weight matrices that are connected from several different input vectors and layer outputs. This will become clear when we introduce the LDRN network. Also, the example in Figure 1 has only two layers; our general LFFN can have an arbitrary number of layers. The layers do not have to be connected in sequence from Layer 1 to Layer M. For example, Layer 1 could be connected to both Layer 3 and Layer 4, by weights $\mathbf{LW}^{3,1}$ and $\mathbf{LW}^{4,1}$

respectively. Although the layers do not have to be connected in a linear sequence by layer number, it must be possible to compute the output of the network by a simple sequence of calculations. There cannot be any feedback loops in the network. The order in which the individual layer outputs must be computed in order to obtain the correct network output is called the *simulation order*.

B. LAYERED DIGITAL RECURRENT NETWORK

We now introduce a class of recurrent networks that are based on the LFFN. The LFFN is a static network, in the sense that the network output can be computed directly from the network input, without the knowledge of initial network states. A Layered Digital Recurrent Network (LDRN) can contain feedback loops and time delays. The network response is a function of network inputs, as well as initial network states.

The components of the LDRN are the same as those of the LFFN, with the addition of the tapped delay line (TDL), which is shown in Figure 2. The output of the TDL is a vector containing current and previous values of the TDL input. In Figure 2 we show two abbreviated representations for the TDL. In the case on the left, the undelayed value of the input variable is included in the output vector. In the case on the right, only delayed values of the input are included in the output.

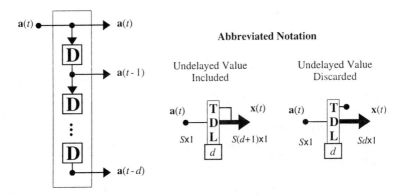

Figure 2. Tapped Delay Line

Figure 3 is an example of an LDRN. Like the LFFN, the LDRN is made up of layers. In addition to the weight matrices, bias, summing junction, and transfer function, which make up the layers of the LFFN, the layers of the LDRN also include any tapped delay lines that appear at the input of a weight matrix. (Any weight matrix in an LDRN can be proceeded by a tapped delay line.) For example, Layer 1 of Figure 3 contains the weight $\mathbf{LW}^{1,2}$ and the TDL at its input. Note that all of the layer outputs and net inputs in the LDRN are explicit functions of time.

The output of the TDL in Figure 3 is labeled $\mathbf{a}^{2,2}(t)$. This indicates that it is a composite vector made up of delayed values of the output of Subnet 2 (indicated by the second superscript) and is an input to Subnet 2 (indicated by the first superscript). (A subnet is a series of layers which have no internal tapped delay lines. The number of the subnet is the same as the number of its output layer. These concepts are defined more carefully in a later section.) These TDL outputs are important variables in our training algorithm for the LDRN.

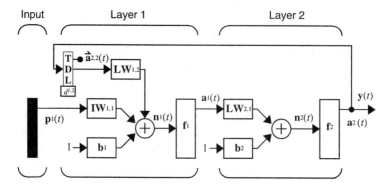

Figure 3. Layered Digital Recurrent Network Example

In the LDRN, feedback is added to an LFFN. Therefore, unlike the LFFN, the output of the network is a function not only of the weights, biases, and network input, but also of the outputs of some of the network layers at previous points in time. For this reason, it is not a simple matter to calculate the gradient of the network output with respect to the weights and biases (which is needed to train the network). This is because the weights and biases have two different effects on the network output. The first is the direct effect, which can be calculated using the standard backpropagation algorithm [Hagan *et al.*, 1996]. The second is an indirect effect, since some of the inputs to the network, such as $\vec{\mathbf{a}}^{1,2}(t)$, are also functions of the weights and biases. In the next section we briefly describe the gradient calculations for the LFFN and show how they must be modified for the LDRN. The main development of the next two sections is a general gradient calculation for arbitrary LDRN's.

III. PRINCIPLES OF DYNAMIC LEARNING

Consider again the multilayer network of Figure 1. The basic simulation equation of such a network is

$$\mathbf{a}^k = \mathbf{f}^k\left(\sum_i \mathbf{IW}^{k,i}\mathbf{p}^i + \sum_j \mathbf{LW}^{k,j}\mathbf{a}^j + \mathbf{b}^k\right), \tag{2}$$

where k is incremented through the simulation order.

The task of the network is to learn associations between a specified set of input/output pairs: $\{(\mathbf{p}_1, \mathbf{t}_1), (\mathbf{p}_2, \mathbf{t}_2), \dots, (\mathbf{p}_Q, \mathbf{t}_Q)\}$. The performance index for the network is

$$F(\mathbf{x}) = \sum_{q=1}^{Q} (\mathbf{t}_q - \mathbf{y}_q)^T (\mathbf{t}_q - \mathbf{y}_q) = \sum_{q=1}^{Q} \mathbf{e}_q^T \mathbf{e}_q \tag{3}$$

where $\mathbf{y}_q$ is the output of the network when the qth input, $\mathbf{p}_q$, is presented, and $\mathbf{x}$ is a vector containing all of the weights and biases in the network. (Later we use $\mathbf{x}^i$ to represent the weights and biases in Layer i.) The network should learn the $\mathbf{x}$ vector that minimizes F.

For the standard backpropagation algorithm [Hagan et al., 1996] we use a steepest descent learning rule. The performance index is approximated by:

$$\hat{F} = \mathbf{e}_q^T \mathbf{e}_q, \tag{4}$$

where the total sum of squares is replaced by the squared errors for a single input/output pair. The approximate steepest (gradient) descent algorithm is then:

$$\Delta w_{i,j}^{k,l} = -\alpha \frac{\partial \hat{F}}{\partial w_{i,j}^{k,l}}, \quad \Delta b_i^k = -\alpha \frac{\partial \hat{F}}{\partial b_i^k} \tag{5}$$

where α is the learning rate. Define

$$s_i^k \equiv \frac{\partial \hat{F}}{\partial n_i^k} \tag{6}$$

as the sensitivity of the performance index to changes in the net input of unit i in layer k. Using the chain rule, we can show that

$$\frac{\partial \hat{F}}{\partial iw_{i,j}^{m,l}} = \frac{\partial \hat{F}}{\partial n_i^m} \times \frac{\partial n_i^m}{\partial iw_{i,j}^{m,l}} = s_i^m p_j^l, \quad \frac{\partial \hat{F}}{\partial lw_{i,j}^{m,l}} = \frac{\partial \hat{F}}{\partial n_i^m} \times \frac{\partial n_i^m}{\partial lw_{i,j}^{m,l}} = s_i^m a_j^l,$$

$$\frac{\partial \hat{F}}{\partial b_i^m} = \frac{\partial \hat{F}}{\partial n_i^m} \times \frac{\partial n_i^m}{\partial b_i^m} = s_i^m \tag{7}$$

It can also be shown that the sensitivities satisfy the following recurrence relation, in which m is incremented through the *backpropagation order*, which is the reverse of the simulation order:

$$\mathbf{s}^m = \dot{\mathbf{F}}^m(\mathbf{n}^m) \sum_i (\mathbf{LW}^{i,m})^T \mathbf{s}^i \tag{8}$$

where

$$
\mathbf{\dot{F}}^m(\mathbf{n}^m) = \begin{bmatrix} \dot{f}^m(n_1^m) & 0 & \cdots & 0 \\ 0 & \dot{f}^m(n_2^m) & \cdots & 0 \\ \vdots & \vdots & & \vdots \\ 0 & 0 & \cdots & \dot{f}^m(n_{S^m}^m) \end{bmatrix}
\tag{9}
$$

and

$$
\dot{f}^m(n_j^m) = \frac{\partial f^m(n_j^m)}{\partial n_j^m}
\tag{10}
$$

This recurrence relation is initialized at the output layer:

$$
\mathbf{s}^M = -2\mathbf{\dot{F}}^M(\mathbf{n}^M)(\mathbf{t}_q - \mathbf{y}_q).
\tag{11}
$$

The overall learning algorithm now proceeds as follows: first, propagate the input forward using Eq. (2); next, propagate the sensitivities back using Eq. (11) and Eq. (8); and finally, update the weights and biases using Eq. (5) and Eq. (7).

Now consider an LDRN, such as the one shown in Figure 3. Suppose that we use the same gradient descent algorithm, Eq. (5), that is used in the standard backpropagation algorithm. The problem in this case is that when we try to find the equivalent of Eq. (7) we note that the weights and biases have two different effects on the network output. The first is the direct effect, which is accounted for by Eq. (7). The second is the indirect effect, since some of the inputs to the network, such as $\mathbf{a}^{1,2}(t)$, are also functions of the weights and biases. To account for this indirect effect we must use dynamic backpropagation.

To illustrate dynamic backpropagation [Yang et al., 1993, Yang, 1994], consider Figure 4, which is a simple recurrent network. It consists of an LFFN with a single feedback loop added from the output of the network, which is connected to the input of the network through a single delay. In this figure the vector $\mathbf{x}$ represents all of the network parameters (weights and biases) and the vector $\mathbf{a}(t)$ represents the output of the LFFN at time step t.

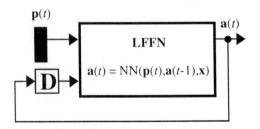

Figure 4. Simple Recurrent Network

Now suppose that we want to minimize

$$F(\mathbf{x}) = \sum_{t=1}^{Q} (\mathbf{t}(t) - \mathbf{a}(t))^T (\mathbf{t}(t) - \mathbf{a}(t)) \tag{12}$$

In order to use gradient descent, we need to find the gradient of F with respect to the network parameters. There are two different approaches to this problem. They both use the chain rule, but are implemented in different ways:

$$\frac{\partial F}{\partial \mathbf{x}} = \sum_{t=1}^{Q} \left[\frac{\partial \mathbf{a}(t)}{\partial \mathbf{x}} \right]^T \times \frac{\partial^e F}{\partial \mathbf{a}(t)} \tag{13}$$

or

$$\frac{\partial F}{\partial \mathbf{x}} = \sum_{t=1}^{Q} \left[\frac{\partial^e \mathbf{a}(t)}{\partial \mathbf{x}} \right]^T \times \frac{\partial F}{\partial \mathbf{a}(t)} \tag{14}$$

where the superscript e indicates an explicit derivative, not accounting for indirect effects through time. The explicit derivatives can be obtained with the standard backpropagation algorithm, as in Eq. (8). To find the complete derivatives that are required in Eq. (13) and Eq. (14), we need the additional equations:

$$\frac{\partial \mathbf{a}(t)}{\partial \mathbf{x}} = \frac{\partial^e \mathbf{a}(t)}{\partial \mathbf{x}} + \frac{\partial^e \mathbf{a}(t)}{\partial \mathbf{a}(t-1)} \times \frac{\partial \mathbf{a}(t-1)}{\partial \mathbf{x}} \tag{15}$$

and

$$\frac{\partial F}{\partial \mathbf{a}(t)} = \frac{\partial^e F}{\partial \mathbf{a}(t)} + \frac{\partial^e \mathbf{a}(t+1)}{\partial \mathbf{a}(t)} \times \frac{\partial F}{\partial \mathbf{a}(t+1)} \tag{16}$$

Eq. (13) and Eq. (15) make up the forward perturbation (FP) algorithm. Note that the key term is

$$\frac{\partial \mathbf{a}(t)}{\partial \mathbf{x}} \tag{17}$$

which must be propagated forward through time.

Eq. (14) and Eq. (16) make up the backpropagation-through-time (BTT) algorithm. Here the key term is

$$\frac{\partial F}{\partial \mathbf{a}(t)} \tag{18}$$

which must be propagated backward through time.

In general, the FP algorithm requires somewhat more computation than the BTT algorithm. However, the BTT algorithm cannot be implemented in real time, since the outputs must be computed for all time steps, and then the derivatives must be backpropagated back to the initial time point. The FP algorithm is well suited for real time implementation, since the derivatives can be calculated at each time step.

IV. DYNAMIC BACKPROP FOR THE LDRN

In this section, we generalize the FP algorithm, so that it can be applied to arbitrary LDRN's. This is followed by applications of the LDRN and dynamic backpropagation to problems in filtering and control.

A. PRELIMINARIES

To explain this algorithm, we must create certain definitions related to the LDRN. We do that in the following paragraphs.

First, as we stated earlier, a *layer* consists of a set of *weights*, associated *tapped delay lines*, a *summing function*, and a *transfer function*. The network has *inputs* that are connected to special weights, called *input weights,* and denoted by $IW^{i,j}$, where j denotes the number of the input vector that enters the weight, and i denotes the number of the layer to which the weight is connected. The weights connecting one layer to another are called *layer weights* and are denoted by $LW^{i,j}$, where j denotes the number of the layer coming into the weight and i denotes the number of the layer at the output of weight. In order to calculate the network response in stages, layer by layer, we need to proceed in the proper layer order, so that the necessary inputs at each layer will be available. This ordering of layers is called the *simulation order*. In order to backpropagate the derivatives for the gradient calculations, we must proceed in the opposite order, which is called the *backpropagation order*.

In order to simplify the description of the training algorithm, the LDRN is divided into *subnets*. A subnet is a section of a network that has no tapped delay lines, except at the subnet input. Every LDRN can be organized as a collection of subnets. We define the subnets by proceeding backwards from the last subnet to the first subnet. To locate the last subnet, start at the first layer in the backpropagation order and proceed through the backpropagation order until you find a layer containing delays, which becomes the first layer in the last subnet. The last subnet is then defined as containing all of the layers beginning at the layer containing delays and continuing through the simulation order to the first layer in the backpropagation order (or the last layer in the simulation order). This defines the last subnet. To find the preceding subnet, start with the next layer in the backpropagation order and proceed in the same way until you find the next layer with delays. This process continues until you reach the last layer in the backpropagation order, at which time the first *subnet* is defined. As with the layer simulation order, we can also define a *subnet simulation order* that starts at the first subnet and continues until the last subnet.

For example, the LDRN shown in Figure 5 has thee layers and two subnets. To simplify the algorithm, the subnet is denoted by the number of its output layer. For this network the simulation order is 1-2-3, the backpropagation order is 3-2-1 and the subnet simulation order is 1-3.

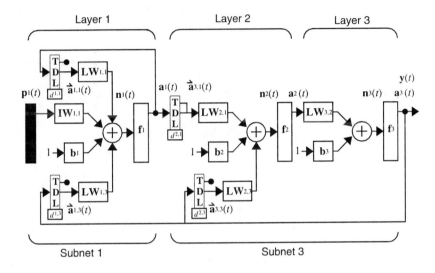

Figure 5. Three-layer LDRN with Two Subnets

B. EXPLICIT DERIVATIVES

We want to generalize the forward perturbation (FP) algorithm of Eq. (13) and Eq. (15) so that it can be applied to an arbitrary LDRN. Notice that we have two terms on the right-hand side of Eq. (15). We have an explicit derivative of the performance with respect to the weights, which accounts for the direct effect of the weights on the performance and can be computed through the standard backpropagation algorithm, as in Eq. (8). We also have a second term, which accounts for the fact that the weights have a secondary effect through the previous network output. In the general LDRN, we may have many different feedback loops, and therefore there could be many different terms on the right of Eq. (15), and each of those terms would have a separate equation like Eq. (15) to update the total derivative through time. For our development of the FP algorithm, we have one term (and an additional equation) for every place where one subnet is input to another subnet. Recall that the subnet boundaries are determined by the locations of the tapped delay lines. Within a subnet, standard backpropagation, as in Eq. (8), can be used to propagate the explicit derivatives, but at the subnet boundaries an equation like Eq. (15) must be used to calculate the total derivative, which includes both direct and indirect effects. In this subsection we describe the computation of the explicit derivatives, and then in the following subsection we explain the total derivative computation.

A backpropagation process to calculate the explicit derivatives is needed for each subnet. These equations involve calculating the derivative of the subnet output with respect to each layer output in the subnet. The basic equation is

$$\frac{\partial^e \mathbf{a}^{jz}(t)}{\partial \mathbf{a}^i(t)} = \sum_k \frac{\partial^e \mathbf{n}^k(t)}{\partial \mathbf{a}^i(t)} \times \frac{\partial^e \mathbf{a}^{jz}(t)}{\partial \mathbf{n}^k(t)} \tag{19}$$

where $\mathbf{a}^{jz}(t)$ represents a subnet output, $\mathbf{a}^i(t)$ is the output of a layer in subnet jz, $\mathbf{n}^k(t)$ is the net input of layer k, which has a connection from layer i. The index i is incremented through the backpropagation order. If we define

$$\mathbf{S}^{k,jz} \equiv \frac{\partial^e \mathbf{a}^{jz}(t)}{\partial \mathbf{n}^k(t)} \text{ , and note that } \frac{\partial^e \mathbf{n}^k(t)}{\partial \mathbf{a}^i(t)} = \mathbf{LW}^{k,i}, \tag{20}$$

then we can write Eq. (19) as

$$\frac{\partial^e \mathbf{a}^{jz}(t)}{\partial \mathbf{a}^i(t)} = \sum_k \mathbf{LW}^{k,i} \times \mathbf{S}^{k,jz}. \tag{21}$$

This recursion, where i is incremented along the backpropagation order, begins at the last layer in the subnet:

$$\frac{\partial^e \mathbf{a}^{jz}(t)}{\partial \mathbf{a}^{jz}(t)} = \mathbf{I}, \tag{22}$$

where $\mathbf{I}$ is an identity matrix whose dimension is the size of layer jz.

C. COMPLETE FP ALGORITHM FOR THE LDRN

We are now ready to describe a generalized FP algorithm for the arbitrary LDRN. There are two parts to the FP algorithm: Eq. (13) and Eq. (15). Eq. (13) remains the same for the LDRN as for the simple network in Figure 4. Eq. (15), however, must be modified. For the general case we have one equation like Eq. (15) for each subnet output. Each of these equations has a term for the explicit derivative and one additional term for each subnet output.

The complete FP algorithm for the LDRN network is given in the following flowchart. It contains three major sections. The first section computes the explicit (static) derivatives, as in Eq. (21), which are needed as part of the dynamic equations. The second section computes the dynamic derivatives of the subnet outputs with respect to the weights, as in Eq. (15). The final section computes the dynamic derivatives of performance with respect to the weights, as in Eq. (13).

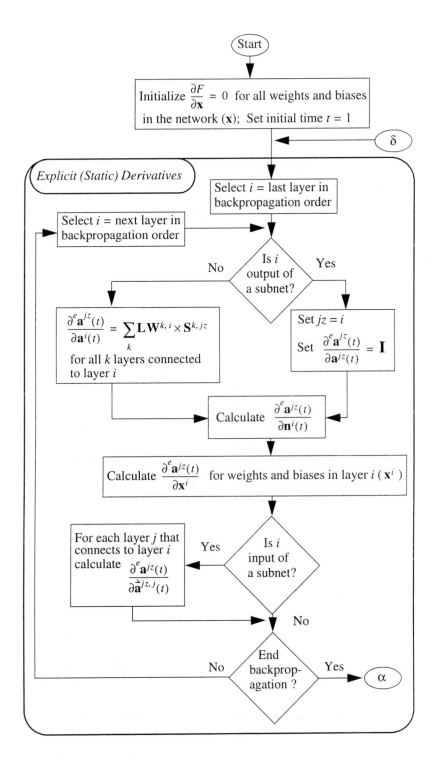

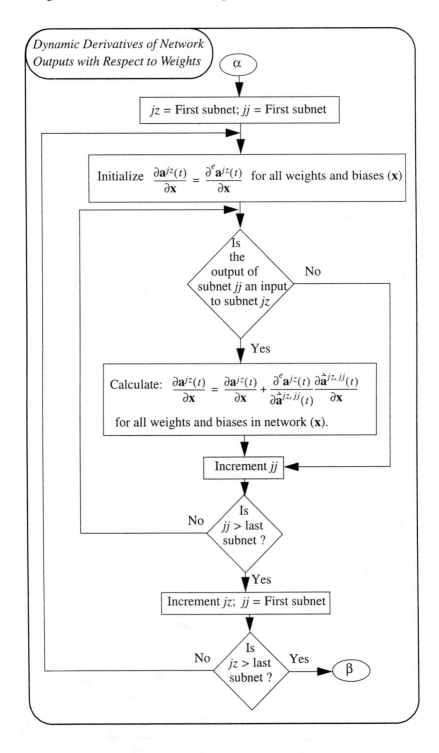

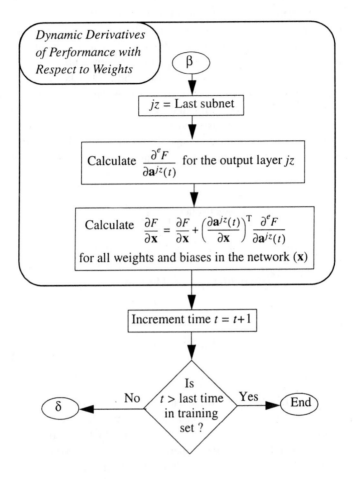

V. NEUROCONTROL APPLICATION

In this section we illustrate the application of the LDRN and dynamic backpropagation to a control problem. We wish to control the output of an acoustic transmitter, whose schematic diagram is shown in Figure 6.

Binary data is transmitted via acoustic signals from one pipeline location to another. Acoustic stress waves are imparted into the pipeline by the acoustic transmitter. The stress waves propagate through the pipeline to the acoustic receiver, which receives the transmitted signal. Tone bursts of different frequencies are used to represent either a 1 or a 0. The acoustic channel provided by the pipeline causes heavy distortion in the transmitted signal. There are often extraneous unwanted acoustic stress waves created by external sources, such as engines, geartrains, and pumps, that are imparted into the pipeline. The inherent channel distortion and the unwanted external noise can degrade the transmitted signal such that signal detection and interpretation at the receiver are unreliable or impossible. One method of enhancing communication performance is to equalize the effects of the transmission channel by adjusting the transmitter output so that the measured signal imparted to the pipeline at a short distance from the transmitter is the desired signal. Ideally, the feedback measurement of this signal is taken at the receiver. Of course, in practice, the feedback signal is measured near the transmitter. To alleviate the effects of unwanted disturbance noise, the transmitter can actively cancel the disturbance noise by way of destructive interference. The transmitter creates stress waves that are out of phase with, and of equal magnitude to, the undesired signals. In this example, a neural network controller is used as both a channel equalizer and an active noise canceller.

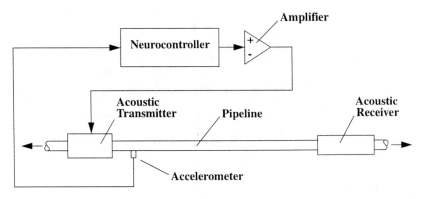

Figure 6. Schematic of Acoustic Transmitter/Receiver System.

In addition to illustrating dynamic backpropagation on the neurocontroller for the acoustic transmitter, this section also demonstrates the effect of training with approximations to true dynamic derivatives. The evaluation is based on squared error performance and floating point operations. When approximations are used, the computational burden can be reduced, but the errors generally increase.

Figure 7 is a schematic of the control system. In this system, model reference adaptive control (MRAC) [Narendra, 1990] is applied to the control of the acoustic transmitter. The plant model is used only as a backpropagation path for the derivatives needed to adjust the controller weights; the plant model weights are not adjusted. The plant model is a 2-layer LDRN, with 10 input taps, 50 feedback taps, and 15 hidden neurons. The controller weights are adjusted such that the error $e_c(t)$, between a delayed reference input $r(t)$ and the actual plant output $c(t)$, is minimized. The controller structure consists of 40 input taps, 50 controller feedback taps, 75 plant output feedback taps, and 15 hidden neurons.

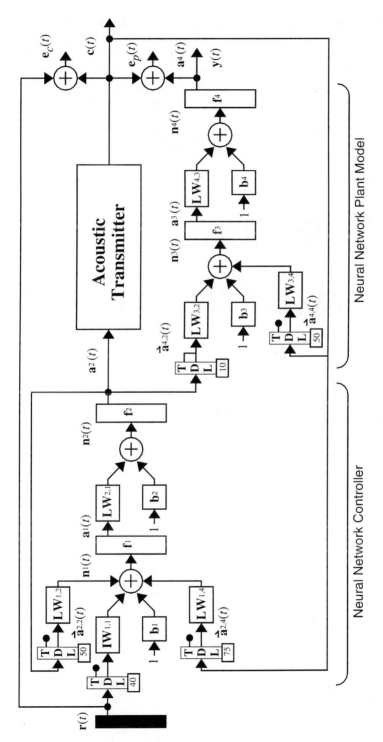

Figure 7. Self-Equalizing Acoustic Transmitter

339

If we apply the concepts described in the previous sections to the system shown in Figure 7, we notice that the total system is an LDRN that can be divided into two subnets. The last subnet (number 4) corresponds to the Neural Network Plant Model (with $\mathbf{a}^4(t)$ as the subnet output). The first subnet (number 2) corresponds to the Neural Controller (with $\mathbf{a}^2(t)$ as the subnet output). The subnets are fully connected, so we have two sets of training equations:

$$\frac{\partial \mathbf{a}^4(t)}{\partial \mathbf{x}} = \frac{\partial^e \mathbf{a}^4(t)}{\partial \mathbf{x}} + \frac{\partial^e \mathbf{a}^4(t)}{\partial \hat{\mathbf{a}}^{4,2}(t)} \frac{\partial \hat{\mathbf{a}}^{4,2}(t)}{\partial \mathbf{x}} + \frac{\partial^e \mathbf{a}^4(t)}{\partial \hat{\mathbf{a}}^{4,4}(t)} \frac{\partial \hat{\mathbf{a}}^{4,4}(t)}{\partial \mathbf{x}} \tag{23}$$

and

$$\frac{\partial \mathbf{a}^2(t)}{\partial \mathbf{x}} = \frac{\partial^e \mathbf{a}^2(t)}{\partial \mathbf{x}} + \frac{\partial^e \mathbf{a}^2(t)}{\partial \hat{\mathbf{a}}^{2,4}(t)} \frac{\partial \hat{\mathbf{a}}^{2,4}(t)}{\partial \mathbf{x}} + \frac{\partial^e \mathbf{a}^2(t)}{\partial \hat{\mathbf{a}}^{2,2}(t)} \frac{\partial \hat{\mathbf{a}}^{2,2}(t)}{\partial \mathbf{x}} \tag{24}$$

We now show how these equations can be developed using our general FP algorithm, which was described in the flowchart in the previous section. We start in the last layer in the backpropagation order (layer 4), obtaining:

$$\frac{\partial^e \mathbf{a}^4(t)}{\mathbf{a}^4(t)} = \mathbf{I} \; ; \; \mathbf{S}^{4,4} \equiv \frac{\partial^e \mathbf{a}^4(t)}{\mathbf{n}^4(t)} = \dot{\mathbf{F}}^4(\mathbf{n}^4)$$

$$\frac{\partial^e \mathbf{a}^4(t)}{\partial \mathbf{b}^4} = \dot{\mathbf{F}}^4(\mathbf{n}^4) \; ; \; \frac{\partial^e \mathbf{a}^4(t)}{\partial \mathbf{L} \mathbf{W}^{4,3}} = \dot{\mathbf{F}}^4(\mathbf{n}^4) \cdot [\mathbf{a}^3(t)]^T$$

Layer 3 is not the output of a subnet, so we apply:

$$\frac{\partial^e \mathbf{a}^4(t)}{\mathbf{a}^3(t)} = \mathbf{L}\mathbf{W}^{4,3} \times \mathbf{S}^{4,4}$$

$$\mathbf{S}^{3,4} \equiv \frac{\partial^e \mathbf{a}^4(t)}{\mathbf{n}^3(t)} = \mathbf{L}\mathbf{W}^{4,3} \times \mathbf{S}^{4,4} \times \dot{\mathbf{F}}^3(\mathbf{n}^3)$$

$$\frac{\partial^e \mathbf{a}^4(t)}{\partial \mathbf{b}^3} = \mathbf{L}\mathbf{W}^{4,3} \times \mathbf{S}^{4,4} \times \dot{\mathbf{F}}^3(\mathbf{n}^3)$$

$$\frac{\partial^e \mathbf{a}^4(t)}{\partial \mathbf{L} \mathbf{W}^{3,2}} = \mathbf{L}\mathbf{W}^{4,3} \times \mathbf{S}^{4,4} \times \dot{\mathbf{F}}^3(\mathbf{n}^3) \times [\hat{\mathbf{a}}^{4,2}(t)]^T$$

$$\frac{\partial^e \mathbf{a}^4(t)}{\partial \mathbf{LW}^{3,4}} = \mathbf{LW}^{4,3} \times \mathbf{S}^{4,4} \times \overset{\cdot 3}{\mathbf{F}}(\mathbf{n}^3) \times [\overset{\wedge 4,4}{\mathbf{a}}(t)]^{\mathrm{T}}$$

Layer 3 has two inputs with delays, therefore it is the beginning of the last subnet, and we calculate:

$$\frac{\partial^e \mathbf{a}^4(t)}{\partial \overset{\wedge 4,2}{\mathbf{a}}(t)} = \mathbf{LW}^{4,3} \times \mathbf{S}^{4,4} \times \overset{\cdot 3}{\mathbf{F}}(\mathbf{n}^3) \times \mathbf{LW}^{3,2}$$

$$\frac{\partial^e \mathbf{a}^4(t)}{\partial \overset{\wedge 4,4}{\mathbf{a}}(t)} = \mathbf{LW}^{4,3} \times \mathbf{S}^{4,4} \times \overset{\cdot 3}{\mathbf{F}}(\mathbf{n}^3) \times \mathbf{LW}^{3,4}$$

Layer 2 in the neural controller is the end of the first subnet. So we apply the equations:

$$\frac{\partial^e \mathbf{a}^2(t)}{\mathbf{a}^2(t)} = \mathbf{I}; \ \mathbf{S}^{2,2} \equiv \frac{\partial^e \mathbf{a}^2(t)}{\mathbf{n}^2(t)} = \overset{\cdot 2}{\mathbf{F}}(\mathbf{n}^2)$$

$$\frac{\partial^e \mathbf{a}^2(t)}{\partial \mathbf{b}^2} = \overset{\cdot 2}{\mathbf{F}}(\mathbf{n}^2); \ \frac{\partial^e \mathbf{a}^2(t)}{\partial \mathbf{LW}^{2,1}} = \overset{\cdot 2}{\mathbf{F}}(\mathbf{n}^2) \cdot [\mathbf{a}^1(t)]^{\mathrm{T}}$$

Layer 1 is not the output of a subnet, so we apply:

$$\frac{\partial^e \mathbf{a}^2(t)}{\mathbf{a}^1(t)} = \mathbf{LW}^{2,1} \times \mathbf{S}^{2,2}$$

$$\mathbf{S}^{1,2} \equiv \frac{\partial^e \mathbf{a}^2(t)}{\mathbf{n}^1(t)} = \mathbf{LW}^{2,1} \times \mathbf{S}^{2,2} \times \overset{\cdot 1}{\mathbf{F}}(\mathbf{n}^1)$$

$$\frac{\partial^e \mathbf{a}^2(t)}{\partial \mathbf{b}^1} = \mathbf{LW}^{2,1} \times \mathbf{S}^{2,2} \times \overset{\cdot 1}{\mathbf{F}}(\mathbf{n}^1)$$

$$\frac{\partial^e \mathbf{a}^2(t)}{\partial \mathbf{LW}^{1,1}} = \mathbf{LW}^{2,1} \times \mathbf{S}^{2,2} \times \overset{\cdot 1}{\mathbf{F}}(\mathbf{n}^1) \times [\overset{\wedge 2,2}{\mathbf{a}}(t)]^{\mathrm{T}}$$

$$\frac{\partial^e \mathbf{a}^2(t)}{\partial \mathbf{LW}^{4,1}} = \mathbf{LW}^{2,1} \times \mathbf{S}^{2,2} \times \overset{\cdot 1}{\mathbf{F}}(\mathbf{n}^1) \times [\overset{\wedge 2,4}{\mathbf{a}}(t)]^{\mathrm{T}}$$

$$\frac{\partial^e \mathbf{a}^2(t)}{\partial \mathbf{IW}^{1,1}} = \mathbf{LW}^{2,1} \times \mathbf{S}^{2,2} \times \dot{\mathbf{F}}^1(\mathbf{n}^1) \times [\vec{\mathbf{r}}(t)]^T$$

Layer 1 has two inputs with delays, so it is the end of the first subnet, and we calculate

$$\frac{\partial^e \mathbf{a}^2(t)}{\partial \vec{\mathbf{a}}^{2,2}(t)} = \mathbf{LW}^{2,1} \times \mathbf{S}^{2,2} \times \dot{\mathbf{F}}^1(\mathbf{n}^1) \times \mathbf{LW}^{1,2}$$

$$\frac{\partial^e \mathbf{a}^2(t)}{\partial \vec{\mathbf{a}}^{2,4}(t)} = \mathbf{LW}^{2,1} \times \mathbf{S}^{2,2} \times \dot{\mathbf{F}}^1(\mathbf{n}^1) \times \mathbf{LW}^{1,4}$$

Now that we have finished with the backpropagation step, we have the explicit derivatives for all of the weights and biases in the system. We are now ready to calculate the dynamic derivatives. We initialize

$$\frac{\partial \mathbf{a}^2(t)}{\partial \mathbf{x}} = \frac{\partial^e \mathbf{a}^2(t)}{\partial \mathbf{x}}$$

and calculate

$$\frac{\partial \mathbf{a}^2(t)}{\partial \mathbf{x}} = \frac{\partial \mathbf{a}^2(t)}{\partial \mathbf{x}} + \frac{\partial^e \mathbf{a}^2(t)}{\partial \vec{\mathbf{a}}^{2,2}(t)} \frac{\partial \vec{\mathbf{a}}^{2,2}(t)}{\partial \mathbf{x}}$$

and

$$\frac{\partial \mathbf{a}^2(t)}{\partial \mathbf{x}} = \frac{\partial \mathbf{a}^2(t)}{\partial \mathbf{x}} + \frac{\partial^e \mathbf{a}^2(t)}{\partial \vec{\mathbf{a}}^{2,4}(t)} \frac{\partial \vec{\mathbf{a}}^{2,4}(t)}{\partial \mathbf{x}} \ .$$

This gives us Eq. (24) for all weights and biases. A similar process is performed for subnet 4 to obtain Eq. (23).

We have now computed all of the dynamic derivatives of the outputs of the subnets with respect to the weights. The next step is to compute the derivatives of the performance function with respect to the weights. We must first calculate

$$\frac{\partial^e F}{\partial \mathbf{a}^4(t)} = -2(\mathbf{r}(t) - \mathbf{a}^4(t)),$$

to obtain

$$\frac{\partial F}{\partial \mathbf{x}} = \frac{\partial F}{\partial \mathbf{x}} + \left(\frac{\partial \mathbf{a}^4(t)}{\partial \mathbf{x}}\right)^{\mathrm{T}} \frac{\partial^e F}{\partial \mathbf{a}^4(t)}$$

for all the weights and biases in the neural controller. The process is repeated for each sample time in the training set.

The LDRN was trained using the preceding equations. Now we demonstrate the performance of the closed-loop acoustic transmitter system. The reference input used in the simulation consisted of a random sequence of tone burst pulses, as shown in Figure 8. The tone bursts are evenly spaced and appear randomly at one of two frequencies. In order to investigate the robustness of the controller, a periodic disturbance noise was added to the plant input, representing extraneous acoustic stress waves created by external sources. The open-loop plant response, with no controller, is shown in Figure 9. The closed-loop response, after the controller was trained to convergence, is shown in Figure 10.

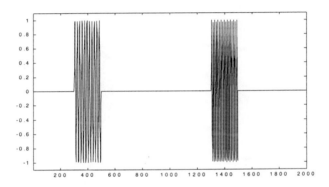

Figure 8. Tone Burst Reference Input

In the next test, dynamic backpropagation was used in plant model, but was not used in backpropagating derivatives in the controller. Only static backpropagation was used in the controller. (In Eq. (24) only the explicit derivative terms are calculated.) This procedure requires less computation than the full dynamic backpropagation but may not be as accurate. The results are shown in Figure 11.

For the last test, dynamic backpropagation was only used to compute a dynamic derivative across the first delay in the tapped-delay line between the plant model and the controller. All other derivatives were computed using only explicit (static) derivatives. The controller weights never converged in this case, so a plot of the results is not shown. The results are summarized in Table 1.

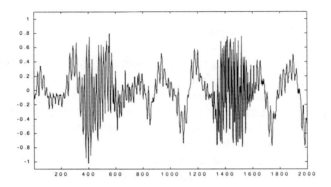

Figure 9. Open-loop Plant Response

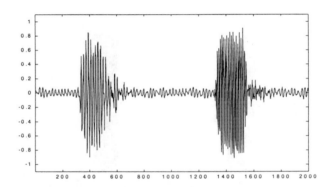

Figure 10. Closed-Loop System Response (Full Dynamic Training)

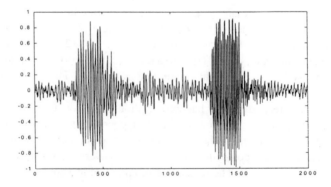

Figure 11. Response without Dynamic Controller Training

Table 1 provides a summary of the performance results for all three tests. These results highlight the increased computational burden when calculating dynamic derivatives instead of simply static derivatives. In this example, reasonable performance was possible even when dynamic derivatives were used only in the plant model. This derivative approximation decreased the computational burden by approximately 65%. Using essentially no dynamic derivatives in training reduced the computational burden by approximately 98%. However, performance in this case was unacceptable.

Derivative Method	Flops/Sample	Sum Squared Error
Full Dynamic	9.83×10^5	43.44
Plant Only Dynamic	3.48×10^5	55.53
No Dynamic	1.85×10^4	127.88

Table 1. Simulation Results for the Neural Controller

VI. RECURRENT FILTER

This section provides a second example of the application of the LDRN and dynamic backpropagation. We use a multi-loop recurrent network to predict an experimental acoustic signal. The prediction of acoustic signals is crucial in active sound cancellation systems. Acoustic environments are often very complex, due to the complexity of typical sound sources and the presence of reflected sound waves. The dynamic nature of acoustical systems makes the use of recurrent filter structures of great interest for prediction and control of this type of system.

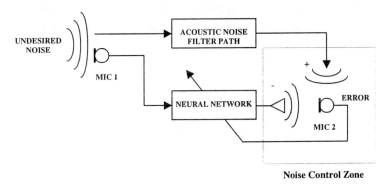

Figure 12. Active Noise Control System

Figure 12 depicts a typical Active Noise Control (ANC) system. An acoustic noise source creates undesirable noise in a surrounding area. The goal of the active noise suppression system is to reduce the undesirable noise at a particular location by using a loudspeaker to produce "anti-noise" that attenuates the unwanted noise by destructive interference. In order for a system of this type to work effectively, it is critical that the ANC system be able to predict (and then cancel) unwanted sound in the noise control zone.

In the first part of this section we develop the dynamic training equations for the ANC system. Then we present experimental results showing the prediction performance.

Figure 13 shows the structure of the LDRN used for predicting the acoustic data. In this network there are 3 cascaded recurrent structures. If we follow the methods described in Section IV, we see that the system is composed of three subnets. Therefore, we have three sets of training equations:

$$\frac{\partial \mathbf{a}^6(t)}{\partial \mathbf{x}} = \frac{\partial^e \mathbf{a}^6(t)}{\partial \mathbf{x}} + \frac{\partial^e \mathbf{a}^6(t)}{\partial \vec{\mathbf{a}}^{6,4}(t)} \frac{\partial \vec{\mathbf{a}}^{6,4}(t)}{\partial \mathbf{x}} + \frac{\partial^e \mathbf{a}^6(t)}{\partial \vec{\mathbf{a}}^{6,6}(t)} \frac{\partial \vec{\mathbf{a}}^{6,6}(t)}{\partial \mathbf{x}} \tag{25}$$

$$\frac{\partial \mathbf{a}^4(t)}{\partial \mathbf{x}} = \frac{\partial^e \mathbf{a}^4(t)}{\partial \mathbf{x}} + \frac{\partial^e \mathbf{a}^4(t)}{\partial \vec{\mathbf{a}}^{4,2}(t)} \frac{\partial \vec{\mathbf{a}}^{4,2}(t)}{\partial \mathbf{x}} + \frac{\partial^e \mathbf{a}^4(t)}{\partial \vec{\mathbf{a}}^{4,4}(t)} \frac{\partial \vec{\mathbf{a}}^{4,4}(t)}{\partial \mathbf{x}} \tag{26}$$

$$\frac{\partial \mathbf{a}^2(t)}{\partial \mathbf{x}} = \frac{\partial^e \mathbf{a}^2(t)}{\partial \mathbf{x}} + \frac{\partial^e \mathbf{a}^2(t)}{\partial \vec{\mathbf{a}}^{2,2}(t)} \frac{\partial \vec{\mathbf{a}}^{2,2}(t)}{\partial \mathbf{x}} \tag{27}$$

Notice that in Eq. (27) there is only one dynamic term. This is because there is only one tapped-delay input that comes from a subnet.

We now show how these equations can be developed using our general FP procedure, which was described in the flowchart of Section IV. We start in the last layer in the backpropagation order (Layer 6) to get the following equations:

$$\frac{\partial^e \mathbf{a}^6(t)}{\partial \mathbf{a}^6(t)} = \mathbf{I} , \ \mathbf{S}^{6,6} \equiv \frac{\partial^e \mathbf{a}^6(t)}{\partial \mathbf{n}^6(t)} = \dot{\mathbf{F}}^6(\mathbf{n}^6)$$

$$\frac{\partial^e \mathbf{a}^6(t)}{\partial \mathbf{b}^6} = \dot{\mathbf{F}}^6(\mathbf{n}^6) , \ \frac{\partial^e \mathbf{a}^6(t)}{\partial \mathbf{LW}^{6,5}} = \dot{\mathbf{F}}^6(\mathbf{n}^6) \cdot [\mathbf{a}^5(t)]^{\mathrm{T}}$$

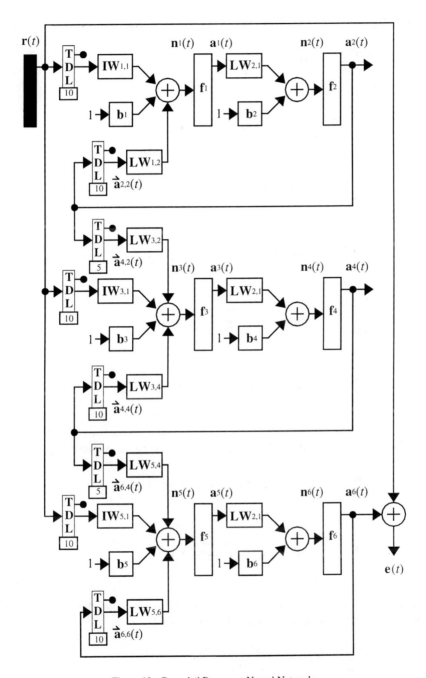

Figure 13. Cascaded Recurrent Neural Network

Layer 5 is not the output of a subnet, so the resulting equations are:

$$\frac{\partial^e \mathbf{a}^6(t)}{\partial \mathbf{a}^5(t)} = \mathbf{LW}^{6,5} \times \mathbf{S}^{6,6}$$

$$\mathbf{S}^{5,6} \equiv \frac{\partial^e \mathbf{a}^6(t)}{\partial \mathbf{n}^5(t)} = \mathbf{LW}^{6,5} \times \mathbf{S}^{6,6} \times \dot{\mathbf{F}}^5(\mathbf{n}^5)$$

$$\frac{\partial^e \mathbf{a}^6(t)}{\partial \mathbf{b}^5} = \mathbf{LW}^{6,5} \times \mathbf{S}^{6,6} \times \dot{\mathbf{F}}^5(\mathbf{n}^5)$$

$$\frac{\partial^e \mathbf{a}^6(t)}{\partial \mathbf{LW}^{5,4}} = \mathbf{LW}^{6,5} \times \mathbf{S}^{6,6} \times \dot{\mathbf{F}}^5(\mathbf{n}^5) \times [\vec{\mathbf{a}}^{6,4}(t)]^T$$

$$\frac{\partial^e \mathbf{a}^6(t)}{\partial \mathbf{IW}^{5,1}} = \mathbf{LW}^{6,5} \times \mathbf{S}^{6,6} \times \dot{\mathbf{F}}^5(\mathbf{n}^5) \times [\vec{\mathbf{r}}(t)]^T$$

$$\frac{\partial^e \mathbf{a}^6(t)}{\partial \mathbf{LW}^{5,6}} = \mathbf{LW}^{6,5} \times \mathbf{S}^{6,6} \times \dot{\mathbf{F}}^5(\mathbf{n}^5) \times [\vec{\mathbf{a}}^{6,6}(t)]^T$$

Layer 5 has two tapped-delay inputs from subnets, so we must calculate the explicit derivatives of the subnet output with respect to these inputs to yield:

$$\frac{\partial^e \mathbf{a}^6(t)}{\partial \vec{\mathbf{a}}^{6,4}(t)} = \mathbf{LW}^{6,5} \times \mathbf{S}^{6,6} \times \dot{\mathbf{F}}^5(\mathbf{n}^5) \times \mathbf{LW}^{5,4}$$

$$\frac{\partial^e \mathbf{a}^6(t)}{\partial \vec{\mathbf{a}}^{6,6}(t)} = \mathbf{LW}^{6,5} \times \mathbf{S}^{6,6} \times \dot{\mathbf{F}}^5(\mathbf{n}^5) \times \mathbf{LW}^{5,6}$$

Layer 4 is the end of the second subnet, so we now calculate the explicit derivatives with respect to the second subnet output.

$$\frac{\partial^e \mathbf{a}^4(t)}{\partial \mathbf{a}^4(t)} = \mathbf{I} \; ; \; \mathbf{S}^{4,4} \equiv \frac{\partial^e \mathbf{a}^4(t)}{\partial \mathbf{n}^4(t)} = \dot{\mathbf{F}}^4(\mathbf{n}^4)$$

$$\frac{\partial^e \mathbf{a}^4(t)}{\partial \mathbf{b}^4} = \dot{\mathbf{F}}^4(\mathbf{n}^4)\,;\ \frac{\partial^e \mathbf{a}^4(t)}{\partial \mathbf{LW}^{4,\,3}} = \dot{\mathbf{F}}^4(\mathbf{n}^4) \cdot [\mathbf{a}^3(t)]^T$$

Layer 3 is not the output of a subnet, so the resulting equations are:

$$\frac{\partial^e \mathbf{a}^4(t)}{\partial \mathbf{a}^3(t)} = \mathbf{LW}^{4,\,3} \times \mathbf{S}^{4,\,4}$$

$$\mathbf{S}^{3,\,4} \equiv \frac{\partial^e \mathbf{a}^4(t)}{\partial \mathbf{n}^3(t)} = \mathbf{LW}^{4,\,3} \times \mathbf{S}^{4,\,4} \times \dot{\mathbf{F}}^3(\mathbf{n}^3)$$

$$\frac{\partial^e \mathbf{a}^4(t)}{\partial \mathbf{b}^3} = \mathbf{LW}^{4,\,3} \times \mathbf{S}^{4,\,4} \times \dot{\mathbf{F}}^3(\mathbf{n}^3)$$

$$\frac{\partial^e \mathbf{a}^4(t)}{\partial \mathbf{LW}^{3,\,2}} = \mathbf{LW}^{4,\,3} \times \mathbf{S}^{4,\,4} \times \dot{\mathbf{F}}^3(\mathbf{n}^3) \times [\overset{\wedge}{\mathbf{a}}^{4,\,2}(t)]^T$$

$$\frac{\partial^e \mathbf{a}^4(t)}{\partial \mathbf{IW}^{3,\,1}} = \mathbf{LW}^{4,\,3} \times \mathbf{S}^{4,\,4} \times \dot{\mathbf{F}}^3(\mathbf{n}^3) \times [\overset{\wedge}{\mathbf{r}}(t)]^T$$

$$\frac{\partial^e \mathbf{a}^4(t)}{\partial \mathbf{LW}^{3,\,4}} = \mathbf{LW}^{4,\,3} \times \mathbf{S}^{4,\,4} \times \dot{\mathbf{F}}^3(\mathbf{n}^3) \times [\overset{\wedge}{\mathbf{a}}^{4,\,4}(t)]^T$$

Layer 3 has two delayed inputs from other subnets, so we must compute the following explicit derivatives:

$$\frac{\partial^e \mathbf{a}^4(t)}{\partial \overset{\wedge}{\mathbf{a}}^{4,\,2}(t)} = \mathbf{LW}^{4,\,3} \times \mathbf{S}^{4,\,4} \times \dot{\mathbf{F}}^3(\mathbf{n}^3) \times \mathbf{LW}^{3,\,2}$$

$$\frac{\partial^e \mathbf{a}^4(t)}{\partial \overset{\wedge}{\mathbf{a}}^{4,\,4}(t)} = \mathbf{LW}^{4,\,3} \times \mathbf{S}^{4,\,4} \times \dot{\mathbf{F}}^3(\mathbf{n}^3) \times \mathbf{LW}^{3,\,4}$$

Layer 2 is the end of the first subnet, so we apply the equations

$$\frac{\partial^e \mathbf{a}^2(t)}{\partial \mathbf{a}^2(t)} = \mathbf{I}\,;\ \mathbf{S}^{2,\,2} \equiv \frac{\partial^e \mathbf{a}^2(t)}{\partial \mathbf{n}^2(t)} = \dot{\mathbf{F}}^2(\mathbf{n}^2)$$

$$\frac{\partial^e \mathbf{a}^2(t)}{\partial \mathbf{b}^2} = \overset{\cdot 2}{\mathbf{F}}(\mathbf{n}^2) \; ; \; \frac{\partial^e \mathbf{a}^2(t)}{\partial \mathbf{LW}^{2,1}} = \overset{\cdot 2}{\mathbf{F}}(\mathbf{n}^2) \cdot [\mathbf{a}^1(t)]^\mathrm{T}$$

Layer 1 is not the output of a subnet, so we apply

$$\frac{\partial^e \mathbf{a}^2(t)}{\partial \mathbf{a}^1(t)} = \mathbf{LW}^{2,1} \times \mathbf{S}^{2,2}$$

$$\mathbf{S}^{1,2} \equiv \frac{\partial^e \mathbf{a}^2(t)}{\partial \mathbf{n}^1(t)} = \mathbf{LW}^{2,1} \times \mathbf{S}^{2,2} \times \overset{\cdot 1}{\mathbf{F}}(\mathbf{n}^1)$$

$$\frac{\partial^e \mathbf{a}^2(t)}{\partial \mathbf{b}^1} = \mathbf{LW}^{2,1} \times \mathbf{S}^{2,2} \times \overset{\cdot 1}{\mathbf{F}}(\mathbf{n}^1)$$

$$\frac{\partial^e \mathbf{a}^2(t)}{\partial \mathbf{IW}^{1,1}} = \mathbf{LW}^{2,1} \times \mathbf{S}^{2,2} \times \overset{\cdot 1}{\mathbf{F}}(\mathbf{n}^1) \times [\overset{\rightarrow}{\mathbf{r}}(t)]^\mathrm{T}$$

$$\frac{\partial^e \mathbf{a}^2(t)}{\partial \mathbf{LW}^{1,2}} = \mathbf{LW}^{2,1} \times \mathbf{S}^{2,2} \times \overset{\cdot 1}{\mathbf{F}}(\mathbf{n}^1) \times [\overset{\rightarrow}{\mathbf{a}}{}^{2,2}(t)]^\mathrm{T}$$

Layer 1 has one delayed input from another subnet, so we calculate

$$\frac{\partial^e \mathbf{a}^2(t)}{\partial \overset{\rightarrow}{\mathbf{a}}{}^{2,2}(t)} = \mathbf{LW}^{2,1} \times \mathbf{S}^{2,2} \times \overset{\cdot 1}{\mathbf{F}}(\mathbf{n}^1) \times \mathbf{LW}^{1,2}$$

At this point, we have the explicit derivatives for all the weights and biases in the system. These explicit derivatives are used with Eq. (25) – Eq. (27) to compute the dynamic derivatives we need for training the network. Notice that the solution to Eq. (27) is an input to Eq. (26) and Eq. (27) on the following time step. The solution to Eq. (26) is an input to Eq. (25) and Eq. (26) on the following time step. Finally, the solution to Eq. (25) is an input to Eq. (25) on the following time step.

After all the dynamic derivatives of the output of the system with respect to the weights and biases have been computed, we must calculate

$$\frac{\partial^e F}{\partial \mathbf{a}^6(t)} = -2(\mathbf{r}(t) - \mathbf{a}^6(t))$$

We can then compute the derivative of the cost function with respect to all the weights and biases using

$$\frac{\partial F}{\partial \mathbf{x}} = \frac{\partial F}{\partial \mathbf{x}} + \left(\frac{\partial \mathbf{a}^6(t)}{\partial \mathbf{x}}\right)^{\mathrm{T}} \frac{\partial^e F}{\partial \mathbf{a}^6(t)}$$

The process is repeated for each sample time in the training set.

After the network was trained, it was used to predict experimentally recorded noise. The result is shown in Figure 14. The data was collected in an acoustically "live" environment that was conducive to sound reflection. The prediction results for the LDRN, trained with full dynamic backpropagation, is compared to two other systems. The first comparison system is an LDRN that is trained only with static derivatives. The second comparison system is a non-recurrent LFFN system with a tapped-delay line at the input. Figure 14 shows the actual and predicted signals when full dynamic backpropagation is used to train the LDRN. Figure 15 is a plot of the errors between actual and predicted signals.

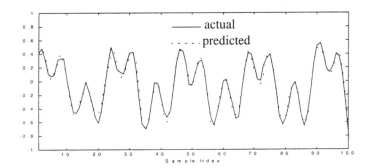

Figure 14. Prediction Results for LDRN with Full Dynamic Training

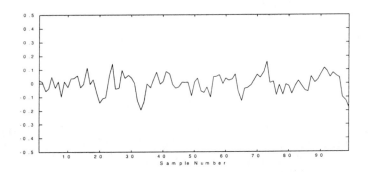

Figure 15. Errors for LDRN with Full Dynamic Training

The next experiment uses the same data, but only explicit (static) derivatives were used. The errors between actual and predicted signals are shown in Figure 16.

351

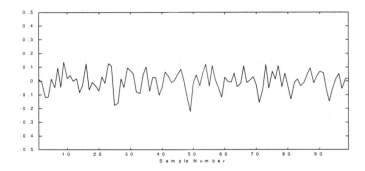

Figure 16. Prediction Errors for Static Training

The results shown in Figure 16 are reasonably good. We can see some degradation in performance, which might be critical in certain situations. In sound cancellation applications, for example, the differences would certainly be detectable by the human ear.

As a final experiment, the data was processed using an LFFN, with TDL input. The network size was adjusted so that the number of weights was comparable to the LDRN used in the previous experiment. The prediction errors for the LFFN are shown in Figure 17.

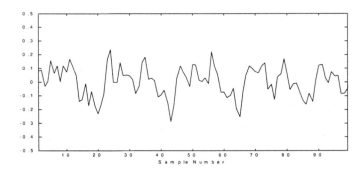

Figure 17. LFFN Prediction Results

The LFFN prediction performance is not too bad, but is significantly worse than the LDRN performance, when trained with full dynamic backpropagation. A summary of the simulation results is provided in Table 2. Notice the dramatic increase in floating point operations required to process each sample when dynamic training is used.

Prediction Method	Flops/Sample	Mean Squared Prediction Error
LDRN Full Dynamic Training	4.32×10^4	.0050
LDRN Static Training	5.19×10^3	.0087
LFFN	1.85×10^3	.0120

Table 2. Simulation Results

VII. SUMMARY

This chapter has discussed the training of recurrent neural networks for control and signal processing. When computing training gradients in recurrent networks, there are two different effects that we must account for. The first is a direct effect, which explains the immediate impact of a change in the weights on the output of the network at the current time. The second is an indirect effect, which accounts for the fact that some of the inputs to the network are previous network outputs, which are also functions of the weights. To account for this indirect effect we must use dynamic backpropagation.

This chapter has introduced the Layered Digital Recurrent Network (LDRN), which is a general class of recurrent network. A universal dynamic training algorithm for the LDRN was also developed. The LDRN was then applied to problems in control and signal processing. A number of practical issues must be addressed when applying dynamic training. Computational requirements for dynamic training can be much higher than those for static training, but static training is not as accurate and may not converge. The appropriate form of training to use (dynamic, static, or some combination) varies from problem to problem.

REFERENCES

Demuth, H. B. and Beale, M., *Users' Guide for the Neural Network Toolbox for MATLAB,* The Mathworks, Natick, MA, 1998.

Hagan, M.T., Demuth, H. B., Beale, M., *Neural Network Design,* PWS Publishing Company, Boston, 1996.

Narendra, K. S. and Parthasrathy, A. M., Identification and control for dynamic systems using neural networks, *IEEE Transactions on Neural Networks,* 1(1), 4, 1990.

Yang, W., *Neurocontrol Using Dynamic Learning,* Doctoral Thesis, Oklahoma State University, Stillwater, 1994.

Yang, W. and Hagan, M.T., Training recurrent networks, *Proceedings of the 7th Oklahoma Symposium on Artificial Intelligence,* Stillwater, 226, 1993.

Chapter 13

REMEMBERING HOW TO BEHAVE: RECURRENT NEURAL NETWORKS FOR ADAPTIVE ROBOT BEHAVIOR

T. Ziemke

Department of Computer Science
University of Skövde, 54128 Skövde, Sweden

I. INTRODUCTION

The use of artificial neural networks (ANNs) in robots and autonomous agents has during the 1990s become the subject of research in various disciplines, and a number of collections on different aspects of this topic have appeared [Bekey, 1993, Brooks, 1998, Omidvar, 1997, Sharkey, 1997, Ziemke, 1998, Ziemke, 1999]. Roboticists and ANN researchers naturally have an interest in neural robot control and learning, but furthermore this type of system has attracted much attention in embodied AI and cognitive science, as well as artificial life and adaptive behavior research. In particular recurrent neural nets (RNNs) have become the focus of much research, due to their capacity for dealing with temporal and sequential information - a capacity essential to any agent continually interacting with its environment.

Different theoretical perspectives on RNN-controlled agents and examples of recent experimental research are discussed in the following section. Section III will then investigate and compare the suitability of both first- and higher-order recurrent control architectures for the realization of adaptive robot behavior. Two experiments, in which the weights in recurrent control networks are evolved to solve tasks requiring the robot to exhibit state- or context-dependent behavior, are used to demonstrate and analyze different recurrent robot control architectures. The final section will summarize the discussion, present some conclusions, and point out directions for future research on RNNs for adaptive robot behavior.

II. BACKGROUND

As mentioned above, RNN-controlled robots have become the subject of interest in a number of fields of research. From an *engineering perspective,* ANNs in general have a number of properties that make them well suited to deal with the problems of robot control. They are typically considered to be robust to noise and capable to handle incomplete data, which allows them, to a higher degree than conventional algorithms, to deal with, for example, the uncertainties of a dynamic environment and the limitations of sensor measurements. Moreover, the capacity for continual adaptation allows ANN robot controllers to adapt to, for example, changing environments or failing hardware. Furthermore, ANNs are *model-free* techniques, i.e., they allow robots to learn from the interaction with their environment, and thus they do not require a designer to provide them with an explicit model of the world *a priori*. As Meeden has pointed out, the capacity for adaptation allows for "bottom-up construction" of robot control systems, i.e., it "allows the task demands rather than the designer's biases to be the primary force in the shaping of the system's development" [Meeden, 1996]. Thus, the flexibility of ANN controllers in many cases reduces the task of the designer to the choice of an appropriate control architecture.

These advantages of ANNs are exemplified well by the ALVINN project [Pomerleau, 1993], in which a vehicle is guided by an ANN. The controller, a feedforward ANN trained with the backpropagation algorithm [Rumelhart, 1986], receives as input the 30x32 pixels of the image obtained from a camera mounted on top of the vehicle and directed at the road ahead (see Figure 1). The network's output determines the steering direction. The network initially 'observes' a human driver and is trained on the data (visual input and steering direction) collected during this phase. After training, the network takes over the role of the human driver and steers the vehicle so as to keep it on the road. ALVINN has been shown to work in the real world, including two- and four-lane roads, crossings, dirt roads, and highway traffic at speeds of up to 55 miles per hour.

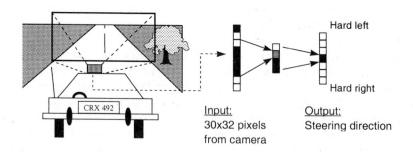

Figure 1. A schematic illustration[1] of the ALVINN vehicle and its control network.

The ALVINN example illustrates the power of standard feedforward networks as well as their limitations. The control network solves a difficult pattern recognition task which certainly would have required complex image preprocessing, the use of line extraction algorithms, etc., if programmed by a human designer. However, due to its use of a feedforward network ALVINN remains a purely reactive system. This means that it has no notion of the

---

[1] In reality ALVINN's control network contains about 1000 units.

temporal aspects of its task and will always react to its visual input in the same fashion, independent of the current context. It neither knows where it came from, nor can it predict what will happen in the future or navigate toward a goal. The reason the systems nevertheless solves a clearly non-trivial task is that the world it is situated in provides it with the necessary continuity: The road is always 'out there' and functions as a scaffold 'guiding' ALVINN such that the 'navigation' task can be solved in a purely reactive fashion.

For most mobile robots, however, the environment is not that benevolent in the sense that the 'solution' is already built into it. Often they have to solve tasks like homing or finding a goal location, but are faced with the problem of *perceptual aliasing*. That means, many locations in the environment look the same from the robot's current point of view, such that they cannot be distinguished without knowledge/memory of where the robot came from. Moreover, as Meeden [Meeden, 1996] has pointed out, robot/agent problems are often defined in terms of abstract goals rather than specific input-output pairs. Thus, moment-to-moment guidance, as provided in ALVINN's case, is typically not available for a learning robot since for a given situation there is not necessarily only one right or wrong action, and even if there were, it would typically not be known *a priori* [Meeden, 1996].

Furthermore, robots often have to exhibit adaptive behavior to deal with requirements changing over time. Meeden [Meeden, 1993, Meeden, 1996], for example, discusses the case of Carbot, a toy-car-like robotic vehicle placed in a rectangular environment approximately 20 times its own size. Apart from the 'low-level' goal of avoiding bumping into the walls surrounding the environment, Carbot's 'high-level' goal periodically changes between having to approach a light source placed in one corner of the environment and having to avoid it. This means that it should, depending on the current goal, maximize or minimize the readings of two light sensors directed towards the front of the vehicle. Apart from that, Carbot is equipped only with digital touch sensors at the front and the back of the vehicle which detect collisions when they occur, but do not give any advance warning. The task is further complicated by the fact that the smallest dimension of the environment is smaller than Carbot's turning radius. The vehicle can therefore only execute a 180-degree turn in a series of backward and forward movements.

Meeden *et al.* [Meeden, 1993] have carried out extensive experimental comparisons of different feedforward and recurrent control architectures for varying Carbot tasks. The basic recurrent control architecture (Figure 2) was similar to Elman's Simple Recurrent Network [Elman, 1990]. The network's inputs came from light and touch sensors (plus in some experiments an extra input indicating the current goal), its outputs controlled the motor settings, and the hidden unit activation values were copied back and used as extra inputs in the next time step. Not surprisingly, the experimental results show that RNNs consistently outperformed feedforward networks.

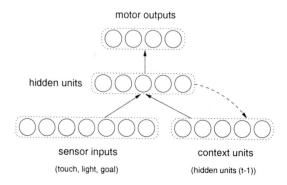

Figure 2. Meeden's recurrent robot control architecture. Solid arrows represent fully connected layer of weights between two layers of units (indicated by surrounding dotted lines). Hidden unit values are fed back via a 1:1 copy connection (dashed arrow) and used as extra inputs in the next time step. Adapted from Meeden [1996].

Meeden *et al.* have analyzed the recurrent control networks and shown that they utilize their internal state (i.e., the hidden unit activation values) to carry out behavioral sequences corresponding to particular motion strategies instead of merely reacting to the current input. For example, to avoid the light the robot would (starting from a position facing the light) first move backwards for a couple of time steps (into the center of the environment) and then carry out a series of alternating forward right and backward left movements until it faces away from the light. Thus, it executes a multi-turn strategy in the center of the environment, which overcomes the problem that the environment's smallest dimension is smaller than its own turning radius. Meeden *et al.* therefore argue that Carbot's behavior is *plan-like* in the sense that (a) it associates abstract goals with *sequences* of primitive actions, (b) the behavior can be described in hierarchical terms (cf. above), and (c) the robot maintains its overall strategy even when flexibly reacting to the environmental conditions. For example, when encountering a wall while carrying out the above light avoidance strategy, it will react to the wall first and then return to its high-level strategy. On the other hand, the behavior is not plan-like in the traditional sense that the robot explicitly anticipates the future, and the number and complexity of Carbot's strategies are admittedly limited. Meeden has further discussed the relation to planning in subsequent work [Meeden, 1994, Meeden, 1996].

For *artificial intelligence* (AI) research the use of ANN-controlled robots, due to their capacity for bottom-up construction of control systems, has received much attention as a methodology for the study of intelligent behavior in artifacts. Traditional AI research, beginning in the mid-1950s, largely ignored earlier work on robotic/cybernetic creatures, such as the work of Grey Walter [Grey Walter, 1950, Grey Walter, 1953]. Instead, AI turned to the computer as a model of mind. In the functionalist framework of *cognitivism* and the *computer metaphor for mind,* having a body, living or artificial, is regarded as a low-level implementational issue. Thus the study of intelligence was largely separated from the interaction between agent and environment, and until the mid-1980s there was relatively little interest in robots in AI research. Instead research focused on internal *representations* corresponding to external objects ('knowledge'), in particular symbolic representations, and the computational, i.e., formally defined and implementation-independent, processes operating on these representations ('thought'). Problems with this disembodied view of intelligence, which separated internal representations in AI programs from the world they were supposed to represent, were not widely recognized until the 1980s. Searle [Searle, 1980] and Harnad [Harnad, 1990] pointed out that, because there are no causal connections between the internal symbols and the external world, purely computational AI systems lack *intentionality*, i.e., the capacity to relate their internal processes and representations to the external world. During the 1980s many AI researchers therefore (re-) turned to the study of the interaction between agents and their environments. Researchers like Brooks [Brooks 1986, Brooks, 1991] and Wilson [Wilson, 1985, Wilson, 1991] suggested a bottom-up approach to AI, also referred to as *New AI* or *behavior-based AI*, as an alternative to the representationalist/computationalist framework of cognitivism. In particular, it was argued that AI should be approached first and foremost through the study of the interaction between *autonomous agents* and their environments by means of perception and action. For a more detailed review of the bottom-up approach to AI see Ziemke [1998].

Brooks therefore approached the study of intelligence through the construction of physical robots, which were embedded in and interacting with their environment by means of a number of behavioral modules working in parallel in a so-called *subsumption architecture*. Each of these behavioral modules was implemented as a finite state machine receiving sensory input from some of the robot's receptors and controlling some of its effectors. While the general idea of a parallel and distributed control architecture was generally accepted, a major criticism of Brooks' original subsumption architecture is that it does not allow for learning. Hence, this type of robot, although autonomous in the sense that during run-time it interacts with the environment on its own, i.e., independent of an observer, still remains heteronomous in the sense that its control mechanism is predetermined by the designer. A number of researchers have therefore pointed out that a necessary element of an artificial agent's autonomy would be the capacity to determine and adapt, at least partly, the mechanisms underlying its behavior [Boden, 1996, Steels, 1995, Ziemke, 1997, Ziemke, 1998]. Much research effort during the 1990s has therefore been invested into making robots 'more autonomous' by providing them with the capacity for self-organization. Typically these approaches are based on the use of computational learning techniques to allow agents to adapt the internal parameters of their control mechanisms. Thus, the use of ANN-controlled robots using learning and/or evolutionary adaptation techniques has become a standard methodology in bottom-up AI research.

From a *cognitive science point of view,* adaptive ANN-controlled robots do not only have the practical advantages described above from an engineering and AI perspective, but they also offer a novel approach to the study of the embodied and situated nature of cognitive processes [Clark, 1997, Sharkey, 1998]. In particular the parallel and distributed nature of weight and unit representations in ANNs, and the fact that these representations can be formed in interaction with an environment, make ANN-controlled robots an interesting approach to the study of cognitive representation. Unlike traditional AI, connectionists do not promote symbolic representations that mirror a pre-given external reality. Rather, they stress self-organization of an adaptive flow of signals between simple processing units in interaction with an environment, which is compatible with an interactivist [Bickhard, 1995] or experiential [Sharkey, 1997] view of representation, and thus offers an alternative approach to the study of cognitive representation.

However, in most connectionist work the 'environment' is still reduced to input and output values. That means, ANNs, unlike real nervous systems, are typically not embedded in the context of an agent and its environment. Thus, although in a technically different fashion, connectionists were, like cognitivists, mainly concerned with explaining cognitive phenomena as separated from agent-world interaction. Hence, they initially focused on modeling of isolated cognitive capacities, such as the transformation of English verbs from the present to the past tense [Rumelhart, 1986] or the prediction of letters or words in sequences [Elman, 1990]. Thus, early connectionism was mostly concerned with the self-organization of weights to match given input-output pairs, whereas making the connection between inputs, outputs, and internal representations and the actual world they were supposed to represent was still left to the observer. The situation, however, changes fundamentally as soon as ANNs are used as robot controllers, i.e., 'artificial nervous systems' mapping a robot's sensory inputs to motor outputs. Then the network can actually, by means of the robot body (sensors and effectors), interact with the physical objects in its environment, independent of an observer's interpretation or mediation. Dorffner [Dorffner, 1997] has therefore suggested the approach of *Radical Connectionism*, i.e., the use of ANNs for control of and learning in robotic agents, as a natural testbed and a step forward from a *connectionist point of view*.

RNNs play a central role in such approaches to the study of cognitive representation. This is because they account for the (long-term) representation of learning experience in connection weights as well as the (short-term) representation of the controlled agent's current context or immediate past in the form of internal feedback. Peschl [Peschl, 1996] has pointed out that RNNs, like real nervous systems, are "structure determined" (also see Maturana [1980]), which means that, unlike ALVINN, their reaction to environmental stimuli always depends on the system's current state (or structure) and thus is never determined by the input alone. Peschl refers to this as the "*autonomy* of a representational system."

III. RECURRENT NEURAL NETWORKS FOR ADAPTIVE ROBOT BEHAVIOR

A. MOTIVATION

The vast majority of recurrent neural architectures for learning and control of robots and autonomous agents (e.g., [Beer, 1990, Biro, 1998, Meeden, 1996, Nolfi, 1999, Tani, 1996, Tani, 1998, Ulbricht, 1996]) make use of *first-order feedback*. That means, certain neuron activation values are, as in Meeden's architecture (see Figure 2), fed back and used as extra inputs to some of the neurons (typically at the input layer) in a later time step (typically the next one). *Higher-order feedback*, on the other hand, typically modulates/adapts connection weights and/or biases (see, e.g., Figure 3). Unlike in other areas, such as (formal) language recognition, there are only very few cases where higher-order networks have been used as robot control architectures. This section will therefore demonstrate and analyze both first- and higher-order recurrent neural robot control architectures experimentally. It should be noted in advance that first- and higher-order networks are computationally equivalent [Siegelmann, 1995, Siegelmann, 1998]. That means, every task solved by a higher-order RNN could also be solved by some first-order net. Hence, in the experiments discussed in the following, higher-order RNN-controlled robots will not do anything that could not, at least in theory, be done by first-order RNN-controlled ones. Computational equivalence of network architectures in theory, however, does not say much about their suitability to solve particular tasks in practice. The latter will therefore be investigated here experimentally.

Some of the author's own work [Ziemke, 1996a, Ziemke, 1996b, Ziemke, 1996c, Ziemke, 1997, Ziemke 1998] has been concerned with recurrent robot control architectures inspired by Pollack's *Sequential Cascaded Networks* (SCNs), also referred to as *dynamical recognizers*, which were originally used for formal language recognition [Pollack, 1987, Pollack, 1991]. This architecture (Figure 3) consists of (a) a *function network* mapping input to output and an internal state, and (b) a *context network* mapping the internal state to the next time step's function network weights (including biases). Thus, this type of network utilizes a second-order, multiplicative type of feedback, with the effect that the function network's input-output mapping can change from time step to time step in a context- or state-dependent fashion. The experiments documented in the following subsections will illustrate how this mechanism can be used to realize adaptive *behavioral dispositions* in robots.

B. ROBOT AND SIMULATOR

The experiments discussed here have been carried out using a simulation of a Khepera miniature mobile robot. The Khepera [Mondada, 1993] has a circular body with a diameter of 55 mm and is equipped with eight infrared proximity sensors with a range of approximately 50 mm, six of them at the front

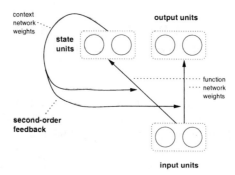

Figure 3. Sequential Cascaded Network (SCN), a second-order recurrent architecture consisting of (a) a function network mapping input to output and internal state, and (b) a context network mapping the internal state to the next time step's function network weights. The solid arrows represent a fully connected layer of weights between two layers of units (indicated by surrounding dotted lines).

the back. It has two motors, which independently control two wheels; one to the right and one to the left. The wheels can spin forward and backward independently, such that the robot can turn on the spot if they spin in opposite directions.

The robot simulator used here is a slightly adapted version of the one presented by Miglino [1995]. The simulation is based on sensor measurements obtained from a real Khepera robot. It has been shown in a number of papers, (e.g., Nolfi, [1997]), that the simulation of infrared sensors and motors is sufficiently realistic to allow the transfer of controllers trained in simulation to the real robot. An additional ground sensor (see details below) has been used here which is not present on the physical robot, such that the experiments presented here could not be validated on the real robot. Random noise, uniformly distributed in the range of +/- 10% of the maximum sensor readings, has been added to all sensor measurements.

C. ROBOT CONTROL ARCHITECTURES

In the experiments documented here the five different ANN architectures shown in Figure 4 have been used to control the Khepera robot. All of the networks receive five inputs from the robot's sensors (normalized to values between 0 and 1; see details below), and they produce two motor outputs directly controlling the robot's wheels. The output units use the logistic activation function, i.e., the outputs are between 0 and 1, with 0 corresponding to full speed backward rotation, 0.5 corresponding to no motion, and 1 corresponding to full speed forward rotation.

Architecture A is a standard feedforward multilayer perceptron with three hidden units. B is a recurrent network with two memory units, which are used as extra inputs in the next time step (first-order feedback). C is similar to B, but uses an additional layer of three hidden units. The hidden units in A and C use the logistic activation function, such that activation values lie between 0 and 1. D is a Sequential Cascaded Network with two state units, like the one shown in

Figure 3. E is a novel variation of the SCN (D), here also referred to as *Extended Sequential Cascaded Network* (ESCN). It has an additional decision unit, which in every time step determines whether to use feedback. The idea behind this extension is that the robot should be able to decide selectively when to change its sensorimotor mapping, instead of (re-) setting the function network weights in each and every time step. Thus, the context network is only used to adapt the function network when the decision unit activation exceeds a certain threshold (here 0.5; the decision unit uses the logistic activation function), otherwise the weights and biases in the function network remain unchanged. The state units in D and E also use the logistic activation function. The output units of the context networks in D and E (cf., Figure 3), however, use a linear activation function such that the function network weights and biases (which are the outputs of the context network) are not limited to values between 0 and 1.

D. EXPERIMENT 1
1. Environment and task

Figure 5 shows the simulated robot in the environment used in experiment 1. The robot is placed in a rectangular environment of 1000 mm x 600 mm, surrounded by walls (the straight lines), which contains a zone (the large circle) outside of which it should keep moving while avoiding collisions, whereas once it has entered the zone it should simply not leave it anymore. The robot is initially placed with a random orientation in a random position outside the zone, and during learning it is punished for collisions and rewarded strongly for every time step it spends in the zone (for details see below). Moreover, while outside the zone, it is rewarded for moving as quickly and straight as possible and keeping away from walls. It uses four infrared proximity sensors at the front[2]

---

[2] The left and the right pairs of the six front sensors are averaged and used as if they were one sensor.

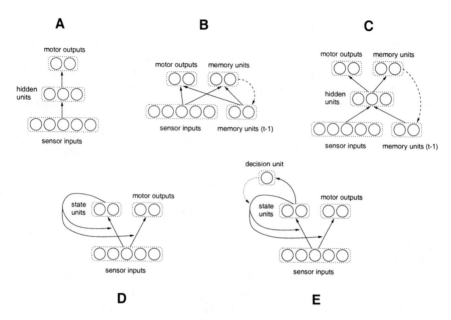

Figure 4. ANN robot control architectures used in the experiments. All networks receive input from the four proximity sensors and the ground sensor and produce two outputs directly controlling the left and right wheels' motors (see text for details). In all cases the solid arrows represent fully connected layer of weights between two layers of units (indicated by surrounding dotted lines). The dashed arrows represent 1:1 copy connections (without weights). A: Feedforward network with three hidden units. B: Recurrent network with two memory units, which are used as extra inputs in the next time step. C: Like B, but with three hidden units. D: Sequential Cascaded Network with two state units (for details see Figure 3). E: Extended Sequential Cascaded Network: like D, but extended with a decision unit, which determines in each time step whether to use feedback.

and a ground sensor,[3] which is only fully active in the time step when the robot passes the black line marking the zone border. As mentioned above, these five sensors provide input to the controller networks (see Figure 4), and the network's two output units directly control the speeds of the two wheels.

The experimental setup is intentionally kept very simple in order to illustrate as clearly as possible the basic mechanisms of behavioral adaptation in recurrent robot controllers. A significantly more complex scenario will be used in experiment 2 below. However, although this task is fairly simple, it clearly requires some form of memory. Since the ground sensor does not tell the robot whether it is inside or outside the zone, but only when it passes the borderline, the robot needs to 'remember' on which side of the border it currently is. This is necessary, for example, in order to be able to react to the absence of significant sensory stimuli in two completely different ways inside and outside the zone (standstill or circling vs. searching forward motion). Hence, the feedforward

---

[3] As mentioned above, the ground sensor is not actually available on the real robot. A possible physical implementation would be a light sensor directed at the ground below the robot, capable of distinguishing white and black ground.

networks (architecture A), in both experiments, cannot be expected to achieve the same level of performance as the recurrent networks. They are nevertheless included in the comparisons to illustrate the difference that the use of feedback makes.

Figure 5. Simulated Khepera robot in environment 1. The large circle indicates the zone the robot should enter and stay in. The small circle represents the robot, and the lines inside the robot indicate position and direction of the infrared proximity sensors used in experiments 1 and 2.

2. Network training

Recurrent networks are known to be difficult to train with, e.g., gradient-descent methods such as standard backpropagation [Rumelhart, 1986] or even backpropagation through time [Werbos, 1990]. They are often sensitive to the fine details of the training algorithm, e.g. the number of time steps unrolled in the case of backpropagation through time (e.g., [Mozer, 1989]). For example, in an autonomous agent context, Rylatt [1998] showed, for one particular task, that with some enhancements Simple Recurrent Networks [Elman, 1990] could be trained to handle long-term dependencies in a continuous domain, thus contradicting the results of Ulbricht [1996] who had argued the opposite. In an extension of the work discussed in the previous section, Meeden [1996] experimentally compared the training of recurrent control networks with (a) a local search method, a version of backpropagation adapted for reinforcement learning, and (b) a global method, an evolutionary algorithm. The results showed that the evolutionary algorithm in several cases found strategies, which the local method did not find. In particular, when only delayed reinforcement was available to the learning robot, the evolutionary method performed significantly better due to the fact that it did not at all rely on moment-to-moment guidance [Meeden, 1996].

In the experiments documented here, all control networks have therefore been trained using an evolutionary algorithm very similar to the one used by Nolfi [1997], a genetic algorithm [Holland, 1975] evolving an initially randomized population of 100 individuals over 5000 generations. For architectures A, B, and C the artificial genotype of each individual encodes all the connection weights (including biases) of a complete control network as a single bitstring. Each real-valued weight (between -10.0 and $+10.0$) is represented by a string of 8 bits. For architectures D and E, in which function network weights change dynamically, the genotype encodes the connection weights in the context network plus initial

365

state unit activation values, such that the initial function network weights can be derived by propagating the initial state through the context network.

To evaluate their fitness each individual of every generation is used to control the robot during a trial period of 400 time steps, starting from a random position outside the zone and with a random orientation. While outside the zone individuals score between 0.0 and 1.0 fitness points per time step, being rewarded for moving as fast and as straight as possible while minimizing encounters with walls. While inside the zone, they simply receive 100 fitness points for every time step they remain inside. To encourage the selective use of feedback in networks of architecture E, they only score fitness points during those time steps when they are not using feedback, i.e., when they are not using the context network to re-set function network weights and biases. For all networks, the points collected during the 400 time steps are summed up at the end of the evaluation period to determine the individual's overall fitness. Of the 100 individuals the 20 'fittest' ones of each generation are selected, and each of them produces five 'offspring' which will be part of the next generation, which thus again consists of 100 individuals. 'Reproduction' is carried out by creating a copy of the artificial genotype with a mutation probability of 1% for each of the bits. The reason that only mutation, but no crossover, is used here is that several researchers, e.g., Meeden [1996], have shown/argued that the use of crossover does not improve performance when evolving ANN robot controllers. This was also the case in the experiments of Nolfi [1997], from whom also the other evolutionary algorithm parameter settings used here (population size, mutation rate, bitstring representation) have been adopted. Initial experiments were carried out with a variety of alternative parameter settings; none of which, however, resulted in significantly better results. For both experiments 1 and 2, ten evolutionary runs, starting from different random initial populations, were carried out for each of the five architectures.

3. Results

Networks of architectures B, C, D, and E quickly evolved to robustly solve the task. The evolutionary process was nevertheless continued for 5000 generations to ensure that evolution had converged. Networks of architecture E exhibit best overall performance, although they are not able/allowed to score points while using feedback (cf. previous subsection). For each of the 5000 generations Figure 6 shows, averaged over all ten evolutionary runs for architecture E, the fitness of the best individual, the mean fitness of the 20 best individuals selected for reproduction, and the mean fitness of all individuals in the population. As the figure shows, the best individuals achieve a fitness score around 30000, corresponding to approximately 300 time steps (out of 400) spent in the zone.

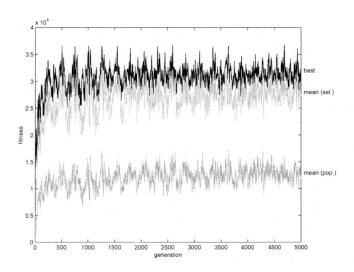

Figure 6. Fitness values for networks of architecture E in experiment 1. For each generation the figure shows the fitness of the best individual ('best'), the mean fitness of the 20 best individuals selected for reproduction ('mean (sel.)'), and the mean fitness of all individuals in the population ('mean (pop.)'). The values shown are rolling averages over three generations, averaged over all ten evolutionary runs.

Table 1 illustrates the performance differences between architecture E and the other architectures using the three fitness measures illustrated in Figure 6. The values shown are the average differences between the architectures during all 5000 generations (and in parentheses the differences during the last 500 generations, which allows the comparison of already trained networks, relatively independent of possible differences in learning speed). Thus, for example, the best individuals in the populations of architecture A have a fitness that is on average 40.8% lower than that of networks of architecture E during all 5000 generations, and 40.1% lower during the last 500 generations.

	Best individuals	mean fitness [20 selected]	Mean fitness [whole population]
A	-40.8% (-40.1%)	-51.2% (-49.5%)	-44.5% (-42.0%)
B	-5.5% (-6.6%)	-1.6% (-2.7%)	+6.6% (+3.8%)
C	-7.0% (-10.4%)	-4.4% (-8.9%)	-10.1% (-14.4%)
D	-2.2% (-3.4%)	-2.1% (-4.7%)	-0.7% (-3.2%)

Table 1. Performance differences between architecture E and other architectures in experiment 1. All differences are stated in percent of the performance of architecture E (as illustrated in Figure 7). Values are averaged over all 5000 generations (in parentheses over the last 500 generations) of all ten evolutionary runs.

Table 1 shows that architectures A, B, C and D perform worse than E according to basically all of the three performance measures. The only exception is that networks of architecture B actually achieve a higher mean fitness when looking at the whole population; they do however achieve lower values when compared to the best networks. Not surprisingly, the feedforward networks (A) perform significantly worse than all recurrent architectures. Because of their lack of feedback they cannot 'remember' whether they have passed the circle border or not. Recurrent architectures B, C, and D, on the other hand, in experiment 1 come relatively close to the performance of E.

4. Analysis

This subsection will present some analysis of different recurrent networks successfully solving the task. All networks analyzed here are taken from the final generations, and they are representative of how networks of the respective architecture evolved to solve the task, although there are of course differences between individuals in a population as well as between populations in different evolutionary runs. Figure 7 illustrates the performance of a successful robot controller of architecture B. The robot's position at each time step is indicated by a circle. The robot in this case starts off facing the wall to the left, moves forward at maximum speed, correctly avoids the walls twice by turning right, finally enters the zone after about 120 time steps, and keeps spinning in place there for the remaining time steps, thus maximizing its fitness.

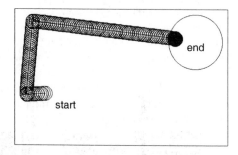

Figure 7. Example trajectory for a robot controller (architecture B) in experiment 1. The robot's position in each time step is indicated by a circle, and its heading by the line inside that circle. The robot correctly avoids the walls twice by turning right, enters the zone, and keeps spinning in place.

Figure 8 further illustrates the robot controller's performance, showing the unit activation values, and the fitness points collected during the 400 time steps. Figure 9 shows the controller network's connection weights (including biases). Together Figures 8 and 9 allow some analysis of how the robot controller solves the task. Initially the robot receives no sensory input, apart from noise, as there are no objects nearby. Due to the strongly positive biases for both left and right motor output unit (see Figure 9), the robot moves forward at maximum speed as long as possible. Twice it quickly avoids walls appearing at the front/left (see Figures 8 and 7), by temporarily inhibiting the right motor using the large negative weights between the sensors and the right motor output unit (see Figure 9). This makes the right wheel spin backwards, which in combination with the left wheel's continued full speed forward motion makes the robot turn away from the wall. So far both memory units have been inactive due to their negative biases. But, when entering the zone, the ground sensor activates memory unit 1 through the large positive weight between the two, and during the remaining time steps (when the ground sensor no longer detects the borderline) memory unit 1 keeps (re-)activating itself using a large positive weight (see Figure 9). Memory unit 1 also inhibits the right motor through a large negative weight (see Figure 9). Thus, the robot in the absence of significant sensory stimuli keeps spinning in place, such that maximum fitness points can be collected for the rest of the evaluation period.

```
output, left motor
output, right motor
sensor, left
sensor, front left
sensor, front right
sensor, right
sensor, ground
memory unit 1
memory unit 2
fitness
```

Figure 8. Activation and fitness values during the 400 time steps of the evaluation trial for the robot controller (architecture B) illustrated in Figure 8 (experiment 1). Activation values are illustrated as vertical black lines whose height corresponds to the represented value. All unit activation values lie between 0 and 1 (full height black line) (NB. In the case of the motors 0 corresponds to full speed backward rotation, 0.5 to no motion, and 1 to full speed forward rotation). The fitness value is either 0 (no line), between 0 and 1 (short line), or 100 (full height black line).

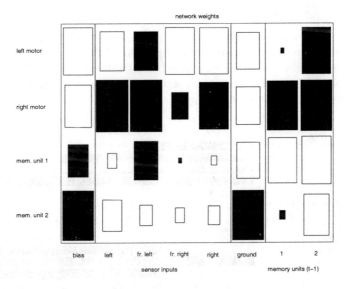

Figure 9. Connection weights (including biases) for the robot controller (architecture B) illustrated in Figures 7 and 8. Positive weights are shown as white rectangles and negative ones in black, with the rectangles' areas corresponding to the weight values.

Networks of architecture C (B plus an additional hidden layer) typically evolved to solve the task in a way very similar the one described above. Since architecture C in experiment 1 actually achieved slightly worse performance than the theoretically less powerful B (see Table 1), it is not discussed in further detail here. Figure 10 instead illustrates the performance of a successful robot controller of architecture D (Sequential Cascaded Network). The robot uses a similar behavioral strategy as the one above, although internally realized differently as we will see. The robot starts off in the same position, moves forward at maximum speed, correctly avoids the walls twice, this time by turning left, finally enters the zone after about 110 time steps, and, as before, keeps spinning in place there.

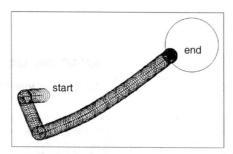

Figure 10. Example trajectory for a robot controller (architecture D) in experiment 1. The robot correctly avoids the walls twice by turning left, then enters the zone and stays there, spinning in place.

Figure 11 further illustrates the robot controller's performance, showing as before the unit activations and fitness values during the evaluation period, but now also the motor units' biases, which in architecture D can be adapted dynamically by the context network. Figures 12 and 13 show the weights in the function network, both outside and inside the zone.

Figure 11. Activation values, motor biases, and fitness points during the 400 time steps of the evaluation trial for the robot controller (architecture D) illustrated in Figure 10 (experiment 1). Biases are shown in the range of –10 (no line) to +10 (full height black line).

Together these figures provide some insight into how the second-order network (D) solves the task. Initially, outside the zone, state unit 1 is inactive, due to a negative bias, while state unit 2 is active, due to a positive bias. The function network, which results from propagating the state unit values through the context network, has strongly positive biases for both left and right motor (see Figure 12). This makes the robot move forward fast in the absence of significant sensory stimuli. When encountering a wall at the front/right the left motor output unit is inhibited by the sensors, such that the robot avoids the wall by turning left. Outside the zone state unit 1 is inactive (see Figure 11), but it is activated by the ground sensor through a large positive weight (see Figure 12) when passing the borderline. The change in state unit activation leads to a different weight configuration (see Figure 13) in the function network from the next time step. Now both state units have positive biases, and the left motor has a negative bias while the bias for the right motor remains strongly positive. Accordingly, the robot now keeps spinning in place inside the zone and thus collects maximum fitness points during the rest of the evaluation period.

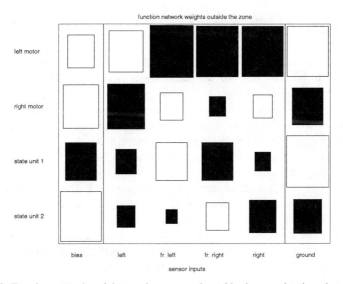

Figure 12. Function network weights as they are used outside the zone by the robot controller (architecture D) illustrated in Figures 11 and 12.

Since the Sequential Cascaded Network (architecture D) makes use of its context network in every time step, the state units have to reflect the current requirements on the function network. In the above case, for example, there have to be two different internal states corresponding to different weight configurations in the function network, embodying appropriate sensorimotor

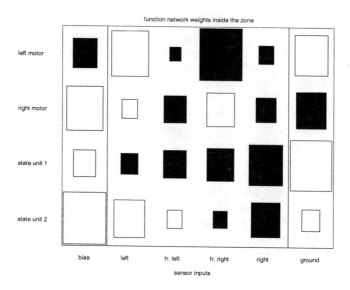

Figure 13. Function network weights as they are used inside the zone by the robot controller (architecture D) illustrated in Figures 10 and 11.

mappings for 'outside' and 'inside.' In the Extended Sequential Cascaded Network (architecture E), on the other hand, where the extra decision unit selectively determines whether to use the context network or not, there is not necessarily a 1-1 mapping between current state unit activations and current function network weight configuration. This is illustrated in the following example of a successful robot controller of architecture E. The trajectory taken by the robot is very similar to the one shown in Figure 7, and therefore not shown here again. Activation and fitness values are shown in Figure 14. It can be seen that state unit 2 is active during both forward motion outside the zone and spinning inside the zone, whereas it is less active during turning/spinning outside the zone. State unit 1, on the other hand, is only fully active while passing the borderline. The decision unit is apparently only active while turning away from walls and while passing the borderline, i.e., feedback through the context network is actually only used in these situations.

Figures 15 and 16 show the function network weight configurations as they are used outside (during forward motion) and inside the zone, respectively. Again, it can be seen that both motors have strongly positive biases during forward motion outside the zone, whereas one of them is negative inside the zone, leading to spinning in place, as in the previous examples. The state units, on the other hand, do not change their biases significantly. State unit 1 is activated slightly by sensory stimuli at the left/front, but only activated fully by the ground sensor through the large positive weight between them (see Figure 15).

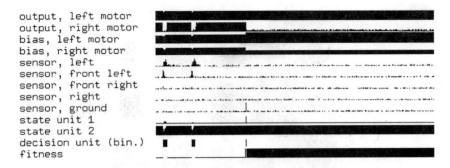

```
output, left motor
output, right motor
bias, left motor
bias, right motor
sensor, left
sensor, front left
sensor, front right
sensor, right
sensor, ground
state unit 1
state unit 2
decision unit (bin.)
fitness
```

Figure 14. Activation values, motor biases, and fitness points during the 400 time steps of the evaluation trial for a robot controller of architecture E (experiment 1). The decision unit is illustrated as rounded to a binary value, with a black line corresponding to an active decision unit (activation exceeds 0.5, in which case the context network will be used) and white corresponding to an inactive decision unit (resulting in no use of feedback).

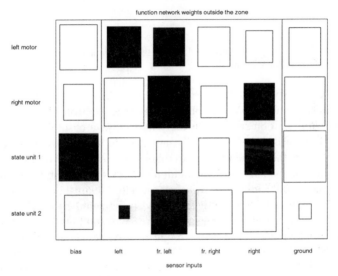

function network weights outside the zone

left motor

right motor

state unit 1

state unit 2

bias   left   fr. left   fr. right   right   ground

sensor inputs

Figure 15. Function network weights as they are used during forward motion outside the zone by the robot controller (architecture E) illustrated in Figure 14.

E. EXPERIMENT 2

1. Environment, task and training

Having illustrated the general workings of first- and higher-order RNN control of adaptive robot behavior with a simple example above, we can now turn to a more complex task. The setup for experiment 2 is illustrated in Figure 18. Again, the robot, using the same sensors and control architectures as in experiment 1, is placed in an environment of 1000 mm x 600 mm, which now contains 11 identical round objects, five of them inside a zone and six of them

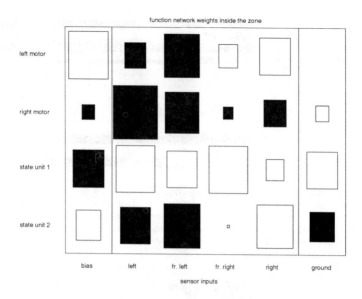

Figure 16. Function network weights as they are used inside the zone by the robot controller (architecture E) illustrated in Figure 15.

outside. As in experiment 1, the robot is initially given a random orientation and placed in a random position outside the zone. The robot's task is to avoid collisions with the objects outside the zone (those are solid objects), but to 'collect' those inside the zone by 'hitting' them, which makes them disappear immediately. In this experiment the robot receives –500 fitness points for collisions outside the zone (possibly multiple times if persisting to bump into the obstacle) and +500 points for 'collisions' inside, but in this case always only once per 'collected' object since it disappears immediately. The robot is not punished for leaving the zone, but inside it receives 0.0 to 4.0 fitness points per time step for moving as fast and as straight as possible and approaching objects. Outside the zone, as in experiment 1, the only positive reward the robot can get is 0.0 to 1.0 fitness points per time step for moving as fast and as straight as possible and staying away from objects.

Apart from the different fitness function/reward scheme, training of the control networks is carried out exactly as described for experiment 1, with the exception that every individual now in each generation is given two evaluation trials of 400 time steps each, starting from different random positions outside the zone.

2. Results

As for experiment 1, the evolutionary process was carried out for 5000 generations, although highly fit and robust control networks evolved far more quickly than that. Again, the Extended Sequential Cascaded Networks (architecture E) exhibited best overall performance. For each of the 5000

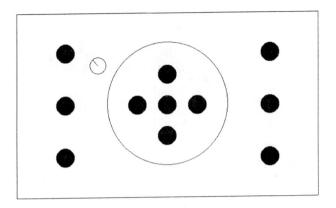

Figure 17. Simulated Khepera robot in environment 2. The black circles represent objects, which are to be avoided outside the zone (indicated by the large circle), but to be 'collected' inside.

generations, Figure 18 shows, averaged over all ten evolutionary runs for architecture E, the fitness of the best individual and the mean fitness of the 20 best individuals selected for reproduction. It turned out that the better an architecture did on these two performance measures, the lower was actually its mean fitness over the whole population. The latter values were strongly negative, due to the fact that some of the controllers in each generation persisted to bump into an object outside the zone, thus collecting −500 points in every time step. This indicates that there is a thin line between highly fit and highly unfit robot controllers, in the sense that a slight mutation of an individual, which achieved high fitness in generation t, can easily result in an individual, which performs very badly in generation t+1. Given the large difference in reward for hitting identical objects inside and outside the zone respectively, this is perhaps not too surprising. The mean fitness of the population was therefore not used as a performance measure in experiment 2. Instead, Figure 19 illustrates the increase in the number of correctly collected objects during the 5000 generations, averaged over the whole population in all ten evolutionary runs for architecture E. It can be seen that the average evolved robot controller collects only about three objects (out of a maximum of ten; five in each of the two evaluation trials). It should, however, be remembered that each generation consists of 100 mutants, i.e., random mutations of (relatively) successful networks, of which only the best 20 are selected. As Figure 18 shows, the 20 best individuals in the end achieve, on average, a fitness score around 3700, corresponding to approximately seven collected objects, and the very best ones often manage to collect all ten objects.

Table 2 illustrates the performance differences between architecture E and the other architectures using the three fitness measures illustrated in Figures 18 and 20. As in Table 1, the values shown are the average differences between the architectures during all 5000 generations (and in parentheses the differences during the last 500 generations, which allows the comparison of already trained networks, relatively independent of possible differences in learning speed).

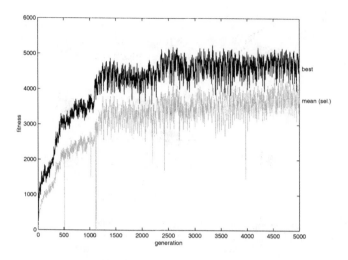

Figure 18. Fitness values for networks of architecture E in experiment 1. For each generation the figure shows the fitness of the best individual (best) and the mean fitness of the 20 best individuals selected for reproduction (mean (sel.)). The values shown are rolling averages over three generations, averaged over all ten evolutionary runs.

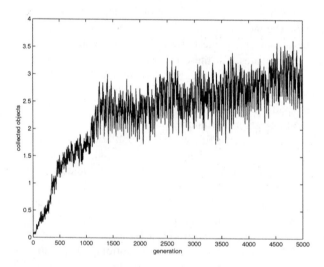

Figure 19. Number of correctly collected objects for networks of architecture E in experiment 2. The values shown are rolling averages over three generations, averaged over all ten evolutionary runs.

Again, architectures A, B, C, and D exhibit worse performance than E according to the three performance measures. The only exception is that, on average, the best networks of architecture C achieve a 1.1% higher fitness during the final 500 generations. However, according to the other performance measures, architecture C, like B and D, performs significantly worse than E. Moreover, architecture B this time outperforms D, but it is no longer clearly better than C. The differences between E and the other recurrent architecture are larger here than in experiment 1, which might be due to the increased complexity of the task. Again, however, all recurrent architectures clearly outperform A due to its lack of feedback.

	best individuals	mean fitness [20 selected]	objects collected [whole population]
A	-68.6% (-69.2%)	-57.2% (-48.1%)	-90.7% (-90.1%)
B	-9.5% (-3.9%)	-10.7% (-11.9%)	-14.6% (-13.8%)
C	-9.6% (+1.1%)	-16.0% (-8.9%)	-32.1% (-26.4%)
D	-23.8% (-20.3%)	-13.8% (-14.7%)	-32.2% (-31.8%)

Table 2. Performance differences between architecture E and other architectures in experiment 2. All differences are stated in percent of the performance of architecture E (as illustrated in Figures 19 and 20). Values are averaged over all 5000 generations (in parentheses over the last 500 generations) of all ten evolutionary runs.

3. Analysis

As for experiment 1, this subsection will present some analysis of successful robot controllers in experiment 2. The analysis will here be limited to networks of architectures E, which exhibited best performance, and B, which evolved similar solutions as C, and is to some degree representative of first-order recurrent networks. Figure 20 illustrates the performance of a successful robot controller of architecture B. To allow better understanding of the robot's behavior during this trajectory the collected objects are shown in their original positions; it should however be noted that for the robot, as discussed above, they disappear upon first contact. The robot starts off facing the upper left obstacle. It turns away from it, faces the wall, and turns away from that also (keeping safe distances in both cases). It enters the zone, collects the left object, and leaves the zone again. When facing the lower wall it starts moving in a curve to the right, which takes it back into the zone. When detecting the upper object on its right it performs a sharp turn to the right to be able to collect that object, and performs another right turn to collect the center object as well. It continues to move straight ahead which allows it to collect the lower object. It leaves the zone, and as before, when detecting the wall ahead starts moving in a curve to the right, which takes it back into the zone. It leaves and enters the zone once more, and eventually the evaluation period ends after 400 time steps.

Figure 21 shows the activation values and fitness points for the robot controller network during this trajectory, and its weights are shown in Figure 22. It can be seen that the network has evolved a strong positive bias for the left motor and a weaker positive bias for the right motor. This gives the robot a tendency to move forward turning slightly to the right in the absence of significant sensory stimuli, at least as long as it outside the zone (see Figure 20). Moreover, the proximity sensors (when active) have a stronger inhibitory effect

377

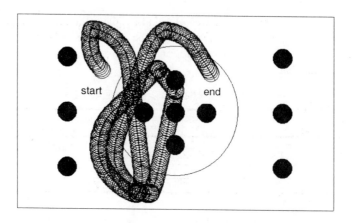

Figure 20. Example trajectory for a robot controller (architecture B) in experiment 2. The robot successfully collects four objects in the zone and correctly avoids objects and walls outside the zone.

on the right motor than on the left. Thus, the robot outside the zone avoids objects by sharp turns to the right. When entering the zone the ground sensor fully activates memory unit 1, but it only slightly activates memory unit 2, which has a larger negative bias and a smaller positive weight. Memory unit 1 keeps (re-)activating itself as long as the robot remains in the zone and it also has a positive influence on the right motor, with the result that inside the zone the robot tends to move forward in a straighter line than outside. As Figure 20 illustrates, inside the zone the robot turns to the right towards objects in order to collect them instead of turning away from them. This is achieved through the combination of the right proximity sensors' strong inhibitory effect on the right motor, memory unit 1's positive influence on the right motor and its slightly negative influence on the left motor (see Figure 22). The latter makes the left wheel slow down slightly too, with the effect that the robot does not turn away from the object before reaching it. When passing the borderline on the way out of the zone, the combination of active ground sensor and active memory unit 1 finally activates memory unit 2. The activity of memory unit 2 during a single time step suffices to trigger a gradual decrease in activity in memory unit 1 over 2-3 steps (see Figure 21), whose self-activation does not suffice to keep itself activated once it is no longer fully active.

For architecture E, roughly speaking, two types of internal organizations evolved in experiment 2. In the one type 'inside' and 'outside' are reflected by distinct state unit activations, whereas in the other type they are only reflected by different function network weight configurations, as demonstrated earlier for a controller network of architecture E in experiment 1. Since the latter type has already been discussed in this paper, a network of the former type will be analyzed in the following. Figure 23 shows a characteristic trajectory of a upper left obstacle. It turns away from it to the left, enters the zone, and collects

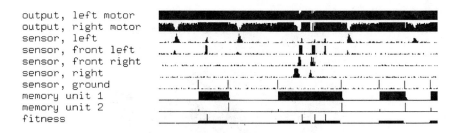

```
output, left motor
output, right motor
sensor, left
sensor, front left
sensor, front right
sensor, right
sensor, ground
memory unit 1
memory unit 2
fitness
```

Figure 21. Activation and fitness values during the 400 time steps of an evaluation trial for the robot controller (architecture B) illustrated in Figure 21(experiment 2). The fitness value is either 0 (no line), between 0 and 1 (short line) outside the zone, between 0 and 4 (slightly longer line) inside the zone, or 100 (full height black line) when correctly 'collecting' an object.

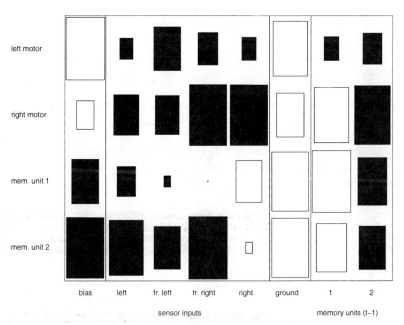

Figure 22. Connection weights for the robot controller network (architecture B) illustrated in Figures 20 and 21.

three objects on its first pass through the zone, turning slightly to the left towards each of them. As soon as it has left the zone it starts moving in a semi-circle to the left, which takes it back into the zone. In the zone it starts moving straight ahead again, takes a slight turn to the right to collect the upper object, and continues straight ahead out of the zone. The same pattern is repeated: as soon as it leaves the zone, it moves in a semi-circle to the left, which takes it back into the zone, where it starts moving straight forward again. Once more it performs a slight turn to the right to collect an object it would otherwise have missed. It

379

continues to move straight ahead, leaves the zone, returns in another semi-circle, enters once more, and moves straight ahead until the evaluation period ends.

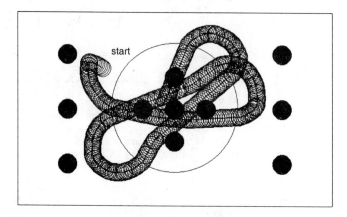

Figure 23. Example trajectory for a robot controller (architecture E) in experiment 2. The robot successfully collects all the objects in the zone, and outside it moves in semi-circles taking it back into the zone.

A look at Figure 24, which illustrates the unit activation and fitness values during the above trajectory, shows that this controller network is slightly smarter than that of architecture B discussed above. Instead of bouncing off obstacles back into the zone as that robot did (see Figures 20 and 21), the one illustrated in Figures 23 and 24 carries out its semi-circle strategy[4] even in the absence of significant sensory stimuli to which it could react.

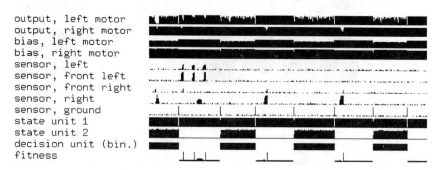

Figure 24. Activation values, motor biases, and fitness values during the 400 time steps of an evaluation trial for the robot controller (architecture E) illustrated in Figure 24 (experiment 2).

That means, in a sense, it 'knows' how to return back into the zone on its own, instead of doing so by merely reacting appropriately to obstacles. Figures 25 and

---

[4] This type of strategy also evolved in networks of architecture B, C, and D in some cases, but not as often as for architecture E.

26 illustrate how this is realized internally, showing the function networks weights as they are used inside the zone and outside in a semi-circle, respectively.

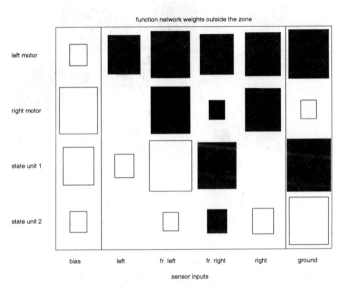

function network weights outside the zone

Figure 25. Function network weights as they are used outside the zone (during a semi-circle) by the robot controller (architecture E) illustrated in Figures 23 and 24.

As shown in Figures 25 and 26, the network has again evolved substantially different biases for use inside and outside the zone respectively. In the former case (see Figure 25) the robot has a strong positive bias for its right motor output unit and a weak positive bias for the left one. As a result the robot moves in a semi-circle to the left in the absence of sensory stimuli, which, as illustrated in Figure 23, is a good strategy for getting back into the zone once the robot has left it. The beginning of the trajectory, however, also shows that the control network does of course not ignore sensory stimuli. The obstacle it faces in the beginning is correctly avoided by a sharp left turn (see Figures 23 and 24), which is caused by the proximity sensors' influence which inhibits the left motor more strongly than the right one (see Figure 25). Outside the zone both state units are active due to their positive biases; the activation of state unit 2, however, varies slightly between 0.8 and 1.0, and with it the speed of the left motor (see Figure 24). Furthermore, the decision unit is actually active all the collect any fitness points during this time. When the ground sensor gets activated it inhibits state unit 1, but activates state unit 2, which results in the function network configuration shown in Figure 26. State unit 2 now has a time while the robot is outside the zone, as a result of which the robot does not negative bias and can only be activated again by a high ground sensor reading.

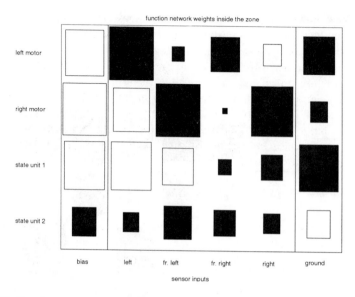

Figure 26. Function network weights as they are used inside the zone by the robot controller (architecture E) illustrated in Figures 24 and 25.

Left and right motors now both have strong positive biases, which results in relatively straight forward motion inside the zone. The connection weights between the proximity sensors are now set such that different sensors inhibit the two motor output units. The left motor is inhibited by the left sensor, which enables the robot to perform (slight) left turns towards objects, as it does during its first pass through the zone when collecting three objects (see Figure 24). The right motor, on the other hand, is inhibited by the sensor on the right. This allows the robot to perform turns to the right in order to collect objects it would have missed otherwise, as it does during its second and third passes through the zone (see Figure 23 and 24).

It should be noted that the robot controller here correctly 'switches' back and forth between different function network configurations several times, and each time the appropriate weights and biases are set or restored. Thus, again the Extended Sequential Cascaded Network (architecture E) realizes the required behavioral adaptation in an interesting way. In this case it switches between two radically different sensorimotor mappings, and thus behavioral dispositions, i.e., at any point in time the robot 'knows' where (on which side of the zone border) it currently is and behaves accordingly. Thus these controllers realize a form of *virtual modularity* through feedback, i.e., they dynamically adapt their behavioral dispositions, such that they act *as if* they were using different modules for different situations/contexts. It is worth noting that this allows the controlled robot to exhibit adaptive, context-dependent responses to otherwise identical stimuli of two types. Firstly, the round objects, which look identical inside and outside the zone, assume different *functional tones* (see von Uexküll [1928], Ziemke [2000]) for the robot. They are therefore correctly attributed different meanings, leading to opposite responses. Secondly, although containing no information about direction whatsoever, the zone border stimulus triggers two opposite responses, switching from an inside behavioral disposition to one for outside, and the other way round. Thus, the robot in this case, unlike ALVINN not able to rely on an external scaffold/structure to guide its behavior, has formed an internal structure that allows it to reliably interact with its environment. This behavioral structure, and the mechanisms realizing it, can be considered *interactive representations* (see Bickhard [1995], Dorffner [1997]), formed by the agent in interaction with its environment, not as an abstract model of the world, but for the purpose of guiding its own behavior.

IV. SUMMARY AND DISCUSSION

This chapter started off with a discussion of the relevance of RNNs for robot learning and control to various lines of research in cognitive science, connectionism, AI, and engineering of robot control systems. In particular it was argued that RNN-controlled robots receive much attention due to their capacity to form internal control structures and representations in interaction with an environment. These issues were then illustrated and analyzed in quite some detail, comparing four different first- and higher-order recurrent robot control architectures in two experiments that required the controlled robot to exhibit context-dependent behavior. The quantitative results showed that best performance in both experiments was achieved by architecture E, the Extended Sequential Cascaded Network (ESCN), a novel variation of Pollack's SCN. However, whether this architecture is actually better suited for robot control or the results are really due to the details of the experimental setups or the evolutionary training procedure (the latter was slightly different for the ESCN), can only be determined by further extensive experimentation.

Further analysis of the experiments showed that the way this type of RNN constructs and utilizes internal structures for adaptive robot behavior closely corresponds to what Peschl in his discussion of RNNs referred to as "representation without representations":

> The internal structures do not map the environmental structures; they are rather responsible for generating functionally fitting behavior which is *triggered* and *modulated* by the environment and *determined* by the internal structure (. . . of the synaptic weights). It is the result of *adaptive* phylo- and ontogenetic processes which have changed the architecture over generations and/or via learning in an individual organism in such a way that its physical structure embodies the dynamics for maintaining a state of equilibrium/homeostasis. [Peschl, 1996]

Thus, RNNs in a sense offer a 'middle way' between (a) the explicit world models of traditional AI, lacking grounding in and interaction with the world they are supposed to represent, and (b) the world-dependence of purely reactive systems, like ALVINN, which rely on the world to 'puppeteer' their behavior. The internal structures and representations formed in RNNs, in the self-organization of adaptive behavior in interaction between a robot and its environment, are the result of a structural coupling between the two, which ensures their structural congruence (see Maturana [1987], Varela [1991]). Thus, they are the result of a constructive process (see Peschl [1996], Ziemke [1999], Ziemke [2000]), and they reflect an agent's *subjective* embedding in the world, allowing it to attribute varying meaning to stimuli according to its own current behavioral disposition.

Apart from the investigation of higher-order RNNs for more complex robot tasks, the author's current work includes further investigations of (a) the practical suitability of first- and higher-order RNNs for different tasks, in particular their amenability to training through backpropagation and evolutionary algorithms, and (b) cognitive and semiotic aspects of representation formation and sign usage in RNN-controlled robots and their implications for the possibilities and limitations of robot autonomy and subjectivity [Ziemke, 2000].

ACKNOWLEDGMENTS

This work has been supported by funding from The Foundation for Knowledge and Competence Development (1507/97), Sweden. The author would like to thank Noel Sharkey, Larry Medsker, Fredrik Linåker, and Henrik Jacobsson for their useful feedback on earlier versions of the work, and Lars Niklasson for providing Figure 1. Moreover, the author would like to thank Henrik H. Lund and Stefano Nolfi who did most of the development of the kepsim simulator, which has been used (in slightly adapted form) to implement the experiments documented in this paper.

REFERENCES

Beer, R. D., *Intelligence as Adaptive Behavior: An Experiment in Computational Neuroethology*, Academic Press, Cambridge, 1990.

Bekey, G. and Goldberg, K. Y., Eds., *Neural Networks in Robotics*, Kluwer, Boston, 1993.

Bickhard, M. H. and Terveen, L., *Foundational Issues in Artificial Intelligence and Cognitive Science - Impasse and Solution,* Elsevier, New York, 1995.

Biro, Z. and Ziemke, T., Evolving visually guided approach behaviour in recurrent artificial neural network robot controllers. *Proceedings of the Fifth International Conference on Simulation of Adaptive Behavior*, MIT Press, Cambridge, 1998.

Boden, M. A., Autonomy and artificiality, in *The Philosophy of Artificial Life*, Boden, M. A., Ed., Oxford University Press, Oxford, 95, 1996.

Brooks, R. A., A robust layered control system for a mobile robot, *IEEE Journal of Robotics and Automation*, 2(1), 14, 1986.

Brooks, R. A., Intelligence without reason, *Proceedings of the Twelfth International Joint Conference on Artificial Intelligence (IJCAII-91)*, Morgan Kauffmann, San Mateo, 569, 1991.

Brooks, R. A., Grossberg, S., and Optican, L., Eds., *Neural Networks*, 11(7-8), 1998. Special issue on *Neural Control and Robotics: Biology and Technology*.

Clark, A., *Being There–Putting Brain, Body and World Together Again*, MIT Press, Cambridge, MA, 1997.

Dorffner, G., Radical connectionism–a neural bottom-up approach to AI, in *Neural Networks and a New Artificial Intelligence*, Dorffner, G., Ed., International Thomson Computer Press, London, 93, 1997.

Elman, J., Finding structure in time, *Cognitive Science*, 14, 179, 1990.

Grey Walter, W., An imitation of life, *Scientific American*, 182, 42, 1950.

Grey Walter, W., *The Living Brain*, Norton, New York, 1953.

Harnad, S., The symbol grounding problem, *Physica D*, 42, 335, 1990.

Holland, J. H., *Adaptation in Natural and Artificial Systems*, The University of Michigan Press, Ann Arbor, 1975.

Maturana, H. and Varela, F., *Autopoiesis and Cognition: The realization of the living*, Reidel, Boston, 1980.

Maturana, H. and Varela, F., *The Tree of Knowledge: The Biological Roots of Human Understanding*, New Science Library, Boston, 1987.

Meeden, L. A., *Towards planning: Incremental investigations into adaptive robot control*, PhD dissertation. Indiana University, 1994.

Meeden, L. A., An incremental approach to developing intelligent neural network controllers for robots, *IEEE Transactions on Systems, Man, and Cybernetics*, 26, 1996.

Meeden, L. A., McGraw, G., and Blank, D., Emergence of control and planning in an autonomous vehicle. *Proceedings of the Fifteenth Annual Meeting of the Cognitive Science Society*, Lawrence Erlbaum, Hillsdale, 735, 1993.

Miglino, O., Lund, H. H., and Nolfi, S., Evolving mobile robots in simulated and real environments, *Artificial Life*, 2(4), 417, 1995.

Mondada, F., Franzi, E., and Ienne, P., Mobile robot miniaturisation: A tool for investigation in control algorithms, *Proceedings of the Third International Symposium on Experimental Robotics*, Kyoto, Japan, 1993.

Mozer, M., A focused back-propagation algorithm for temporal pattern recognition, *Complex Systems*, 3, 349, 1989.

Nolfi, S., Using emergent modularity to develop control systems for mobile robots, *Adaptive Behavior*, 5(3-4), 343, 1997.

Nolfi, S. and Tani, J., Extracting regularities in space and time through a cascade of prediction networks: The case of a mobile robot navigating in a structured environment, *Connection Science*, 11(2), 125, 1999.

Omidvar, O. and van der Smagt, P., Eds., *Neural Systems for Robotics*, Academic Press, Boston, 1997.

Peschl, M., The representational relation between environmental structures and neural systems: Autonomy and environmental dependency in neural knowledge representation, *Nonlinear Dynamics, Psychology and Life Sciences*, 1(3), 1996.

Pollack, J. B., Cascaded back-propagation on dynamic connectionist networks, *Proceedings of the Ninth Annual Conference of the Cognitive Science Society*, 391, 1987.

Pollack, J. B., The induction of dynamical recognizers, *Machine Learning*, 7, 227, 1991.

Pomerleau, D. A., *Neural Network Perception for Mobile Robot Guidance*, Kluwer, Dordrecht, 1993.

Rumelhart, D. E. and McClelland, J., On learning the past tense of English, in *Parallel Distributed Processing: Explorations in the Microstructure of Cognition, Volume 2: Psychological and Biological Models,* Rumelhart, D. E., McClelland, J., and the PDP Group, Eds., MIT Press, Cambridge, 216, 1986.

Rumelhart, D. E., Hinton, G. E., and Williams, R. J., Learning internal representations by error propagation, in *Parallel Distributed Processing:*

Explorations in the Microstructure of Cognition, Volume 1: Foundations, Rumelhart, D. E., McClelland, J., and the PDP Group, Eds., MIT Press, Cambridge, 318, 1986.

Rylatt, M. and Czarnecki, C., Beyond physical grounding and naïve time: Investigations into short-term memory for autonomous agents, *Proceedings of the Fifth International Conference on Simulation of Adaptive Behavior,* MIT Press, Cambridge, 1998.

Searle, J., Minds, brains and programs, *Behavioral and Brain Sciences,* 3, 417, 1980.

Sharkey, N. E., Ed., Neural networks for coordination and control: the portability of experiential representations, *Robotics and Autonomous Systems,* 22(3-4), 1997.

Sharkey, N. E., Ed., *Robotics and Autonomous Systems,* 22(3-4). Special issue on *Robot Learning: The New Wave,* 1997.

Sharkey, N. E. and Ziemke, T., A consideration of the biological and psychological foundations of autonomous robotics, *Connection Science,* 10(3-4), 361, 1998.

Siegelmann, H. T., *Neural Networks and Analog Computation: Beyond the Turing Limit,* Birkhäuser, Boston, 1998.

Siegelmann, H. T. and Sontag, E. D., On the computational power of neural nets, *Journal of Computer and System Sciences,* 50(1), 132, 1995.

Steels, L., When are robots intelligent autonomous agents?. *Robotics and Autonomous Systems,* 15, 3, 1995.

Tani, J., Model-based learning for mobile robot navigation from the dynamical systems perspective, *IEEE Transactions on Systems, Man, and Cybernetics,* 26(3), 1996.

Tani, J. and Nolfi, S., Learning to perceive the world as articulated: an approach for hierarchical learning in sensory-motor systems, *Proceedings of the Fifth International Conference on Simulation of Adaptive Behavior,* MIT Press, Cambridge, 1998.

Ulbricht, C., Handling time-warped sequences with neural networks, in *From Animals to Animats 4–Proceedings of the Fourth International Conference on Simulation of Adaptive Behavior,* Maes, P., Mataric, M., Meyer, J.-A., Pollack, J., and Wilson, S., Eds., MIT Press, Cambridge, 180, 1996.

von Uexküll, J., *Theoretische Biologie*, Suhrkamp, Frankfurt/Main, 1928.

Varela, F. J., Thompson, E., and Rosch, E., *The Embodied–Mind Cognitive Science and Human Experience*, MIT Press, Cambridge, 1991.

Werbos, P., Backpropagation through time: What it does and how to do it, *Proceedings of the IEEE*, 78(10), 1990.

Wilson, S. W., Knowledge growth in an artificial animal, *Proceedings of the First International Conference on Genetic Algorithms and Their Applications*, Lawrence Erlbaum, Hillsdale, NJ, 16, 1985.

Wilson, S. W., The animat path to AI, in *From Animals to Animats–Proceedings of the First International Conference on Simulation of Adaptive Behavior*, Meyer, J.-A. and Wilson, S. W., Eds., MIT Press, Cambridge, 15, 1991.

Ziemke, T., Towards adaptive behaviour system integration using connectionist infinite state automata, in *From Animals to Animats 4–Proceedings of the Fourth International Conference on Simulation of Adaptive Behavior*, Maes, P., Mataric, J.A., Meyer, J.-A., Pollack, J., and Wilson, S., Eds., MIT Press, Cambridge, 15, 1996.

Ziemke, T., Towards autonomous robot control via self-adapting recurrent networks, in *Artificial Neural Networks–ICANN 96*, von der Malsburg, C., von Seelen, W., Vorbrüggen, J. C., and Sendhoff, B., Eds., Springer Verlag, Berlin/Heidelberg, 611, 1996a.

Ziemke, T., Towards adaptive perception in autonomous robots using second-order recurrent networks, *Proceedings of the First Euromicro Workshop on Advanced Mobile Robots*, IEEE Computer Society Press, Los Alamitos, 89, 1996.

Ziemke, T., The "environmental puppeteer" revisited: A connectionist perspective on "autonomy," *Proceedings of the Sixth European Workshop on Robot Learning*, Brighton, UK, 100, 1997.

Ziemke, T., Adaptive behavior in autonomous agents, *Presence*, 7(6), 564, 1998.

Ziemke, T., Rethinking grounding, in *Understanding Representation in the Cognitive Sciences. Does Representation Need Reality*, in Riegler, A., Peschl, M., and von Stein, A., Eds., Plenum Press, New York, 1999.

Ziemke, T. and Sharkey, N. E., Eds., *Connection Science*, 10(3-4), Special Issue on *Biorobotics*, 1998.

Ziemke, T. and Sharkey, N. E., Eds., *Autonomous Robots*, 7(1), Special Issue on *Artificial Neural Networks for Robot Learning*, 1999.

Ziemke, T. and Sharkey, N. E., A stroll through the worlds of robots and animals: Applying Jakob von Uexküll's theory of meaning to adaptive robots and artificial life, *Semiotica*, special issue on Jakob von Uexküll, to appear in 2000.

INDEX

Index